THE CIVILIZATION OF THE AMERICAN INDIAN SERIES

The Cherokees

The
Cherokees

By Grace Steele Woodward

UNIVERSITY OF OKLAHOMA PRESS : NORMAN

By Grace Steele Woodward

*The Man Who Conquered Pain: A Biography of William
  Thomas Green Morton* (Boston, 1962)
The Cherokees (Norman, 1963)

Library of Congress Catalog Card Number: 63–8986

Copyright 1963 by the University of Oklahoma Press,
Publishing Division of the University.
Composed and printed at Norman, Oklahoma, U.S.A.,
by the University of Oklahoma Press. First edition.

To Guy

Contents

Illustrations

xi

Maps

Acknowledgments

THE PREPARATION of this one-volume history of the Cherokees, although a colossal undertaking, has not been accomplished alone. I am indebted to many librarians and other individuals for their patient and painstaking help in this venture. In the summer of 1961 the staff of the Department of Manuscripts, British Museum, searched for and found valuable manuscripts bearing on the Colonial period which they permitted me to use freely during my short stay in London.

In the initial stage of research Miss Carmelita Shea, National Archives, Washington (Indian Records Unit), guided me through the then unmicrofilmed material—tray after tray of it—relating to the Cherokees. When later this material was microfilmed, others of the staff in the Indian Records Unit apprised me of its availability. Mrs. Leila F. Clark, librarian of the Smithsonian Institution, was tireless in her search for both primary and secondary material in the library. The staffs of the Smithsonian, Department of Archives, and of the Library of Congress contributed greatly to my research. At the Library of Congress I was allowed stack privileges, and while in the Smithsonian Archives, I was permitted to examine rare and priceless maps and manuscripts bearing on the Cherokees.

At Gilcrease, in Tulsa, Martin A. Wenger, librarian, called my attention to the Ross Papers and also made available to me other unexplored sources of Cherokee material, cheerfully guiding me through the immense treasures of the Gilcrease archives. Co-operating with me at the University of Tulsa were Miss Eugenia Maddox, librarian; Mrs. Crafton James, head of circulation; and Mr. Winston Weathers of the department of English. Jack Haley of the Division of Manuscripts in the Library of the University of Oklahoma tirelessly searched for lithographs and photographs and other primary materials on the Cherokees.

Of great assistance were Mrs. Mary Givens Bryan, director of the Department of Archives and History, Atlanta, Georgia, and Miss Carroll Hart, assistant archivist. At the Georgia Historical Commission in Atlanta, Mrs. Mary G. Jewett made me welcome and provided data on the Cherokees not to be had elsewhere. My thanks go to Mr. Joseph B. Cumming, chairman of the Georgia Historical Commission, for inviting me to attend the dedication of New Echota in May, 1962.

When I visited the Qualla Reservation at Cherokee, North Carolina, Mose Owl, curator of the Cherokee Museum, literally took me by the hand and conducted me on a tour of the museum. His recitation of tribal stories was invaluable to me, recreating as they did the dark days of the removal of his people.

Another source of inspiration has been Mrs. Carolyn Thomas Foreman, who, during our visits in her Muskogee home, made me appreciate, as she does, all Cherokees. To Mrs. Foreman, the Cherokee people are a noble people and must be understood to be appreciated.

An Oklahoma landmark, the Murrell House, near Tahlequah, contains many relics and pictures of interest to a historian of the Cherokees. To its custodian, Mrs. Marguerite Clay Ross, I render my appreciation for allowing me to examine the Ross family Bible and other interesting material in her custody. The staff of the Northeastern State College Library at Tahlequah kindly allowed me the use of scrapbooks, newspapers, and photographs.

Everett Haymore, not once but several times, flew me daringly low over areas in Tennessee, North Carolina, Georgia, and Alabama associated with the Cherokees' migration, thus permitting me to examine the terrain called by the Cherokees "the trail where they cried."

Particular acknowledgment is made to two persons whose secretarial assistance cannot be over-stressed. They are Mrs. Geraldine Watkins and her sister Miss Shirley Shanks of Bixby, who tirelessly toiled to prepare this manuscript for submission to the University of Oklahoma Press.

GRACE STEELE WOODWARD

Tulsa, Oklahoma
January 2, 1963

The Cherokees

Geo   12
MAth   9
Hist   9

Psg   6

PE   3

CHAPTER I

The Cherokees Today

THE EMERGENCE of any primitive Indian tribe or nation from dark savagery into the sunlight of civilization is a significant event. But in the case of the Cherokees, the event is both significant and phenomenal. Between 1540 and 1906 the Cherokee tribe of Indians reached a higher peak of civilization than any other North American Indian tribe. However, at the beginning, the Cherokees' conquest of civilization was agonizingly slow and uncertain. They were the war lords of the southern Appalachian Highlands, and were therefore loath to expend their energies elsewhere. "We cannot live without war," they told white men who visited their highland strongholds in the eighteenth century. "War is our beloved occupation."[1]

Despairing of the Cherokees' ever taking the first step toward civilization, James Adair, a trader among them for forty years in the eighteenth century, pessimistically predicted around 1775 that the Cherokees' inordinate fondness for war could only result in their complete annihilation.[2] And Major Andrew Lewis, a British Colonial officer sent to the Cherokee country by Governor Dinwiddie of Virginia to gain the Cherokees' support in the French and Indian

[1] John Haywood, *The Natural and Aboriginal History of Tennessee up to the First Settlements Therein by the White People in the Year 1768*, 238.
[2] James Adair, *History of the American Indians*, 227.

War, afterward commented, "They are like the Devil's pigg, they will neither lead nor drive."[3]

But led or driven, the warlike and willful Cherokees, lingering in the Stone Age by choice at the turn of the eighteenth century, were forced by circumstances beyond their control to transfer their concentration on war to problems posed by the white man. For, following their first encounter with the Spaniards in 1540, the Cherokees' recorded history bulges with problems initiated by the white man. Thus, to cope with these unwelcome problems, the Cherokees were —through bleak necessity—forced in the nineteenth century to turn from war to the conquest of civilization. And by so doing, the warlike Cherokees became civilized and mature.

As summed up by W. R. L. Smith, author of *The Story of the Cherokees,* the outstanding events that turned the tide of Cherokee history were:

> First, The coming of the Spanish plunderers under Hernando De-Soto in 1540.
>
> Second, The treaty with England in 1730, in which . . . [Cherokee] lands were ceded to the crown, and the tribe made complete submission to the British empire.
>
> Third, The treaty with the new American Republic in 1785, by the terms of which, mutual friendship was established and the tomahawk was buried forever.
>
> Fourth, The tragedy of an enforced removal to the West, at the hands of the United States government in 1838.
>
> Fifth, The overwhelming misfortunes incident to the Civil War, 1861–65.
>
> Sixth, The dissolution of tribal bonds in 1906, and fusion into the mass of American citizenship. . . .
>
> Between these first and last dates lie . . . three hundred and sixty-six changeful, fateful, transforming years. So terrible were some of the ills through which . . . [the Cherokees] passed . . . [that] sympathetic white friends feared the tribe was fated to perish. . . . [But] in every threaten-

[3] Samuel Cole Williams, *Dawn of Tennessee Valley and Tennessee History,* 177n.

ing crisis . . . [the Cherokees'] indestructible racial vitalities found the way of extrication and survival.[4]

Chronologically three centuries separate early Cherokee conquistadors of civilization from today's Cherokees. But historically they are in spirit one and the same. They display the same basic character traits: humor, persistence, adaptability, and aggressiveness.

For example, the late Will Rogers' humor was the same brand of humor employed by Rogers' Cherokee ancestors, the Vanns, who in 1809 purportedly inscribed the following epitaph on a wooden slab in Georgia to mark the grave of James Vann, killed in a shooting fray by his brother-in-law:

> *Here lies the body of James Vann*
> *He killed many a white man*
> *At last by a rifle ball he fell*
> *And devils dragged him off to hell.*[5]

Will Rogers' humorous comment on epitaphs, some hundred years later, you will recall, was: "When I die my epitaph, or whatever you call those signs on gravestones, is going to read: 'I joked about every prominent man of my time, but I NEVER MET A MAN I DIDN'T LIKE.' I am so proud of that I can hardly wait to die so it can be carved. And when you come around to my grave, you'll find me sitting there, proudly reading it."[6]

Humor or "joshing one another" is as prevalent today among Cherokee full bloods as it was among Cherokees in the southern Appalachians two centuries ago. The strong "will to win" of early Cherokees is also repeated today in their Oklahoma descendants who are athletes, creative artists, business and professional men, scientists, and city, state, and national officials.

To encounter a sizable number of full-blood Cherokees and those carrying a modicum of white blood it is necessary, today, to visit eastern Oklahoma: Adair, Cherokee, Mayes, and Delaware counties.

[4] *The Story of the Cherokees*, 9.

[5] Epitaph of James Vann recently discovered in Georgia. Courtesy Mrs. Mary Jewett, Georgia Historical Commission, Atlanta.

[6] *Oklahoma Today* (Fall, 1959).

In these counties there is a heavy concentration of full-blood Cherokees living on flinty hillsides, alongside streams, or on narrow back roads infrequently traveled by whites. It has been estimated that approximately fifteen thousand full bloods and near–full bloods live in this area on the small and unproductive farms allotted to them, or to their close kin, prior to statehood.

Being the descendants of Cherokees who had lived "from time out of mind" in the beautiful southern Appalachians, eastern Oklahoma full bloods, before statehood, obviously preferred allotments in the flint hills to the more productive allotments in river valleys that went to mixed bloods. Never as prosperous as the mixed-blood valley Cherokees, many of the full bloods in eastern Oklahoma today are lagging woefully behind the mixed-bloods, economically, socially, and morally. They supplement their small income from farms and subsidies from the government with wage work or seasonal jobs in near-by towns or on farms belonging to white men. In May they pick strawberries; in July, beans; and in August and September, cotton. Paid fair wages, this type of worker usually spends his money as quickly as he makes it on whisky, and on cars, washing machines, and other items that, uncared for, soon fall into necessitous disuse. This type of Cherokee is frequently accused by white critics of being shiftless and "no account." But, as in the case of other races, the majority cannot be judged by the minority. There are full bloods in eastern Oklahoma today who own and operate small businesses. Others act as fishing guides to tourists who frequent lake resorts in the area. Among this class of full bloods are found ministers, teachers, and progressive farmers and stockmen. They stress truck-farming, berry- and fruit-growing, and poultry enterprises. This progressive type of Indian will not long remain in the background of the growing and thriving, and comparatively new, state of Oklahoma.

Agents from Mayes, Cherokee, Adair, and Delaware counties report that 4-H clubs in county and rural schools that are predominantly Cherokee are attracting Cherokee members who show considerable leadership. The Cherokee County agent reported in 1959 that there were more than five hundred rural Indian families in his county, and that practically all were of the Cherokee tribe. "Generally the Indian folks, most of them only part Indian blood, participate as well as other folks in our 4-H, FFA [Future Farmers of America] and other farm programs," reported the agent. "Many of our recent top winners are ¼ to ½ Indian blood."[7]

Cherokee 4-H Club and Future Farmers of America members raise Hampshire and Southdown lambs and cattle, and aspire to attend agriculture schools when they reach college age. In the rural areas near Roland, members of Future Farmers of America are today winning prizes at the state and county fairs on Angus, Guernsey, and Shorthorn cattle.

Too, full-blood and near-full-blood Cherokee adults of eastern Oklahoma who have hitherto suffered from poverty are improving their financial status by working in restaurants and motels. A limited number of Cherokee women are working at The Sequoyah Weavers' Association near Tahlequah. Here they are making blankets, piece goods, belts, deerskin hunting jackets, and other sale goods. Four Cherokee women work daily at looms, turning out exquisite work reminiscent of early periods before the tribe came to Oklahoma. Aided by the Indian Arts and Crafts Board of the United States Department of the Interior, the Sequoyah weavers, at present, are the outstanding promoters of domestic crafts among women. Basketmaking, once sponsored by the IACB, apparently has not made headway in eastern Oklahoma. But why this is so the Cherokees themselves do not know. Buckbushes, one of the artisans' favorite materials for baskets, are plentiful. And Cherokee baskets are in demand by Oklahomans.

No account of eastern Oklahoma Cherokees would be complete without mention of the Keetoowah or Nighthawk societies, to which approximately 3,500 Cherokees belong. In 1859, Evan Jones, the Baptist missionary, reorganized the ancient and secret Keetoowah Society, giving as his motive the desire to assist the Cherokees in preserving the best of their ancient tribal traditions. Jones's critics, however, said that his real motive in reorganizing the Keetoowahs was to originate or activate an abolitionist society which could be counted on to support the Union if it became divided by civil war.

[7] Jasper Hare, Cherokee County farm agent, to Grace Woodward, May 21, 1959.

Today the original Keetoowah Society is split into factions, each having its own chief and headmen. At first the Keetoowah's rituals were held at night in the woods. Outsiders knew neither the meeting place nor the nature of the rituals. However, in recent years the various Keetoowah organizations have permitted the public to attend their meetings.

The site of the ceremonies of the largest and possibly the oldest Keetoowah Society in Oklahoma is the "Redbird Smith Place," six miles northwest of Vian, Oklahoma. Here on this site, near the old settlers' capital of Tahlonteskee, two ceremonies are conducted each year. A ceremony on July 19 commemorates the birth date of the late Chief Redbird Smith, who, after the Civil War, reactivated the Keetoowah society. A second annual ceremony is in September, around the date when ancient Cherokees celebrated the green corn busk. Today it is held for the purpose of expressing appreciation for a bountiful harvest. Both celebrations begin at daybreak and continue until the same time on the day following. Cherokee ball-plays, stalk shoots, orations, feasts, and dances reminiscent of the old days accompany these celebrations. But today's celebrants, when dancing, strap small condensed-milk cans filled with pebbles on their legs and ankles in lieu of the turtle shells used by their ancestors. And white people are frequently invited to participate in the dances, provided they do not ridicule the performances. Signs tacked to trees fringing the dance grounds prohibit the bringing in of whisky and other alcoholic beverages by whites or Indians. And an inebriated white man who attracts attention to his condition by his loud and disorderly behavior finds himself lifted unceremoniously by the coat collar by Indian police and dragged to his car, where he is instructed to stay until he can behave himself.

Sacred to the Keetoowahs today is the eternal fire of the Cherokees. Kindled in ancient days at the beginning of each new year, it was kept burning throughout the year in the Cherokees' council houses. Now, according to ancient custom, seven varieties of wood, symbolizing the Cherokees' seven clans, are used in the building of the eternal fire.

Keetoowahs belonging to the Redbird Smith society have in their possession the Cherokees' sacred wampum belt, which relates the history of the tribe from its early beginnings. This society also owns the seal of the original society. Carefully, these secret relics are guarded by Redbird Smith's descendants.

The Keetoowahs in Oklahoma are not enemies of the mixed bloods who after statehood "followed the white man's road." Nor are they enemies of full bloods who are not Keetoowahs.

Full-blood Cherokees—whether Keetoowahs or not—have straight black hair, prominent cheekbones, and are either tall or of small, wiry build. The women have the final say (so mission workers report) in a household. But they are, outwardly, retiring. Full bloods in eastern Oklahoma converse animatedly in Cherokee when among themselves. They also gesticulate when they talk, and laugh at their own jokes. (Stoicism and dead-pan faces are reserved for the white men!)

A common ancestry promotes understanding between Cherokee full bloods and the mixed bloods. They are poles apart in many respects but, under the skin, are still brothers. For one thing, they have Cherokee traditions in common, and no amount of white blood can dilute the remembrance of what happened in centuries past to the Cherokee people.

It is difficult to estimate the number of citizens in Oklahoma who are of Cherokee descent. But it is supposed that there are about 100,000 Cherokee mixed bloods living in all parts of the world, and of this number 47,000 are in Oklahoma. Oklahoma Cherokees, although citizens of the state, have a principal chief and a governing body or council. The principal chief receives no salary, and his tenure of office is four years. Appointed by the President of the United States after a vote of recommendation by the council, the principal chief of the Cherokees is vested with authority to speak and act for the tribe in negotiations with federal, state, and local governments. Approximately 25,000 Cherokees in Oklahoma are under the jurisdiction of the Indian Bureau of the United States Department of the Interior. The original rolls list 41,935 Cherokees, including minors, intermarried citizens, Delawares and Shawnees who bought into the tribe, freedmen, and minor freedmen.

At present the Cherokees—both full bloods and mixed bloods—are deeply interested in the recovery of money which the tribe feels is due it from the 8,144,000 acres of land sold in 1893 to the federal government. This part of their domain, referred to as the "Cherokee Outlet," was sold to the government for $10,212,000, or $1.25 an acre. An expert on the staff of Oklahoma State University has recently testified before the Indian Claims Commission in Washington that the Cherokee Outlet was worth $10.01 an acre at the time the government took it.

Since 1948, Cherokee lawyers and their associates have been attempting to recover the real value of the Outlet land. Expert government witnesses appraised the value of the land as of 1893 at only $1.70 per acre—$3,600,000.00 more than the tribe received for it. The courts, however, have now decided that the Cherokees should have been paid approximately $14,700,000.00 more than was received in 1893. Congress has appropriated the money for payment of the judgment, and distribution is to be made to members of the tribe.

The Cherokee Outlet suit and other federal legislation affecting Cherokees were the subjects discussed in 1959 when full bloods and mixed bloods met at Tahlequah, the old Cherokee National Capital, on September 5, to celebrate the Cherokee National Holiday. An annual event, the Cherokee National Holiday commemorates the signing of the Cherokee constitution in 1839, after the majority of the tribe had completed its migration from east of the Mississippi to present-day Oklahoma.

On September 5, 1959, about two thousand Cherokees attended the Tahlequah celebration. Full bloods came from Flute Springs, Chalk Bluff, Goat Cliff, and Pumpkin Hollow in eastern Oklahoma. Mixed-blood Cherokees, who, in appearance, looked to be white, came from Oklahoma City, Tulsa, and other Oklahoma towns in the central part of the state. Both full bloods and mixed bloods gathered in "Capitol Square" for the program. Centering "the Square" is the old red brick capitol building, now the Cherokee County courthouse. It was a warm, mellow September day and the pollen from goldenrod made some of the Cherokees sneeze—and some of the whites too, for that matter.

From a bandstand under the trees, speeches were delivered by the vice-chief, in the absence of the principal chief, and by the Cherokee lawyers who were representing the tribe in Washington on "the Outlet case." These speeches were punctuated by the crowning of "Miss Cherokee Holiday," an attractive Cherokee high-school senior. A full-blood Cherokee minister delivered the convocation. A band of church singers sang many long hymns.

Between speeches, old-timers reminisced as they placidly sat, Cherokee-fashion, under the trees puffing on pipes. The cornstalk shooters restlessly awaited the World's Champion Cornstalk Shoot, in which Kendall Sorethumb was to compete. On this occasion it was obvious that mixed bloods and full bloods were molded again as of yore into "the body politic." But not for long! At the termination of the ceremonies in the Square, the Cherokees' able and distinguished lawyers left for Washington by plane to pursue the Outlet suit. And the other mixed bloods from Tulsa and Oklahoma City, brushing aside the past, steamed off in bright new cars for homes that in no way resemble the Cherokee mansions of the affluent of early days. Departing too—but more leisurely—were the full-blood and near-full-blood Cherokees, a majority of whom would pick cotton or gather pecans and fruit until after the first frost in eastern Oklahoma. Similar programs were followed in 1960, 1961, and 1962 —the 1962 National Holiday being highlighted by the court's favorable decision in the Outlet case.

But there is yet another band of Cherokee full bloods and near-full bloods in the United States worthy of mention. They are the Eastern Band of Cherokees who live on the Qualla Boundary (or Reservation) in western North Carolina. The Eastern Band of Cherokees do indeed memorialize the past, and they themselves quicken the curiosity of visitors.

Small in stature, Qualla Boundary residents have straight black hair, prominent cheekbones, and eyes frequently reminiscent of the Mongolian race. Prognathism (projecting jaw) is occasionally seen here, as in Oklahoma. When older, the women tend to be heavy-set, but men, old and young, are usually wiry. However, there are exceptions. One of the ballplayers at the Hiwassee Fair in the fall of 1960 bordered on obesity, but his weight did not deter him from leaping into the air, capturing the ball in the pocket of his ball-play stick, and carrying it down the field to the goal post.

Qualla Boundary Cherokees, unlike the Oklahoma Cherokees, have not intermarried to any extent with whites—hence the predominance of full bloods whose blood, when analyzed, is Type I in the method used by anthropologists today to determine racial mixtures. Since intermarriage is common in the tribe, its virility is safeguarded by clan regulation; seven clans are still the divisions of the Eastern Band as they were in ancient days. To safeguard the virility of the Eastern Band of Cherokees, a member of the Wolf Clan does not mate with a member of his clan but chooses a mate from the Deer, Bird, Twister, Blue, Red, or Wild Potato clans. This is the way in which marriages were made by the ancestors of Qualla Boundary Cherokees in centuries past.

These ancestors, you will recall, were the little frenzied band of Cherokees who, eluding the military in 1838, hid for several years in North Carolina caves and mountains adjacent to the site of the present Qualla Boundary, subsisting on roots, berries, and the wildlife around them.

Among this band of several hundred refugees was the Cherokee martyr Tsali (or Charley), who had supposedly killed a soldier whose brutality had provoked his wrath. With Tsali were two companions also accused by the military of committing murder. To effect the rescue of the refugees, William Thomas, a white man who had long been the Cherokees' friend, persuaded Tsali and his companions to give themselves up to federal officials. And this Tsali and his companions did, paying with their lives for the purported crimes they had committed—but only on the provision that, following their execution, the band of refugees hiding in caves be permitted to remain in North Carolina.

Today contradictory legends about Tsali run rampant in western North Carolina.[8] But whether Tsali was old, young, married, or a

[8] One version of the Tsali story tells of the attempted rape of Anawaggia and

bachelor does not detract from his heroism. Tsali is the beloved idol of the Eastern Band of Cherokees, and William Thomas is nearly as popular. For after the execution of Tsali and his companions for a crime which many eastern Cherokees do not believe they committed, William Thomas again intervened with the federal government in behalf of the Indians. Out of the funds allowed them by the government for confiscated lands and improvements, Thomas

her companion by two soldiers ironically assigned to guard Cherokee captives en route from North Carolina Valley Towns to the stockade at Bushnell. The assault occurred after dark, when all the prisoners—save Anawaggia, her friend, and Tsali, a twenty-nine-year-old Cherokee mountaineer—were asleep. These three heard the two soldiers stealthily approaching their campsite. Anawaggia quickly snatched Tsali's hatchet from his belt, and when one of the soldiers tried to pull her into the bushes, she let fly the hatchet—killing first her assailant and then his confederate.

Then Anawaggia gave the weapon back to its owner. And Tsali, knowing that, when the murders were discovered, he would be searched, hid the blood-stained hatchet inside his blouse. "I will have to pay for this," the chivalrous Tsali is purported to have muttered to Anawaggia. "But you need not worry; I will not give out your name."

Later when accused of the murders, Tsali was among the three hundred Cherokee captives who eluded their guards after reaching the Bushnell stockade and escaped to the mountains. By hiding in caves, these escapees eluded capture for several years after the mass of the Cherokees had been removed, thus becoming the nucleus of today's residents of the Qualla Reservation. Tsali's deed and its aftermath remain fresh in the remarkable memories of the Qualla Reservation Cherokees. For Tsali, influenced by Colonel William Thomas, eventually gave himself up. Stoically, he agreed to pay for Anawaggia's offense, provided that Cherokee cave dwellers would be permitted by the federal government to live peaceably in North Carolina. Two other Cherokee men wanted for similar crimes came in with Tsali to be put to death. The execution of the three was accomplished—at their request—by their friend, a Cherokee Methodist preacher, and not by a white man. Fearlessly, Tsali and his companions, with arms folded over their chests, stepped into their respective newly dug graves to await death.

This hitherto unpublished account of the murders of the two soldiers was told to me recently by Moses Owl, the custodian of the Cherokee Museum at Cherokee, North Carolina. Moses Owl's grandmother was a witness to these murders, and in later years told him the story. Moses says his grandmother—she could even have been Anawaggia—belonged to the same clan (the Long Hairs) that Tsali belonged to. She was twenty-nine, the same age as Tsali. She knew Tsali to be a bachelor and not the middle-aged, married man with a family represented by historians of former years. Tsali's hatchet is in the museum. Moses Owl contends that this is the true story of Tsali.

13

bought for the eastern Cherokees small farms in Swain and Jackson counties.

There they built rude log huts and attempted to wrest a living from soil that yielded small crops of corn, beans, and tobacco. So wretched was their poverty that they did not attempt to participate in the activities of the state of North Carolina, of which they were then citizens. After the Civil War—in 1889—they were recognized as a corporate body under the laws of the state of North Carolina, and as wards of the United States, were supervised by the Indian Bureau. The land occupied by their descendants today is known as the Qualla Boundary.

Today's Eastern Band of Cherokees numbers approximately 4,500 persons. Like the Oklahoma Cherokees, they have a chief who is appointed by the President of the United States following his recommendation by the vote of a council. And today they are prospering.

Improved mountain roads in western North Carolina are greatly responsible for the Eastern Band of Cherokees' recent progress. Since 1931 tourists have been attracted to the Qualla Boundary, which embraces approximately 56,000 acres of picturesque country. Stimulated by tourist trade, the Qualla Arts and Crafts Mutual, Incorporated, was organized in 1947; today it markets the products of 175 Cherokee craftsmen. Organized in 1950, the Cherokee Indian Farmers' Co-operative today affords farmers markets for products that hitherto went to waste for lack of outlets. In 1950 the Boundary Tree Tourist Enterprise opened for year-round business. Sources of additional income to the tribe are the Mountainside Amphitheater, the Oconaluftee Village, the Cherokee Museum, and the many curio shops whose wares are temptingly displayed.

A visit to the Qualla Boundary, in this writer's opinion, is equivalent to a semester's college course in Cherokee history, provided the visitor applies himself to its thorough exploration. Here today are monuments to the Cherokees from the beginning of their recorded history not found elsewhere. As reported by Cherokee authority William Gilbert, Jr., the Qualla Boundary and its residents are a living, breathing re-creation of the past, a study of the present progress of a backward band of Indians, and an adventure which travelers to North Carolina should not miss:

Today the traveler coming into the Qualla Boundary may approach from Asheville on the east or from Knoxville on the north. Coming from Asheville by car he will be impressed by the memorable mountain scenery and by the carefully engineered road by which, through a series of magnificent curves, he proceeds over the ridge through the Soco Gap and down into the valley of the Oconaluftee River, where the Cherokee agency is situated. Here he is impressed by the many tourist courts. Approaching the reservation from Knoxville, he proceeds through Seviersville, through the fine curves upward to Newfound Gap, where a magnificent panorama of both Tennessee and North Carolina is to be viewed. Proceeding down the road he follows a lively and beautiful mountain stream, the Oconaluftee River, which dashes over rocks and through glades of delicate and sylvan character. Further on as he enters the reservation he passes the fine Boundary Tree Tourist Court built and maintained by the tribe. At length he arrives at the outdoor amphitheater built into the mountainside for the annual summer-long performance of the spectacular drama of Cherokee life, "Unto These Hills." After this he arrives at the modern and well-kept Agency buildings and the Tribal Council Hall in the center of the reservation.

To rescue and preserve for posterity the unique cultural and other contributions of the Cherokees to the world's resources in ways of living, a typical tribal village of 1750 has been reconstructed in recent years near Mountainside Amphitheater, called Oconaluftee Village. Inside the village during the summer Cherokees carry on the ancient way of life, practicing basket weaving, aboriginal cooking, beadwork, pottery, and weapon making. Dugout canoes are hollowed out of poplar logs with primitive ax and fire, and other arts are pursued.

Near the Tribal Council Hall a Museum of the Cherokees has been established since 1948, in which are housed tools, household utensils, ornaments, primitive money, and weapons. Household and daily-used artifacts made of cane, stone, bone, shell, and wood are on display. Others items to be seen include an ancient rifled blow-gun with its poised dart, a large bow which could hurl its arrows more than 400 yards, grotesque hand-carved masks of the medicine men, arrowheads of quartz and flint, stone axes, celts, chisels, stone hammers, and ritual pipes of stone and clay and catlinite. Here, too, are pictures of the great Cherokee chiefs shown wearing their colorful costumes and turbans.

In the same way in which the turbulence of the ancient seas was frozen into great rock strata of the Appalachian folds, so the turbulence of the frontier life and the Indian way of life have been frozen into the present-day Cherokee Reservation in North Carolina. The Indians who can be seen there today memorialize the past in a very real and vivid manner.[9]

Aware of the memorialization of the past on the Qualla Boundary, a visitor frequently pauses in his examination of baskets, beaded belts, ball-play sticks, or other articles for sale in the sidewalk curio shops at Qualla to stare wonderingly at the Cherokee craftsman from whom he is contemplating purchasing the articles. Suddenly the craftsman, and not the purchases, becomes important to the visitor. He is indeed mystifying when thus studied. Of the present and yet of the past, the Cherokee craftsman has an old-world face, an old-world aura. The visitor's curiosity quickens. Who is he? What is his true origin? Does he himself know?

[9] "The Cherokees of North Carolina: Living Memorials of the Past," in *Smithsonian Institution, Annual Report to the Board of Regents*, 529, 532. *Pub. 4272.* Washington, 1956.

CHAPTER II

Savages and Spaniards in 1540

THE ORIGIN of the Cherokees is a mystery even to themselves. But certainly Cherokees of the historic age know that their people did not originate from the clouds nor spring from the earth, as some of their eighteenth-century forebears presumably remarked to white men.[1] According to William P. Ross, a nineteenth-century chief, "No response comes down the gallery of time from the silent recesses of the past. Echo alone replies, where and whence came they [the Cherokees]!"[2]

Highly proficient in preserving their vast collection of tribal records—begun in 1540 by De Soto's four chroniclers[3] and brought up to the present by college-educated Cherokees—Cherokees of the historic age may well lay the obscurity of tribal origin at the wigwams of prehistoric ancestors. Obviously not history-minded, these ancestors differed from other ancient North American Indian tribes

[1] See Alexander Hewatt, *An Historical Account of the Rise and Progress of the Colonies of South Carolina and Georgia.*

[2] Mrs. William P. Ross, ed., *The Life and Times of Honorable William P. Ross,* 233.

[3] Unless otherwise specified, all of the material on De Soto in this chapter is from the *Final Report of the United States De Soto Expedition Commission,* 76 Cong., 1 sess., *House Exec. Doc. No. 71.* De Soto's chroniclers were, as listed in this report, Rodrigo Ranjel, Ruiz Hernando de Biedma, Hidalgo de Elvas (a gentleman of Elvas), and Garcilaso de la Vega.

who, before the coming of the Unakas or white men, pictured their history on sticks, wove it into wampum, or imbedded it deeply in the memories of descendants. Thus, lacking records of their origin, Cherokees of the historic age are compelled to reconstruct their prehistoric past from foundation to capstone out of traditional, archaeological, and linguistic data.

Tribal traditions assert that the powerful and warlike Cherokees have always held the vast mountainous region of the southern Alleghenies in what is today southwest Virginia, western North and South Carolina, eastern Tennessee, northern Georgia, and the northeastern hip of Alabama. Allowing for fluctuations of boundaries resulting from tribal wars, the Cherokees' mountainous domain once embraced approximately forty thousand square miles.

Questioned by white men in the eighteenth century, the Cherokees stoically maintained that their domain had been given to them by the Great Spirit (Asga-Ya-Galun-lati), to whom the whole earth belonged. And oddly enough, this tradition withstood the wear and tear of time. For in January, 1830, this legend reappeared in the Cherokees' petition in the Supreme Court of the United States:

> That the Cherokees were the occupants and owners of the territory in which they now reside before the first approach of the white men of Europe to the western continent; 'deriving their title from the Great Spirit [Asga-Ya-Galun-lati] who is the father of the human family, and to whom the whole earth belongs.' Composing the Cherokee Nation, they and their ancestors have been and are the sole and exclusive masters of this territory, governed by their own laws, usages, and customs.[4]

But, even though Cherokees of the historic age cannot explain their origin, tribal orators at one time referred frequently to a migration period. Until the nineteenth century venerable chiefs recited the history of Cherokee tribal migration at every Great Green Corn Festival in the fall. On these important occasions, the orators would allude to "the towns of people in many nights' encampment re-

[4] United States Supreme Court Reports, *Cherokee Nation v. Georgia*, 5 Peters 1.

moved."[5] Then, for some reason, the history of Cherokee migration was deleted from orations delivered by the chiefs; thus, by the nineteenth century this facet of oral Cherokee history was barely remembered by the oldest member of the tribe.

However, Delaware traditions do mention a prehistoric migration of the Cherokees. According to the Delawares' Walum Olum (ancient sticks painted with hieroglyphics depicting the Delaware's history from their creation to the coming of the white man), the Delawares fought the Tallegwis or Cherokees throughout the reign of three Delaware chiefs at a time when the Delawares were inhabitants of the Eastern seaboard. And eventually, according to the Walum Olum, the Cherokees were conquered. After the Cherokees had been defeated by the Delawares, aided by the Iroquois (thought to be the Tallegwis' kinsmen) from the Great Lakes, the Delawares wrathfully drove the Tallegwis southward beyond the Ohio River.[6]

When reinforced by archaeological and linguistic data, this ancient Delaware tradition of victory over the Cherokees gains momentous impact. Archaeologists have discovered Indian burial mounds in Ohio, Illinois, Virginia, and Tennessee, presumably built by the Tallegwis or ancient Cherokees en route to the southern Alleghenies. In the center and at the base of them were found pipes similar to the ones used in a later era by southern Allegheny Cherokees. Imbedded in layers of earth from their base to apex were found fragments of charred crematory posts similar to those of southern Allegheny Cherokees. Set in hard clay saucer-like depressions, these post fragments were accompanied by artifacts and residue of bones thought to have belonged to the Tallegwi or ancient Cherokees, the builders of these mounds.

Further evidence of an early habitation of the ancient Cherokees in what is now the Great Lakes region of the United States comes from linguists who have discovered that the Cherokee and Iroquoian languages are in many respects similar; as a result of this discovery, many linguists now classify the Cherokees as a branch of the Iroquoian family originating in the north. However, this theory has

---

[5] John Haywood. *Natural and Aboriginal History of Tennessee*, 236f.
[6] Leander Leitner, ed., *The Walum Olum*, Pt. 4.

not been adopted *in toto* by anthropologists. The late Frank G. Speck, for one, theorized to the contrary that the Cherokees, and perhaps the Iroquois, too, originated in the Orinoco and Amazon River basins in South America. Speck contended that none of the southern tribes —save the Cherokees and possibly the Catawbas—rimmed their baskets with a thin oak loop bound fast with a hickory fiber withe, a characteristic of baskets made by the natives in the Orinoco and Amazon basins. Both Cherokees and South Americans employed the double-weave and the chain and diagonal pattern. This mode of weaving linked the Cherokees' ancestry with that of basket-weavers in the Orinoco and Amazon areas.[7] And certainly today's Cherokee basket-makers living on the Qualla Reservation in North Carolina employ the double-weave, the diagonal and chain pattern, and the rimming method mentioned above. But, even assuming that basketry definitely links the ancient Cherokees with South America in prehistoric times, the Cherokees could easily have migrated to North America via Mexico. Crossing the Mississippi, they could have traveled northward until they encountered the Iroquois on the Great Lakes. After settling among this tribe, the ancient Cherokees could have adopted the Iroquoian language or parts of it.

Another eminent authority, W. H. Holmes, also saw a similarity in the art of the Cherokees and that of the Caribbeans. But in this case pottery, instead of basketry, provided the clues. According to Holmes, ancient Cherokees, using primitive wooden paddles, stamped their pottery while yet damp with curves and scrolls as did the Caribbeans who reportedly once had island kinsmen whose name resembled the Cherokees'.[8]

Also attempting to learn about the mysterious origin of the Cherokees was James Adair, an eighteenth-century trader and historian who lived among the tribe for forty years. After completing a study

[7] See Frank G. Speck, *Decorative Art and Basketry of the Cherokees.*

[8] William Eubanks, Cherokee, to Professor Holmes relative to the origin of the American Indians, particularly the Cherokees, Unpublished MS No. 3706, Smithsonian Institution, Bureau of American Ethnology (hereinafter referred to as B. A. E.), Washington, D. C.

of their customs and rituals, Adair advanced the theory that the Cherokees were one of the ten lost tribes of Israel.[9] But Adair's theory is not accepted by today's ethnologists, who state conclusively that "the Cherokees were once a powerful detached tribe of the Iroquoian family" and that "they originated in the North, but they were found in possession of the southern Allegheny region when first encountered by De Soto in 1540."[10]

Paralleling the mystery of the Cherokee origin is that of the Cherokee name. By some ethnologists and historians, the word Cherokee is conceded to be a corruption of *Tsalagi* or *Tsaragi*. But does this concession conclusively prove that *Tsalagi* is a mnemonic signifying "Ancient Tobacco People" issuing from *tsalu*, the Cherokee name for tobacco, and *agaawli*, "old or ancient"? Or rather, is *Tsalagi* a derivative of *A-tsila-gi-ga-i*, whose Cherokee meaning is "Red Fire Men"? The Cherokee emblem of bravery was the color red, and bravery was believed by the Cherokees to emanate from the East where rose the sun. In this instance *Tsalagi* could well mean "Children of the Sun" or "Brave Men."[11]

Nor is the riddle of the Cherokee name solved by the Cherokees' neighbors, the Choctaws, who in early days called the Cherokees *Chalakki*. But *Chalakki*, too, is controversial. For, according to the *Final Report of the United States De Soto Expedition Commission*, *Chalakki* does not, as many historians over the years have contended, refer to inhabitants of "the Province of Chalique" (or Cheleque) mentioned by De Soto's chroniclers. As identified by the Commission, the "Province of Chalique" was a Siouan province on the Savannah River in South Carolina. Therefore, concludes the Commission, *Chilakee* is a Creek word signifying "People of a Different Speech," and so is the proper name to apply to Chalique inhabitants. By the same token *Chilakki* or *Chilakee*, a Choctaw word meaning "Cave

[9] Adair, *History of the American Indians*, Chaps. I and II.

[10] Smithsonian Institution, B. A. E., *Bulletin No. 30* (pamphlet). See also Grant Foreman, *The Five Civilized Tribes*, 18.

[11] John P. Brown, *Old Frontiers*, 528. See also Muriel H. Wright, *A Guide to the Indian Tribes of Oklahoma*, 56f.

People" which stems from *chiluk* or *chuluk,* better applies to early Cherokees of the upper dialects living in the mountainous area of western North Carolina.[12]

Simpler to explain are the names which early-day Cherokees gave to themselves. Since Kituhwa (today near Bryson City, North Carolina) is conceded to be the Cherokees' mother settlement in the southern Alleghenies, it seems right and proper for early-day Cherokees to have referred to themselves as *Ani Kitu Hwagi,* "People of Kituhwa." Another Cherokee favorite was *Ani-Yun Wiya,* "Real or Principal People," but the origin of this Cherokee name, too, is unknown. However, historians of Cherokee history recall that in 1775 at Sycamore Shoals, Dragging Canoe, a Cherokee chief, referred to his people as *"Ani-Yun Wiya."* On the occasion Dragging Canoe, in protesting the Cherokees' cession of land to Richard Henderson's Transylvania Company, said:

> We had hoped that the white men would not be willing to travel beyond the mountains. . . . Finally the whole country, which the Cherokees and their fathers have so long occupied, will be demanded, and the remnant of *Ani-Yun Wiya,* The Real People, once so great and formidable, will be compelled to seek refuge in some distant wilderness.[13]

This mysterious tribe—whose origin is lost and whose name is inexplicable—later became avid historians, seeking out every possible bit of historical evidence concerning its past.

The Cherokees' impressive recorded history narrating their phenomenal advancement, retarded at times by tragedy and misfortune, actually began with the arrival of Hernando de Soto in their country in 1540.

Armored in steel, and clad in rich silks and velvets, De Soto's cavalry entered the Cherokees' country on Tuesday, May 25, 1540, spending the night at a "little forest" near the site of Highlands in

---

[12] Wright, *A Guide to the Indian Tribes of Oklahoma,* 56f.
[13] Williams, *Dawn of Tennessee Valley and Tennessee History,* 407.

western North Carolina. Behind the cavalry marched De Soto's foot soldiers—numbering between five and seven hundred when counted with the cavalry—and behind them came several hundred Tamemes or Indian slaves carrying on their backs heavy "hanegas" of maize, quintals of cassavas, shoulders of bacon, mattocks, and spades.

The Tamemes, wearing collars of iron and in chains, were the proud Indians captured by De Soto following his disembarkation at Tampa Bay on June 3, 1539. Of both sexes, the Tamemes, taken between Tampa and the Cherokee country, were in the main Tamucuan, Muskogean, and Siouan stock. A goodly number had been purchased by De Soto from their chiefs with trade goods—looking glasses, plumes adorned with silver, bells, glass beads, false pearls, caps of yellow satin, velvet aprons, and knives. A Tameme's burdens were not light, but if he attempted to escape them, he was set upon by De Soto's pack of vicious bloodhounds and ofttimes torn into pieces by the animals.

A captive of another caliber, however, was the "Lady of Cofitachequi." Commandeered by De Soto to guide the expedition northward to Guasili in the Cherokees' country where De Soto hoped to find gold, the Lady of Cofitachequi was the niece of the chieftainess of Cofitachequi, a province near the site of Silver Bluff, South Carolina.

Departing from Cofitachequi on May 13, the Lady of Cofitachequi, borne on a litter by slave women, led the De Soto expedition northward over a trail that topped the high divide between the Savannah and Saluda rivers. Thus guided, the expedition passed without mishap through the Siouan provinces of Chalique and Gualquila. The unclad residents of Gualquila gave De Soto for food hundreds of wild hens, a little maize, and a goodly number of dogs that could not bark (maybe opossums).

After passing through Xuala, a Siouan town inhabited by Indians who called themselves "Cheraws," the Lady of Cofitachequi, on May 25, led the expedition northward into the mountains over the ancient Winding Stair Trail. This trail crossed a high ridge in the foothills of the southern Alleghenies, ran alongside White River, skirted Glade Mountain, and turning west, reached the site of Highlands where, on May 25, the De Soto expedition spent the night.

On the following day, Wednesday, May 26, De Soto's expedition, with its drove of squealing swine (estimated at around two hundred) and its pack of vicious bloodhounds, resumed its journey. Descending Cullasaja Gorge, it crossed the Little Tennessee River to a plain near the site of Franklin, where De Soto's chroniclers complained of the cold. The Gentleman from Elvas also noted that on the night of May 26 the Lady of Cofitachequi deserted the expedition, taking with her a casket of valuable pearls:

> The Governor [De Soto] set out from Xualla for Guaxule [Guasili], crossing over very rough and lofty mountains. Along this way, the cacica or cutifachiqui whom the governor brought as aforesaid for the purpose of taking her to Guaxule . . . stepped aside saying that she had to attend to her necessities. Thus she deceived them and hid herself in the woods; and although they sought her she could not be found. In five days the Governor arrived at Guaxule. The Indians there made him service of three hundred dogs, for they observed that the Christians liked them and sought them to eat; but they were not eaten among them. In Guaxule and along all that road there was very little maize.[14]

The escape of the Lady of Cofitachequi is of little moment to Cherokee historians. What is important is De Soto's visit to Guasili, and the chroniclers' allusion to the visit. For Guasili, it has been estimated by the United States De Soto Expedition Commission, was the one town visited by De Soto in 1540 whose residents were "real Cherokees"—unless Tanasqui, on the Tennessee River, was in 1540 inhabited by Cherokees.[15] Thus, Guasili (thanks to De Soto's

[14] James Alexander Robertson, *True Relations of the Hidalgo of Elvas, 1557,* II, 98–118.

[15] See *Final Report of the United States De Soto Expedition Commission,* 50. "If there is one place on De Soto's route which there is some reason to regard as Cherokee, it would be Guasili or Guasule. It has already been suggested that this may be explained by Cherokee *Ayuhwasi* plus a locative ending. . . . The name given by Pardo was probably Tocar (or perhaps Tocare), though we also find it sometimes spelled Tocax and Tocal." John Swanton, *The Indians of the Southeastern United States,* 110.

24

chroniclers) could appropriately be called the birthplace of the Cherokees' recorded history.

To reach Guasili from the site of Franklin, it is assumed that De Soto's expedition—minus its lady guide—blundered onto an old Indian trail that ascended the valley of the Cartoochaye, crossed Black Gap, and led down the valleys of Shooting Creek and Hiwassee to the town of Guasili situated at the juncture of Peachtree Creek and the Hiwassee (today Murphy, North Carolina).

After arriving at Guasili early on Sunday, May 30, Elvas reported the Cherokees' gift of dogs and corn. Garcilaso, as was his wont, exaggeratingly stated that Guasili contained three hundred houses and that the chief's house was "on a high elevation like all other similar ones which we have described. All around it was a public walk along which six men could pass abreast." Ranjel, considered trustworthy, wrote that they arrived early on Sunday at Guasili, whereupon "messengers of peace appeared . . . and they gave them Tamemes, many little dogs and corn; and since this was a fine stopping place, the soldiers afterwards in throwing dice called out 'The house of Guasili,' or a good throw." Biedma confirmed Elvas' assertion that there was little corn at Guasili. But all four chroniclers spelled *Guasili* differently. And Garcilaso, differing with Ranjel who wrote that De Soto spent but a fraction of a day at Guasili, extended the time of De Soto's stay to four days.

Plainly their encounter with the Spaniards of De Soto's expedition was not very important to Guasili Cherokees. Cherokee traditions thereafter made no mention of De Soto's visit nor of the visits of Don Pardo in 1566–67. But possibly De Soto's and Pardo's visits were not rendered disagreeable and tragic by the rape of Indian women, the burning of Tamemes at the stake, and the rifling of houses and temples by the expedition, as was the case in visits to other southeastern tribes made by De Soto.

A century passed, a century of Cherokee history unrecorded by white men and only orally recited by the Cherokees. These oral recitations of Cherokee history, omitting De Soto's and Pardo's visits, doubtlessly recalled the memorable deeds of Cherokee chiefs and warriors, and the defeat of enemies in general. Even so, the expe-

25

ditions did mark the beginning of the Cherokees' historical period, their emergence from the mysterious and engulfing darkness whence they had come.

CHAPTER III

Appraisal of the Cherokees
by the Colonists

EARLY IN THE HISTORICAL PERIOD, on July 15, 1673,—over one hundred years after De Soto's expedition—the Cherokees came in contact with the people whose influence was to provide their first major outside stimulus. On July 15, 1673, there arrived at Chota on the Little Tennessee River two white men, James Needham and Gabriel Arthur. They had been dispatched to the Cherokees' Overhills capital of Chota by Abraham Wood, a Virginia trader at Fort Henry (the site of Petersburg, Virginia), for the express purpose of opening a trading path between Chota and the Virginia colony, a colony that was in sore need of the Cherokees' peltries, beeswax, and bears' oil for export to England.

Arriving at Chota, via the Blue Ridge and Unaka Mountains, Needham and Arthur were well received by the chief of Chota— possibly because they were accompanied by a band of Occaneechis. Standing by to interpret what they had to say to the chief was Indian John, described by Abraham Wood as being "a fatt thick bluff faced fellow."[1] Also vouching for Needham and Arthur were their Occaneechi guides, who were on friendly terms with the Weesocks, a few of whom lived with the Cherokees at Chota. Thus did Needham

---

[1] Clarence Walworth Alvord and Lee Bidgood, *The First Explorations of the Trans-Allegheny Region by the Virginians, 1650–1674*, 215–18.

and Arthur succeed not only in exploring the Tennessee Valley (hitherto unexplored by the English) but also in making friends with the chief of one of the most feared and ferocious tribes then living in the southeastern section of North America.

Needham and Arthur's arrival having greatly excited his people, the chief of Chota ordered his warriors to remove the white men and their interpreter to a scaffold, where they could be seen but not crushed by the citizenry, to whom white men were obviously an oddity.

Given this excellent opportunity to examine his surroundings, Needham entered the following description of Chota in his letter book, a letter book that Abraham Wood later utilized in his correspondence with John Richards in London:

> The town of Chote is seated on ye river side, having ye clifts on ye river side on ye one side being very high for its defence, the other three sides trees of two foot or over, pitched on end, twelve foot high, and on ye topps scaffolds placed with parrapets to defend the walls and offend theire enemies which men stand on to fight, many nations of Indians inhabit downe this river . . . which they the Cherokees are at warre with and to that end keepe one hundred and fifty canoes under ye command of theire forts. Ye leaste of them will carry twenty men, and made sharpe at both ends like a wherry for swiftness, this forte is four square; 300: paces over and ye houses sett in streets.[2]

In his letter to Richards, Abraham Wood also referred to the Cherokees' kind treatment of Needham and Arthur, even "to addoration." And sharing in this "addoration" was Needham's horse, the sole equine survivor of the expedition:

> A stake was sett up in ye middle of ye towne to fasten ye horse to, and aboundance of corne and all manner of pulse with fish, flesh, and bears oyle for ye horse to feed upon and a scaffold sett up before day for my two men . . . that theire people might stand and gaze at them and not offend them by theire throng.[3]

[2] Samuel Cole Williams, ed., *Early Travels in the Tennessee Country*, 27–28.
[3] *Ibid.*

Having made friends with the chief, Needham left Arthur at Chota to learn the Cherokee language and hastened to Wood's Post, intending to return to the Cherokees' Overhills capital shortly with trading goods—guns, axes, metal tomahawks, cloth, beads, warriors' looking glasses, and ribbons. But, after procuring the goods from Abraham Wood and getting as far as the Yadkin River with them, Needham was murdered by Indian John, with whom he had previously quarreled. Indian witnesses to the murder were Needham's Occaneechi guides and several Cherokees from Chota who had accompanied Needham to Virginia—presumably to bind the trade agreement between Wood and their people. Their gruesome version of the murder (according to Wood) was:

> [Indian John, after quarreling with Needham] . . . catched up a gunn, which he himself had carried to kill meat for them to eate and shot Mr. Needham near ye burr of the eare and killed him. . . . [whereupon] Indian John drew out his knife, stepped across ye corpse of Mr. Needham, ript open his body, drew out his hart, held it in his hand and turned and looked to ye eastward, toward ye English plantations and said he valued not all ye English.[4]

Having done away with Needham, Indian John sent a message to the chief of Chota by the Cherokees that Arthur should be killed as well. But, arriving at Chota, the Cherokees found the chief away, and so instead delivered Indian John's message to the people, some of whom were for killing Arthur, and others, against it. Presumably, the Indians who heeded Indian John's advice were the Weesocks or Waxhaws living with the Cherokees. Binding Arthur to a stake, they heaped combustible stalks of cane and brush around him, preparatory to setting them afire.

> [But] Before ye fire was put too ye [Arthur] ye King came into ye towne with a gunn upon his shoulder . . . and ye King ran with great speed to the place and said who is that that is goeing to put fire to the English man. A Weesock borne started up with a fire-brand said that am I. Ye King forthwith cockt his gunn and shot ye Weesock

[4] Alvord and Bidgood, *First Explorations*, 215.

dead, and ran to Gabriel and with his knife cutt the thongs that tide him and had him goe to his house.[5]

So rescued, Arthur remained with the Cherokees at Chota for almost a year. Disguised as a Cherokee, Arthur accompanied the chief of Chota and his warriors on war raids to Spanish settlements in Florida, to enemy Indian communities on the Atlantic seaboard, and to Shawnee towns on the Ohio River.

But sometime in 1674 the Shawnees wounded, then captured Arthur in their own country. Arthur's career as a Cherokee warrior abruptly ended when the Shawnees discovered that, under his coating of clay and ashes, he was a white man. Following this discovery, the Shawnees—for some unknown reason—did not kill Arthur but, instead, permitted him to return to Chota when his wound was healed.

Arriving safely at Chota, Arthur was shortly afterward accompanied by its chief and his warriors to Virginia. There, on June 18, 1674, the chief delivered Arthur to Abraham Wood, who welcomed both Cherokees and Arthur warmly but apparently did not attempt to renew trade relations with the Cherokees at Chota.

Arthur's contribution to Cherokee recorded history was his letter book, utilized by Wood but not made available in after years to Cherokee historians. However, from Arthur's known adventures, Cherokee historians derive the valuable information that as early as 1673 the Cherokees possessed guns, which they presumably acquired when raiding Spanish settlements in Florida. Too, Arthur's mention of such raids in Florida disputes the assumption of many historians that between De Soto's visit in 1540 and Arthur's and Needham's in 1673 the Cherokees' contacts with white men were nonexistent.

Following Arthur's and Needham's contact with the Cherokees of Chota in 1673–74, a vast amount of information relating to the Cherokees issued from the quills of white men who, from that date on, came in contact with the Cherokees. In the main this informa-

[5] *Ibid.*, 218.

tion was supplied by colonists from Charlestown. Mention was made of the Cherokees by Henry Woodward, for one. In 1674, Woodward, after making his will, chose to travel from Charlestown to Virginia over a trail that brought him to "Chorakae" settlements on the "head branches" of the Savannah River.[6] Woodward's observation, though brief, clearly indicated that the Cherokees, since De Soto's visit in 1540, had moved into an area that at an earlier period was inhabited by people of Siouan stock. Cherokee settlements on the head branches of the Savannah (the Keowee River and its tributaries) thereafter were referred to by Charlestown colonists as "The Lower Towns of the Cherokees."

Cherokee chiefs, from "Toxawa and Keowa," referred to vaguely by Charlestown officials in 1684 as the signatories of a treaty "said to have been made" between the Cherokees and the South Carolina colony, were from these Lower Towns settlements and possibly from the Middle Towns of the Cherokees as well.[7]

Another early reference to the Cherokees was made by James Moore and Colonel Maurice Matthews, who, in 1690, bravely ventured into the then dark and mysterious Cherokee country in search of gold but "retired on account of trouble with the Indians."[8] Three years later, in 1693, the "trouble with the Indians" experienced by Moore and Matthews did not deter the hostile Cherokees from going to Charlestown and demanding firearms from the governor of Charlestown to use in wars against the Esaws (Catawbas), Savanahs (Shawnees), and other enemy tribes.

That war was the Cherokees' principal occupation until the nineteenth century was the unanimous conclusion of white men with whom they came in contact. The journals, letters, and official records of Charlestown and Georgia colonists, of English and Scottish emissaries of the crown, of traders and missionaries, and even of a

---

[6] John R. Swanton, *The Indians of the Southeastern United States*, B. A. E., *Bulletin No. 137* (1946), 110–12.

[7] *Ibid.*

[8] *Ibid.*, James Mooney, *Myths of the Cherokee*, B. A. E., *Nineteenth Annual Report* (1897–98), Pt. 1, 31.

Quaker botanist from Philadelphia who visited the eighteenth-century Cherokees—all attest to the Cherokees' inordinate fondness for war.

Around 1730, English emissaries of the crown strove to make peace between the Cherokees and the Tuscaroras. But the Cherokee chiefs said: "Should we make peace withe the Tuscaroras . . . we must immediately look for some other with whom we can be engaged in our beloved occupation."[9]

Sent to the Cherokees' Lower, Middle, and Overhills towns by the crown in 1725 to regulate Cherokee-British trade, and at the same time to alienate the Cherokees from the French, Colonel George Chicken noted the Cherokees' fortifications:

> We set away from home [Charlestown] & went to old Estatoe a large town & very well fortified all around with punchins and also ditched on the Outside of the sd [said] Punchins (wch Ditch) is stuck full of . . . spikes so that if the Enemy should . . . fall therein, they must without doubt receive a great deal of Damage by those Spikes— I also observe that there are sevl [several] new flankers made to the fortifications of the Town & that the Town House is also enforted.[10]

Tellico or "Great Terriquo" was also described by Chicken as being fortified. All of Tellico's houses had been made "muskett proof," and its Town Houses (Council Houses), "enforted." "Otherwise," observed Chicken, the residents of Tellico "would be cut off by the enemy who are continually within a mile of the town lurking about the skirts thereof."[11]

As described by Chicken, the Cherokees' fortified towns in 1725 resembled Chota in 1673.

Supporting his predecessors' observations of the warlike Cherokees, William Fyffe, a plantation owner of Charlestown, wrote to his brother in 1761:

[9] Haywood, *Natural and Aboriginal History of Tennessee*, 238.

[10] Public Record Office, London, Journal of the Commissioner of Indian Affairs (Colonel George Chicken's Journal, 1725), MS (copy) in the Thomas Gilcrease Institute of American History and Art, Tulsa, Oklahoma.

[11] *Ibid.*

"War is their [the Cherokees] principal study & their greatest ambition is to distinguish themselves by military actions . . . even the old men who are past the trade [age] themselves use every method to stirr up a martial ardour in the youth. The women (as among the whites know how to persuade by Praises or Ridicule the young men to what they please) employ their art to make them warlike. . . . Their young men are not regarded till they kill an enemy or take a prisoner. Those houses in which there's the greatest number of scalps are most honoured. A scalp is as great a Trophy among them as a pair of colours among us.[12]

Other eighteenth-century white men who were associated with the Cherokees noted the Indians' methods of perpetuating and fanning to frenzy the war spirit of the tribe. Parents taught a Cherokee boy that he was dishonored unless he avenged an insult. And, fearful that drastic punishments would blunt their warlike dispositions, Cherokee tribal government did not provide laws for such punishment of villainous youths. Thus, miscreants were merely "dryscratched" with briers or snake teeth, publicly ridiculed, or simply ignored. As noted by William Fyffe in 1761:

Their punishments are voluntary acts of justice done by the Father or Head of the cabin upon any offender in his cabin. They are so regular that quarrels & murders (their almost only vices among themselves) happen very seldom. Without laws & punishments to force them they adhere punctually to what their fathers practice before them.[13]

In order to keep alive tribal fondness for war, Cherokees taught youths to endure hunger and pain; to witness stoically the torture of war captives; and to listen courteously to chiefs and headmen who at public gatherings, year in and year out, recited their own war deeds or the war deeds of ancient forebears.

To aggrandize war, the honorary war titles of "Outacite" (Man-

---

[12] William Fyffe to Brother John, February 1, 1761, original MS in Gilcrease Institute.
[13] *Ibid.*

Killer) or "Colonah" (The Raven) were conferred on young warriors who distinguished themselves in battle. And women who had distinguished themselves in war were given the title of "Ghighau" (Beloved Woman) and made members of the Cherokee war council.

As the war lords of the southern Alleghenies, and even of all the southeastern section of the United States, eighteenth-century Cherokees were constantly at war either with neighboring enemies or with Indian enemies of the English, the latter repaying the Cherokees for war services with firearms and gifts. Thus, between 1711–13, according to South Carolina records, 310 Cherokees assisted the English at Charlestown in driving the Tuscaroras out of the southeastern part of the United States northward beyond the Great Lakes, where the Tuscaroras became the sixth nation in the Iroquoian Confederacy. And, as a letter written by Major Charles Gale to officials in London amply demonstrated, the colonists of South Carolina, in 1711, would never have avenged the murders of 137 settlers on the Roanoke by the Tuscaroras without Cherokee help. "I must inform your honours ye governors of . . . Carolina are not in a condition to take a full (I might say any) satisfaction on ye neighboring Indians nor to prevent their further progress," Major Gale explained to London officials—officials who possibly did not realize the colonists' dependence on Indian allies for their very survival.[14]

If not engaged in wars initiated by the colonists or in legitimate wars of their own, Cherokees in the eighteenth century would start wars with neighbors admittedly to provide practice for warriors. The method employed by the Cherokees in this instance was to invade settlements of neighboring tribes whose warriors were away and, swooping down upon the aged and young, carry them back to Cherokee settlements.

Eighteenth-century white men noted the adverse effects of war on the Cherokee tribe but saw also its benefits. William Fyffe be-

---

[14] Major Charles Gale to English correspondent, November 2, 1711, in "F. Fairfax Discourse of Witchcraft," Unpublished MS No. 32,496, in Department of MSS, British Museum, London.

moaned the fact that the war-loving Cherokees frequently confounded barbarity with courage. But at the same time Fyffe admitted that the Cherokees' recitations of war deeds encouraged their youths to become orators who even surpassed those of ancient Greece and Rome:

> Among themselves Every warrior is an orator & they have publick gatherings frequently to give them an opportunity of boasting of their exploits. This they do with such Enthusiasm that the young are catch'd with it & eager to emulate them. This is an excellent way to whet the courage of their youth.[15]

The decrease in the Cherokees' population was attributed to war by white men.[16] Although the Cherokees boasted in the middle of the eighteenth century that they could on short notice set six thousand warriors on the war trail, this force seemed likely to diminish since Cherokee women as a rule produced but small families—three or four children being considered by them a sizeable family.

Second to war, the Cherokees' beloved occupation was the hunt. It was enjoyed by both sexes, according to eighteenth-century white observers. Other occupations of Cherokee men, not so favored but deemed to be necessary, were the making of bows, tomahawks, war clubs, canoes, and earthen ware. To women and "useless fellows" was relegated such work as gardening, the care of hogs and poultry, the smoking of venison and other meats procured on the hunt, the tanning of hides, the manufacture of clothing, and the rearing of the young.[17]

According to William Fyffe, a Cherokee woman was never idle and had no time to tattle or to create mischief. And Lieutenant Henry Timberlake, Fyffe's contemporary, declared Cherokee women to be excellent cooks, especially of bread. "After making a fire on the hearthstone," wrote Timberlake in his *Memoirs,* "they sweep the embers off, laying a loaf smooth on it; this they cover with a sort

[15] William Fyffe to Brother John, *loc. cit.*
[16] *Ibid.*
[17] *Ibid.*

of deep dish, and renew the fire upon the whole, under which the bread bakes to as great perfection as in any European oven."[18]

To eighteenth-century white men historians are indebted for descriptions of the appearance of Cherokees of this era; of their dress, deportment, customs, and religion (or lack of it); of the organization of their government and the linguistic divisions of the nation; and for general descriptions of the Cherokees' towns, public buildings, and private dwellings.

In describing the Cherokees to his brother John in far-off Dundee, William Fyffe wrote:

> An Indian [Cherokee] is much of the colour of the orange that's painted for a Sign to your Toy shops especially after it's a little dirtied black. Have straight limbs & [are] generally taller than whites. They are a hardy people tho' their hardiness consists rather in bearing much exercize than labour. The men have no Hair on their chin or lips & both sexes shave it off their privities. Their education consists chiefly in learning to bear cold Hunger Fatigue & pain of which they have enough from their method of life.[19]

Lieutenant Henry Timberlake's description of the Cherokees in the main agrees with Fyffe's:

> The Cherokees are of middle stature, of an olive colour, tho' generally painted, and their skins stained with gunpowder pricked into it in very pretty figures. The hair of their head is shaved . . . except a patch on the hinder part of the head, about twice the bigness of a crownpiece, which is ornamented with beads, feathers, wampum, stained deers' hair, and such baubles. . . .
>
> They that can afford it wear a collar of wampum, which are beads cut out of clam-shells, a silver breastplate, and bracelets on their arms and wrists of the same metal, a bit of cloth over their private parts, a shirt of English make, a sort of cloth-boots, and mockasons, which are shoes of a make peculiar to the Americans, ornamented with porcupine-quills; a large mantle or matchcoat thrown over all compleats

[18] P. 30.
[19] William Fyffe to Brother John, *loc. cit.*

their dress at home; but when they go to war they leave their trinkets behind, and the mere necessaries serve them. . . . Both men and women were streight and well-built, with small hands and feet.[20]

William Bartram, a Philadelphia botanist, noted the dress of Cherokee women:

> The dress of the females is somewhat different from that of the men; their flap or petticoat, is made after a different manner, is larger and longer, reaching almost to the middle of the leg, and is put on differently; they have no shirt or shift but a little short waistcoat, usually made of callico, printed linen, or fine cloth decorated with lace, beads & c. They never wear boots or stockings, but their buskins reach to the middle of the leg. They never cut their hair, but plait it in wreathes, which is turned up, and fastened on the crown, with a silver broach, forming a wreathed top-knot.[21]

According to another authority (Wah-ne-nau-hi, or Mrs. Lucy L. Keyes), eighteenth-century Cherokee women wore skirts and short jackets with leggings and moccasins. "Their hair was combed smooth and close then folded into a club at the back of the head and tied very tight with a piece of dried eel-skin which was said to make the hair grow long."[22]

Cherokee dress always suited the occasion. A chief, for example, wore a gold-dyed buckskin shirt and leggings with matching feather headdress when he performed a special dance for his people every seventh year. And the ceremonial dress of a woman chief was a knee-length skirt woven from feathers and edged at the bottom with down plucked from the breast of a white swan.[23]

We have it from William Bartram that Cherokee maidens, when picking strawberries, wore little or nothing, "disclosing their beauties to the fluttering breeze, and bathing their limbs in the cool, flitting

[20] Williams, *Dawn of Tennessee Valley and Tennessee History*, 75, 77.

[21] *Travels*, 319.

[22] Wah-ne-nau-hi, Unpublished MS No. 2191, B. A. E.

[23] See replicas of clothing on display in Council House at Oconaluftee Village, Cherokee, North Carolina.

streams."[24] But when performing the friendship dance at the Town House, according to Bartram, Cherokee maidens were dressed in robes of chaste white deerskin, totally unlike their habitual dress—short skirts, buskins reaching to the mid-calf of the leg, and short jackets secured with silver broaches exposing several inches of midriff.

Cherokee children, when small, went unclad. But female children, upon reaching the age of ten, wore garments similar to those worn by their mothers. A youth frequently went unclad until he reached puberty.

The deportment of eighteenth-century Cherokees was also observed and recorded by white men. Timberlake noted that "they seldom turn their eyes on the person they speak of, or address themselves to, and are always suspicious when peoples' eyes are fixed on them."[25] Fyffe was impressed also by the Cherokees' grave and "judicious Behaviour on all publick occasions. This seems an exception to their character which is impetuous & ungovernable."[26] And Fyffe, after witnessing a chief's diplomatic handling of an obtuse South Carolina governor in 1761, declared this chief capable of outwitting both Richlieu and Walpole, and the Cherokees as a whole, the superiors of Europeans in politics. "They laugh at the Europeans," he said, "for being so ready to talk & tell their minds & interrupt one another."[27]

Originating nicknames and laughing at Europeans and at themselves were evidently the favorite diversions of eighteenth-century Cherokees. To "a dull stalking fellow," Adair noted, the Cherokees gave the name of Sooreh, "the Turkey Buzzard"; to a cross, waspish fellow, the name Kana Cheesteche or "the Wasp." A loquacious English trader was known to the Cherokees of one town as Sekakee, "the Grasshopper." "The Ugly White Man" was a common nickname for Europeans. But the Cherokees' nickname "The

[24] *Travels*, 225f.
[25] *Memoirs*, 55.
[26] William Fyffe to Brother John, *loc. cit.*
[27] *Ibid.*
[28] Adair, *History of the American Indians*, 193.

Old Rabbit" bestowed on Eleazar Wiggan, early-day interpreter and trader, was inspirited by affection, not ridicule.[28]

Rarely did a Cherokee raise his voice in public or private, unless intoxicated by the white men's rum. To a Cherokee, silence was golden. But, according to Adair, the Cherokees did have the unfortunate habit of calling people liars. "As there is no alternative between a falsehood and a lie, they usually tell any person, in plain language, 'you lie,' as a friendly negative to a reputed truth."[29]

Fyffe thought that the Cherokees acted more naturally in family matters than did the whites. "Their men & women confine themselves to their proper spheres while we in general act otherwise."[30]

The Cherokees' hospitable deportment toward white men they liked was noted by Colonel George Chicken, who, when in their country in 1725, was fanned with eagle tails by welcoming Cherokees,[31] and by Lieutenant Timberlake,[32] to whom the Cherokees proffered their pipes (estimated by Timberlake to number between 170–80) at a council at Settico. At Cowee in May, 1775, winsome Cherokee maidens insisted on sharing with William Bartram and his guide the wild strawberries which they had been picking. "We accepted a basket, sat down and regaled ourselves on the fruit, encircled by the whole assembly of the innocently jocose nymphs," Bartram afterward wrote in his memoirs.[33]

Possibly the most honored visitor to the Cherokee country was His Majesty Louis Philippe of France, who, in 1797, traveled incognito with his two brothers through the Cherokee country on horseback. At Chota, His Majesty (at that time, the Duke of Orleans) was accorded the great privilege of sleeping in the chief's quarters between the chief's grandmother and grandaunt.

Louis Philippe's brothers, being entertained by the sight of their august kinsman sleeping on a mat between two such venerable "ladies," wrote to their sister Princess Adelaide that "They [the

[29] *Ibid.*, 50–51.
[30] William Fyffe to Brother John, *loc. cit.*
[31] Journal of the Commissioner of Indian Affairs, *loc. cit.*
[32] Timberlake, *Memoirs*, 39.
[33] *Travels*, 226.

Cherokees] received us with great kindness. . . . And After them, we found the Falls of Niagra the most interesting object of our journey."[34]

The customs—especially concerning marriage—of eighteenth-century Cherokees have long been both incomprehensible and intriguing to historians. As described by Adair and others, Cherokee marriage ceremonies of this period were brief and simple. The ritual merely entailed the exchange of gifts, in lieu of vows, between a bride and her groom, and lasted but half an hour. Meeting at the center of the Town House, the groom gave the bride a ham of venison and in exchange received from her an ear of corn, whereupon the wedding party danced and feasted for hours on end. The groom's gift of venison symbolized his intention to keep his household supplied with game from the hunt, and the bride's ear of corn signified her willingness to be a good Cherokee housewife.[35]

The fact that Cherokees frequently made three marriages within one year struck eighteenth-century white men as peculiar. Adair's comment was that Cherokee women, "like the Amazons . . . divorce bed-fellows at their pleasure."[36] But William Fyffe seemed to approve and even envy the Cherokee husband's privilege of punishing a wife for incontinency as he saw fit.[37]

Deploring the Cherokees' practice of admitting women to their war councils and of giving them freedom accorded women of no other red race that he had known, James Adair accused Cherokee men of living under petticoat government. Henry Timberlake, too, in his *Memoirs*, refers unenthusiastically to the Cherokee custom of permitting women chiefs (usually successors to chieftain husbands) to decide the fate of prisoners and, by the "wave of a swan's wing, deliver a wretch condemned by the council, and already tied to the stake."

[34] Williams, ed., *Early Travels in the Tennessee Country*, 433–38.

[35] Adair, *History of the American Indians*, 127; William Fyffe to Brother John, *loc. cit.*; Timberlake, *Memoirs*, 65.

[36] *History of the American Indians*, 146.

[37] William Fyffe to Brother John, *loc. cit.*

The Cherokees' war habits were a source of interest to both Fyffe and Timberlake. Fyffe observed that when it was decided among the chiefs and headmen to strike the war trail, the "war hatchet" was sent to all the towns in the nation and to all the Cherokees' allies. Whereupon, "there's nothing heard but war songs and howlings."[38] To prepare for war, the warriors blacked their faces and streaked them with vermillion, and dressed their hair with feathers while the chief struck the war pole with his club and sang the war song. As recorded by Timberlake, the chief's war song began as follows:

> *Where 'er the earth's enlightened by the sun,*
> *Moon shines by night, grass grows, or waters run,*
> *Be 't known that we are going like men, afar,*
> *In hostile fields to wage destructive war.*[39]

When finished with his song, the chief led his warriors to a site selected by him for the exchange of ceremonial war dress for that of actual war. Awaiting the arrival of the warriors at this site were Cherokee women who had in their possession the warriors' oldest breechcloths and blankets. The warriors, after donning these articles of apparel, delivered to the women their ceremonial clothing and, as observed by William Fyffe, then headed down the war trail "like a string of geese," with the chief in the lead.

The Cherokees' torture of war captives upon their return from these raids was a custom deplored by eighteenth-century white men. The laceration of a prisoner's flesh, the ripping off of his toe- and fingernails, and the subjection of the mangled stumps of his extremities to fire before ending his life were tortures too horrible to contemplate. However, well-read white men, recalling the Spanish Inquisition, prayed that in time the Cherokees might be delivered from this dark practice, even as the Spaniards had been.

Lieutenant Henry Timberlake, for one, was permitted to see another facet of Cherokee life that presumably diverted his mind from

[38] *Ibid.*
[39] *Memoirs,* 56f.

their heinous torture of captives. The following account by Timber-lake of the Cherokees' treatment of their own indigent members contrasts oddly with Cherokee cruelty:

> When any [of their people] are hungry, as they term it, or in distress, orders are issued out by the headmen for a war-dance, at which all the fighting men and warriors assemble; but here, contrary to all their other dances, one only dances at a time, who, after hopping and caper-ing for near a minute, with a tommahawke in his hand, gives a small [w]hoop, at which signal the music stops till he relates the manner of taking his first scalp, and concludes his narration, by throwing on a large skin spread for that purpose, a string of wampum, piece of plate, wire, paint, lead, or anything he can conveniently spare; after which the music strikes up, and he proceeds in the same manner through all his warlike actions: then another takes his place, and the ceremony lasts till all the warriors and fighting men have related their exploits. The stock thus raised, after paying the musicians, is divided among the poor.[40]

But obviously the Cherokees' unique method of helping their weak and indigent was not inspirited by religion. White men among them reported that eighteenth-century Cherokees had no formal religion to guide their actions. William Fyffe's comment was:

> Some of them have a confused notion of good and evil spirits but seem more attentive to the latter, than to apply to the former. They're strongly affected with dreams & run to their conjurers for an explana-tion, they likewise depend on their conjurers to foretell to them what success they'll have in Hunting & all their concerns. They [the con-jurers] also act as their physicians using charms & conjuration tho' they have a universal Remedy which they use for all Disorders which is to put the sick in a close hutt [a Cherokee hothouse] in which is placed a large stone. This is made very hot and water thrown on it till by the steam & his own sweat the patient is well soak'd & then they hurry him to the nearest river and throw him in. . . . This is the remedy for their acute Disorders, but they're said to be more skilled in the vir-

---

[40] *Ibid.*

tues of vegetables in the cure of Lues Venera & other chronic disorders.[41]

As in all matters pertaining to their life, conjurers or Adawehis held important positions in the Cherokees' government. Custom decreed that Adawehis be present at every council to prevent evil spirits from entering the Town House, the seat of government. Wearing animal or bird masks, the Adawehis also served as the chief's counselors, and by signs, portents, and ancient formulas directed his movements.

Each Cherokee town was governed by two chiefs—a White Chief for peace time and a Red Chief for wartime. The chief in power occupied an ottoman in the "holy area" or west half of the Town House. The Red Chief or war chief, when in power, sat closer to the sacred fire that burned in the center of the Town House than did the White Chief, the Red Chief being considered the more important of the two. This of course was because war, to the Cherokees, was infinitely more important and desirable than peace.

When the Cherokees were embroiled in war, their Red Chief (Danawaga-we-u-we) was reckoned the most powerful Cherokee in the town or nation, albeit his office was more uncertain and temporary than the White Chief's. The duration of the Red Chief's office depended entirely upon the vital outcome of wars, while the White Chief's merely depended on his ability to attend to inconsequential ecclesiastical and civil matters.

Custom dictated that an assemblage of war women or Pretty Women be present at every war council. And since the war women had themselves won previous honors in wars and were the mothers of warriors, they played an important role in Cherokee war councils. Seated in the "holy area," these women sagely counseled the Red Chief on strategy, time of attack, and other weighty matters related to war.

Seated on "sophas," or seats, in the Town House were the common Cherokees, who at councils attentively listened to the chiefs

[41] William Fyffe to Brother John, *loc. cit.*

and headmen orate for hours. "Toeuhah" or "it is true" was their comment when the orator was finished.[42]

In ancient days Cherokee Town Houses had seven sides, one for each of the seven clans. Occupants of the "sophas" or seats were clansmen, custom decreeing that members of a clan sit together at council. Consequently, children, who always belonged to the clan of the mother, sat with their mother and her clan, and their father sat with his. But by the middle of the eighteenth century the Town Houses (or at least the ones noted by Timberlake and Bartram) were rounded in shape, albeit the symbolism of seven remained.

Detailed descriptions of both the exterior and interior of Cherokee Town Houses were recorded. But—as in all descriptions of people, places, or buildings—these descriptions reflect the moods and viewpoints of the narrators and thus frequently vary. For example, to Lieutenant Henry Timberlake the exterior of the Town House at Chota, "the metropolis of the country," had the appearance of a small mountain, its top or roof being covered with earth. "It is built in the form of a sugar loaf," Timberlake wrote in his *Memoirs*, "and [is] large enough to contain 500 persons."[43] But Louis Philippe referred to the same Town House as being "hexagonal" and made of logs.[44]

William Bartram's description of the Town House at Cowee, in the Cherokee Middle Towns, emphasized construction:

> The Rotunda is constructed in the following manner: They first fix in the ground a circular range of posts or trunks of trees about six feet high, at equal distances, which are notched on top, to receive into them, from one to another a range of beams or wall plates; within this is another circular order of very large and strong pillars, about twelve feet high, notched in like manner at top to receive another range of wall plates, and within this is yet another or third range of stronger and higher pillars, but fewer in number, and standing at a greater

[42] Adair, *History of the American Indian*, 50; Bartram, *Travels*, 233.
[43] Samuel Cole Williams, ed., *Lieut. Henry Timberlake's Memoirs*, 59.
[44] Williams, ed., *Early Travels in the Tennessee Country*, 433, 438.

distance from each other; and lastly in the centre at top, these rafters are strengthened and bound together by cross beams and laths, which sustain the roof; which is a layer of bark . . . tight enough to exclude the rain, and sometimes they cast a thin superficies of earth over all.[45]

Written while he was nauseated by the tobacco which he had smoked in Cherokee Town Houses at Chota and at Settico, Timberlake's account of the interior of one is somewhat prejudiced:

The Town House in which are transacted all public business and diversions . . . [is] extremely dark, having besides the door, which is so narrow that but one at a time can pass, and after much winding and turning, but one small aperture to let the smoak out, which is so ill-contrived, that most of it settles in the roof of the house. Within it has the appearance of an ancient amphitheater, the seats being raised one above another, leaving an area in the middle, in the center of which stands the fire; the seats of the head warriors are nearest it.[46]

Unlike Timberlake, Bartram does not complain of either the entrance to or "smoak" within the Town House at Cowee:

There is but one large door which serves at the same time to admit light from without and the smoak to escape when the fire is kindled; but as there is but a small fire kept . . . and that fed with dry small sound wood divested of its bark, there is but little smoak; all around the inside of the building, betwixt the second range of pillars and the wall, is a range of . . . sophas . . . in theatrical order, where the assembly sit.[47]

The fire alluded to by both Timberlake and Bartram corresponded to an altar in the white men's cathedrals. It was kindled atop a cone-shaped mound of earth in the center of a Town House. The history of the Cherokees' ceremonial fire was inexplicable to men like Wil-

---

[45] *Travels,* 232f.
[46] Williams, ed., *Lieut. Henry Timberlake's Memoirs,* 59.
[47] *Travels,* 233.

liam Fyffe, who observed that Cherokee history must needs be recited, sung, or recorded in wampum, "for they [the Cherokees] know nothing of writing."[48]

Understandably, the Town House was the largest and most important structure in a Cherokee town. And since it was estimated by James Adair, in 1735 or 1736, that there were approximately sixty-four towns and villages in the Nation, the same number of Town Houses presumably existed at that date.[49]

Being a trader, this data must have helped Adair to determine the amount of English goods that he would need for trade with the Cherokees. Too, a knowledge of Cherokee towns and their populations enabled Adair to estimate the number of peltries he could count on from the Cherokees for export—an important item, when one considered that the Cherokee Nation's annual yield of peltries had climbed from 50,000 in 1708 to nearly 1,000,000 in 1735, the year in which James Adair completed his Cherokee census. On the basis of Adair's count of Cherokee towns, it has been estimated by James Mooney that the population of the Cherokee Nation in Adair's time was between sixteen and seventeen thousand persons.

Adair's survey of Cherokees' towns yielded other important information—later to be incorporated by Adair in his *History of The American Indians*—that gives one a picture of eighteenth-century towns.

Certain Cherokee towns, Adair observed in his history, were referred to by the residents as "Towns of Refuge." These, as their name implies, were refuges for murderers whose lives were demanded elsewhere by relatives of the deceased. Thus, a murderer, to avoid paying for his crime under the ancient Cherokee unwritten law of blood for blood, postponed his death by sojourning in a Town of Refuge, where the ancient blood-for-blood law could not be enforced. His return to the scene of his crime was an open invitation to relatives of the deceased to "take their satisfaction."[50]

[48] William Fyffe to Brother John, *loc. cit.*

[49] Adair, *History of the American Indians;* Mooney, *Myths of the Cherokee, loc. cit.,* 34.

[50] *History of the American Indians;* William Fyffe to Brother John, *loc. cit.*

The Cherokees also had Mother Towns that served as headquarters for their seven clans. But whether they were Mother Towns or Towns of Refuge, Cherokee towns were laid off in approximately the same manner and according to the same plan.[51] In the center of each town stood the Town House—presumably on elevated ground. And in front of the Town House was the Square, a level area used by the Cherokees for dances, games, and celebrations of all kinds.

Near the Town House and Square were the public granary and community gardens. And clustered around these public areas were the private homes of the Cherokees, with their "dependencies"—a hothouse adjacent to the dwelling, poultry houses, and hogpens.[52]

It is not difficult to procure descriptions of Cherokee houses. Adair and Bartram have both graphically described mid- and late-eighteenth-century ones. According to Adair, early Cherokee houses were made of logs, roofed with bark, had but one door, and were windowless. A fire burned in the center of the earliest houses, and its smoke was ushered out through a small aperture in the roof. These houses were brightened inside by rugs woven from hemp, then painted in gay colors with bird, animal, and flower motifs. Buffalo-hide chests, cane seats, and baskets of every shape and size constituted their furnishings.

Bartram gives the following description of Cherokee dwellings:

> The Cherokees construct their habitations on a different plan from the Creeks, that is but one oblong four square building, one story high; the materials consisting of logs or trunks of trees, stripped of their bark, notched at their ends, fixed one upon another, and afterwards plaistered well, both inside and out, with clay well tempered with dry grass, and the whole . . . roofed . . . with the bark of the Chestnut tree or long broad shingles. The building is . . . partitioned transversely, forming three apartments which communicate with each other by inside doors; each house . . . has besides a little conical house, covered

---

[51] A. S. Gatchet (collector) from Richard F. Wolfe, Unpublished MS No. 388, B. A. E.

[52] See Adair, *History of the American Indians*; Bartram, *Travels*; and Mooney, *Myths of the Cherokee, loc. cit.*

with dirt, which is called the winter or hot-house; this stands a few yards distance from the mansion-house, opposite the front door.[53]

A typical Cherokee town or village contained between thirty and sixty houses. But Bartram estimated in 1775 that there were one hundred dwellings at Cowee, each having its own garden, orchard, hogpens, and hothouse. Bartram also discovered that in the Cherokees' orchards there was manure evenly spread around "plumb" and peach trees.

Linguistic differences among the Cherokees were noted by eighteenth-century white men. The three dialects spoken then in the Nation have been classified by Mooney as Eastern, Middle, and Western.

According to Mooney, the Eastern or Lower dialect was spoken "in all the towns and settlements on the Keowee and Tugaloo, headstreams of Savannah River, in South Carolina and the adjacent portion of Georgia." Now extinct, the Eastern dialect was the only Cherokee dialect having the *r* instead of the *l* sound.

The Middle or Kituhwa dialect was spoken in towns on the Tuckasegee and the headwaters of the Little Tennessee, in the very heart of the Cherokee country. (And, today, the Middle or Kituhwa dialect is spoken on the Qualla Reservation in western North Carolina.)

The Western dialect was used in most of the towns in what is today eastern Tennessee and upper Georgia, and areas on the Hiwassee and Cheoah rivers in present North Carolina.[54]

In the seventeenth and eighteenth centuries, when the Cherokees were making their first acquaintance with the British colonists and with the white man's way of life, they still maintained naturally enough their own cultural habits—habits which were not entirely to disappear or perceptibly to change for centuries to come, and which embraced not only warfare but a whole host of diversions.

Six great festivals enlivened and punctuated the Cherokees' year,

[53] *Travels*, 231f.
[54] Mooney, *Myths of the Cherokee, loc. cit.*, 16f.

aboriginally a year of twelve or thirteen months.[55] First came the great festival that commemorated the first new moon of spring and the welcome appearance of green grass. A second great festival, *Sah, looh, stee-knee, keeh steh steeh*, marked the ecstatic season when young corn could be tasted. Then, some forty or fifty days later, the third festival, *Tung, nah, kaw, HOON GH-ni*, celebrated the maturity of the corn and its readiness for harvest. A fourth festival, *Nung, tah, -tay-quah*, coincided with the wondrous appearance of the first new moon of autumn and the begining of the *gola* winter months. And a fifth—celebrated ten days later—marked the highly important propitiation or cementation festival, referred to by the Cherokees as *Ah, tawh, hung, nah*.

Great preparations were made by the Cherokees for celebrating *Ah, tawh, hung, nah*, for the fifth festival gave every member of the tribe the opportunity to "begin over" and start life anew. Thus, when the time for the celebration approached, Cherokees discarded old clothing and house furnishings for new, burning old possessions in a communal bonfire in the Square. The Adawehis extinguished the sacred fire in the Town House and with much ceremony built a new fire atop a mound of fresh earth in the center of the "holy area." Whereupon the people of the town, having extinguished the fires in their dwellings and swept these dwellings clean, came to the Town House and from the Adawehis received embers from the sacred fire with which to rekindle new fires.

The Square was swept clean like the dwellings, and the exterior of the Town House was whitened all over with clay. And, since this was the season when transgressions were forgiven, murderers returned from Towns of Refuge to dwell in peace with townsfolk whose kin they had murdered—knowing that the ancient law of blood for blood no longer applied to them, now that *Ah, tawh, hung, nah* was here.

Purification was achieved by all members of the tribe by drinking

[55] Frank G. Speck and Leonard Broom in collaboration with Will West Long, *Cherokee Dance and Drama*, 7f.

great quantities of physic (the black drink) and by bathing in the nearest stream both before and after the social dances that lasted for approximately a week. Participated in by both men and women, the social dances of the Cherokees were actually dramatizations of friendship, neighborliness, and the intimacy of the sexes, and were referred to as the "Beginning," "Friendship," and "Round or Running Dances."[56]

Following the celebration of *Ah, tawh, hung, nah,* there was an interval before the sixth great festival of *Eelah, wahtah, lay-kee.* And so the Cherokees, while awaiting its arrival, turned to other diversions. They celebrated a war victory, got ready for a hunt, enjoyed various games, or regaled the young with imaginative tales told to Cherokee children by elders from time immemorial.

No diversion excited the Cherokees more than the celebration of a war victory, its highlight being the "Scalp" or "Victory Dance" that sometimes lasted for weeks and was participated in by both sexes. Frenzied women and warriors, waving hoops adorned with scalps, wildly danced and whooped nightly in the torchlighted Square adjacent to the Town House—much to the horror of eighteenth-century white men, who pronounced the proceedings "revolting" and more of an orgy than a dance.

Less gruesome were the Cherokees' animal dances commemorating the hunt—a diversion second in the Cherokee's affections to war. The Raccoon and Beaver Dances dramatized the killing of these animals, the skinning of their carcasses, and the stretching and treatment of their hides. A Buffalo Hunt Dance was performed by men and women impersonating cows and bulls. Wearing buffalo masks, the dancers realistically pawed the earth with make-believe hoofs, emitted great bellows, and, head downward, charged would-be slayers. Another favorite animal dance of the Cherokees was the Bear Dance. It was performed with great gusto and sincerity in late autumn or winter by hunters because, as every hunter knew, the bears had, at one time, been human like themselves—an eighth clan. Wan-

---

[56] *Ibid.,* 19–84; Swimmer, Unpublished MS No. 2242, "Cherokee Dance Songs, etc.," B. A. E.

dering off from the tribe, this clan had eventually assumed the guise of bears, and thus bears must be accorded great respect by hunters before and during a hunt. Cherokee tradition decreed that hunters appease a bear (or any animal, for that matter) by first asking its permission for the act of killing it. If, for some reason, permission was withheld by the animal, the hunter would be visited immediately by crippling rheumatism, and the family of the hunter would be likewise attacked. So preceding a hunt, the Bear Dance and all other superstitions relating to a bear hunt were strictly observed by Cherokee hunters, both men and women.

A ball-play ranked high among Cherokee diversions. Even though it was only a contest or a game, when a ball-play was scheduled between two towns, young and old were present to celebrate the event with feasts, dances, and wagers placed on certain players.

Similar to lacrosse, the ball-play, as it was played by Cherokees in eighteenth century, was certainly no game for women or white men. Its players—sometimes fifty on a side—captured a small deer-skin-covered ball in mid-air and, carrying it down the playing field in the webbed curve of their ball-play stick, hurled it over a goal post, thereby winning a point for their side. But en route to the goal post, the player was likely to be kicked, punched, or even killed by opponents, who went unpenalized. But even though they were bloody affairs, the Cherokee ball-plays were never so spectacular as those of the Choctaws, the Cherokees' neighbors, whose great ball-plays were played by teams having several hundred on each side.

A Cherokee ball-play was celebrated beforehand by dances in the Town House. These dances were designed to give the players courage and strengthen their "will to win." Of this celebration preceding a ball-play at Cowee in the Middle Towns, William Bartram wrote in 1775:

> The people being assembled . . . and the musicians having taken their station, the ballplay [dance] opens, first with a long harangue or oration, spoken by an aged chief, in commendation of the manly exercize of the ball-play. . . .
>
> This prologue being at an end, the musicians began, both vocal and

instrumental, when presently a company of girls, hand in hand, dressed in clean white robes and ornamented with beads, bracelets, and a profusion of gay ribbands, entering the door, immediately began to sing their responses in a gentle, low and sweet voice, and formed themselves in a semicircular file or line, in two ranks, back to back, facing the spectators and musicians, moving slowly round and round; this continued about a quarter of an hour, when we were surprised by a sudden very loud shrill whoop, uttered at once by a company of young fellows, who came in briskly . . . with rackets and hurls in one hand. These champions . . . were . . . painted and ornamented with silver bracelets, gorgets and wampum . . . [with] high waving plumes in their diadems, who . . . formed themselves in a semicircle rank also, in front of the girls, when these changed their order, and formed a single rank parallel to the men, raising their voices in responses to the tunes of the young champions, the semicircles continually moving round.[57]

The musicians who played for the Ball-Play Dance and other dances performed in the Town House or Square occupied a special place in the center of the building—presumably a place near the fire. Cherokee musical instruments consisted of a wooden water drum, a cane flute, a long-handled gourd rattle, and tortoise-shell leg rattles. A water drum was usually made from a hollowed-out section of buckeye trunk and was approximately eleven by eight inches in size. The drumhead was a water-soaked woodchuck skin "held down by a hickory loop ¾ inch wide."[58] Stained with red clay, pokeberry juice, or juice of the sumac berry, Cherokee water drums were colorful in appearance. Gourd rattles made a gratifying noise when shaken properly by a Cherokee musician. The leg rattles' effectiveness depended upon the ability of the dancer and, if he were agile and active, could make about as much noise as a gourd rattle.

Chungke was another favorite Cherokee game, even though it was not as spectacular as the ball-play. Every town and village had its chungke yard, comprising approximately an acre of leveled ground, onto which was rolled the discus-shaped chungke stone—

[57] *Travels*, 233f.
[58] Speck, Broom, and Long, *Cherokee Dance and Drama*, 20.

a stone which Cherokee men frequently worked for a year to perfect.

Chungke was played by two or more players. Each cast marking poles after the rolling chungke stone, the second player attempting to strike the rolling stone, and the first to intercept his opponent's pole while in flight. Sharp eyesight and skill, coupled with the will to win, were the marks of a good chungke player. The player whose pole fell nearest to the stone where it came to rest won two points, one hundred points being the game. The poles were seven feet long, marked in spaces for measuring throws. As in the ball-play, wagers were made at chungke games—by both players and spectators. The inventor of the game is said to have once bet his wife on the result of a throw, and lost.

Although Cherokees of the historic period did not know their own origin, they knew how the earth had been created. Tribal story-tellers (Adawehis) had explained this thing to them:

> The earth is a great island floating in a sea of water, and suspended at each of the four cardinal points by a cord hanging down from its sky vault, which is of solid rock. . . .
>
> When all was water, the animals were above in Galun lati, beyond the arch; but it was very much crowded, and they were wanting more room. They wondered what was below the water, and at last Dayunisi, "Beaver's Grandchild," the little Water-Beetle, offered to go and see if he could learn. It darted in every direction over the surface of the water, but could find no firm place to rest. Then it dived to the bottom and came up with some soft mud, which began to grow and spread on every side until it became the island which we call the earth. It was afterwards fastened to the sky with four cords, but no one remembers who did this.[59]

According to this Cherokee legend, the Great Buzzard made the Cherokees' mountains by roughing up the earth when it was still soft and wet. Sent out by the animals in Galun lati to see if the earth was ready for occupancy, the Great Buzzard flew over all the

[59] Mooney, *Myths of the Cherokees, loc. cit.,* 236–320.

earth and when tired alighted in the Cherokee country to rest. Wherever his giant wings "struck the earth there was a valley, and where they turned up again there was a mountain."

> The world was cold until the Thunders (Ani-Hyuntikwala ski) who lived also in Galun lati sent their lightning and put fire into the bottom of a hollow sycamore tree which grew on an island. The animals knew it was there . . . but they could not get to it on account of the water, so they held a council to decide what to do. This was a long time ago.

In attempting to recover fire from the sycamore, Raven's feathers were scorched black. Wa huhu, the little screech owl, got his eyes nearly burned out. The eyes of Hooting Owl (U guku) and of Horned Owl (Tskili) became ringed with ashes that they couldn't remove. And, in attempting to recover fire, there were many other bad aftereffects on animals, reptiles, and birds living then in Galun lati. However, fire was eventually recovered by Kanane ski Amai yehi, the Water Spider, who "spun a thread from her body and wove it into a tusti bowl, which she fastened on her back." By putting one little coal of fire in her bowl, she succeeded in bringing back fire. And, so Cherokee storytellers told their people, "ever since we have had fire, and the Water Spider still keeps her tusti bowl."

Tales about the rabbit, terrapin, bear, otter, and various other animals were delightful diversions of the Cherokees, and are assumed to have existed at the time of De Soto's visit in 1540.

To understand the Cherokees' diversions, customs, formulas for disease, superstitions, and the tremendous influence of the Adawehis on their lives, it is absolutely essential that one make the acquaintance of the "Stone Man" or Nun Yunu wi, a legendary monster whose skin was of stone. For this unpleasant and unsavory monster holds the key to the Cherokees' past, he having (according to Cherokee legend) bequeathed to the Cherokees when dying all of their ceremonials and rites. Since the Stone Man is of so much consequence, this version of his life and death is repeated here in detail:

> Once when all the people of the settlement were out in the moun-

tains on a great hunt one man who had gone on ahead climbed to the
top of a high ridge and found a large river on the other side. While
he was looking across he saw an old man walking about on the opposite
ridge, with a cane that seemed to be made of some bright, shining rock.
The hunter watched and saw that every little while the old man would
point his cane in a certain direction, then draw it back and smell the
end of it. At last he pointed it in the direction of the hunting camp on
the other side of the mountain, and this time when he drew back the
staff he sniffed it several times as if it smelled very good, and then
started along the ridge straight for the camp. He moved very slowly,
with the help of the cane, until he reached the end of the ridge, when
he threw the cane out into the air and it became a bridge of shining
rock stretching across the river. After he had crossed over the bridge
it became a cane again, and the old man picked it up and started over
the mountain toward the camp.

The hunter was frightened and felt sure that it meant mischief,
so he hurried on down the mountain and took the shortest trail back
to the camp to get there before the old man. When he got there and
told his story the medicine-man said the old man was a wicked cannibal
monster called Nun' Yunu' wi, "Dressed in Stone," who lived in that
part of the country, and was always going about the mountains looking
for some hunter to kill and eat. It was very hard to escape from him,
because his stick guided him like a dog, and it was nearly as hard to
kill him, because his whole body was covered with a skin of solid rock.
If he came he would kill and eat them all, and there was only one way
to save themselves. He could not bear to look upon a menstrual woman,
and if they could find seven menstrual women to stand in the path
as he came along, the sight would kill him.

So they asked among all the women, and found seven who were sick
in that way, and with one of them it had just begun. By the order of
the medicine-man they stripped themselves and stood along the path
where the old man would come. Soon they heard Nun' Yunu' wi' coming through the woods, feeling his way with his stone cane. He came
along the trail to where the first woman was standing, and as soon
as he saw her he started and cried out: "Yu! my grandchild; you
are in a very bad state!" He hurried past her, but in a moment he met
the next woman, and cried out again: "Yu! my child; you are in a
terrible way," and hurried past her, but now he was vomiting blood.
He hurried on and met the third and the fourth and the fifth woman,

but with each one that he saw his step grew weaker until, when he came to the last one, with whom the sickness had just begun, the blood poured from his mouth and he fell down on the trail.

Then the medicine-man drove seven sourwood stakes through his body and pinned him to the ground, and when night came they piled great logs over him and set fire to them, and all the people gathered around to see. Nun' Yunu' wi was a great Ada' wehi and knew many secrets, and now as the fire came close to him he began to talk, and told them the medicine for all kinds of sickness. At midnight he began to sing, and sang the hunting songs for calling up the bear and the deer and all the animals of the woods and mountains. As the blaze grew hotter his voice sank lower and lower until at last, when daylight came, the logs were a heap of white ashes and the voice was still.[60]

These, then, were the late seventeenth- and early, middle, and late eighteenth-century Cherokees, as seen through the eyes of the people, principally the English, who encountered them. That the Cherokees' advancement was at first painfully slow is a matter of record. The Cherokees of this era were proud and independent Stone Age people, who, at first, did not welcome suggestions from white men but clung tenaciously to their own culture, which, to them, was sufficient.

"I look upon these Savages," William Fyffe apprised his brother in Dundee in 1761, "to be much the same State as our Forefathers were perhaps in Alex the Great's time or, if Scotland was not enhabited then (tho' it must have been) in Julius Caesar's time."[61]

Content with their culture and way of living, the Cherokees would possibly have remained in the state of "Alex the Great's time" but for the English, French, and Spanish colonists who, in the last decade of the seventeenth and throughout the eighteenth century, kept the Cherokee Nation in a furor.

[60] *Ibid.*, 319f.
[61] William Fyffe to Brother John, *loc. cit.*

CHAPTER IV

"The King, Our Father"

SATISFIED WITH THEIR STATE, the warlike Cherokees through-out the Colonial period, by choice, remained savages. To the Reverend Martin, who, in the eighteenth century, zealously attempted to Christianize them, the Cherokees vehemently declared "that they knew very well that if they were good they would go up; if bad down; that he could tell them no more; that he had long plagued them with what they noways understood and they desired him to depart the country."[1]

Guns, war paint, and rum, provided by white men, were infinitely more appealing to eighteenth-century Cherokees than the white man's religion or other civilizing forces. Even so, Adair maintained that Jesuit priests from French colonies succeeded in gaining a few converts among the Cherokees in the Colonial period.

The Cherokees received guns from Charlestown officials in 1711 on condition that they fight against the Tuscaroras, who had recently murdered 137 colonists on the Roanoke. Between 1711–13, serving in Moore's expedition under Captains Harford and Thurston, about 300 Cherokee warriors assisted the English in driving the Tuscaroras out of the Southeast to Lake Oneida in New York, where they became the Sixth Nation in the Iroquoian Confederacy.

[1] Timberlake, *Memoirs*, 63f.

Furnished guns from then on by Charlestown colonists, the Cherokees zestfully waged many wars against the Creeks, Congarees, Esaws (Catawbas), Pedees, and other ancient enemies. Uniting with the Chickasaws in 1715, they drove the mighty Shawnees out of the beautiful and fertile Cumberland River Valley to an area beyond the Ohio River. Both Cherokees and Chickasaws afterward used the Cumberland River Valley for fishing, hunting, and grazing preserves.

At the outbreak of the Yamassee War, around 1715, some seventy Cherokee warriors joined the Yamassees and their allies, the Catawbas, in fighting Charlestown colonists—turning English guns on residents of Charlestown, and killing plantation owners who had settled areas adjacent to the town. But eventually the Cherokees broke their alliance with the Yamassees and in 1716, or thereabouts, made peace with the Colonists.[2]

The Cherokees' break with the Colonists at Charlestown in 1715 was provoked in part by the Colonists' shipment of Cherokee war prisoners to the West Indies as slaves. To procure Indian slaves for export in the Colonial period, Charlestown colonists (including governors and their aides) deliberately fomented wars between southern tribes; clandestinely issued guns and ammunition to both sides, on the condition they both deliver all war prisoners to colony slave-traders; and, upon the delivery of prisoners, immediately removed evidence of slave transactions from the investigative and indignant eyes of chiefs by shipping Indian prisoners in wholesale lots to West Indian slave markets.

Protesting the enslavement and export of their people throughout the latter part of the seventeenth and most of the eighteenth century, Cherokee chiefs were usually told by bewigged and pompous Charlestown governors that they had no knowledge of the export of Cherokees; or, admitting that Cherokees had been exported, the governors would hypocritically assure the chiefs that they would

---

[2] For an account of war activities of the Cherokees in the early Colonial period, see John Swanton, *The Indians of the Southeastern United States*, B. A. E., *Bulletin No. 137*; and Ross, ed., *The Life and Times of Honorable William P. Ross*, 234.

shortly be returned to their homes.[3] Thus, relations between the Cherokees and the Charlestown colonists were frequently strained to the breaking point, and war at times was averted only by the Cherokees' peace chief, Attakullaculla or the Little Carpenter, whose diplomacy was declared by Charlestown colonist William Fyffe to be superior to that of either Richelieu or Walpole.

Attempting to come to an understanding with Charlestown colonists on matters outside the realm of slavery, in 1721 thirty-seven Cherokee chiefs met with Governor Nicolson, the first royal governor of Charlestown. Both sides settled many of their difficulties at this meeting. The boundary line between the Cherokees' country and the South Carolina colony was clearly defined. And the chiefs agreed to elect one of their number to represent the Cherokees in all future dealings relating to trade with the Charlestown government. This was clearly a step upward for the Cherokees, who, until then, had been represented at Charlestown by all of their chiefs, each of whom held a different view of Cherokee-Colonial trade relations. Frequently in disagreement over this or that trade policy, the chiefs' divergent views were noted by Charlestown officials, and taken advantage of accordingly.

Having received complaints from the chiefs that Charlestown traders were frequently "very abuseful" to the Cherokees,[4] Governor Nicolson suggested that the chiefs permit an English commissioner of trade to operate in all their towns—come and go as he pleased, and to supervise the traders and see that they did not short-measure the Cherokees. Other regulatory standards of trade between the Cherokees and the Charlestown government would also be taken over by the new commissioner. The chiefs perceived at once the advantages in this arrangement and gave it their sanction.

Perhaps the greatest milepost in the Cherokees' historical meet-

---

[3] References to enslavement of Cherokees and other southern Indians during the Colonial period are from the following sources: Letter from Major Charles Gale to English correspondents, *loc. cit.;* and Hewatt, *The Rise and Progress of the Colonies,* I, 297f.

[4] Hewatt, *The Rise and Progress of the Colonies,* I, 297f.

ing with Governor Nicolson in 1721 was the land cession made by the chiefs to the English, it being the Cherokees' first land cession to white men in the history of the tribe. On this date, the chiefs ceded the English a slice of land between the Santee, Saluda, and Edisto rivers—land that the Cherokees seldom used but, because of its proximity to the South Carolina border, was extremely valuable to the expanding Charlestown colony.[5]

Upon returning to their respective towns, following this historic meeting with Governor Nicolson in 1721, the chiefs notified the Cherokee people of the election by the chiefs of Chief Wro-setas-atow[6] as head of the Cherokee-Colonial trade in their country and of Governor Nicolson's appointment of Colonel George Chicken to the office of English commissioner of trade among the Cherokees. It was impressed upon the people by their chiefs that Colonel Chicken was coming to help them and, therefore, was to be permitted freedom in the Cherokees' Lower, Middle, and Upper Towns.

That he was given this freedom by the Cherokees is attested to by the entries in Colonel Chicken's journal made while performing his duties as English commissioner among them. Hospitably received everywhere he went in the mysterious country which had been so feared by white men at the onset of the Colonial period, Colonel Chicken took advantage of this opportunity to turn the Cherokees against the French. Having already won over the Choctaws and Creeks, the French, too, were making a strong play for the Cherokees' trade. But because of Chicken's efforts, the Charlestown colony was able to get a stronger foothold on Cherokee trade than the French.

Nine years later, in 1730, the Cherokees reaffirmed the trade agreement which their chiefs had made with Governor Nicolson at Charlestown in 1721, and, through the efforts of Sir Alexander

---

[5] *Ibid.*; Royce, *Cherokee Nation*, in B. A. E., *Fifth Annual Report*, 144.

[6] Since Mankiller headed the delegation of thirty-seven chiefs who met with Governor Nicolson in 1721, it is assumed by some historians that he was "Wro-setas-atow," the name Mankiller being a general name of chiefs, but actually this assumption is questionable. See Hewatt, *The Rise and Progress of the Colonies, passim.*

Cuming, an unofficial envoy of His Majesty King George of England, acknowledged the complete sovereignty of England over their people.

No event in Cherokee history is more dramatic and colorful than this acknowledgment by the Cherokees of their alliance to King George II. Even eyewitnesses to the event—English traders mostly —were unable at first to believe that haughty Cherokee war lords had actually relinquished their cherished freedom to the imperious stranger, Sir Alexander Cuming, who arrived at Keowee (near present-day Clemson, South Carolina) on March 23, 1730.

Armed with three cases of pistols, a gun, and a sword, Cuming, on the night of March 23, attempted to enter the Town House at Keowee, wherein sat approximately three hundred Cherokees who had been summoned there to hear his "Big Talk." But at the entrance of the Town House a trader detained Sir Alexander.

"Your Excellency," the trader explained, "the Indians do not come into this house with arms on their persons, and do not permit anyone else to do so."

At this, Sir Alexander reportedly thundered: "It is my intention if any of the Indians refuse the King's health to take a brand out of the fire that burns in the center of the room and set fire to the house."

Sir Alexander's wild speech did not set well with traders like Ludovic Grant, the scion of a proud Scottish family, nor with other traders who heard Sir Alexander that night.

"This strange speech, which I and the other Traders heard him make did not give some of them . . . a very favourable impression of him," was Grant's terse comment.

Sir Alexander's interpreter, William Cooper, declared that "if he had known beforehand what Sir Alexander would have order'd him to have said, he would not have ventured into the Town House to have been the interpreter, nor would the Indian Traders have ventured to have been Spectators, believing that none of them could have gone out of the Town House without being murdered, considering how jealouse that People had always been of their liberties."

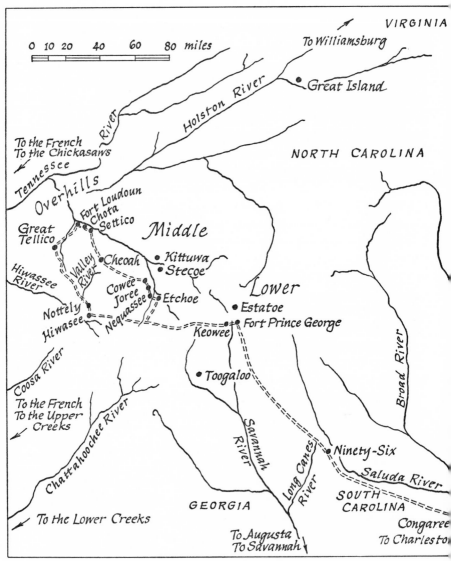

From The Cherokee Frontier, *by David H. Corkran*

THE CHEROKEE COUNTRY, 1740–62.
Dotted line marks the main trail across the Cherokee Nation.

Leaving Keowee in the Cherokees' Lower Towns, the following morning Sir Alexander visited the Cherokees' Middle and Over-hills Towns and exacted the same promise from their inhabitants by the selfsame methods he had used at Keowee.

Stopping at Tellico, en route to Nequassee (today Franklin, North Carolina), Sir Alexander received Chief Moytoy's pledge of loyalty to His Majesty King George. Thereupon Sir Alexander arranged for Moytoy's election as principal chief, or emperor of the Cherokees, when the council assembled at Nequassee on April 3, 1730. And, on this occasion, Sir Alexander required white men to set down in writing the phenomenon they had witnessed, just as he had at Keowee.[7]

As described by Sir Alexander, who referred to himself in the third person in his journal, the crowning of Moytoy was an event worth noting:

> This was a Day of Solemnity the greatest that ever was seen in the Country; there was Singing, Dancing, Feasting, making of Speeches, the Creation of Moytoy Emperor, with the unanimous consent of all the headmen assembled from the different Towns in the Nation, a Declaration of their resigning their Crown, Eagles, Tails, Scalps of their Enemies, as an Emblem of their all owning his Majesty King George's Sovereignty over them, at the Desire of Sir Alexander Cuming, in whom an absolute unlimited Power was placed.[8]

An item not to be overlooked when appraising Sir Alexander's success with the Cherokees is his cultivation of the Adawehis. At every stop he made in the Cherokee country, the traders noted that Sir Alexander always made friends with the Adawehis, who were known to wield tremendous influence over the people. Unless they had been advised by the Adawehis to do exactly what Sir Alex-

---

[7] The account of Sir Alexander Cuming's conquest of the Cherokees is from the following sources: Williams, ed., *Early Travels in the Tennessee Country*, "Journal of Sir Alex. Cuming," 115–43; and Hewatt, *The Rise and Progress of the Colonies*, II, 3, 9, 11.

[8] *Ibid.*

ander asked them to do, the people would never have behaved as they did toward a stranger.

To prove to His Majesty King George II that he had actually won the Cherokees' allegiance to the crown, Sir Alexander succeeded in taking seven Cherokees and their trusted interpreter Eleazar Wiggan ("The Old Rabbit") back with him to England. Only two of the Cherokees were chiefs, but the other five were prominent members of the tribe. The seven blanketed and besilvered Cherokees who with The Old Rabbit were conducted by Sir Alexander up the gangplank of the man-of-war *Fox* at Charlestown on May 4, 1730, were Oukah-Ulah, a chief suggested by Moytoy (detained at home by the illness of his wife); Oukandekah (or Oukanaekah), shortly to be called "Attakullaculla" (or the Little Carpenter); Kettagusta; Tathtiowie; Clogittah; Collanah; and Ounakannowie.[9]

Arriving at Dover on June 5, the Cherokees went from there to London, where they were quartered by Sir Alexander in basement rooms in the house of Mr. Arne, an undertaker, in Kingstreet, Covent Garden. There the chiefs were properly coached and otherwise prepared for their audience with King George II on June 18 at Windsor Castle, where His Majesty was then holding court.

Knowing the Cherokees' fondness for calling people liars, Sir Alexander presumably warned them to refrain from using this popular expression when in the presence of His Majesty, lest they be run through by a guardsman's sword. And, instead of taking His Majesty's hand, as the chiefs had learned to do when introduced to white men, they were probably instructed by Sir Alexander and Wiggan to kiss His Majesty's hand and to kneel properly when presented at court.

London newspapers of the day reported that the Cherokees' audience with His Majesty went off splendidly, the seven so-called savages from North America kneeling, as did Sir Alexander, at the proper time. As related by Sir Alexander in his journal, he (Sir Alexander) "laid the Crown of the Cherokee Nation at His Majesty's Feet, with the five Eagle Tails, as an Emblem of His Majesty's

---

[9] Carolyn Thomas Foreman, *Indians Abroad*, 45.

Sovereignty, and four Scalps of Indian Enemies; all of which His Majesty was pleased to accept of."[10]

As "Emperor Moytoy's" representative, Chief Oukah-Ulah (referred to by the London press as "the King") was dressed for his court presentation in a scarlet jacket and knee-length satin trousers, but his companions were naked, save for their breechcloths, each of which were decorated in the back with horse tails. Befeathered and painted with green, red, and blue dots, one carried a bow, another a "Musqueton." Making a picturesque group, all seven of Sir Alexander's wards stood, as directed, near His Majesty at dinner. The Cherokees' answers to King George's questions were discreetly translated by The Old Rabbit so as not to offend His Majesty's sensibilities.

When afterward the group was conducted to the gallery over the terrace, one Cherokee carrying a bow caught sight of an elk in the park below and had to be restrained from demonstrating his marksmanship to his royal host. Later, at the command of His Majesty, Cuming's wards were provided a banquet of leg of mutton and saddle and loin of mutton at "The Mermaid." This repast was unquestionably devoured without the aid of cutlery, since the Cherokees of that era always ate with their fingers or from a communal gourd or horn spoon.

After their royal reception at Windsor Castle, the Cherokees became the rage of London. Wined, feted, and followed by great crowds, they visited the Tower, attended theatrical performances, fairs, and were entertained sumptuously by a group of London merchants interested in South Carolina trade at the Carolina Coffee House in Birchin Lane. Habited in rich garments laced in gold presented to them by His Majesty, they strolled through St. James's Park, visited Westminster Abbey and the Houses of Parliament, and sat for a group portrait and single portraits for His Grace the Duke of Montague. And, in early September, they were grandly driven in two coaches to Whitehall, escorted "by a sergeant of the Foot Guards and file and a half of grenadiers," to meet the Lords Com-

[10] Williams, ed., *Early Travels in the Tennessee Country*, 129.

missioners, who acquainted them with the Articles of Agreement drawn up to regulate trade in their country—articles of agreement that would bind the Cherokee Nation to England for the next fifty years.

A ceremony of a kind accompanied the discussion of the Articles of Agreement between the Cherokees and the Lords Commissioners. On this occasion Oukanaekah, who could speak a little English, acted as spokesman for the Cherokees. Oukanaekah was then a slight young man of about thirty. He was not very tall, but his speech and manner were impressive. Addressing the Lords Commissioners, Oukanaekah said: "We look upon the Great King George as the Sun, and as our father, and upon ourselves as his children. For though we are red, and you are white yet our hands and hearts are joined together. What we have seen, our children from generation to generation will always remember it. In war we shall always be with you."

Dramatically, Oukanaekah laid the eagle feathers brought by the Cherokees to England on the table in front of the King's representatives. "This is our way of talking," he said, "which is the same thing to us as your letters in the book are to you, and to your beloved men we deliver these feathers in confirmation of all we have said."[11]

The Articles of Agreement (or Friendship and Commerce) were not signed by the Cherokees until some days later. Actually, they were signed on the night of September 23, at Sir Alexander Cuming's lodgings in Spring Garden, Westminster, in the presence of Governor Robert Johnson and the Secretary of the Board of the Charlestown colony. The author of the Articles was Sir William Keith of Pennsylvania, who happened to be in England at the time. Familiar with the ways of the red men, Sir William used imagery freely in composing the Articles, which committed the Cherokees to exclusive trade with England; guaranteed white offenders in the Cherokee country a trial in English courts; and pledged the Chero-

---

[11] Carolyn Thomas Foreman, in *Indians Abroad*, gives a detailed and graphic account, based on English news stories, of the Cherokees' stay in England. For a discussion of the manner in which the Cherokees were entertained by the English, *Indians Abroad* cannot be surpassed.

kees to English military service exclusively if England should engage in a war or wars with the French or any foreign power.

Following the signing of the trade agreements on September 23, the Cherokees departed for America under the chaperonage of Governor Johnson, Sir Alexander Cuming being detained in England to answer serious charges of fraud and embezzlement filed against him by colonists at Charlestown. But to his Cherokee wards, Sir Alexander was not guilty of fraud, embezzlement, or any misdemeanor. When the Cherokees thereafter spoke of Cuming, they termed him "a man whose talk is upright and who came to the Cherokees like a warrior from his Majesty."

Upon their return to their country, the Cherokees were sharply questioned by the people concerning the promises they had made to "The Man who lives across the Great Water." Had they given away the Cherokees' land, theirs from time out of mind? Assured by The Old Rabbit of the loyalty of the seven Cherokees, the people were willing to listen to Oukanaekah's prolonged accounts of the English visit, a visit that he never tired of recounting. Elected the Cherokees' peace chief and renamed Attakullaculla or the Little Carpenter, the former Oukanaekah would not tolerate criticism from any source against the English, especially from the young men, who were prone to belittle them at times.

Around 1736, some five years after the Indians' English visit, the French sent emissaries to all the Cherokee towns to try to win the Cherokees away from the English. The French had Fort Toulouse on the Coosa River in the heart of the Creek Nation (a few miles above the present Montgomery, Alabama). It was mounted with fourteen guns and filled with provisions which the French made available to the Choctaws, Creeks, and Cherokees.

But Attakullaculla would have nothing to do with the French. He cautioned his people to close their ears to the French emissaries who asked the Cherokees when their crops failed: "Why do you go naked when you can come to the French Fort [Toulouse] and be clothed as are the Creeks and Choctaws."[12]

---

[12] Brown, *Old Frontiers*, 49.

One of the Frenchmen who came to the Cherokee country and established headquarters there around 1736 was Christian Gottlieb Priber, who represented himself as a Jesuit priest. Priber donned Cherokee apparel and, outwardly at least, adapted himself to all the Cherokee ways and customs, thus winning a number of converts to the French cause. Oconostota, the war chief, was one of Priber's converts, and so persuaded many of his people to support Priber's erratic plan to make a communistic republic out of the Cherokee Nation. Taking the title of "His Majesty's Principal Secretary of State," Priber asserted that he had received from Moytoy, the Cherokee emperor, this title and permission to organize the tribe into the form of government just mentioned. In this government, all Cherokees were to be equal; goods were to be held in common; children were to be the property of the state; marriage was to be abolished; and each Cherokee was to work for the common good of the Nation, his only personal property to be books, paper, pen, and ink.

However, Priber's influence on Oconostota and other converts was weakened by his capture in 1739 by English traders, when he was en route to Fort Toulouse to render a report of his activities to the French. Priber was turned over to officials in the Georgia colony, and spent the remainder of his life in the Frederica prison. However, Priber's influence, though diminished, lived on in certain Cherokee settlements for some years. Priber converts, for example, blamed the scourge of smallpox in 1738, that reduced the Cherokee population by half, on the English, whom Priber had taught the Cherokees to hate. Priber converts also accused the English of planting smallpox germs in the trading goods sold to the Cherokees.

But the Adawehis told the Cherokees that this was a "lie." The English had not sent the disease; it had been sent by the Great Spirit to punish the wicked who drank the white man's rum and afterward mistreated their wives and children.

Attacked by smallpox, Oconostota, the war chief, grew increasingly hostile toward the English. A large, handsome man, Oconostota, after recuperating from his illness, had but to gaze at his pitted reflection in his warrior's mirror to fly into a rage against the English.

And soon it came to Attakullaculla's notice that Oconostota spent much of his time with the French at Fort Toulouse. When reprimanded by the Little Carpenter for this defection, Oconostota replied: "What Nation or people am I afraid of? I do not fear the forces which the Great King George can send against me to these mountains."[13] Thereafter the French had the support of Oconostota and several young chiefs who, to taunt the Little Carpenter, would fly the French standard from the roofs of their Town Houses. But a substantial number of peace chiefs in the Nation supported the Little Carpenter by promoting English trade between the Cherokees and the Georgia colony as well as the colony at Charlestown.

Willingly the Cherokees living in what is now northern Georgia permitted Andrew Duché, a young potter, in 1738, to carry back to his home in Savannah great quantities of white clay, out of which Duché baked the first white china ever baked on the North American continent. Duché recognized the Cherokee clay as being petuntse and kaolin (the ingredients used by the Chinese to make their exquisite porcelain) and continued to procure it from the Cherokees after severing connections with the Georgia colony, whose officials frowned on his venture. Sold to a London firm by Duché, Cherokee clay (or "earth," as it was referred to then) started England's first porcelain factories.[14]

In addition to trading with the Georgia colonists, the Cherokees, in 1740, furnished Georgia with one thousand warriors to repulse the Spaniards at St. Augustine. But Cherokee relations with the Virginia colony did not materialize until the eruption of the French and Indian War in America around 1754, a war that Lieutenant Colonel George Washington said could not be won by the English without the help of the Indians.

Fomented by the French colonists in North America (who, in

[13] *Ibid.*, 12.

[14] The fact of the baking of china from Cherokee clay by Duché has not been greatly publicized, and is not generally known in England or the United States today. Sources confirming Duché's porcelain-making as related to the Cherokees are the Will of Andrew Duché, City Hall, Philadelphia; *Colonial Records of Georgia* (Candler edition), IV, V; and *The Chronicle of the Early American Industries Association* (November, 1934, and January, 1935).

turn, were prodded into war with English colonists and their Indian allies by the French in Europe who were allies of the Austrian Empress Maria Theresa, at war with Prussia), the French and Indian War inspirited Virginia colonists to ask the Cherokees for a fighting force. But the Cherokees, not having had many contacts up to then with the Virginians, refused. Thereupon, as suggested by Lieutenant Colonel George Washington, Nathaniel Gist was sent to the Cherokee country by Governor Dinwiddie of Virginia to beg the Cherokees' aid in a counteroffensive against the Shawnee towns. Gist's mission was successful only because the Cherokees were bitter enemies of the Shawnees. One hundred warriors under Ostenaco offered to fight the Shawnees, who were allies of the French.

Washington was elated by Gist's success. But he cautioned Governor Dinwiddie to treat the Cherokee warriors with respect, since "They will be of particular service—more than twice their number of white men. . . . It is a critical time," Washington declared. "They [the Cherokees] are very humorsome, and their assistance is very necessary. One false step might not only lose us *that*, but even turn them against us."[15]

(That English colonists did not heed Washington's warning in regard to the Cherokees is a matter of record. Throughout the French and Indian War, English colonists took an incredible number of false steps which eventually, in 1759–60, led them into a war with the Cherokees, a war that came close to annihilating the tribe.)

Urged by Nathaniel Gist, one hundred Cherokee warriors from Chota and its adjacent settlements agreed, as allies of the English, to attack the Shawnees in the Ohio River region, provided the English would build forts in their country for the protection of their families against the French while they were away. Thereupon, coincident with General Braddock's defeat and death at Fort Duquesne, Governor Glen of South Carolina agreed to build two forts in Cherokee country—Fort Prince George on the Savannah River,

---

[15] John Frederick Schroeder and B. J. Lossing, *Life and Times of Washington*, I, 350f.

a gunshot's distance from Keowee in the Lower Towns, and Fort Loudoun at the confluence of the Little Tennessee and Tellico rivers near Chota in the Overhills Towns. These forts were to be garrisoned by the English and paid for by the services of Cherokee warriors in the French and Indian War. A treaty negotiated with Attakullaculla and other Cherokee chiefs by Governor Glen on this occasion netted the crown approximately forty million acres of rich plantation land between the Wateree and Santee rivers; furnished the English with land in the Cherokees' country upon which to build the proposed forts; strengthened England's trade agreement with the Cherokees; and elicited from Attakullaculla this pledge: "We fear not the French. Give us arms and we will go to war against the enemies of the Great King."[16]

A third fort was built by the Virginians in 1756 on the north bank of the Little Tennessee across from Chota under the supervision of Major Andrew Lewis. Unnamed and ungarrisoned, this fort was referred to merely as "the Virginia Fort." Upon its completion, Cherokee warriors headed by Ostenaco and under the command of Major Lewis amiably departed from Chota in January, 1756, headed for the Shawnee settlements on the Ohio.

But, en route to the Shawnee country, a series of calamities befell the Cherokees. In attempting to cross an ice-jammed river, boats containing their provisions were overturned and the Cherokees' provisions lost. Prevented by swollen, ice-jammed rivers from reaching the Shawnees' settlements, the Cherokees headed for Chota via the back country in Virginia. Compelled to kill their horses for food, the Cherokees received no help from Richard Pearis, their interpreter, who drowned his disappointment with Monongahela and rum. Left to forage for themselves, the Cherokees appropriated stray horses in the Virginia back country and helped themselves to the Virginians' poultry and other edibles in smokehouses and storage cellars. Thereupon the Virginians, unaware of the Cherokees' dilemma or the fact that they were allies, ambushed them and killed twenty-four. And, since Governor Dinwiddie had agreed to pay a bounty to colonists for enemy scalps, the Virginians presumably took the Cherokee scalps in to Dinwiddie's headquarters and collected for them. When apprised of their blunder, the Virginians defended their action by accusing the Cherokees of theft of both horses and provisions.

Apologies and gifts to the relatives of the slain warriors and to the chief of Chota by Governor Dinwiddie followed. But the tragedy was not forgotten by war chiefs or peace chiefs. Attakullaculla, vowing vengeance against the Virginians, bided his time to demand satisfaction for the murders of Ostenaco's warriors. To Captain Raymond Demere, the commandant at Fort Loudoun, Attakullaculla confided that what had occurred in Virginia had set his people against the English, especially the Virginians. Cherokee warriors no longer wanted to be Virginia's allies, even though they were expected to pay for Fort Loudoun's construction by fighting the French.

Letters from Governor Dinwiddie containing criticism mixed with praise for the Cherokees' co-operation in the war further irritated Attakullaculla. "I do not know what to make of Governor Dinwiddie's letter," Attakullaculla told Captain Demere on one occasion." "[For] he has sent us a good talk and a bad one together. If he complains of the few men in Virginia, pray what might he expect of the great number he desires?"[17]

Thereafter, vengeance was written on the faces of warriors who left Cherokee towns to fight Indian enemies of the English. Messages sent to Attakullaculla and the other chiefs from Dinwiddie confirmed the reports from runners that Cherokee warriors were setting fire to settlers' cabins in the back country of Virginia, and scalping women and helpless children. And, en route back to Cherokee country, they repeated these atrocities in Yadkin River settlements in North Carolina.

Halfheartedly, Attakullaculla, Old Hop (by then very feeble), and Willinawaw sent apologies to the governors of Virginia and North Carolina. But apparently these apologies were merely gestures of penitence; for the warriors who committed the crimes were

[17] *Ibid.*, 65.

permitted to hold scalp dances and riotous celebrations upon their return from the settlements they had ravaged, and the scalps on their hoops were unmistakably English.

Meanwhile, at Keowee (in 1759) in the Lower Towns, Salouee, the young chief of Ettowee, incited a band of wild, reckless warriors to murder twenty-four settlers in the back country of South Carolina in payment for the murder of the twenty-four warriors by the Virginians. This fiendish act of revenge bestirred Governor Lyttelton, Governor Glen's successor, to demand that Attakullaculla deliver to him at Charlestown the same number of Cherokees, preferably the settlers' assassins. Of this dark and feverish period of revenge and retribution between the colonists and the Cherokees, William Fyffe wrote the following account to his Dundee kin on February 1, 1761:

> Attacullaculla whom we call the Little Carpenter, promised to deliver up the murderer to the number demanded by Governour Lytellton which was 24. He brought in 3 & was in Quest of more when Salouee . . . stirr'd up the young Fellows to rescue some the Little Carpenter was bringing in. Attacullaculla told the Governor there was such a ferment in the Nation that it was impossible to get the rest which made our governour detain 21 of those Indians He had in his camp as Hostages till a like number of murderers were brought in. These he left at Fort Prince George, patch'd up a hasty Peace with the Cherokees & return'd. I believe . . . he was glad to get off with so much Honour for . . . the Indians had begun to collect in a Body for as yet the Nation was not unanimous against us, but the rash young Fellows only. Our people were no sooner return'd than they begun to murder and destroy openly the long cane settlers. A number of 30 or 40 families who lived nighest . . . them were attacked & almost wholly destroy'd. The Indians finding little or no Resistance in these Skirmishes begun to hold us in contempt & Salouee with his associates sent the most insulting messages to our commanders of Forts & even to the Governour.[18]

In desperation Governor Bull, who succeeded Lytellton after the latter had made a temporary peace with the Cherokees, applied to

[18] William Fyffe to Brother John, *loc. cit.*

General Amherst, the new commander in chief of the English army, for troops to subdue the recalcitrant and savage Cherokees, who had now struck the war pole full force against the English.

In response to Governor Bull's frantic request, General Amherst sent him a battalion of Highlanders and four companies of Royal Scots commanded by Colonel Montgomery.

A few weeks after disembarking at Charlestown in the latter part of April, 1760, Montgomery marched to the Congaree, where he was joined by the whole force of the province. From there the English troops invaded the Lower Towns, burning them all to the ground and killing sixty Cherokees and taking forty prisoners.

Of this Cherokee invasion by Montgomery and the general situation in America, Washington wrote to his London agent on May 10, 1760:

> The French are so well drubbed, and seem so much humbled in America, that I apprehend our generals will find it no difficult matter to reduce Canada to our obedience this summer. But what may be Montgomery's fate in the Cherokee country I cannot so readily determine. It seems he has a prosperous beginning . . . and he is now advancing his troops in high health and spirits to the relief of Fort Loudoun. But let him be wary. He has a crafty, subtle enemy to deal with that may give him most trouble when he least expects it.[19]

As predicted by Washington, Montgomery did indeed find the Cherokees "a crafty, subtle enemy." After relieving Fort Prince George, Montgomery planned to march into the Cherokees' Overhills country to relieve Fort Loudoun, whose garrison was starving. But five miles from Etchoe, the lowest town in the Cherokees' Middle country, Montgomery's troops found themselves entrapped in a deep valley whose steep clay sides were covered by vegetation.

From behind this vegetation sprang hordes of shrieking, painted Cherokee warriors. Firing at Montgomery's advance guard of rangers led by Captain Morrison, the warriors killed Morrison and a number of his men. Upon entering the valley, Montgomery's Royal

[19] Schroeder and Lossing, *Life and Times of Washington,* I, 470.

Scots encountered the warriors' fire and several were killed. But, by marching toward the left, the Highlanders sustained the infantry and grenadiers and eventually forced the Cherokees to retreat.

However, this victory did not blind Montgomery, who had been wounded, to the hazards he would encounter if he attempted to push on through the Cherokees' wild and rugged country to Fort Loudoun. For Montgomery had noted that the Cherokees possessed rifled-barreled guns which carried farther than the smooth-bored guns that had been issued Montgomery's troops. Too, some of Montgomery's troops had contracted smallpox when at Fort Prince George, and the disease seemed to be spreading. Taking stock of these difficulties, Montgomery marched his men back to Charlestown, where he announced to Governor Bull that—with the exception of four hundred men—he and his troops would "take shipping" for New York.

William Fyffe, as were all the colonists at Charlestown, was infuriated over Montgomery's refusal to relieve the garrison at Fort Loudoun. But General Amherst reportedly sanctioned Montgomery's abandonment of the Overhills fort—or so William Fyffe reported to his brother:

> The poor garrison of Fort Loudon was soon after obliged to capitulate to these savages [the Cherokees] rather than starve. The terms were: to be conducted in safety out of the Nation and have a sufficient Number of Indians to hunt for them to supply them with fresh meat during their march. Upon these conditions the men march'd out & left the powder and shot with some cannon to the Indians. The Garrison had their arms. They marched 2 or 3 days having the Indian chiefs who signed the capitulation [Chiefs Oconostota and Cunigatogae] accompany them but these left them on various pretenses and in the morning as they were beginning to march the advanced guard gave the alarm by saying they saw some naked Indians. Some of the officers ran toward a rising ground to look out but the Indians by this time had crept among the long grass close up to them. Some they kill'd and scalp'd, among these Capt. Demere and other officers, the rest are prisoners in the Nation.[20]

[20] William Fyffe to Brother John, *loc. cit.*

Captain John Stuart, a Scot, was one of the prisoners who was returned to Fort Loudoun after the massacre of Demere and other members of the garrison. Prior to the evacuation of the fort, Stuart, who was a close friend of Attakullaculla, had with great effort arranged with the chiefs at a council held at Chota to evacuate Fort Loudoun on August 7 and permit the garrison to return to Fort Prince George under Cherokee escort. Back at the fort, Stuart's freedom was purchased from Oconostota by Attakullaculla, who, in exchange for Stuart, gave Oconostota his arms and all of his clothing with the exception of his breechcloth. Attakullaculla also effected the release of William Shorey, an interpreter, and of a private. Both Stuart and Shorey were married to Cherokee women—Stuart, to the former Susannah Emory, Ludovic Grant's quarter-blood granddaughter, and Shorey (a Scot like Stuart) to Ghigooie, a full-blood member of the Bird clan.[21]

(In years ahead, John Stuart was to play an important role in Cherokee affairs. Certainly no white man who ever sojourned among the Cherokees was more beloved by them than John Stuart. Renamed Bushyhead by the Cherokees because of his shock of reddish-brown hair, Stuart's distinguished mixed-blood descendants took the Bushyhead name, an honored name today in Oklahoma.)

Reporting on the situation in the Cherokee country following the evacuation in August of Fort Loudoun, Ostenaco wrote the following letter to Governor Bull:

> The Man Killer and Saloue say there is no peace belt in the world strong enough to hold them; that they are coming down with all the cannon from Fort Loudoun and all the white men with them, and 200 Creeks from the lower towns, and 200 from the upper, and the Mortar with them.
>
> The Man Killer says he does not want to hurt you, and it would be very good for you to go off in the night, and take such prisoners as will serve you to the settlements, and you will not be hurt, not one of you.[22]

---

[21] Emmet Starr, *History of the Cherokee Indians,* 474.
[22] Brown, *Old Frontiers,* 105.

However, Fort Prince George escaped the vengeance of the Cherokees. Perhaps the chiefs decided they had evened the score with the British, for even though the French encouraged them to continue their war against the English, the Cherokees, instead, asked for peace. At Nequassee, on September 26, 1760, the English colors were raised, and two thousand Cherokees heard Oconostota and Ostenaco speak for peace. Englishmen who came into the Nation were not to be molested, declared the chiefs. The hatchet that had been bloody would be buried forever deep in the earth, and again the English and Cherokees would be brothers.

But to the Cherokees' chagrin, peace was refused them by the English military. The English had recently taken Canada from the French; therefore, North America was to be under English rule. General Amherst—although he must have realized that had Fort Loudoun not been built the Cherokees might have joined up with the French and the war might then have taken a different turn—refused the Cherokees' pleas. The surrender of Fort Loudoun to the Cherokees had wounded his British pride.

"I must own I am ashamed," he wrote Governor Bull, "for I believe it is the first instance of His Majesty's troops having yielded to the Indians."[23]

In the spring of 1761, General Amherst dispatched Colonel James Grant to Charlestown with two thousand men to invade the Cherokee country, for the sole purpose of wiping out the insult inflicted by the Cherokees upon His Majesty's arms.

It was June, called by the Cherokees "Da-tsalunee," or "Green Corn Month," when Colonel Grant, who had been Colonel Montgomery's aide the year before, destroyed fifteen of the Cherokees' Lower and Middle Towns. Burning the communities to the ground, Grant's men went on to lay waste approximately fifteen hundred acres of corn, beans, and peas—after which five thousand starving Cherokees fled to the canebrakes and forests, where they subsisted on berries, acorns, and the game they could kill out of hunting season.

In the face of such devastation, the Little Carpenter met the Eng-

---

[23] *Ibid.,* 107.

lish at Fort Prince George on May 27 and, putting aside his pride, again asked for peace. Grant refused. The Cherokees first had to be punished for the Fort Loudoun massacre, Grant said.

Hearing this, the Cherokees repaired to Etchoe Pass, where they ambushed Grant, Francis Marion and his Carolina Rangers, and Captain Kennedy and his ninety provincials. In a frenzy, the Indians killed eleven and wounded fifty of Grant's men, and only a lack of ammunition forced them to withdraw. From their retreat the Cherokees saw Colonel Grant and his troops cross the river, carry the wounded into the Council House at Etchoe, and then burn the town.

By September or Dulu-stinee, Nut Month, the Cherokees' Lower and Middle Towns had been laid waste by Grant's men, and the people were on the brink of starvation. No longer able to endure the sight of their suffering people, Attakullaculla, Ostenaco, the Raven of Chota, Old Caesar of Hiwassee, and fifteen minor chiefs went to Fort Prince George to sign a treaty of peace prepared by Grant.

One clause in Grant's treaty affronted the Little Carpenter: "Four Cherokee Indians shall be delivered to Colonel Grant to be put to death in front of his camp; or four green scalps be brought to him in the space of twelve nights." Because of this one clause, the Little Carpenter refused to sign the treaty. Instead, he asked Grant's permission to go to Charlestown to confer with Governor Bull.

"Attakullakulla, I am glad to see you," the Governor said. "As you have always been a good friend of the English, I take you by the hand, and not only you, but those with you, as a pledge of their security while under my protection."

Strings of wampum (one for each of the Cherokee towns) were presented to Governor Bull by the Little Carpenter. Between presentations, the chief made diplomatic overtures to the English: "I am come to see you as a messenger from the whole Nation . . . and hope we shall live as brothers together."

The wampum strings looked like a bead bouquet in the Little Carpenter's wrinkled brown hand. ". . . As to what has happened, I believe it has been ordered by the Great Father above. We are of a different color from the white people . . . but one God is the father of all. . . . I hope that the path, as the Great King told me, will never be crooked, but straight and open for all to pass."[24]

Following the Little Carpenter's visit with Governor Bull, this news story appeared in the *Carolina Gazette* on September 23, 1761:

> On this day Attacullaculla . . . signed the treaty of peace and received an authenticated copy under the great seal. He earnestly requested that Captain John Stuart might be made chief white man (Indian agent) in their nation. "All the Indians love him," he said, "and there will never be any uneasiness if he is there." His request was granted. This faithful Indian afterward dined with the governor and tomorrow sets out for his own country.[25]

Two months later the Cherokees signed a separate peace treaty with the Virginians at the English fort on the Great Island of the Holston River. Present at the signing of the treaty were Colonel Stephens, commandant of the fort, and his staff and four hundred Cherokees headed by Standing Turkey or Cumnacatogue, Old Hop's successor.[26] Following the signing of the treaty, Standing Turkey told Colonel Stephens that he had one more favor to beg of him and that was to send an officer back with him to his country as that would convince the Nation of the good intentions of the English toward the Cherokees.

But Colonel Stephens was hesitant about sending an emissary into the Cherokee country, believing that it would endanger his life. However, Lieutenant Henry Timberlake stepped forward and volunteered to accompany the chief and his people—thus freeing Stephens from the responsibility of making a selection.

Timberlake's six-month residence in that part of the Cherokee country which had been unfriendly to the English helped immeasurably to heal the breach between England and the Cherokee Na-

[24] *Ibid.*, 112f.

[25] *Ibid.*

[26] The spelling of the name of this chief varies. Timberlake spelled it "Kanagatucko"; Fyffe's spelling was "Cunnacatoque." Mrs. Foreman refers to him as "Stalking Turkey," other authors as "Standing Turkey."

tion. A genial guest, Timberlake got along so famously with Chiefs Ostenaco (who lived in the Overhills Town of Tamali), Pouting Pigeon, and Stalking Turkey that they insisted upon escorting him as far as Williamsburg, the capital of the Virginia colony, when Timberlake made preparations to return to civilization. En route to Williamsburg in the early spring of 1762, Timberlake and his Indian escort were joined by William Shorey, the interpreter, at Fort Lewis.

Arriving at Williamsburg, Timberlake and his company were invited to sup with Mr. Horrocks at William and Mary College. When Ostenaco was shown the portrait of King George III at the College, he studied it with particular attention. Then, turning to Timberlake, Ostenaco said: "Long have I wished to see the King my father; this is his resemblance, but I am determined to see himself. I am now near the sea, and never will [I] depart from it till I have obtained my desires."

On the following day when Ostenaco repeated what he had said at the College to Governor Fauquier, the Virginia Governor gave his consent to the chiefs' going to England under the chaperonage of Timberlake. It was also arranged for William Shorey to act as the Cherokees' interpreter.

The evening before Timberlake's party sailed (May 15) on the *Epreuve* from Hampton, Ostenaco made a farewell speech that was particularly appreciated by nineteen-year-old Thomas Jefferson, then a student at the College. It was not the first time young Tom Jefferson had encountered Ostenaco, for the chief had been entertained frequently when in the Williamsburg area by Jefferson's father, Peter Jefferson, at Shadwell on the Rivanna, the Jeffersons' home. But young Jefferson never forgot this particular speech of Ostenaco.

About sixty years old at the time of his departure for England in 1762, Ostenaco insisted on decking himself out in feathers and paint for the voyage. And, upon arriving at Plymouth on June 5, Ostenaco chanted loudly the dirgelike songs of his forebears— thus thanking in his way the good spirits for their watchful care over him while crossing the ocean. Attracted by these unfamiliar sounds

ATTAKULLACULLA, at the far right, and six other Cherokees who accompanied Sir Alexander Cuming to England in 1730.

CUNNE SHOTE in London, in 1762.
From a painting by Francis Parsons.

OSTENACO, one of the Cherokees who visited London in 1762.

GEORGE LOWREY, cousin of Sequoyah and second chief of the
Eastern Cherokees.

From a painting by George Catlin.

THE WESTERN CHEROKEE CHIEF "DUTCH," OR TAHCHEE.
From a painting by George Catlin.

The Cherokee Historical Association, Inc.

AT OCONALUFTEE VILLAGE, NORTH CAROLINA, a man burns and hacks out a canoe from a poplar tree (above), and a woman stands at the doorway of her model early eighteenth-century house (below).

The Cherokee Historical Association, Inc.

Two scenes from *Unto These Hills:* the ancient Cherokee Eagle Dance (above), and Tsali and his two companions marching off to be shot (below).

GIDEON BLACKBURN, the first Presbyterian missionary to the Cherokees. From a painting by R. Street.

and by the bizarre appearance of Timberlake's wards, crowds of gaping spectators thronged the wharf, making it almost impossible for Timberlake to get the chiefs from ship to chaise. But eventually this was accomplished, and the chaise engaged by Timberlake to take the chiefs to London got under way.

One of the reasons given Governor Faquier by Ostenaco at Williamsburg for wanting to go to England was to see the English King, so that Ostenaco and his companions might judge for themselves whether the Little Carpenter had told them "lies" concerning his visit abroad in 1730. Therefore, Timberlake, shortly after arriving in London, sought an audience with King George III for his wards.

But here Timberlake encountered difficulties. For one thing, deputations of North American Indians were more commonplace in 1762 than they had been in 1730. Consequently, Timberlake was three weeks getting an audience with His Majesty, a fact that made Ostenaco restless and prone to drown his disappointment in spirits. Intoxicated, Timberlake's wards became a problem, a problem that Sir Alexander had not had, for the seven chiefs had been temperate in the use of intoxicants while in London in 1730.

However, the three chiefs eventually were accorded an audience by King George III at St. James's Palace on July 8. One cause for delay, as noted in a London news story, was the death of William Shorey while en route to England. But Shorey's interpreting duties were taken over by Sir Alexander Cuming and two British officers who had mastered the Cherokee language when sent to the Nation years before.

Presumably, Stalking Turkey was the subject for Francis Parsons' portrait of "Cunne Shote" painted in 1762 in London. This magnificent portrait was titled: "Cunne Shote . . . a great Warrior of the Cherokee Nation," and may be seen today in the Thomas Gilcrease Institute of American History and Art in Tulsa, Oklahoma. Sir Joshua Reynolds, too, did a group portrait of the Cherokees and a single portrait, presumably of Ostenaco, which was titled "Syacust Ukah."

On sight-seeing tours, Timberlake's wards visited the same points of interest in London seen by Attakullaculla and his companions thirty years before. But "official England," having already gained the Cherokees' trade in 1730 and recently regained their allegiance, did not put forth undue effort to entertain the wards of Timberlake, who were supervised by Lord Egremont. Despite this fact, the chiefs had many distinguished visitors, among whom was Sir Oliver Goldsmith.

Arriving at the chiefs' quarters, a rented house on Suffolk Street near the Haymarket, Oliver Goldsmith was kept waiting for three hours while Ostenaco made his toilet. When eventually he was presented a gift by Goldsmith, Ostenaco gave the poet a French embrace that left Goldsmith's face streaked with paint. Thus Goldsmith, painted like a savage, evoked laughter from the crowd in the street upon emerging from the chiefs' quarters.

Timberlake's prestige suffered greatly both in America and in England when he was accused by the English press of accepting money for exhibiting the chiefs to the public. Protesting his innocence, Timberlake inferred that Mr. Caccanthropos, who had been instructed by Lord Egremont to see that the chiefs were well taken care of, was to blame for the attack on him. Caccanthropos, according to Timberlake, had encouraged their public exhibition, an exhibition that frequently cast aspersions on the entire Cherokee Nation, since, on numerous occasions, the chiefs appeared in public disgustingly intoxicated.[27]

On August 25, 1762, the three chiefs were firmly elbowed onto a boat for America by Timberlake, who remained behind because he did not have sufficient funds for passage, since the Cherokees had required more financing than he had anticipated. A later trip to England with a Cherokee delegation resulted in disaster for Timberlake and marked the end of his brilliant military career. After this second experience, Timberlake solaced himself by writing his memoirs, which were published in London in 1765.

Following the Treaty of Paris on February 10, 1763, all of the Indian tribes east of the Mississippi came under the jurisdiction of

[27] Timberlake's experiences as given here are from his *Memoirs*, and from Carolyn Thomas Foreman, *Indians Abroad*, 65–81.

England—or so the English contended. The tribes themselves held a different point of view. But under English jurisdiction or not, the Cherokees were faced, as were all these tribes, with postwar problems originated by the whites and not by themselves. Disputes over boundaries, encroachment of whites on Indian lands, the increase of crimes committed by whites, and the latter's unreasonable demand for more and more land harassed the Cherokees and, as usual, brought out their savagery, a savagery that was noted by Adair, the trader.

According to Adair, Cherokee morals, health, government, and population all suffered tremendously from their contacts with whites in the Colonial period. Of this period, a Princeton-educated nineteenth-century Cherokee chief, about 1880, sadly remarked: "It was an Ishmaelitish period when tribe was against tribe and nation against nation, when cunning met cunning, cruelty retaliated cruelty, and perfidy circumvented perfidy and deeds of desperate heroism defied the sword, the scalping knife, the fagot and torture."[28]

Tendered a vote of thanks by the South Carolina Assembly, together with a reward of 1,500 pounds for his heroic but hopeless defense of Fort Loudoun, Captain John Stuart, after the French and Indian War, was appointed British superintendent of Indian affairs south of the Ohio River. Through Stuart, the Cherokees were persuaded to sign a peace treaty with their old enemy kinsmen, the Iroquois, at Fort Stanwix, New Jersey, in 1764. Representing the Cherokees at Fort Stanwix, Chiefs Attakullaculla, Oconostota, and the Raven of Nequassee conceded the Iroquois's ownership of all territory north of the Tennessee River.

A few weeks later Attakullculla, meeting with the Shawnees, Delawares, and other Ohio River tribes at Fort Pitt, attempted to make peace with these former enemies but failed. Noted for his diplomacy, Attakullaculla—called "the Little Carpenter" because, like a carpenter, he could make every notch and joint in a controversy fit smoothly—was disconcerted by his failure at Fort Pitt, a

---

[28] Ross, ed., *The Life and Times of Honorable William P. Ross*, 234. See also Adair, *History of the American Indians, passim.*

failure which hurt his pride but which Superintendent Stuart apparently did not criticize.

Always mindful of his delivery from imprisonment by Attakulla-culla, Superintendent John Stuart from his headquarters at Mobile (and later Pensacola) kept in close touch with the Cherokees—now only one of the southern tribes under his jurisdiction. To help them with their postwar problems, Stuart sent the Cherokees two able Deputy Commissioners of Indians Affairs, Alexander Cameron and John McDonald, both of whom were Scots like Stuart.

Arriving in the Cherokees' territory around 1766, Cameron took a Cherokee wife and settled on Little River in the Long Canes country (today in Abbeville County, South Carolina) on land given him by the tribe. When informing Stuart of the Cherokees' gift to Cameron, Oconostota explained that "we have given him [Cameron] a large piece of land, which we hope will be agreeable with our father." Oconostota also explained to Stuart that Cameron had done the Cherokees justice, told them the truth, and they all loved him. "Mr. Cameron has got a son by a Cherokee woman. We desire that he may educate the boy like the white people, and cause him to be able to read and write, that he may resemble both white and red, and live among us when his father is dead."[29]

John McDonald, Stuart's second deputy, arrived at Charlestown in 1766 at the age of nineteen. Born in Inverness, Scotland, McDonald did not remain long at Charlestown but adventuresomely pushed on to Savannah, where he worked for a time in a mercantile establishment that carried on a thriving trade with the southern Indians. Sent by his Georgia employers to Fort Loudoun to trade with the Cherokees, McDonald there married Anna Shorey, the half-blood daughter of William Shorey, the interpreter—the McDonald's daughter Molly, some years later, became the wife of Daniel Ross and the mother of Chief John Ross.

With this background, John McDonald was, by 1768, an acknowledged defender of the Cherokees and, as estimated by Superintendent Stuart, a dependable deputy. Certainly both McDonald and

[29] Brown, *Old Frontiers,* 128.

Cameron (or "Scotchie," as the Cherokees called him) saw the Indian side of a question when matters had to be adjusted between red men and white. Particularly did Cameron see the Cherokee side when a serious controversy developed between the traders and the Cherokees. "No nation," Cameron wrote to Stuart shortly after he took up residence among the Lower Towns Cherokees, "was ever infested with such a set of villains and horse thieves. . . . A trader . . . will invent and tell a thousand lies; and he is indefatigable in stirring up trouble against all other white persons that he judges his rivals in trade."[30]

With Stuart, Cameron, and McDonald all in sympathy with them, the Cherokees' turbulent affairs were kept well in hand. For the next fifteen years—or until the outbreak of the American Revolution—the Cherokee did not noticeably progress, but neither did they retrogress. During this period marriages with Scots, English, Germans, and Irish were possibly more numerous than in previous years. Prior to the American Revolution, Edward Graves married Lah-to-tau-yie and converted her to Christianity. Lah-to-tau-yie recited stories from the Bible to her neighbors and relatives. Quite often they assembled in her cabin for prayer services. Because she wished to please her husband by dressing herself and her children like the whites, Lah-to-tau-yie's husband made her a loom, sent to England for a spinning wheel, cards, and cotton, and then taught her how to spin and weave cotton into cloth for wearing apparel.[31]

John Adair, from Ireland, married Mrs. Ge-ho-ga Foster, a full-blood Cherokee of the Deer Clan. George Lowrey married Nannie of the Holly Clan, and their son George (born about 1770) figured prominently in the affairs of the Nation until his death in 1852. Married to Bryan Ward, Nancy, a member of the Wolf Clan, was a Ghigau or Beloved Woman, having won this honor when she was

---

[30] *Ibid.*, 125.

[31] Wah-ne-nau-hi (Mrs. Lucy L. Keyes), "Historical Sketches of the Cherokees," in Unpublished MS No. 2191, B. A. E. Parts of this manuscript are quoted by James Mooney in *Myths of the Cherokee, loc. cit.*, where it is referred to only by the author's name.

married to Kingfisher, whose place she took when he was killed in a bloody battle with the Creeks.

From mixed-blood unions consummated in the Colonial period came future Cherokee leaders, saints, and sinners. But not all mixed-blood consortia were legalized by even the pretense of a Cherokee wedding ceremony. A case in point was Nathaniel Gist's union with Wurteh, a sister of Chiefs Doublehead, Onitositah, and Pumpkin-head, which resulted in the birth of Sequoyah around 1760. Alone and unassisted, Wurteh raised her gifted son in her little cabin in the rugged Overhills country. Sequoyah was not recognized by the blue-blooded Gists of Virginia until after he had won the acclaim of the world for inventing the Cherokee syllabary. In the Colonial period "The Ridge," a full blood, married mixed-blood Susie Wickett, and The Ridge's brother, "Oowatie," married Susannah Reese, a mixed-blood Cherokee.[32]

Hundreds of other mixed-blood marriages or consortia strongly influenced the Cherokees, encouraging them to abandon savagery for civilization. But understandably the real steps toward civilization were taken in the nineteenth century by the talented offspring of Cherokee mixed-blood unions. Until then, the majority of the Nation remained, by choice, uncivilized.

As the Colonial period neared its end and Revolutionary War clouds darkened the land, turning their beautiful country again into a veritable inferno, the Cherokees, nearly all of whom were Tories, realized the importance of holding onto their land. To avoid conflicts with English emigrants, Superintendent Stuart frequently advised the Cherokees to make land cessions to England. Such a cession was consummated between Cherokees and English at Hard Labour, South Carolina, in 1768, involving one hundred square miles between the Wateree and Santee rivers. "We have now given the white men enough land to live on," Chief Oconostota ferociously warned Superintendent Stuart following this transaction.[33]

---

[32] The genealogy of Cherokee families is mainly from the B. A. E. Archives; from Starr, *History of the Cherokee Indians;* and from Ross, ed., *Life and Times of Honorable William P. Ross.*

[33] Brown, *Old Frontiers,* 127f.

But barely six months later Deputies Cameron and McDonald had it from the Cherokees that emigrants from Virginia were occupying Cherokee lands on the Watauga River. Encouraged by Daniel Boone, the Robertsons, Beans, Carters, Honeycuts, and many other white families were boldly building cabins and clearing Cherokee land on the Nolichucky River and on streams in the Holston Valley. Warned by the Cherokees to move, the whites remained where they were. In addition to settling on land that was not theirs, the whites were known by the Cherokees to be talking against His Majesty the King, their father. As for the Cherokees, the whites frequently referred to them as "varmints."

CHAPTER V

War and Peace with the Colonists

It meant little to the Cherokees gathered in council at Sycamore Shoals in March, 1775, that in far-distant Boston, John Mal-
comb had been tarred and feathered by the Sons of Liberty; that
342 chests of His Majesty's tea had been dumped by rebel colonists
into Boston Harbor; or that in a month's time rebel colonist Paul
Revere would be making his famous midnight ride to Lexington.
On March 17, 1775, His Majesty's portended war with rebel American colonists did not deter the Cherokees gathered at Sycamore
Shoals (today upper Tennessee) from negotiating with the Transylvania Company the biggest land cession in frontier history.

The tract of land which the Cherokees sold or ceded to Richard
Henderson and Nathaniel Hart, who represented the Transylvania
Company, lay between the "Kaintuckee" and Tennessee rivers, and
embraced what is today Kentucky and middle Tennessee. For this
land, Henderson and Hart offered the Cherokees £2,000 sterling
or £10,000 in trading goods. The trading goods—guns and ammunition mostly—were on display in a log cabin adjacent to the Cherokees' council ground, a grove of greening sycamores alongside the
beautiful Watauga River. A cabin stacked to its capacity with firearms and powder proved irresistible to Chief Oconostota, the war
chief who had sanctioned the land sale, as had Chiefs Attakullaculla

and Savanooka. For at Old Fields the Cherokees had recently been defeated by the Chickasaws because they were short of guns and powder.

Violently opposing the land sale were Dragging Canoe, Attakulla-culla's headstrong son who was the chief of Big Island Town; Willi-nawaw; Tuckasee; the Terrapin; and the Tanase Warrior. Dragging Canoe was against selling the land because he hated the whites and resented their acquisition of any of the Cherokee's holdings. The other chiefs who sided with Dragging Canoe presumably did so because they were under his dominance. Deputies Cameron and Mc-Donald would have certainly joined with Dragging Canoe to protest the consummation of the land sale, had they been present; but neither Cameron nor McDonald, it seems, had been told of the intended sale or cession and so were absent.

Actually, the Cherokees had no right under the Articles of Agreement made with England in 1730 to sell or cede their lands to any buyer save the crown. And assuredly the chiefs knew this, since Attakullaculla had been one of the signatories of the Articles of Agreement. Attakullaculla and the chiefs had also witnessed the near recall by the crown of Superintendent Stuart and Cameron in 1768. Another argument against the sale of the land—ignored but unquestionably known by both Attakullaculla and Oconostota—was that the tract purchased by Henderson and Hart took in the Cumberland River Valley, which the Cherokees and Chickasaws had wrested from the Shawnees in 1715 but to which the Shawnees still laid claim.

At the council at Sycamore Shoals, Dragging Canoe did everything in his power to prevent his ninety-year-old father, Attakulla-culla, and the aged Oconostota from affixing their marks to the treaty providing for the cession of land to the Transylvania Company. Six feet tall and muscular, Dragging Canoe purportedly made an eloquent appeal to the council to abandon the sale. Then, seeing that the chiefs could not be swayed by argument, Dragging Canoe stalked out of the council but later returned to berate both the old chiefs and Henderson for signing the treaty. Allegedly, Dragging

Canoe pointed dramatically in the direction of "Kaintuckee" and, addressing Henderson, said: "You will find its settlement dark and bloody."[1]

A letter from John Stuart informed the chiefs, upon their return from the council at Sycamore Shoals, of His Majesty's serious trouble with "his children," the colonists. Because of this trouble, Charlestown was now occupied by rebel colonist General Charles Lee and his southern troops. Lee had recently cut off the Cherokees' supplies, threatened Stuart's life, and confiscated Stuart's elegant mansion on Tradd Street in Charlestown, where the chiefs had visited. Stuart, having fled to St. Augustine in one of His Majesty's ships, was now domiciled there. Sick and infirm, Stuart was unable to visit his Cherokee friends. But, to relieve their distress, he wrote that he was sending thirty horseloads of ammunition for their protection (in the event of a rebel invasion) to Chota by Henry Stuart, his brother. The latter would, for the time being, take over Superintendent Stuart's duties. Upon arriving at Chota, Henry Stuart would further explain the trouble between His Majesty and the colonists to the Cherokees.

When he reached Chota around April 24, 1776, Henry Stuart was confronted with problems that would have been difficult for an experienced man to solve. Having had little or no experience with Indians, Stuart was disconcerted by the theft of nine loads of ammunition by the band of Illinois Indians whom he had encountered on the Tennessee when en route to Chota. Dragging Canoe's animosity toward the Wataugans was another source of anxiety to Stuart, who had been cautioned by his brother to avert, if possible, war between the Cherokees and the Wataugans. (There were loyalists as well as rebels among the Wataugans, and Stuart felt that they would suffer or be destroyed by a Cherokee-white war.)

Cameron, meeting Stuart upon his arrival at Chota, raged and fumed against the recent treaty made at Sycamore Shoals, insisting

---

[1] This oft-quoted but disputed speech by Dragging Canoe can be found in John P. Brown's *Old Frontiers,* 12.

that it be repudiated. However, Cameron, Oconostota, Henry Stuart, and Attakullaculla all felt it necessary to prevent the war party, headed by Dragging Canoe, from striking the war pole against the Wataugans. Preaching neutrality to the council, white and red pacifists (among the latter was Nancy Ward, the ghigau, who was a niece of Attakullaculla) persuaded Dragging Canoe to defer any action against the Wataugans until Stuart and Oconostota had tried to remove them from Cherokee lands by means of diplomacy.

Consequently, both Stuart and Oconostota sent letters to the Wataugans calculated to induce their removal. Chief Oconostota suggested that, to avoid war, the Wataugans withdraw at least into the limits of their alleged purchase. Stuart, in his letter, suggested that the Wataugans would find living in west Florida more to their liking than their present settlements.

But to these diplomatic overtures the Wataugans gave evasive answers and stayed where they were. To further confuse and evade the issue, members of the Watauga settlements circulated a forged letter from Stuart inviting loyalists to join the Cherokees in a frontier war against the rebels. As nearly as Stuart could figure out, he had made a mistake by turning over the two bona fide letters which he and Oconostota had written for delivery to a trader who later was discovered to be a rebel spy.

From then on, it seemed, Henry Stuart ran into entanglements where the Cherokees were concerned, and these entanglements deterred him from visiting the other southern tribes as frequently as had his brother. Dragging Canoe was Stuart's thorn in the flesh. Determined to strike the war pole against the Wataugans, Dragging Canoe paid little heed to Stuart's caution concerning the necessity of the Cherokees' remaining neutral in the "King's War" with the colonists. Dragging Canoe's attention was focused only upon the hated Wataugans, who yet had not moved from the Cherokee's land.

Possibly a Cherokee-white war could have been averted had not the residents of Chota received a visit in mid-May, 1776, from a delegation of Shawnees, Delawares, Mohawks, Nancutas, Ottawas, and others of the Iroquois Confederation, headed by Cornstalk, the noted Shawnee chief. Encouraged no doubt by the British in the north, Cornstalk's deputation was traversing the country from Canada to the Gulf, urging Indians everywhere to unite in a giant movement to exterminate the white race.

In a council at Chota, northern chiefs told the Cherokees that "the King's troops would soon fall on their enemies toward the sea, and if they united and fell upon them on this side they would find them as nothing."[2] At the conclusion of a speech made by one of the Shawnee deputies, the Shawnee vehemently declared that "Now is the time to begin; there is no time to be lost."[3]

Cameron, Henry Stuart, and other traders at the council noted that Dragging Canoe and his followers were becoming wrought up by these talks. Alarmed, Stuart sent James Colbert, a loyalist Chickasaw agent, to Pensacola for one hundred horseloads of ammunition, in the event that Dragging Canoe incited border warfare following the council.

It was noted by Stuart and other loyalists at the council that Nancy Ward, the ghigau who headed the women's council, treated the northern Indians coolly. Attakullaculla and Oconostota, seated on their ottomans in the "holy area," looked sad and dejected throughout the council, and, when presented with the northern Indians' war belts, both chiefs silently refused them. Dragging Canoe and his hotbloods—Doublehead, Young Tassel, Bloody Fellow, and Osiotto—excitedly accepted the war belts, however, and shortly afterward they struck the war pole against the Wataugans.

Feeling his oats, Dragging Canoe commanded his warriors to detain the traders at Chota and commandeer their war-trade goods. Three of the traders who had yards at Chota were Isaac Thomas, Jarrett Williams, and William Fawling. Dragging Canoe sneeringly reminded Henry Stuart that the Cherokees had saved his brother John's life. He then proceeded to upbraid Stuart for having sent

---

[2] Samuel Cole Williams, *Tennessee during the Revolutionary War*, 31.
[3] *Ibid.*

the letters to the Wataugans which, according to Dragging Canoe, had provoked a war between Cherokees and whites.[4]

Alarmed by Dragging Canoe's hostility toward Stuart, Oconostota advised him, if he valued his life, to return to his home. And Stuart took this advice. But before leaving Chota, Stuart called a council of his own and gave the northern Indians a straight talk:

> You northern Indians have proper white men to direct you, but the Cherokees have not. If they go over the border and kill women and children, and fall on the King's friends as well as his enemies, they will draw against themselves all the forces that were intended to be used against the King's troops; and will rouse the resentment of those who otherwise might have been their friends.
>
> Your father (Captain Stuart) is willing to support you while you pay regard to his talks; but we do not consider it time for the Cherokees to go out until they are certain an army is coming. We therefore cannot give our consent to their going to war.[5]

Disregarding Stuart's talk at council, Dragging Canoe, grotesquely painted, headed for the Kentucky Road. Returning with four fresh scalps of white men secured to his hoop, Dragging Canoe presented them to the northern Indians as a going-away gift. To Stuart, Dragging Canoe was extremely insolent, berating him for leaving Chota, and condemning him for this or that action during his superintendency.

Stuart was promised by Oconostota before his departure from Chota that Oconostota would call a council and take a firm stand against Dragging Canoe. But before the council could be convened, Oconostota received word that the Cherokees of the Lower Towns, possibly influenced by Dragging Canoe and the northern Indians, had already attacked the South Carolina frontier.

A runner overtook Stuart in the Creek country, following his departure from Chota on July 12, to give him a message from Cameron

---

[4] The account of Henry Stuart's experiences at Chota are from Williams, *Tennessee during the Revolutionary War*, 20–30; Williams, *The Lost State of Franklin*, 157; Brown, *Old Frontiers, passim;* and R. S. Cotterill, *The Southern Indians*, 39.

[5] Brown, *Old Frontiers*, 146.

that the one hundred loads of ammunition had been received at Chota and had been appropriated by Dragging Canoe and his war party. "All our rhetoric could no longer dissuade them from taking up the hatchet," Cameron's message read.[6]

Meanwhile, on the night of July 8, 1776, Nancy Ward prepared the black drink, a service expected of a ghigau when warriors purified themselves for war. The war kettle, which previously had been set on the council fire in the Town Touse, was filled with approximately twenty gallons of river water. Then the Ghigau, after taking a handful of what appeared to be salt out of a deerskin bag and flinging part of it at the war chief's feet and the remainder into the fire, flourished a swan's wing over the kettle while chanting the age-old chant bequeathed ancient Cherokees by the Stone Man. Again delving into the deerskin bag, the Ghigau procured a branch of the yaupon shrub, which she threw into the war kettle to simmer and make the physic or black drink which the warriors would later drink. Having done this, the Ghigau returned to her seat next to the warriors and headmen.[7]

From the warriors' conversation, the Ghigau derived the information that Dragging Canoe intended to strike the white settlements near the Great Island of the Holston and those in near-by Virginia on July 20. On the same day Abram of Chilhowee would strike on the Nolichucky and Watauga rivers, and the Raven of Chota would attack settlements in Carter's Valley.

After the purification ceremonies, the Ghigau hastened through the darkness to the trading yards of Thomas, Williams, and Fawling, where she revealed Dragging Canoe's plans. Urging the three traders to sound the alarm from Wolf Hills (Abingdon, Virginia) westward, the Ghigau helped the three to make their escape from Chota. Known to be a friend to both whites and Indians, the Ghigau desired to avert bloodshed and save the lives of her people as well as those of the settlers.[8]

---

[6] *Ibid.*, 148.

[7] The preparation of the physic or black drink is described by Timberlake in his *Memoirs*.

[8] "Nancy Ward was a character of such consequence," according to a footnote

Thus forewarned, Fort Caswell on the Watauga was filled to capacity with settlers' wives and children, among whom were Mrs. Bean and her brood, including her eldest son, Russell, who had been the first white child born in the Watauga settlement (later Tennessee). Fort Caswell was under the able command of Colonel John Carter, Captain James Robertson, and Lieutenant John Sevier. Fort Lee having been abandoned, Fort Caswell now sheltered many of its residents.

At Island Flats, five or six miles below the junction of the Holston's dual forks, five companies of militia and 175 hardy frontiersmen, having been forewarned, awaited Dragging Canoe's attack. Carter's Valley was also prepared for the scheduled Cherokee attack. Alerted by Nancy Ward's emissaries, Carter's Valley males had fled to Eaton's across the North Fork of Holston, and their wives and children had gone to the present Wythe County in Virginia.

Unaware that the enemy had been warned of his arrival, Dragging Canoe and his men swept down the great war trail on July 20, heading for the Great Island of the Holston. When within six miles of the fort, Dragging Canoe's advance guard, sighting the enemy marching toward them in single-file columns, fired. Thereupon the whites scattered and made for the woods, and the guards turned back to inform Dragging Canoe of the enemy's retreat. Upon receipt of this news, Dragging Canoe beckoned his men on. "Come on," he yelled lustily. "The Unakas [whites] are running, come on and scalp them!"[9] But Dragging Canoe had not reckoned on the enemy's employment of Indian bushfighting; he, himself, had planned to fight on this occasion like the whites in the open. But now the tables were turned! Dragging Canoe was in full view on the trail, and the enemy, firing furiously from the forest, was bulwarked and protected by gigantic trees.

on page 36 of Williams' *Tennessee during the Revolutionary War*, "as to deserve ampler treatment than she has so far received." Other descriptions of Nancy Ward are in Timberlake's *Memoirs;* Mooney's *Myths of the Cherokee, loc. cit.;* Haywood's *Natural and Aboriginal History of Tennessee*, 278; and Starr's *History of the Cherokee Indians, passim.*

[9] Williams, *Tennessee during the Revolutionary War*, 41; Theodore Roosevelt, *Winning of the West*, I, 289.

At the first fire, Dragging Canoe fell; a ball pierced both thighs, and he was carried on a litter to the rear. By his orders, the Indians retreated with their wounded, leaving behind thirteen dead.

Savagely, Dragging Canoe ordered the warriors to break up the carefully thought up formation and, in Indian style, go in small parties to the Clinch, Powell, and Holston valleys and there "take hair (scalps) and horses." And his warriors, knowing that Dragging Canoe must avenge the thirteen deaths or lose face in the Nation, massacred eighteen whites and then looted and burned their cabins.

The Raven of Chota made little headway at Carter's Valley and, after burning a few deserted cabins there, returned to Chota. Following a futile siege of Fort Caswell at Watauga, old Abram took a few prisoners, and then he, too, gave up. Among Abram's prisoners were Mrs. Bean and Samuel Moore. As was customary at Fort Caswell, the women left the fort at daybreak to milk the cows. And it was when Mrs. Bean, lagging behind the other women, was heading for the fort, presumably with her pail of milk, that she was captured. Samuel Moore, a young boy, was captured outside the fort when getting boards with which to cover a cabin inside the stockade.[10]

Taken into the Cherokee country, Moore was burned at the stake; but Mrs. Bean, rescued by Nancy Ward, was taken to the Ghigau's house. There Mrs. Bean instructed Cherokee women and the Ghigau's slaves how to make butter and cheese—the Ghigau purportedly being the first Cherokee in the Nation to own cattle. Shortly after her capture, Mrs. Bean was permitted to return to her home.

Dragging Canoe and his war party, having suffered defeat at the hands of the hated whites, became more vengeful than ever—"taking hair and horses" of frontiersmen at every opportunity. To punish the Cherokees, Colonel Samuel Jack with a force of 200 Georgians destroyed Cherokee towns on the Chattahoochee and Tugaloo rivers in July, 1776. In August and September, Colonel Andrew Williamson with 1,100 Carolinians made short work of the Lower

---

[10] The story of the attacks by the Cherokees on the forts and the capture of Mrs. Bean and Samuel Moore are from Williams, *Tennessee during the Revolutionary War*, 35–47; J. G. M. Ramsey, *Annals of Tennessee*, 157; Roosevelt, *Winning of the West*, I, *passim*; Brown, *Old Frontiers*, *passim*.

Towns, burning "Locaber," Alexander Cameron's handsome estate near the ruins of Fort Prince George. Williamson then joined General Griffith Rutherford and his 2,000 North Carolinians, who had already laid waste the Middle Towns, in destroying the Valley Towns. Meanwhile, Colonel Christian with his 1,800 Virginians took the Overhills Towns without a struggle. Christian reported later that the abandoned Overhills contained 40,000–50,000 bushels of corn and approximately 50,000 bushels of potatoes.[11]

The Cherokees from Lower, Middle, and Valley Towns sought shelter among the British in West Florida or with the Creeks. In March, 1777, the homeless inhabitants of Big Island Town (Dragging Canoe's town), Settico, Tellico, and Chilhowee, rather than rebuild their ravaged towns, removed to Chickamauga Creek. There they built new homes—named for the old—centered around Deputy John McDonald's Commissary and home (near present-day Chattanooga, Tennessee). Referred to afterward as "secessionists," the Chickamaugans no longer pretended to be a party to the transactions of the old conservative peace faction but became a disturbing law unto themselves.

The removal of Dragging Canoe's secessionists to the Chickamaugan area enabled the old chiefs of the conservative party to negotiate a peace treaty with South Carolinians and Georgians at De Witt's Corner on May 20, 1777. Two months later, on July 20, a peace treaty was negotiated by the same conservative party with the Virginians at the Great Island of the Holston. All told, these two treaties took from the Cherokees 5,000,264 acres of valuable land—an unconscionable price, the old chiefs argued, to pay for a war uselessly fomented by Dragging Canoe and his hotbloods.

The peace party's relinquishment of present-day Greenville, Anderson, Pickens, and Oconee counties in South Carolina on May 20 at De Witt's Corner caused many of the Lower Town refugees to join Dragging Canoe's "Chickamogees," as they were called by

---

[11] Accounts of the punitive expeditions of the Americans may be found in Mooney, *Myths of the Cherokee, loc. cit.*; Ramsey, *Annals of Tennessee*; Brown, *Old Frontiers*; Roosevelt, *Winning of the West*, I; Cotterill, *The Southern Indians*; and in many other places.

frontiersmen. The ceders lived in the Overhills and were therefore not actually the owners of the land, according to the Lower and Middle Towns. Relinquishment of the land north of Nolichucky— Great Island excepted—infuriated "the Chickamogees."

Dragging Canoe showed his contempt for both the peace party and the despised white treaty-makers by stealing horses and taking scalps in the vicinity of the treaty grounds. When preliminaries for the forthcoming treaties were taking place at Fort Patrick Henry in April, Dragging Canoe stole ten horses from James Robertson and scalped Frederick Calvitt a mile and a half from Calvitt's dwelling. Tempestestuously moving over to Carter's Valley, Dragging Canoe murdered David Crockett, the grandfather of David Crockett of Alamo fame, killed Crockett's wife and several of his children, and took two sons—Joseph and James—whom he kept as prisoners for seventeen years. Dragging Canoe's depredations were straws in the wind that real peace was a long way off between his element and the whites.[12]

In the Great Island treaty of 1777, the Cherokees reserved Great Island for the use of Nathaniel Gist, Sequoyah's father. The Cherokees said that they desired that Gist "might sit down upon it when he pleased, as it belongs to him and them to hold good talks on." But Gist (up to that time a Tory) by then had decided to join Washington's army and so did not use Great Island. On his return to Virginia in January, 1777, Gist was commissioned a colonel in the continental army on the recommendation of General Washington, with whom he had been friends for years. After the signing of the treaty, about seventeen warriors, led by the Pigeon, accompanied Gist back to Virginia to serve as scouts in Washington's army.[13]

After the signing of the Treaty of Great Island, North Carolina commissioners appointed James Robertson Indian commissioner to the Overhills, and Virginia commissioners appointed Joseph Martin to the same office to represent their state. Thereafter Robertson lived,

[12] Williams, *Tennessee during the Revolutionary War*, 64f.

[13] The Pigeon, it will be recalled, was one of the chiefs who went to England with Timberlake in 1762. The account here given of the treaty of Great Island is from Williams, *Tennessee during the Revolutionary War*, 71.

until removing in 1779 to the Cumberland Valley, at the mouth of Big Creek (in present Hawkins County, Tennessee); and Joseph Martin, married to Betsy, the daughter of Nancy and Bryan Ward, lived on Great Island.

Both Robertson and Martin were disturbed, after the Great Island treaty had been signed, by the impoverishment in the Overhills, where lived the chiefs who had signed the treaty. Stuart and Cameron had cut off most of the Overhills' supplies and were diverting them to the Chickamaugans. And it was rumored that the Overhills were thinking of joining the Chickamaugans. As American patriots, the commissioners were apprehensive of the Overhills' being forced to go to Stuart for help, since the Americans had not aided them after the treaty. (The Americans were not willfully neglectful of the Cherokees, but were financially hard-pressed at this time themselves.)

Stuart and Cameron, quite obviously, kept the Chickamaugans supplied with food and ammunition, hoping to weld them into an effective British fighting force (with Creeks, Shawnees, and Chickasaws) when Sir George Prevost invaded Georgia. To add to the woes of Commissioners Robertson and Martin, the Wataugans were not living up to their treaty obligations but were again infuriating both Overhills and Chickamaugans by trespassing on the Cherokees' lands.

Onitositah or Old Tassel sent the following protest from the Overhills to Commissioner Martin, requesting him to send it on to the governor of North Carolina:

> BROTHER: I am now going to speak to you. We are a poor distressed people, that is in great trouble. . . . Your people from Nolichucky are daily pushing us out of our lands. We have no place to hunt on. Your people have built houses within one day's walk of our towns. We don't want to quarrel with our elder brother; we therefore hope our elder brother will not take our lands from us, that the Great Man above gave us. He made you and he made us; we are all his children. . . . We are the first people that ever lived on this land; it is ours.[14]

[14] Ramsey, *Annals of Tennessee* (Fains Index), 271.

No action in regard to Old Tassel's letter seems to have been taken by the governor of North Carolina. The Wataugans' violation of the Treaty of Great Island continued, and the retaliation of Dragging Canoe's forces became more savage.

To punish the Chickamaugans, Governor Patrick Henry of Virginia directed Colonel Evan Shelby on January 8, 1779, to "raise three hundred men in his district to go at once to Chickamauga and totally destroy that and every settlement near it which the offending Indians occupy."[15]

Shelby, in April, 1779, invaded the Chickamaugans' towns with a force of six hundred North Carolinia and Virginia volunteers. He burned eleven towns, carried off twenty thousand bushels of corn, and confiscated John McDonald's winter yield of peltries and the ammunition stores of the British. Shelby's overthrow of the Chickamaugans' towns required little effort since the warriors were away from home, fighting in behalf of the British on South Carolina and Georgia borders.

Feeling a little sheepish, no doubt, Evan Shelby and his men, who would be needed soon for fighting Patrick Ferguson at Kings Mountain, headed for that area. The force under Captain John Montgomery that had assisted Shelby followed the Ohio River to its mouth, there joining George Rogers Clark's forces to protect the northwest.

Dragging Canoe and his followers did not attempt to rebuild all of their towns destroyed by Shelby's forces but accepted land from the Creeks and started new settlements at the base of "Chatanuga" Mountain. Called the "Five Lower Towns," these settlements soon became more notorious than their predecessors. They were Nickajack (today near Shellmound, Tennessee); Running Water (below the present Hale's Bar Lock and Dam); Long Island (the site of present Bridgeport, Alabama); Crow Town (now near Stevenson, Alabama, on Crow Creek); and Lookout Town, on the east side of Lookout Creek, which became the rendezvous of Dragging Canoe, Doublehead, Pumpkin Boy, Bench, red-haired Will Webber, Bloody

---

[15] Williams, *Tennessee during the Revolutionary War*, 91.

Fellow, Glass, the Bowl, Middlestriker, John Watts (or Young Tassel), Little Owl, the Badger, and other Cherokees who hated the whites.

A short time before Shelby's attack on the Chickamaugan towns John Stuart died at Pensacola, and Cameron took his place. Stuart, therefore, was spared the knowledge that Henry Hamilton, British governor of the Northwest Territory with headquarters in Detroit, had been arrested. With Prevost and Cameron, Stuart had been aiding Hamilton in his plan to crush the rebels by a pincers movement extending from Canada to the Gulf. The plan called for Hamilton to bring both the northwestern and southern Indians into joint action by the spring of 1779. Hamilton's pincers movement was somewhat similar in scope to the scheme proposed by the northern Indians to the southern in 1775. But there was this difference: Had the northern Indians' plan succeeded in 1775, the Indians would have held the balance of power in North America. Now, if Hamilton's plans bore fruit, North America would be British-ruled, with the Indians continuing to be English wards; the Indians would have acted merely as England's allies.

But Hamilton's plans were smashed by George Rogers Clark when Clark took Kaskaskia and Fort Vincennes in Illinois. And although Hamilton recaptured Fort Vincennes, it was snatched from him by Clark in his winter campaign. In a surprise attack on Vincennes, Clark seized the fort and arrested Hamilton, sending him in irons to a Virginia war prison.

Ferguson's defeat at Kings Mountain; the fall of British-held Pensacola to the Spaniards, who, as allies of the French, had declared war on England at the onset of the American Revolution; Cornwallis' defeat at Yorktown—all of these momentous events contributed to the termination of the war between England and her colonies.

When negotiating the peace treaty in Paris in November, 1782, England returned Florida to Spain, who claimed it by conquest. But in so doing, she neglected to define Florida's northern boundary, a fact which was later the basis of a terrific controversy between Spain and new America.

Already in possession of lands west of the Mississippi, Spain now aspired to possess all the eastern valley of the Mississippi River as well. With this in view, she began to court the southern Indians, who were at loose ends since they were no longer dominated by either the English or the French.

Six months later Don Esteban Miró, the new governor of Florida, artfully invited the Choctaws, Chickasaws, Creeks, and Chickamaugans to Pensacola, At an open council Miró gave them this advice:

> Do not be afraid of the Americans. You our brothers, the red men, are not without friends. The Americans have no King, and are nothing of themselves. They are like a man that is lost and wandering in the woods. If it had not been for the Spanish and French, the British would have subdued them long ago.[16]

Governor Miró urged Dragging Canoe and his Chickamaugans to give the Cumberland settlers no rest. He promised these Indians a Spanish trading post on the Tennessee from which they could procure arms and ammunition.

Miró's words were music to Dragging Canoe. Still obsessed by the idea of forming a confederation of Indians from the Great Lakes to the Gulf Coast who would eventually exterminate the whites, Dragging Canoe was not averse to accepting arms and ammunition from any source.

In January, 1784, he was visited by two Shawnees, emissaries of the British at Niagara, and, hypocrite that he was, Dragging Canoe accepted their gifts and views with the same alacrity as he had accepted the Spaniards'. Avidly, he and his followers listened to the Shawnees' message, which foreshadowed the war of 1812:

> BROTHERS; We are glad to see so many of our friends, the red people. We shall let you know everything that is passing amongst us. We have the war hatchet still in our hands, but are going to lay it down, and we want our brothers who fought with us in this war to lay

[16] Brown, *Old Frontiers*, 222.

it down with us. We do not expect that it will be still very long, as we expect the Long Knife will be settling your country soon. If so, we will then assist you, and you shall want for nothing. In the meantime, visit all our brothers, the red men, and make everything straight and strong.[17]

Alienated from the Chickamaugans, the Upper Towns refused to deal with either the English or the Spanish. Old Tassel, their head chief, and Hanging Maw, their war chief, were doing their utmost to get along with the whites, who, since the war, had settled in greater numbers than ever on Cherokee lands. Recently five hundred families—the heads of whom were Revolutionary War soldiers— had crossed the French Broad and had built cabins along Boyd's Creek, only a day's walk from Chota, the Cherokees' capital.

Now the conservative Cherokees' head chief, Old Tassel, respected for his honesty and strict adherence to the truth, had futilely appealed to the governors of both Virginia and North Carolina to help him prevent bloodshed by moving the whites off Cherokee lands. But it seems that these officials did not possess the power to grant his request. The governor of North Carolina shifted the blame for white encroachment upon handsome, hard-riding, fast-shooting John Sevier, referred to by the whites as "Nolichucky Jack" but by the Cherokees as "Little John."

On December 17, 1784, John Sevier and his Indian-hating friends (living mostly in Washington, Sullivan, and Greene counties) broke away from North Carolina and, out of the western lands she had ceded to Congress to defray Revolutionary War debts, formed the state of Franklin. Elected its governor, John Sevier obeyed no laws save his own. When Governor Martin of North Carolina asked Sevier to jail one Major James Hubbard, a Franklinite who in the fall of 1784 had murdered Noonday (Butler) at Settico without provocation, Sevier refused. Sevier also ignored Bloody Fellow of Tuskegee, who sent him this warning: "White men from Nolichucky are planting crops on lands over French Broad River. As soon as the leaves grow a little, if your government does not make

---

[17] *Ibid.*, 246.

them move off, I will come with a party and kill every man, woman, and child that shall be found over the river."[18]

Old Tassel himself had protested a treaty purportedly made between several of his people and the Franklinites in the spring of 1785. Upon receiving an invitation to meet Sevier's representatives at Dumplin Creek to enter into "A Treaty of Amity and Friendship," Old Tassel sent Ancoo of Chota in his place. And Ancoo, being inexperienced in treaty-making, did not understand the exact meaning of the document. Signed by Ancoo and his delegation of young chiefs on May 31, 1785, near the mouth of Dumplin Creek on the bank of French Broad River, the treaty "established the ridge dividing the waters of Little Tennessee as the dividing line between the possessions of the delegation ceding all claims to lands south of the French Broad and Holston, lying east of that ridge."[19]

Old Tassel explained, as best he could, to the governor of North Carolina the circumstances that surrounded the signing of the Treaty of Dumplin Creek. But the governor had little influence with John Sevier. In fact, Sevier had previously refused Governor Martin's order to dissolve the state of Franklin.

On November 18, 1785, Old Tassel carried the Dumplin treaty difficulty and other problems of his people to Hopewell on the Keowee, where the Cherokees were to negotiate their first treaty with the United States. A benign and peaceful man, Old Tassel, aided by Hanging Maw, had assumed the responsibilities of the Nation following Attakullaculla's death in 1780 and Oconostota's death in 1782. An eloquent orator, Old Tassel has been credited with the pithy remark that "Truth is, if we had no lands, we should have fewer enemies."[20] The settlers' lust for Cherokee land obviously disgusted Old Tassel, and in 1785 he was looking forward to the Cherokees' meeting at Hopewell with "the Great men of the thirteen states," to whom he intended to air his grievances.

[18] *North Carolina Colonial Records*, XVI, 924; Brown, *Old Frontiers*, 246.

[19] Ramsey, *Annals of Tennessee*, 299; Charles Royce, *The Cherokee Nation of Indians*, B. A. E., *Fifth Annual Report*, Pt. 2, 152.

[20] This remark was made to Governor Randolph of Virginia by Corn Tassel or Old Tassel. See Williams, *Tennessee during the Revolutionary War*, 267n.

The Treaty of Hopewell, finalized on November 28, 1785, marked another important milestone in Cherokee history, since it initiated a new era in the relations between whites and Cherokees that would effect great changes in the Cherokee Nation.

Upon arriving at Hopewell with 36 chiefs and 918 of his people, Old Tassel was informed by United States Commissioners Hawkins, Pickens, Martin, and McIntosh[21] of the change of sovereignty from Great Britain to Congress that had taken place in the country as a consequence of the successful termination of the Revolution. The commissioners further informed the Cherokees that Congress wanted none of the Indians' lands, nor anything else that belonged to them, but that if the Cherokees had any grievances, to state them freely, and Congress would see justice done them.

Thereupon Old Tassel and the chiefs drafted a map showing the limits of the Cherokees' country, which included the land in Kentucky and Tennessee illegally ceded (or sold) to the Transylvania Company in 1775. But when shown the Henderson deed signed by both Attakullaculla and Oconostota, the chiefs relinquished their claim to this land without much ado, agreeing that the line "from the mouth of Duck River to the dividing ridge between the Cumberland and Tennessee Rivers, should be continued up that ridge and from thence to the Cumberland in such a manner as to leave all the white settlers in the Cumberland country outside of the Indian limits."[22]

Dragging Canoe and his war party were conspicuously absent at the Treaty of Hopewell. But Nancy Ward, the ghigau or Beloved Woman, was there and, at the request of Old Tassel, spoke at the council that preceded the signing of the treaty:

> I have a pipe and a little tobacco to give to the commissioners to smoke in friendship. I have seen much trouble in the late war. I am now old, but hope yet to bear children who will grow up and people

---

[21] Benjamin Hawkins, Andrew Pickens, Joseph Martin, and Lachlan McIntosh.

[22] The text of the Hopewell treaty with the Cherokees is in Charles J. Kappler's *Indian Affairs: Laws and Treaties*, II, 8–11. A discussion of the Hopewell treaty may be found in Royce, *The Cherokee Nation of Indians, loc. cit.*, Pt. 2, 153.

our Nation, as we are now under the protection of Congress and have no more disturbances. The talk that I give you is from myself.[23]

After the Treaty of Hopewell, the Cherokees' affairs worsened. As provided by the treaty, the Cherokee-white conflict was referred to the Congress of the new American republic for settlement. And, from the very start, Congress furnished both Cherokees and frontiersmen with ample proof of its inadequacy in dealing with conflicts of this nature. Ordered to move from Cherokee lands (as provided in the Treaty of Hopewell) or forfeit the protection of the United States, frontiersmen and their families either remained where they were or encroached on Cherokee lands closer to the Overhills, thereby inviting retaliation from Dragging Canoe and his Chickamaugans. Unlike John Stuart, the American Superintendent of Southern Indians, James White, had little understanding of the peculiarities or needs of his wards. White paid little attention to the Choctaws, Cherokees, and Chickasaws, and spent most of his time with the Creeks near the Spanish border. Eventually, his association with the Spaniards, as well as with the Creeks, prompted White to resign the superintendency and lend his support to the Spanish project of colonizing the Mississippi Valley.

Richard Winne from South Carolina, who took over the superintendency on February 29, 1788, also proved to be unequal to the arduous duties assigned him. By the time Winne's term expired, the Upper, Middle, and Lower Towns of the Cherokees were cauldrons of violence. To combat this violence, inspirited mainly by the settlers' continued occupancy of Cherokee land between the forks of the Holston and the French Broad, Congress issued a proclamation on September 1, 1788, forbidding white intrusion on Cherokee land.

The Dumplin Creek treaty and a second treaty forced on the Cherokees by the Franklinites after the Treaty of Hopewell added fuel to Cherokee fires. Naïvely relying on their right to deal with

[23] Brown, *Old Frontiers*, 250n. This was not the first time that Nancy Ward had spoken to commissioners. See Williams, *Tennessee during the Revolutionary War*, 200f.

trespassers as they willed—as stated in the Treaty of Hopewell—
the Cherokees killed several guilty whites. For this last offense, the
Nation was forced by the Treaty of Coyatee to surrender all its
remaining land north of the Little Tennessee.

The unauthorized settlement of 3,500,000 acres of land near
Muscle Shoals between 1788–91 by a Tennessee land company first
drew fire from Dragging Canoe and the Chickamaugans. By act of
the Georgia legislature, the state had disposed of 3,500,000 acres of
vacant land lying south of the Tennessee River to a Tennessee land
company. But when this association undertook to effect a settlement
on the land, it was protested by the Secretary of War and the President. A proclamation from the President declared that the Tennessee company's persistence in settling the Muscle Shoals area would
place them outside the protection of the United States and expose
them to attacks from the Indians who, under the Treaty of Hopewell, had a perfect right to break up the settlement.

As anticipated by the President and his Secretary of War, Dragging Canoe laid siege to the Muscle Shoals settlement, burned its
fortifications, drove its Franklin settlers out of the Chickamauga
area, and pursued them to their former homes. Tearing down the
Kentucky Road, the Chickamaugans killed John Donelson, who had
surveyed the Big Bend settlement. Chickamaugans ranging northward scalped and killed Colonel William Christian. Invading
Greene County, two warriors from Coyatee, an Upper Town, were
paid by the Chickamaugans to procure two scalps in order to assuage
the anger of a Chickamaugan whose two sons had been killed by
Sevier.

Seven or eight months later the Chickamaugans' raids had become so widespread, and so deadly, that Governor Sevier called out
the Franklin militia, and there ensued a full-dress war between the
state of Franklin and the blood-hungry Cherokees.

On August 3, 1788, the Franklin militia, numbering 250 men,
sought out Old Tassel and Hanging Maw and charged them with
the murders of Christian, Donelson, and the two warriors from
Coyatee. Patiently, Old Tassel—still bent on keeping peace—said:

BROTHERS: . . . They are not my people that spilled the blood and spoiled the good talks. My town is not so; they will use you well whenever they see you. The men that did the murders are bad and no warriors. They live at Coyatee, at the mouth of the Holston River. They have done the murders.

My Brother, Colonel Christian, was a good man and took care of everybody. . . . I loved Colonel Christian and he loved me.[24]

In vain did Old Tassel struggle to keep the Upper Towns neutral, but both the Franklin militia and Dragging Canoe's forces defeated his efforts. The Franklin militia marched to Coyatee, found the two Indians who had committed the Greene County murders, and killed them. When the militia returned to Chota, it informed Old Tassel and Hanging Maw that a treaty had been made at Coyatee whereby the state of Franklin had been ceded the Cherokees' land between the French Broad and the Little Tennessee.

To Old Tassel, this unconscionable action was not worthy of recognition. Wisely he ignored it. But his peace program was soon dealt another blow—this time by his own people. Two of his chiefs, Bloody Fellow and the Fool Warrior, avenged the deaths of relatives at the hands of the Franklin militia and Colonel Logan by taking fifteen scalps in the Dumplin settlement, burning and pillaging houses, killing cattle, and stealing horses. (Horses and Negro slaves gained from these raids were considered rich plunder by the Cherokees. Prisoners were valuable when exchanged for Indians captured by the whites.)

Following his raid on the Dumplin settlement, Bloody Fellow sent this message to John Sevier (it was left beside one of his victims): ". . . I did not wish for war, but if the white people want war, that is what they will get."[25]

Hanging Maw, too, began to seethe with anger. Forgetting his pledge of peace, Hanging Maw attacked John and Ephraim Peyton and their crew of surveyors north of the Cumberland, but they out-

[24] Brown, *Old Frontiers,* 255.
[25] *Ibid.,* 253.

ran him and thus escaped his hatchet. After helping himself to their abandoned supplies and horses, Hanging Maw gleefully broke their compasses (called "land stealers" by the Cherokees) by smashing them against a tree. Broken into bits, the compasses would never again aid the whites in measuring the Cherokees' lands.

In June, 1788, a catastrophe—so terrible that it shocked even the callous Chickamaugans—occurred at Chilhowee when Old Tassel, along with Hanging Maw, Abram, and Abram's son were killed by Franklinites while under a flag of truce. The assassinations of Old Tassel and his companions were effected to avenge the murders of all but two members of an entire family. John Sevier led the avenging Franklin militia into the Overhills, where they burned the town of Hiwassee. This accomplished, Sevier returned to his home, leaving Major James Hubbard behind to supervise the ghastly assassinations.

As a result of these crimes, the Upper Towns moved their beloved capital from Chota to Ustanali (the present Calhoun, Georgia). Established on the Coosawattee River, a few miles above its juncture with the Conasauga, the Cherokees' new capital was east of the Chickamauga towns to which the followers of Old Tassel repaired to renew relations with the Chickamaugans.

Notified of the assassinations, Old Tassel's brothers, Doublehead and Pumpkin Boy, with his grandnephews, Tail and Bench, vowed that they would avenge Old Tassel's murder.

When told of Old Tassel's murder, Governor Johnson of North Carolina, who since the beginning of his term had been looking for an excuse to bring the so-called Governor of Franklin to account, issued a warrant for Sevier's arrest, charging him with treason. "I fear that we shall have no peace in the western counties," Johnson declared, "until this robber and free booter is checked."[26]

That the "free booter" was only temporarily checked by his arrest is a matter of record. No longer governor of the state of Franklin, Sevier, when released, turned to Indian-fighting. This activity in-

[26] *Ibid.*, 278.

dubitably took his mind off his troubles, for in his absence from Franklin, many of its people took the oath of allegiance to North Carolina and were received back into its fold.

In November, 1788, the North Carolina General Assembly passed an act forgiving "all Franklinites who would take the oath of allegiance to North Carolina." But it was noted that "this shall not entitle John Sevier to the enjoyment of any office of profit, of honor, or trust in the State of North Carolina."[27]

Repudiated, John Sevier sought aid from the Spaniards for the resuscitation of the state he had governed. But his efforts apparently did not produce results, for on February 17, 1789, he too took the oath of allegiance to North Carolina.

Memories on the frontier being short and forgiving, Sevier was elected to the North Carolina Senate from Greene County in the fall of 1789. And, in addition to this, his title of brigadier general was restored—much to his satisfaction.

The North Carolina Assembly in 1789 passed a second act ceding to Congress all its lands lying west of the Alleghenies. These lands were thereafter known as "The Territory South of the River Ohio," and had pompous, bewigged William Blount as their governor. Blount, taking over his duties in June, 1790, faithfully promised to carry out the Indian program of George Washington, the first President of the United States, who had taken his oath of office the year before on April 30, 1789.

President Washington and his Secretary of War, General Henry Knox, worked together to treat the American Indians fairly, and as far as possible remedy the wrongs done to them during the haphazard Confederation period.

Shortly after Washington's inauguration, the President received a letter from Knox which read:

> The disgraceful violation of the Treaty of Hopewell with the Cherokees requires the serious consideration of Congress. If so direct and manifest contempt of the authority of the United States be suffered with impunity, it will be vain to attempt to extend the arm of govern-

[27] *Ibid.*, 295.

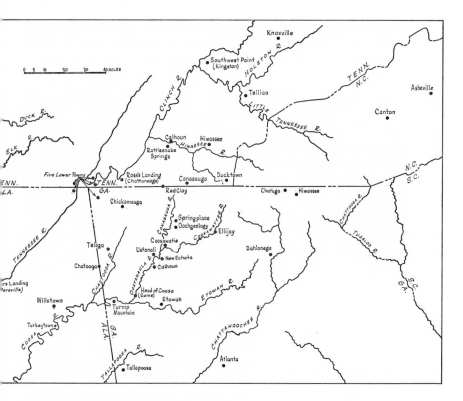

Cherokee towns and settlements in the federal period, 1785–1838.

ment to the frontiers. Indian tribes can have no faith in such imbecile promises, and the lawless whites will ridicule a government which shall, on paper only, make Indian treaties and regulate Indian boundaries.[28]

Largely as a result of this report from Secretary of War Knox, the Cherokees were summoned, by order of the President, to a treaty council at White's Fort (the site of Knoxville) on the Holston River. There, on July 2, 1791, the Treaty of Holston was negotiated between the Cherokees and the United States. Intended by Washington and Knox to end the Cherokee-white conflicts, the Treaty of Holston proved to be a great boon to both Cherokees and frontiersmen. The treaty gave the United States the exclusive right of regulating trade with the Cherokees, and prohibited diplomatic relations with any other "foreign power, individual State, or with individuals of any State." It defined boundaries between the United States and the Cherokees (the definition of boundaries excluded forever the Cherokees' claim to the Cumberland Valley and certain settlements of the whites on the Watauga). Affirming "Perpetual peace between the United States and the Cherokee Nation," the treaty also forbade inhabitants of the United States to hunt on Cherokee lands, or to pass over the same without a passport from the state or territory or other persons authorized by the President of the United States to grant the same. Cherokees committing crimes against citizens of the United States were to be punished by United States law, but inhabitants of the United States committing crimes or transgressions against Cherokees were to be tried and punished by Cherokee laws. And, finally, Cherokees were "to give notice of designs against the peace and interests of the United States."

Article XIV of the Treaty of Holston was to be of immense consequence to Cherokees in the next century, since it paved the way for the Cherokees' nineteenth-century civilization program:

That the Cherokee Nation may be led to a greater degree of civi-

[28] Royce, *The Cherokee Nation of Indians, loc. cit.*, Pt. 2, 160f.

lization, and to become herdsmen and cultivators, instead of remaining in a state of hunters, the United States will from time to time furnish gratuitously the said nation with useful implements of husbandry. And further to assist the said nation in so desirable a pursuit, and at the same time to establish a certain mode of communication, the United States will send such, and so many persons to reside in said nation as they may judge proper, not exceeding four in number, who shall qualify themselves to act as interpreters. These persons shall have lands assigned by the Cherokees for cultivation for themselves and their successors in office; but they shall be precluded exercising any kind of traffic.[29]

Twelve hundred Cherokees and forty chiefs participated in the Holston treaty, negotiated at White's Fort on July 2, 1791. Among those Cherokees present at this auspicious gathering were Dragging Canoe and his Chickamaugans. Chiefs Bloody Fellow, Doublehead, Lying Fawn, and John Watts (Old Tassel's nephew) mingled freely with Little Turkey (Old Tassel's successor) and the old conservative party at this council. But the attendance of Dragging Canoe at the council did not, as it appeared to do, presage the immediate end of his reign of terror.

To obtain ammunition and supplies, Dragging Canoe fraternized with the Spaniards, even though he had accepted with alacrity the goods distributed among the Cherokees at the Treaty of Holston. Dragging Canoe, at the height of his power between 1788–92, and his followers were also assured supplies from John McDonald, who was now associated with the Spaniards—Tory McDonald had chosen to affiliate with Miró in preference to the hated Americans. When Dragging Canoe died in 1792, John Watts stepped into his blood-stained moccasins. Watts thereafter moved his residence to Willston in order to be nearer to Pensacola and Spanish supplies—at the same time keeping in close touch with the Tory McDonald. Bloody Fellow, too, was dealing with both Americans and Spaniards at this date. Hypocritically, Bloody Fellow wrote to Spanish Governor Caronde-

---

[29] Kappler, *Indian Affairs*, II, 29–31.

let (Miró's successor) after the Treaty of Holston, "I will let go the hand of the Americans, and will take hold of that of the Spaniards."[30]

Bloody Fellow and a party of his choice took advantage of Article XII in the Treaty of Hopewell (which permitted the Cherokees "to send a deputy to Congress of their choice whenever they think fit")[31] and went to Philadelphia to see President Washington. Arriving there on December 28, 1791, Bloody Fellow's deputation, according to the official records of the United States, were not presented to Secretary of War Knox "until cloathed."

So well did Bloody Fellow and his outlaw deputation acquit themselves when they were presented to President Washington and Secretary Knox that a treaty was negotiated by the delegation between the Cherokee Nation and the United States government on February 17, 1792. This treaty provided that, instead of $1,000, the sum of $1,500 be paid the Cherokee Nation annually by the United States.

To seal the bargain, the President gave Bloody Fellow the new name of Iskagua or Clear Sky, as well as an American flag and a brigadier general's uniform—to be worn with a medal that had been especially struck for him at the President's orders.

On his return from Philadelphia, Bloody Fellow flew the American flag from his Town House, and became infuriated when it was fired on by Dragging Canoe's outlaws. Bloody Fellow's future fellowship with Carondelet, however, gave the lie to his defense of the American flag, a defense that coincided with the distribution of the annuity and trade goods promised the Cherokees. Nor were other members of Bloody Fellow's deputation to Philadelphia known to be loyal to the United States thereafter. Still identified with the Chickamaugans, they kept the frontier terrorized. Especially did the Chickamaugans harass settlers of the Cumberland Valley.

Because of their depredations, travelers on the Wilderness Road were accompanied by the militia. A mail carrier from Knoxville

[30] Brown, *Old Frontiers,* 339.
[31] Kappler, *Indian Affairs,* II, 8–11.

to Nashville received fifty dollars for one trip, so great were the hazards attending his occupation.

An atrocity greater than any hitherto committed by the Chickamaugans rocked the white frontier in 1793, when Doublehead, Pumpkin Boy (his brother), and Bench (their nephew) ambuscaded Captain William Overall and a companion named Burnett at the Dripping Spring in the barrens of Kentucky. After scalping the two, their assailants drank their whisky, then stripped the flesh from their bones and devoured it when roasted. The only excuse they gave for committing this horrendous crime was that since Overall and Burnett had bravely defied them, the Cherokees partook of their flesh, hoping that it would endow them with their victims' courage.

In order to stir the Nation to war, Doublehead exhibited Burnett's and Overall's scalps at Lookout Town, Willston, Turnip Town, and Coosawattee. So contagious was the mob spirit that towns hitherto friendly to the United States joined in the scalp dances initiated by Doublehead.

An attempt was made by Washington and Knox to win over Doublehead in June, 1794. Conveyed to Philadelphia in an American warship, Doublehead and a deputation of Chickamaugans met with the President and his Secretary of War as had Bloody Fellow two years before. Every effort was made by Knox and the President to make law-abiding Cherokees out of the Chickamaugans.

In the treaty that resulted from this meeting at Philadelphia, Doublehead managed to boost the Cherokees' annuity from $1,500 to $5,000, in goods paid for in advance by the United States. The date of this treaty was June 26, 1794. Although the meeting ended pleasantly enough, the resultant treaty did not greatly benefit the Nation. Upon arriving home, Doublehead called a council at Oconee Mountain and divided the trade goods among his followers, keeping the choicest for himself. The Overhills were not even notified by Doublehead of the distribution of trade goods. And Little Turkey and his people were no longer able to fraternize with the Chickamaugans, who, at this point, seemed infinitely more barbaric than their forebears of the past century.

Eventually, the Chickamaugans had to be subdued by force. Taking matters into his own hands, Brigadier General James Robertson directed Major James Ore to destroy the towns of Running Water and Nickajack but to spare women and children. In Ore's assault on Nickajack, the Breath was killed and Ore's men found on his body a letter from Carondelet advising the Cherokees of the Spaniards inability to furnish them with war goods. Since Spain was now forced to guard her European frontiers against Napoleon, no more supplies could be shipped to North America. This news, with the news that General Anthony Wayne had defeated the northern Indians, who for years had been stirring up the Chickamaugans against the Americans, helped break the fearsome power of the Chickamaugans. After the burning of their towns, the Chickamaugans notified Governor Blount that they were ready to make peace with the whites.

The ensuing council held at Tellico Blockhouse in October, 1794, was attended by both the conservative and war parties. Said Bloody Fellow: "I want peace, that we may . . . sleep in our houses, and rise in peace on both sides." Bloody Fellow's sentiments were echoed by all the Cherokees present, among whom were Bear at Home, Thick Legs, Broom, Little Turkey, John Watts, Glass, Pathkiller, Stallion, and Tallatuskee. Approximately forty chiefs signed the treaty proffered them by the American commissioners.

Optimistically, Governor Blount issued this statement: "Peace with the Indians exists now not only in name or upon paper in form of treaty but in fact, and he who shall violate it shall deserve the severest punishment of the laws and execrations of his fellow citizens."[32]

That peace with the whites was pleasant to the Cherokees became evident almost immediately after the signing of the treaty at Tellico Blockhouse. A new tranquillity enveloped the Cherokees' villages, where now one heard the tinkle of bells on Indian ponies, the low mooing of cattle, and within log cabins the whirring wheels of the women as they spun cotton and flax grown by their men.

[32] Brown, *Old Frontiers,* 440.

CHAPTER VI

Federalization of the Cherokees

"To LIVE SO THAT we might have gray hairs on our heads" had long been the Little Turkey's ambitious desire for his people.[1] And now that President Washington—by the Treaty of Holston— had shown a high regard for Cherokee rights, the Little Turkey's wish was to come true. It will be recalled that Bloody Fellow had been interested in the Chickamaugan's rights under the Treaty of Holston. When in Philadelphia in 1791–92, Bloody Fellow had unabashedly reminded Secretary of War Knox:

> The treaty mentions ploughs, hoes, cattle, and other things for a farm; this is what we want; game is going fast away among us. We must plant corn and raise cattle, and we desire you to assist us. . . .
> We wish you to attend to this point. In former times we bought of the traders goods cheap; we could then clothe our women and children; but now game is scarce and goods dear, we cannot live comfortably. We desire the United States to regulate this matter. . . . We came to Philadelphia with our eyes full of tears. But since we have seen General Washington, and heard him speak through you, our tears are wiped away, and we rejoice in the prospect of our future welfare, under the protection of Congress.[2]

[1] Gilbert E. Govan and James W. Livingood, *The Chattanooga Country*, 67.
[2] *American State Papers*, Indian Affairs, Vol. IV, Class II, 205f.

In 1796, President Washington appointed Benjamin Hawkins "Principal Temporary Agent for the Southern Indians." Thereupon, in the late fall and winter of 1796, Hawkins visited the Cherokee country and reported to James McHenry, the new secretary of war, on conditions there.

At Falling Creek in the latter part of November, 1796, Hawkins saw two Cherokee women driving "10 very fat cattle" to white settlements for sale. He also encountered, shortly afterward, traders "bringing down [from the mountains] 30 wagon loads of skins" on one trip. Upon reaching Etowah on December 1, Hawkins found the town nearly deserted, since its chiefs and warriors were away on a hunt. After assembling the Cherokee women, Hawkins talked to them. He wrote McHenry:

> I visited with them in the evening and conversed with them on the plan for bettering their conditions. . . . They said they would follow the advice of their great father General Washington, they would plant cotton and be prepared for spinning as soon as they could make it, and they hoped they might get some wheels and cards as soon as they should be ready for them, they promised also to take care of their pigs and cattle. . . . They told me they would make corn enough but that they never could sell it. That they were willing to labour if they could be directed how to profit by it.[3]

Hawkins found Cherokee women in the Pine Log settlements also eager to learn how to spin and weave cotton into cloth. They told Hawkins that they had made some cotton, and would make more "and follow the instruction of the agent and the advice of the President." Eager to impress Hawkins with what they could do, Pine Log women showed him the baskets of cane which they had made, patterned after those of their forebears. "The dies of the splits were good and workmanship not surpassed in the United States by white people," Hawkins commented.

But one poor old woman, who had frequently moved to new set-

---

[3] *Letters of Benjamin Hawkins, 1796–1806,* in *Collections* of the Georgia Historical Society, Vol. IX, 21.

tlements after the recent wars, told Hawkins she "knew not where to fix down."[4] A deep scar on her arm, inflicted by white people at Tugaloo, made a vivid impression on Hawkins.

Little Cherokee children, too, carried invisible war scars in their memories and would run and hide at the sight of a white man. Hawkins reported that in one settlement a boy of eight "could not be kept from screaming . . . until I got out the door, and then he ran and hid himself." The screaming child had not actually known the horrors of recent Cherokee-white wars but had heard them discussed by elders, Hawkins was told.

From the Terrapin, Hawkins heard a more pleasant side of the Cherokee story. The Terrapin told Hawkins that he had some cotton ready for market and would soon send it to Tellico Blockhouse. "He wished to know when they might expect plows, and such other implements. The Terrapin said he raised some cattle of 1,200 lbs. near Limestone Creek."[5] At Limestone Creek, Hawkins learned that Cherokee women made a maple sugar every year, using wooden troughs and earthen kettles.

In other sections of the country Hawkins saw fenced farms, orchards, plowed fields, sizable stocks of cattle and hogs, comfortable dwellings, and a goodly number of fine horses. Of "Halfbreed Will's," where he spent the night, Hawkins reported:

> They gave me good bread, pork, and potatoes for supper, and ground peas [peanuts] and dried peaches. I had corn for my horses. The hut in which I lodged was clean and neat. In the morning I breakfasted on corn cakes and pork. They had a number of fowls, hogs and some cattle, the field of 4 acres for corn fenced, and half an acre for potatoes.[6]

Getting practically nothing for what they raised seemed to be a stumbling block to Cherokee advancement; full-grown fowls brought only about one cent apiece in 1796. According to Hawkins, a Cherokee woman carrying a bushel and a half of chestnuts on her back

[4] *Ibid.*, 18.
[5] *Ibid.*
[6] *Ibid.*, 23.

received in exchange for them a petticoat. One bushel of corn brought but a quart of salt, an item the Cherokees were greatly in need of in 1796.

During his forty-year sojourn in Cherokee country, Adair noted the natural resources of the Nation. "Within twenty miles of the late Fort Loudon," he wrote in his *History of the American Indians,* "there is great plenty of whetstones for razors, of red, white, and black colours. The silver mines are so rich that by digging about ten yards deep, some desperate vagrants found . . . so much rich ore, as to enable them to counterfeit dollars, to a great amount."[7] That there were precious stones in the country at West's Mill and near present-day Franklin was known by white men of this date. But the commercial value of the stones could not be realized because of the Cherokees' superstitions—they considered it bad luck to dispose of even semiprecious stones to traders. The great deposits of iron ore in the Cherokee country had not been utilized by the Cherokees when Hawkins visited them. Hawkins did not press the matter but, instead, emphasized the great value of agriculture, animal husbandry, and household arts to the Cherokee people, some of whom, including Half Breed Will, the Terrapin, and several other mixed-blood families, were already fairly well-to-do farmers.

Hawkins encountered mixed bloods in practically all Cherokee settlements but noted that the mountain settlements had the smallest number. By 1796 the Doughertys, Galpins, and Adairs from Ireland had married Cherokees and had mixed-blood families. The Rosses, Vanns, and McIntoshes were of Scottish origin. The Waffords and other intermarried whites were originally from the Georgia and Carolina colonies. At one settlement Hawkins met Thomas Pettit's half-blood wife and quarter-blood daughter and described Pettit's daughter as having "white hair and a beautiful rosy complexion."[8]

It was quite apparent to Hawkins that the Chickamaugans and their allies living in western and southwestern Cherokee settlements had received more trade goods than the mountain Cherokees. Chiefs

---

[7] *History of the American Indians,* 236.

[8] *Letters of Benjamin Hawkins, loc. cit.,* 19.

of mountain towns several years later complained to Hawkins that the Chickamaugans "had received more than their share of spinning wheels and cards, and were consequently more advanced in making their own clothing as well as in farming."[9] When confronted by these accusations, Chiefs Doublehead, Will, and John Watts callously said: "Those who complain came in late. We have got the start on them, which we are determined to keep."[10]

In 1797–98, Silas Dinsmoor, appointed by President John Adams to reside among the Cherokees and instruct them "in the raising of stock, the cultivation of land, and the arts," also reported to the Secretary of War on the progress made by the Cherokees.[11] In one place Dinsmoor saw "42½ yards of good homespun and some ready for the loom."

But Hawkins' first laudatory report of Cherokee progress made to the Secretary of War early in December, 1796, ironically coincided with a resolution brought to the House of Representatives in Philadelphia. Andrew Jackson, a tall, gaunt, blue-eyed representative from Tennessee, America's newest state, introduced a resolution which would reimburse Tennessee for the expense of John Sevier's unauthorized campaign of 1793 against the Cherokees.

Congressman Jackson's bitter denunciation of the Cherokees flatly contradicted the Secretary of War's recent report about their progress. Boldly Jackson declared Sevier's unauthorized Cherokee campaign to have been necessary. "The knife and the tomahawk were held over the heads of women and children. . . . It was time to make resistance. Some of the assertions of the Secretary of War are not founded on fact," he said.[12]

Jackson's resolution was "shelved" for the time being, but not shelved was its author's prejudice against the Cherokees. Jackson's prejudice prodigiously multiplied and, in later years, struck cruelly

[9] Mooney, *Myths of the Cherokee, loc. cit.*, 82.

[10] *Ibid.*

[11] In 1798, President Adams wrote the Cherokees: "You must, moreover, be convinced, that the United States can have your good only in view in keeping Mr. Dinsmoor in your Nation." See *American State Papers, Indian Affairs*, IV, 640–41.

[12] Marquis James, *Andrew Jackson*, 81.

at the heart-core of the once powerful Cherokee Nation. Prior to his election to Congress, Jackson had bitterly fought the Cherokees, after which he had acquired much of their land. In 1795 he had gone to Philadelphia to sell thirty thousand acres purportedly belonging to him—fifty thousand were held jointly with John Overton, and eighteen thousand were on commission for Joel Rice. "Be canded [*sic*] and unreserved with the purchasers," Overton had worriedly cautioned Jackson then. "And particularly inform them that the 'fifty thousand' acres are situate[d] without the [boundaries of land open to white settlement as fixed by the] treaty of Holston."[13]

It is small wonder that Jackson, heartily disliking President Washington, suggested his impeachment. Land speculators of Jackson's caliber constituted one of President Washington's gravest problems. Notified by Knox at the beginning of his term that in some instances speculators were paying less than one cent an acre for ill-gained Cherokee land, Washington threatened to send the regular army to the Indian country to uphold the Indians' rights. To avert this, the Treaty of Holston was negotiated.

President Washington's rejection of a third term boded ill for the Cherokees. Never again would they know the kind and just protection of a President whose Indian policy was designed to defend rather than offend the American aborigines.

Despite the fact that Washington's successors did not always adhere to his high-minded Indian policy, the Cherokee Nation continued to make untoward progress in agriculture, animal husbandry, mechanical skills, and also in new fields of education and government. Their progress was furthered by agent-appointees of Presidents Washington and Adams—Silas Dinsmoor and Return Jonathan Meigs furnishing notable examples. These agents, as provided by the Treaty of Holston, resided among the Cherokees and engaged carpenters, wheelwrights, smiths, and weavers to teach the Cherokees various crafts.

But Cherokee advancement in education and government, although encouraged by the federal government, had to be initiated

[13] *Ibid.*, 74.

by the Cherokee chiefs and the council, who, up to the nineteenth century, had resisted education and any changes in the tribal government. The white man's religion, until now, had also been rejected by the Nation. However, at the beginning of the nineteenth century, the Cherokees' attitude toward education, religion, and, eventually, tribal government all underwent a drastic and revolutionary change. Even as early as 1799, Little Turkey was advocating to the council that it permit Moravian missionaries to establish a school in the Nation. Consequently, in 1801, the Moravians established such a school at Springplace, obtaining the land from "Rich James Vann." But missionaries were told by the council that if they did not educate Cherokee children, they would have to leave the Nation within six months, and that the white man's religious teachings were not welcome unless accompanied by instructions in the three *R*'s.

Around 1803 the chiefs and headmen agreed to let the Reverend Gideon Blackburn, a young Presbyterian minister from Maryville, Tennessee, establish a mission school in the wild Overhills country near Tellico. Blackburn held the view that Cherokee children were worthy of being educated and Christianized, even though John Sevier, when conducting military raids against the Cherokees in the past, had declared Cherokee children to be the "nits that make lice" and instructed his men to exterminate them along with their elders.

Not subscribing to this idea of Sevier's, the Reverend Blackburn, although under the military command of Sevier, had in 1794 estimated Cherokee children to be the key to the problem of civilizing the tribe. Adult Cherokees, reasoned Blackburn, would be difficult to civilize for they were steeped in warlike tribal traditions. But not so, the naked, brown-skinned children, who ran wild in the woods. Blackburn had noted Cherokee children's bright, alert eyes and their quick observant manner. If Christianized and educated, they would grow up to be a blessing to the world instead of a curse, argued Blackburn. A born educator, Blackburn had given his project much thought prior to his going to the chiefs and outlining his plan for educating their children.

Blackburn presented his plan to two thousand Cherokees, including all the chiefs of the Nation, at their October council. After having gained permission from the council to educate Cherokee children, Blackburn next energetically set out to interest the Presbyterian General Assembly and President Jefferson in the project. The President fell in with Blackburn's plan and agreed to furnish him with funds, as provided by the Treaty of Holston for civilizing the Cherokees. The Assembly, too, encouraged Blackburn, bestowing upon him the title of "Superintendent of Education Among the Cherokee Indians." But the combined financial support from the federal government and the Assembly proved to be insufficient for building and operating the Cherokee Overhills school as Blackburn wished. Consequently, Blackburn toured the country soliciting additional funds. In less than a year he had succeeded in raising around $5,000—a sufficient sum to insure the Overhills school's continuance for a year or so after its establishment in 1804. Of the rude log mission-school in the wild and rugged Overhills country, Blackburn wrote the following account to a ministerial friend:

> A school-house, and a house for the teacher were immediately erected. The school-house was so constructed that it might serve the children to eat in, and be comfortable for the lodging of males. The females were appointed to sleep in the master's family. . . . all things now fully prepared, the school was opened in the spring of 1804. . . .
> In the course of the first week we had twenty-one children, who all gave flattering evidence of promising geniuses.[14]

As Blackburn had anticipated, Cherokee children learned their three R's with astonishing ease and rapidity. Presbyterian doctrine, when simplified, also was readily absorbed by Blackburn's "Little Cherokees," as he was pleased to call them. Disciplinary problems were referred to the council. And when children lost or discarded clothing issued them by the school, the council paid for the loss out of the Cherokees' annuities. Blackburn's curriculum stressed study,

---

[14] "An Account of the Origin and Progress of the Mission to the Cherokee Indians; in a Series of Letters from the Rev. Gideon Blackburn, to the Rev. Dr. Morse," Letter II, *The Panoplist* (July, 1807), 85.

but it also emphasized personal cleanliness, the use of cutlery at table, and strict adherence to a schedule.

A year after the opening of the Overhills school, Blackburn triumphantly exhibited his "Little Cherokees" at a council held on July 4, 1805, on the Hiwassee River. Upon debarking from poplar canoes, the little Cherokees, arrayed in white children's clothing furnished by Blackburn's parishioners, proudly marched in twos between an aisle of gaping and skeptical whites and the wondering chiefs and headmen of the Cherokee Nation.

Sedately seated in a semicircle, the little Indians glibly read from the white man's books, sang hymns in English from *Watt's Hymnal* and *Rippon's Selections,* and demonstrated their ability to spell and cipher. It was an awesome performance, in view of the fact that Blackburn's "Little Cherokees" had once been referred to by Governor Sevier as "nits that make lice."

Ironically enough, Governor Sevier witnessed the performance of the Cherokee children on that July day in 1805, and was impressed by it. Having disengaged himself from his companions, Sevier held out his hand to the Reverend Blackburn. Tears dampened Sevier's furrowed, weather-beaten face as he grasped Blackburn's hand and shook it roughly. "I have often stood unmoved amidst showers of bullets from the Indian rifles," he said, "but this effectually unmans me. I see civilization taking the ground of barbarism, and the praises of Jesus succeeding the war whoop of the savage."[15]

Governor Sevier's former boast—doubtlessly recalled by Blackburn on this occasion—that out of the thirty-five battles which he had fought against the Indians he had lost but two, paled into insignificance when compared to his statement on this memorable occasion. "Little John," as the Cherokees called Sevier, had been taught a great lesson by the children, who would someday be Cherokee statesmen, diplomats, and educators.

Frequently, after this exhibition, the chiefs and members of the council conferred with the Reverend Blackburn about their government. And Blackburn strongly urged them to change it. Tribal laws,

[15] Letter IV, in *ibid.* (Feb., 1808), 417.

then unwritten, should be revised and written, Blackburn told the Cherokees. The time had come for the Cherokee Nation, he said, to abolish its "blood-for-blood" laws pertaining to criminals. Instead, miscreants should be properly tried by courts.

After considerable discussion, the Cherokee council decided to follow Blackburn's suggestion and reorganize its government, patterning the new government somewhat after that of the United States. This momentous decision was reached by the council at Broom's Town in the fall of 1808. Thereupon Blackburn gave the news to the Reverend Jedidiah Morse, who, in turn, gave it to the press. The *Panoplist* published Blackburn's letter, an excerpt from which follows:

> The period has at last arrived on which I have long fixed my eager eye. The Cherokee nation has at length determined to become men and citizens. Towards this my exertions have been unremittingly directed since the commencement of my mission to them. A few days ago, in full council, they adopted a constitution, which embraces a simple principle of government. The legislative and judicial powers are vested in a general council, and lesser ones subordinate. All criminal accusations must be established by testimony; and no more executions must be made by the avenger of blood; the infliction of punishment is made a governmental transaction. Small companies [a Captain, a Lieutenant, and four light-horsemen] in each district are to have the power of our sheriffs to apprehend supposed criminals; and to execute according to the decree of the council. This could not be done as with us by an individual, there being no way properly to bind him; it must therefore be done by a company. . . .
>
> They have actually made some laws and entered them on record to stand as written laws of the nation; and you would have been astonished at the etiquette with which they performed this business; from council to council messages were passing and repassing according to the rules of parliament. One law is that no murderer shall be punished until he has been proved guilty before the council. Another that all Indians who have stock to a certain number specified shall pay two dollars annually to support their national government; that every white man in the nation, of every description, shall pay one dollar per annum for the same purpose. . . .

That all Indians shall be obliged to pay for crossing at ferries in the nation, as the whites do; that all ferries are to be taxed for the same purpose, some as high as fifty dollars, some thirty, some twenty. . . . The laws are in the following style, "Be it enacted by the General Council of the Cherokee nation. . . ."

Thus far are the Cherokees advanced; further I believe than any other nation of Indians in America. . . . This is the most critical period I have ever seen . . . and a time which calls forth all the energy in the minds of the Indians.[16]

The land cessions which the Cherokee Nation was pressed into making with the federal government in the latter part of the eighteenth and the first quarter of the nineteenth centuries did not please the Cherokees. The methods used by the various administrations between 1798–1819 were disillusioning to a people who had written laws and were seeking to pattern their government after that of the United States.

President Adams' administration sought to gain land cessions from the Cherokees by settling their overdue debts with trading companies or with the government-operated store or factory at Tellico. The Cherokees had bought more goods and supplies than they could pay for, from both private trading companies and the Cherokee factory at Tellico. Adams' commissioners artfully arranged with the council to revoke Cherokee debts in exchange for cessions of land. Pressed in this way, the Indians had no alternative but to cede their land from time to time to the federal government. Thus, between 1791–1819 the Cherokees negotiated twenty-five land cessions with the federal government.

This manner of settling their debts nettled the majority of the Cherokees. And, since the government goods sold to them at the factory were frequently things that had been damaged in their conveyance from the east, the Cherokees asked Presidents Adams and Jefferson to discontinue the factory and permit them to buy their supplies from traders as in the early days. But both Adams and Jefferson refused to do this.

[16] *Ibid.* (Dec., 1808), 325f.

Instead (during Jefferson's administration particularly), factory goods were forced on the Cherokees by the factor (storekeeper), who had instructions from Jefferson to keep the Cherokees in debt so that their lands could more easily be obtained by the government. An examination of Jefferson's official correspondence relating to Indian trade proves conclusively that Jefferson's favorite method of gaining land from all the southern Indians was identical to that which he employed with the Cherokees.[17]

Another method employed by Jefferson and his successors to obtain land from the Cherokees was to corrupt their chiefs by bribery. Return Jonathan Meigs, surprisingly enough, was frequently the vehicle employed by Jefferson to gain land cessions from the unsuspecting tribesmen, the majority of whom thought highly of Meigs. The Cherokees affectionately referred to Meigs as "White Path" and gratefully acknowledged his help. Certainly no Indian agent had ever been more outwardly solicitous of the Cherokees' welfare! During his stay among them, Meigs set an example for Cherokee farmers by his own farming methods. And he was also active in promoting animal husbandry and the development of mechanical skills in the Nation. Meig's death in 1823 at the age of eighty-three is said to have resulted, in fact, from his insistence on giving up his bed to a visiting Cherokee chief in the dead of winter while he slept in a tent in his yard.

Even so, President Jefferson's Secretary of War, Dearborn, utilized Meigs in 1804 to gain the small tract of land in northeast Georgia, commonly known as "Wafford Settlement." And in 1805, Meigs helped Dearborn obtain three other valuable tracts of land. One of these, ceded by the Cherokees to the federal government on October 25, 1805, was north of the Tennessee River in Kentucky and middle Tennessee. The second, ceded to the government on October 27, was Southwest Point (now Kingston, Tennessee). The third, negotiated on the same day, was the "First Island in the Tennessee River." The Cherokees' beloved Great Island of the Hol-

---

[17] By far the best secondary authority on the United States Indian factory system is Ora Brooks Peake. Her *History of the United States Factory System: 1795–1822* is based almost entirely on National Archives records.

ston River, their old treaty ground, went to the federal government on January 7, 1806.

Aware that the land cessions, if made, would have to be negotiated with the lawless Chickamaugans, Meigs secretly promised Doublehead two tracts of land, a square mile each, at the mouths of the Clinch and Hiwassee rivers and Doublehead's brother-in-law, Tahlonteskee, a similar tract at the mouth of Duck River if they would help the United States commissioners push through the treaties.

For the Wafford Settlement, the Cherokees were paid $5,000 in goods and $1,000 in annuities. For the Tennessee and Kentucky lands, they were paid $15,600 and $3,000 in annuities.

Rich James Vann, a town chief living across the road from Springplace, the new Moravian mission (near present-day Chatsworth, Georgia), supposedly joined chiefs Doublehead and Tahlonteskee in receiving bribes in 1806 for assenting to the cession of a large section of the Cherokees' beloved country lying between the Duck and Tennessee rivers.[18] Vann's own rich red land, farmed by Negro slaves, was in the path of a road due to connect Augusta with Nashville. Called the Georgia or Federal Road, it branched off above James Vann's property on the north—one prong going to Tellico on the Little Tennessee and the other heading northwest to Stone's River, where it connected with the road to Nashville. Since Vann owned a mill and ferry on the Conasauga River, the road benefited him considerably.

The treaty consummated in December, 1806, in Washington City, incensed conservative Upper Towns Cherokees. Wrathfully, they accused the Chickamaugans' treaty-makers with willful violation of the ancient Cherokee law prohibiting the cession of lands without the National council's consent, reminding them that the punishment for violating this sacred unwritten law was death.

Doublehead's murder or execution for treason by "the Ridge," Alex Saunders, and John Rogers followed in June, 1807. Relent-

[18] Sources for land cessions of the Cherokees are Kappler, *Indian Affairs*, II; and Mooney, *Myths of the Cherokee, loc. cit.*

lessly pursued by his executioners, who had already wounded him, Doublehead sought shelter in the loft of Gideon Blackburn's school, which had recently been moved to Tellico Blockhouse. Close behind whooped the Ridge, who with one vengeful plunge of the hatchet finished his grim job. And, because of his participation in the 1806 treaty, Inali or Black Fox (Little Turkey's successor) was deposed but was later reinstated.

After this, the anti-cession party unhappily noted that annuities were paid and goods were distributed by United States commissioners exclusively to the Chickamaugans. The council at Ustanali received no notice of when and where the distribution was to be made. Outraged by this turn of events, the legitimate Cherokee National Council voted to send a deputation to Washington City to request division of the nation, with the Hiwassee Mountains serving as the dividing line between the Upper Cherokees and the Chickamaugans.

Influenced by Gideon Blackburn, now the superintendent of two Cherokee mission schools (one at Tellico Blockhouse and a second at the mouth of Sale Creek), the deputation informed President Jefferson that the Cherokees whom they represented would like to become citizens of the United States. This gave President Jefferson the opening which he had been eagerly awaiting. Quickly he suggested that, if the Cherokee minority could not agree upon the Nation's division, it could remove to lands west of the Mississippi. Some years before—in 1802—the Jefferson administration had made a dangerous pact with Georgia whereby that state was to cede her western lands to the United States and receive in payment for the same $1,250,000, along with the guarantee that the United States would extinguish at their own expense, "for the use of Georgia, as early as the same can be peaceably obtained upon reasonable terms, the Indian title to the lands lying within the limits of that state."[19] Certainly no meaner blow could have been dealt the Cherokees during President Jefferson's reign than the Georgia Compact of 1802.

---

[19] Possibly because of his legal background, John P. Brown in *Old Frontiers* explains the Compact of 1802 more clearly than some other historians. This quotation, however, comes from Henry Thompson Malone, *Cherokees of the Old South*, 65f.

It threatened, for three decades, to sever the Cherokee and Creek Nations from their ancient homelands. And President Jefferson, knowing the worth of the Compact to the federal government as well as to Georgia, was not averse to using it, if it became necessary to remove unwanted Indian tribes west of the Mississippi.

However, in 1808, the Compact of 1802 was not needed to effect the removal of some 1,130 Chickamaugans to lands west of the Mississippi (today Dardanelle, Arkansas, in Pope County). Jefferson had merely to suggest to Tahlonteskee and other Chickamaugans that if they did not care to remain in the same country with their enemy countrymen, they could remove to Dardanelle Rock. Thus, in the spring of 1808, Tahlonteskee—fearing assassination—notified President Jefferson that his people were ready to migrate. Following their migration, Tahlonteskee's band of Cherokees called themselves "Cherokees West" or "Old Settlers."

Engaged in clearing land, building homes, and fighting the truculent Osage tribe, which resented the occupancy of land that they claimed was theirs, the Cherokees West did not attempt to compete with the governmental, economic, educational, and religious progress made by the Cherokees east of the Mississippi. Occasionally they visited the tribesmen in the east, and possibly were amazed by their cultural advancement—much of which had developed since their departure for Arkansas.

However, in 1813–14, a demand from the United States that they take up arms against the hostile Creeks dealt a severe blow to the Eastern Cherokees' cultural advancement. Between six and seven hundred Cherokees, serving under Colonel Gideon Morgan, Major Ridge (the Ridge), John Lowrey, and Captain Richard Brown, fought the Creeks and acquitted themselves nobly at the battles of Horseshoe Bend, Talladega, Emuckfaw, and Enotachopco. Among this number were John Ross, George Gist (Sequoyah), John Drew, Whitepath, Arch Campbell, Going Snake, Chief Junuluska, George Fields, Charles Hicks, and many other mixed bloods and full bloods who were soon to play an important part in their nation's phenomenal advancement.

George Gist even then was toying with the idea of an alphabet.

Trained to be a silversmith, Gist had asked Charles Hicks to write Gist's Indian name—Sequoyah—on the white man's "talking leaf" so that he could stamp its facsimile on the wondrously beautiful silver spurs, bracelets, and other pieces he had learned to make. This led Sequoyah to observe the curious lettering, with an eye to utilizing its form in building a written language for his people.

Young John Ross, tutored by whites hired by Daniel Ross to teach his children, had completed his higher education at Kingsport, Tennessee, when ordered to the Creek country. Ross was twenty-three years old, and though only an eighth-blood, was inwardly all Cherokee.

Ironically, these potential Cherokee leaders, while serving under General Jackson in the Creek war, were given ample opportunity to observe their future political foe. Familiar to them were Jackson's blazing blue eyes, his shrill voice, and the sight of his gaunt figure drooped over a tree during an attack of dysentery. On those occasions, Jackson alternately retched and raged and stubbornly urged his men onward.

Familiar to Cherokee warriors also were Jackson's harsh peace terms. Having defeated the Creeks (or Red Sticks), Jackson demanded 23,000,000 acres of their land after "an unprovoked, inhuman and sanguinary war waged by the hostile Creeks against the United States hath been repelled, prosecuted and determined successfully on the part of the said states in conformity with the principles of national justice and honorable warfare."[20]

Seemingly insensitive to Cherokee deeds of heroism (Chief Junuluska and his warriors swam the Tallapoosa River to the enemies' rear and took all the hostile canoes beached there in readiness for the Creeks' getaway; then, utilizing these same canoes, Junuluska's force pressed into the battle and fought valiantly with Jackson's victorious forces) Jackson, at the close of the war, maintained an attitude toward his Cherokee allies that was anything but commendable. To President Madison and the Secretary of War, William Craw-

[20] Cotterill, *The Southern Indians,* 191.

132

ford, Jackson audaciously suggested that while the United States troops were yet on the field it might be well to force cessions of all Tennessee lands from both Chickasaws and Cherokees. But neither Madison nor his Secretary of War would countenance this unethical procedure. And when Crawford next wrote to Meigs, he instructed him to take care of the Cherokees' interests when the boundary line was run. Apparently Crawford knew that Jackson would be difficult to curb when he learned that the Chickasaws and Cherokees claimed 4,000,000 acres of the 23,000,000 demanded by Jackson from the Creeks.

Anticipating a future campaign against the Spaniards, Jackson invited the Cherokees to enroll for that campaign, but they flatly refused. Giving as an excuse the fact that it was time for annuities to be paid, they turned their boundary settlement over to the head chiefs and Meigs. And Meigs in this particular instance fiercely defended the Cherokees' rights to lands included in the Creek cession which had been occupied by the Cherokees for a good many years.

The treaty negotiated in the Creek council house at Fort Jackson on August 9, 1814, between Cherokee and Creek chiefs and the United States displeased Major General Jackson; nevertheless, it stood until it was made final in Washington a year and a half later.

The Cherokee delegation, who (in the vernacular of the day) "waited on President Madison" in February and March, 1816, to settle difficulties arising from the Creek war, won the respect and admiration of Washington officials. Colonel John Lowrey, spokesman for the Cherokee council, was an older brother of George Lowrey and had George's gifts of integrity and wisdom. Others of the deputation were equally noted for their mannerly conduct and sharp perception. They were old Major Ridge, Captain John Walker, Captain Richard Taylor, Cheucunsenee, and Adjutant John Ross.

John Ross, a slight young man of medium stature, with blue eyes and brown hair, could easily have passed for a white man. And the Ridge (or Major Ridge, as he was then called), with his snow-white hair, amber skin, and dark piercing eyes, cut a fine figure as he strode down the streets of Washington City or sat stiffly erect in a coach, possibly drawn by a lively span of livery-stable horses hired by the deputation to conduct them in proper style to the Secretary of War's office and to the White House.

The following ceremonious conversation between John Lowrey and President Madison (taken down verbatim by either Richard Taylor or John Ross) furnishes irrefutable evidence that the headmen of the Cherokee nation were becoming civilized and also learning to fight the white man with his own weapons—smooth diplomacy:

> COLONEL LOWREY: Father I now have the pleasure to be in your presence. I am directed by my National Council to take you our Father by the hand. This day was appointed by the Great Spirit for us to see one another. It makes my heart as glad to enter your house as it does when I enter my own house. . . . HIS EXCELLENCY JA. MADISON: I was apprised of your coming before you arrived at this place. It always gives me great pleasure to receive my friends in my house especially my red Brethren the Cherokees who have fought by the side of their White Brethren and spilt their blood together.[21]

Before leaving the Nation, the deputation had been carefully instructed by the council to obtain pensions for Cherokees wounded in the Creek War, to ask for more smith-shops and the erection of ironworks, to request the removal of intruders encouraged to settle on their land by Jackson before the final boundary settlement was made, and to demand payment for damages done to Cherokee property by troops passing through the Nation en route to the Creek war.

Meticulously worded, these written requests were signed with the X mark by Colonel John Lowrey, Major Ridge, Captain John Walker, and Cheucunsenee, but Richard Taylor's signature was affixed to them with a fine flourish, as was John Ross's. With Meigs's assistance, this deputation negotiated the first land cession in a decade with the United States in Washington on March 22, 1816. The ces-

---

[21] "Conversation between President Madison and Col. John Lowrey, Feb. 22, 1816," in Ross Papers, Thomas Gilcrease Institute of American History and Art.

sion constituted a triangular wedge of land—the Cherokees' last—in South Carolina.

A second treaty of the same date awarded the Cherokees who had filed claims for troop damages $25,600 in payment for same. Other terms of this agreement clarified the Cherokee-Creek boundary between the Coosa and Tennessee rivers by recognizing Cherokee land claims south of the Tennessee. The treaty also granted to the United States the right to lay off, open, and have the free use of all roads through the Cherokee country necessary to convenient intercourse between the states of Tennessee and Georgia and Mississippi Territory, as well as the free navigation of all rivers within the Cherokee territory.

This last agreement possibly appealed to the Cherokee deputation because it permitted their people to erect "stands" (taverns) or other public buildings along these roads and thus to increase their earnings.

When officially notified of the Cherokee boundary settlement, Jackson termed it a "wanton, hasty, useless thing" and said it was the "hight" [*sic*] of his diplomatic ambition to "undo it."

Jackson's chance to "undo it" eventually came. Appointed a commissioner, together with David Meriwether and Jesse Franklin, Jackson secured the abrogation of the boundary treaty made in Washington by bribing eight Cherokee chiefs. The chiefs—Pathkiller, Glass, Boat, Sour Mush, Chulioa, Dick Justice, Richard Brown, and Chickasautchee—could not resist the presents offered to them by Jackson. After deliberating for two days, they agreed to relinquish the Cherokees' claim to the controversial tract of land south of the Tennessee, which was claimed also by the Chickasaws, for $5,000 cash and $60,000 to be paid the Nation over a period of ten years.

To protect themselves from the wrath of the council, the delegation of twelve who signed the treaty with Jackson did so with the understanding that the Cherokee National Council must ratify it before it became final.[22]

---

[22] Cotterill, *The Southern Indians*, 200.

Jackson's explanation to the Secretary of War of how he over-came the chiefs' aversion to the treaty was: "In concluding the treaty with the Cherokees, it was found both well and polite to make a few presents to the chiefs and interpreters."

The same method was employed to buy the Chickasaws' claims. Jackson wrote to the Secretary of War:

> It was soon found that a favorable result to the negotiation was not to be anticipated unless we addressed ourselves feelingly to the predominant and governing passions of all Indian tribes, i.e., their avarice or fear. Our instructions pointed to the former and forbade the latter: we therefore were compelled . . . to apply the sole remedy in our power. It was applied and presents offered to the influential chiefs, amounting to $4,500, to be paid on the success of the negotiations.[23]

Shortly after this, Agent Meigs was required by the War Department again to bring pressure to bear on the Cherokees to cede their North Carolina lands to the United States. But, confused and angered by the ratification of the October treaty, the Cherokees refused. Thereupon President Monroe's Secretary of War, John Calhoun, turned the matter over to Andrew Jackson, Joseph McMinn, and John Coffee, and they went at the job with a vengeance. Boldly they broached the subject of removal to the Cherokees, suggesting that they exchange their eastern land for western, thereby acquiring new hunting grounds to replace the old.

This argument did not make sense to one Cherokee, who declared:

> The Indians say they don't know how to understand their Father, the President. A few years ago he sent them a plough & a hoe—said it was not good for his red children to hunt—they must cultivate the earth. Now he tells them there is good hunting at the Arkansas: if they go there he will give them rifles.[24]

Bribes followed. A minority in the Nation again agreed to treaty terms as set forth by the wily commissioners in a convention at the

[23] *Ibid.*
[24] Malone, *Cherokees of the Old South*, 69.

new Calhoun Agency on the Hiwassee. Present at this convention were only fifteen chiefs from Arkansas, who had stopped off en route to Washington City.

A week later an antagonistic Cherokee National Council listened to Jackson's explanation of the cessions demanded by the United States. The first was to compensate the United States for land already settled by 3,700 Cherokee migrants in the Arkansas River country. The second comprised the Cherokees' remaining lands in the east, which would be exchanged for lands west of the Mississippi.

Stunned, the council refused. Sixty-seven chiefs signed the protest against emigration that was presented to the commissioners by the council. Upon its receipt, Jackson's hot Irish temper flared up, and he ordered the signers to repudiate it.

Worn down by his vehemence and perhaps by bribery, Tuckasee and Glass joined the Arkansas delegation. And eventually the council followed suit by ceding two tracts of land in Georgia and Tennessee to the United States.

Chisholm, from the western delegation, and Glass and Utsala, from the eastern, were known to have received bribes for their part in this transaction, and the other signers of the minority treaty, signed on July 8, 1817, were suspected of it. The agreement ceded a tract in Tennessee, two in Alabama, and one in Georgia for the equivalent in land on the Arkansas and White rivers "bordering on the Osage nation."

The old weakness—that of a loose confederation of headmen of the Nation—had again proved that what the Cherokee Nation need-ed was a head chief who would weld the nation into "a body politic." Too late the Cherokee National Council appointed a committee of thirteen to safeguard their nation against future land cessions made without the consent of a full council of chiefs. Too late did Path-killer (now the Cherokees' principal chief) and Charles Hicks (their second chief) send a carefully selected deputation to Washington to present a memorial to President Monroe in protest of the 1817 treaty. In Washington the delegation was told by a spokesman for the War Department that the Secretary of War had already arranged for boats to transport emigrants west of the Mississippi. According to the 1817 treaty, each male emigrant was to be furnished a blanket, rifle, brass kettle, and lead; and, purportedly, 3,500 Cherokees had already agreed to emigrate.

Over a year later, on February 27, 1819, the United States demanded the Cherokees' peripheral lands as compensation for past and future emigrations. Following this cession the Cherokees received assurances by the War Department that, since they had already paid for past and future emigrants, Cherokee migration cessions would be discontinued. But was not the state of Georgia demanding that the United States government enforce the Georgia Compact of 1802 and move the Cherokees off their lands in the Georgia area so that these lands could be settled by the people of the state? And had not the United States government between 1794–1819 pressed the Cherokee Nation into making twenty-four treaties involving small and large land cessions

To answer these questions, the Cherokees had but to review their past, and also to note with chagrin and grief that their once vast domain had been reduced—by treaties first with England and then with the United States—from approximately 40,000 square miles to nearly half that area. Measured by the white man's "land stealer" or compass, the Cherokee Nation measured now but 200 miles east to west and 120 miles north to south, its greater portion lying in the Georgia area wherein were concentrated approximately two-thirds of the Nation's population. On the white man's map the Cherokees' holdings of approximately 10,000,000 acres resembled a small, wind-blown leaf bleakly clinging to a wet stone.

Acutely aware of the impending disastrous enforcement of Georgia's Compact of 1802, the Cherokee Nation, between 1819–27, firmly adopted as its main objective the preservation and protection of its remaining lands. Pushing aside minor matters pertaining to its government, the Nation pursued its objective with zeal and persistence, deeming the preservation of the land bestowed upon the Cherokee Nations eons ago by Asga-Ya-Galun-lati to be that Nation's most sacred and demanding duty.

CHAPTER VII

"The Body Politic"

IN A SUPREME EFFORT to forestall the removal of their people from ancestral homelands promised to the state of Georgia by the Compact of 1802, progressive Cherokee leaders, many of whom were mixed bloods, undertook an ambitious and aggressive program that would further Cherokee education and religion; replace ancient Cherokee culture with that of the educated and Christianized white man; and—of utmost importance—convert the Cherokees' tribal government (already altered by the written laws of 1808) into a republic substantially patterned after that of the United States. By adherence to this program, the Cherokees hoped to convince the United States government that the Cherokee Nation merited respect. So convinced, that government would then, they hoped, bring its compact with Georgia to a close by compromise or by some method other than that of extinguishing the Cherokees' title to their lands.[1]

But, ironically, the Cherokees' phenomenal advancement—unparalleled between 1819–27 by any of the other American aborig-

---

[1] "We do sincerely hope that measures may be adopted by the United States and the State of Georgia so as to close their compact without teasing the Cherokees anymore for their lands." See Cherokee Delegation to His Excellency John Q. Adams, Pres. of the United States, March 12, 1825, (copy), in File 2, Loose Papers—Ross, John, in the Georgia Department of Archives and History, Atlanta.

ines—hastened, instead of deterred, enforcement of the Compact. For, upon perceiving the Cherokees' advancement, which, in some respects, outpaced her own, Georgia flew into a mighty rage. Denouncing the Cherokees as savages, Georgia abandoned both dignity and ethics and through her government, press, and courts began, in 1820, a vicious attack upon the Cherokees that was to continue for eighteen years, or until the Cherokees' final removal west of the Mississippi in 1838–39.

But Georgia's tactics did not deter the Cherokees from carrying forward their program of educating, Christianizing, and governing the Nation by the white man's methods and standards. Furthering education, in particular, in the first quarter of the nineteenth century were John Ridge, the son of old Major Ridge, and John's cousin, Elias Boudinot (Buck Oowatie). Both of these mixed-blood Cherokees had attended the mission school at Cornwall, Connecticut, and both had married Cornwall girls. John Ridge had married Susan B. Northrup and Elias Boudinot, Harriet R. Gold, thereby incurring the wrath of Cornwall's bluestocking citizenry to the extent of their closing the mission school and burning John Ridge and his bride in effigy. Among other mixed-blood protagonists of Cherokee education were John Ross, who had been educated by tutors and at an academy at Kingsport, Tennessee; Charles and Elijah Hicks; George Lowrey; Walter Adair; and W. S. Coodey.

Encouraged by these leaders, Cherokee mission schools multiplied in the Nation until, by 1826, there were eighteen of them. Supported partially by a government fund for civilizing American aborigines and partially by the religious funds of Presbyterian, Baptist, Moravian, and Methodist denominations and by the Cherokees themselves, mission schools formed the base of nineteenth-century Cherokee education.

In 1817, Brainerd mission school, staffed by highly educated and dedicated New Englanders sent out by the American Board of Commissioners for Foreign Missions in Boston, opened its doors to male and female Cherokees. Located on the site of John McDonald's former home on Chickamauga Creek (the scene of many a bloody battle between whites and Chickamaugans), Brainerd flourished. Its curriculum embraced Presbyterian doctrine and elementary education for all, mechanical skills for the males, and household skills for the females. All of the students were treated like sons and daughters by the New England teachers. The Indian girls, especially, received kindly treatment from the wives of the missionaries, who taught them how to cook, spin, weave, sew, mold candles, and sip tea sedately in the mission parlor.

The Reverend Blackburn's two schools had been discontinued because of Blackburn's illness about seven years before Brainerd's establishment, and the Moravian school at Springplace had during that time been the only educational center in the Nation. But Springplace, although an excellent influence on Cherokees living in its area, had not been able to reach the Indians elsewhere in the Nation. Nor had the Moravians stressed female education, as did Brainerd.

Never considered inferior to males by the Cherokees, women in ancient times had been respected and accorded consideration in the Nation for the simple reason that they were the mothers of warriors. But, in 1817, they were respected because they were the mothers, or potential mothers, of Cherokee statesmen and leaders. Therefore, women must not only learn household skills but must also be taught from the Bible so that they could, in time, teach their children and others the white man's religion. A striking example of the effect of mission teaching on females in the Nation was Catherine Brown, who, upon completing her education at Brainerd, established a mission school at Creek Path (today in Alabama) where she taught for years.

Associated with Brainerd's faculty at various periods were Cyrus Kingsbury, Daniel Sabin Buttrick, Ard Hoyt, Elizur Butler, and Samuel Austin Worcester. Sent to Brainerd in 1825 by the American Board of Commissioners for Foreign Missions, Worcester was to play an important role in Cherokee affairs until his death in 1852. Between Brainerd's establishment in 1817 and the closing of its doors by the removal of the Nation in 1838–39, its distinguished faculty— graduates of Williams, the University of Vermont, Princeton, and other noted eastern colleges—did more to further the Cherokees' educational program than that of any other mission school in the Nation.

Upon leaving Brainerd, the majority of the faculty established, or taught, mission schools elsewhere in the Nation. Branches of Brainerd mission were established by its former teachers at Taloney (Carmel), Wilstown, Haweis, Candy's Creek, Etowah, and Creek Path. The faculties of these schools served the Cherokees as translators, interpreters, and doctors. Samuel Austin Worcester helped the Cherokees establish an Indian newspaper, the first in North America.

But Brainerd was not the only new mission school established in the Cherokee Nation in 1817. In October of that year the Baptist Board of North Carolina sent Humphrey Posey to Valley Town on the Hiwassee River to establish a mission. But either the Cherokees were not receptive to Posey's preachments or Posey became discouraged by lack of funds, because he did not stay in the Cherokee territory for very long; in 1821, Evan Jones, a native of Wales, took over there, assisted by Isaac Clever, a blacksmith, and John Farrier, a weaver. Deserted after a short time by these assistants, Jones carried on alone until about 1822, when Duncan O'Bryant arrived to open a Baptist mission at Tinsawattee, sixty miles south of Valley Town in present-day Georgia. Jones's circuit also included Notley, a mission sixteen miles southwest of Valley Town.

Even though he possessed little education and limited funds, Evan Jones attracted converts. Through Jones's evangelical labors, Kaneeda, a full blood, was converted and, in 1829, ordained a Baptist minister, the first native Baptist minister in the Cherokee Nation. Kaneeda's ordination was followed in 1830 by that of Jesse Bushyhead, a descendant of John Stuart. Born in present-day Cleveland, Tennessee, Bushyhead had attended an academy in Tennessee and was prepared to teach as well as preach to his people.

Methodist missions were not established in the Cherokee Nation until 1825, possibly because the Methodists prior to this date had devoted their attention solely to evangelical work. But after 1825, Methodist mission schools were opened at Wills Valley and Oostanaula, Coosawattee, Mount Wesley, Ashbury, Chattooga, Sullacoie, Neeley's Grove, and Conasauga. The Methodists' first Cherokee minister was Turtle Fields, a veteran of the Creek war. Identified with Methodism in the Cherokee Nation were Richard Riley, a half blood living at Fort Deposit near what is today Guntersville, Alabama; W. S. Coody; John Ross; Edward Gunter; Turtle Fields; Joeseph Blackbird; and other Cherokee leaders.

The Moravians, who from the beginning of their mission work at Springplace had stressed education, seized the opportunity to utilize Sequoyah's invention of the alphabet in both educational and religious fields. In 1821 the Moravians established a second mission at Oochgeelogy, about fifteen miles south of Springplace, and both Springplace mission and Oochgeelogy mission served the Cherokees until their removal in 1838. To the Moravians, today's Cherokees pay great tribute. Emotionally stable themselves, the missionaries imparted this stability to Cherokee scholars, who, upon leaving Moravian mission schools, strove hard to stamp out illiteracy among their people.[2]

Illiteracy, following Sequoyah's invention of the Cherokee alphabet or syllabary in 1821, was not difficult to stamp out. Young and old Cherokees soon discovered that they could learn to read and write in a very short time by mastering the new invention. Noting the gratifying consequences of Sequoyah's invention, the Cherokee Legislative Council voted to establish a national newspaper and a national seminary in the Nation.

In a meeting at New Town the Legislative Council, in 1825, resolved "to receive donations in money from individuals or societies throughout the United States for the object of establishing and supporting a national academy and for procuring two sets of types to fit

---

[2] Sources of information on Cherokee education in this period are *Memoir of Catherine Brown* (ed. by Rufus Anderson); Mission Reports (1818–25), in unpublished MS. No. 3153, B. A. E.; Eugene Coke Routh, "Early Missionaries to the Cherokees," *Chronicles of Oklahoma, Vol.* XV, 449–65; Malone, *Cherokees of the Old South*, 91–117; Adelaide L. Fries, ed., *Records of the Moravians; Boudinot's Address to the Whites* (printed by W. Geddes in Philadelphia, 1826); and unclassified letters relating to missionaries and Cherokees, in Georgia Department of Archives and History, Atlanta.

one press, to establish a printing office at New Town . . . one set to be composed of English letters, the other of Cherokee characters, the invention of George Guest [Gist], a Cherokee."[3]

The Legislative Council also voted in October, 1825, to appoint Elias Boudinot as the Cherokees' representative. Boudinot was empowered to collect money from eastern lectures for the national academy and newspaper.

On his eastern lecture tour in 1826, Boudinot held Philadelphia and New York audiences spellbound as he recited the achievements of his people and expressed their great desire for education by means of a national newspaper and an academy. Cognizant of his audiences' lack of knowledge concerning his people's advancement from savagery to civilization in a quarter of a century, Boudinot gave them the census returns. In 1824–25—so recited Boudinot—the Cherokees owned 22,000 cattle, 7,600 horses, 46,000 swine, 2,500 sheep, 762 looms, 2,488 spinning wheels, 172 wagons, 2,943 plows, 10 sawmills, 31 gristmills, 61 blacksmith shops, 8 cotton machines, 18 schools, 18 ferries, and a number of public roads.[4]

Boudinot's fund-raising tour financed a newspaper, *The Cherokee Phoenix*, as planned by the Legislative Council. Samuel Worcester procured a printing press for the *Phoenix* in Boston, with type for both the Cherokee and English languages. The *Phoenix* made its debut on February 21, 1828, and caused quite a stir all over America and in some parts of Europe. Its editor, Elias Boudinot, assisted by Worcester, did not use restraint in publishing accounts of Cherokee progress. And in both languages the first issue of the *Phoenix* notified readers that:

> The laws and public documents of the Nation, and matters relating to the welfare and condition of the Cherokees as a people, will be faithfully published in English and Cherokee. . . . We will invariably state the will of the majority of our people on the subject of the present

---

[3] *Laws of the Cherokee Nation . . . at Various Periods* (published in 1852). On microfilm at Emory University.

[4] *Boudinot's Address to the Whites, loc. cit.*

controversy with Georgia, and the present removal policy of the United States Government.[5]

But the reorganization of their government—begun in 1817 and completed in 1827—was the Cherokees' crowning achievement. Retaining their principal chief as the titular head of the Nation, the Cherokees created an elective bicameral legislature by making the National Committee of thirteen members co-ordinate with the National Council. Roughly, the National Committee corresponded to the United States Senate and the National Council to the United States House of Representatives.

Intent less on legislation than on justice, the Cherokees divided the Nation into eight judicial districts, in each of which a judge, marshal, and local council were to apply the laws. For every two districts there was a circuit judge, who, at first, was accompanied on his rounds by a company of "Light Horse" whose duty it was to execute the judge's decisions and, perhaps, protect the judge's life. The marshal collected, on commission, taxes—the principal tax being a poll tax of fifty cents levied on each single man under sixty.[6]

The creation of a National Superior Court, authorized by the Legislative Council at New Town in the fall of 1822, marked another milestone in Cherokee governmental reorganization. As provided for by Cherokee law in 1822, a National Superior Court was ordered to be held during the annual sessions of the Legislative Council in October and November to review cases appealed from the district courts. The law also provided that the court empanel a jury of honest, God-fearing men to decide the cases before the court.

At its first term in October, 1823, the Cherokee high court reviewed twenty-one cases, the majority being civil cases involving debt, damages, or ejectment from property. Criminal cases included grand larceny, such as hog-stealing and other similar crimes.

On October 12, 1824, the Legislative Council decreed that "suits

[5] Malone, *Cherokees of the Old South*, 158.
[6] *Laws of the Cherokee Nation*, loc. cit.

which have been appealed from the District Courts to the Superior Court in cases of debt, the persons non-suited, or against whom judgement shall be given . . . shall pay a cost of six per cent on the amount of the judgement issued, which per cent shall be collected for the benefit of the treasury of the Cherokee Nation." In 1824 the council further decreed that witnesses subpoenaed to appear before the Superior Court must either obey the summons or pay a ten-dollar fine to the person or persons who would have derived benefit from their testimony. Witnesses answering the court's summons were to be paid fifty cents for each day they attended court, this amount "to be levied off the person or persons against whom judgement may be issued."[7]

Antedating the Supreme Court of the state of Georgia by twenty years, the Cherokees' Supreme Court (as their Superior Court came to be called) reviewed 246 cases in its thirteen years of existence, the majority continuing to be civil rather than criminal cases. Debts, bigamy, the sale of improvements by Arkansas emigrants, the vending of "spirituous liquors," and a great variety of other civil and criminal cases were appealed to the National Supreme Court up until 1835, when the Cherokees' titles to their eastern lands were extinguished by the United States with the help and blessing of the state of Georgia.

Fearful, in 1822, that the Cherokees' progress—their stepped-up program of education, their adoption of white culture, and the recent creation of a National Supreme Court—would soon lead to the Indians' demanding citizen-status in the United States, the state of Georgia intensified and expanded its efforts to extinguish Cherokee land titles in the Georgia area. Thus, to facilitate the Cherokees' removal from lands adjacent to Georgia proper, Georgia delegations in the United States Congress and Georgia state officials continued to harangue the President to close the Compact of 1802 and to demand the Cherokees' land.

To appease those Georgians who feared Cherokee progress, the Secretary of War, in 1822, notified the Cherokees that United States

---

[7] Laws quoted throughout this chapter are from *ibid.*

commissioners, empowered by the President and his cabinet to treat with them for their Georgia lands, would soon be in their country to negotiate a treaty of land cession. Upon receipt of this disquieting notice, the Legislative Council, convening at New Town in 1822, passed a resolution that the Nation intended to make no more land cessions with the United States. "Expecting a visit from the commissioners, the head chiefs requested the judges to ascertain wishes, sentiments, and disposition of citizens of respective districts. [And the citizens] unanimously with one voice [expressed] their determination to hold no treaties with any Commissioners of the U. S. . . . being resolved not to dispose of even one foot of ground."[8] On all other matters not pertaining to land cessions, the council agreed to confer with United States "Commissioners or agents with friendship and cordiality, and will ever keep bright the chain of peace and friendship which links the Cherokee nation and the government of the United States."[9]

For a year the Cherokees were not bothered by United States commissioners. Then, on October 23, 1823, the Creek chief, William McIntosh, who was an emissary of the United States commissioners, attempted to bribe John Ross, then president of the Legislative Council, Charles Hicks, the second chief, and Alexander McCoy, clerk of the council, to influence the Cherokee people to make land cessions to the United States. Contemptuously, Ross, Hicks, and McCoy refused McIntosh's $12,000 offer of bribery.

Meeting with the commissioners afterward, the Cherokees became increasingly irritated by their repeated assertion that the Hopewell treaty of 1785 made the Indians mere tenants of their lands and that, therefore, they had no alternative but to cede their lands to the United States.

Stoically, the Cherokees closed the conference.

But, after the commissioners had gone, Indian agent Joseph McMinn (Meigs's successor), continued to harass members of the Legislative Council. At every opportunity, McMinn chided council

---

[8] Council Record, 1822, in Ross Papers, *loc. cit.*
[9] *Ibid.*

members for not co-operating with the United States. Consequently, in January, 1824, the council dispatched John Ross, George Lowrey, Elijah Hicks, and Major Ridge to Washington to ask President James Monroe to abrogate the Georgia Compact of 1802 and also to demand that McMinn be removed from the Nation. Other matters to be attended to in Washington were the payment to the Cherokees, promised the Nation in 1804, for the tract of land known as "The Wafford Settlement" in northeast Georgia; the relocation of the Cherokee agency; and the enlistment of the federal government in collecting taxes levied on white traders.

Upon reaching Washington, the Cherokee delegation engaged room and board at Tennison's Hotel. Seated at table across from a member of Congress from Georgia who, on the floor of the House, had rudely referred to the Cherokees as "savages subsisting upon roots, wild herbs, disgusting reptiles," George Lowrey in a loud voice repeatedly requested that the Negro waiter bring him "some of those roots" (a dish of sweet potatoes). When the sweet potatoes were passed to him, Lowrey took only a small portion, thereby attracting the attention of the dining room. Thereafter, each time that Lowrey repeated his request for "those roots" and accompanied it with the remark, "we Indians are very fond of roots," the diners burst into hilarious laughter.[10]

Official Washington was further impressed by the Cherokee delegation's crisp and pointed reply to the Georgians' accusation (published in the *Georgia Journal*) that the Cherokees were not capable of writing the letters which they had submitted to the President and the Secretary of War upon their arrival. White men were thought to have written the polished letters. Angrily, the Cherokee delegation replied to the charge in the *National Intelligencer*:

> . . . That letter and every other letter was not only *written* but dictated by an Indian. We are not so fortunate to have such help. The white man seldom comes forward in our defense. Our rights are in our own keeping. . . . We felt the necessity of our case and we have

[10] See Ross, ed., *The Life and Times of Honorable William P. Ross.*

endeavored to improve it, our letters are our own—And if they are thought too refined for "Savages" let the white man take it for proof that, with proper assistance, Indians can think and write for themselves. We refer the Georgia delegation, and the Editor of the *Georgia Journal* to our correspondence with their own commissioners. . . .

. . . We are not ignorant of the Convention of 1802. We know every one of its promises. . . . If, however, these are to be violated and the . . . war whoop . . . be raised against us to dispossess us of our lands we will gratify the delegation of Georgia in their present earnestness to see us removed or destroyed by adding additional fertility to our lands by a deposit of our bodies and our bones—*For we are resolved never to leave them but by a parting from them and our lives together.* How the Christians of America and the world will [justify] their attempts upon our rights . . . it is not for us Indians to say—but our cause is with God and good men, and there we are willing to leave it.[11]

President Monroe's reaction to the delegation's demands is interesting to note. Startled by their request for payment of the $1,000 annuity promised the Cherokees by the treaty of 1804, both Monroe and McKee, the secretary of war, denied that such a treaty had ever been made. But the delegation had proof. They produced a duplicate of the original treaty signed by President Jefferson and John McKee. Thereupon McKee again scrabbled through the War Department's files and found the original 1804 treaty.

The delegation's request for the abrogation of the Compact of 1802 was accompanied by its suggestion that the United States give Florida to the state of Georgia in lieu of the Cherokees' land. But neither this suggestion nor the other items in the delegation's agenda met with favor from Monroe and his Secretary of War, who, although impressed with the delegation's diplomacy and sagacity, yet advocated Cherokee removal.

Stalemated, the conference came to an end. The Cherokee delegation went home, and Monroe notified Governor Troup that he had been unable to secure the Cherokee land cession. Troup's accusatory

[11] To Gales and Seaton, April, 1824, from the Cherokee Delegation, in Ross Papers, *loc. cit.*

reply that the President had not kept his word to the Georgia delegation forced from Monroe the defensive statement to Congress that the Compact of 1802 did not provide for the Cherokees' removal by the employment of force. And so, because of this clause, the evil day of Cherokee removal was miraculously postponed. However, the Cherokees apparently did not feel that postponement entitled them to any rest. Menaced by Georgia, the Nation strove harder than ever to strengthen itself from within.

Painfully aware of the susceptibility to bribery of chiefs in the past, the Legislative Council of the Cherokees decreed in 1825 that:

> . . . The Principal Chiefs of the nation shall in no wise hold any treaties or dispose of public property in any manner without the express authority of the Legislative Council in session. . . . The two principal chiefs of the nation shall not, jointly or separately, have the power of arresting the judgments of . . . the courts or of the legal acts of the National Committee and Council, but that the judiciary of the nation shall be independent, and their decisions final, and conclusive; provided always that they act in conformity to the foregoing principles or articles, and the acknowledged laws of the Nation.[12]

In 1825 the Legislative Council decreed that to amend and modify articles of the Cherokees' civil and criminal codes, a quorum was necessary in both the National Committee and Council. In 1825, too, the Legislative Council decreed that "all gold, silver, lead, copper or brass mines, which may be found within the limits of the Cherokee Nation, shall be the public property of the Cherokee Nation, and should the Legislative Council deem it profitable and expedient, to have such mine or mines worked, then, in that case, the discoverer or discoverers shall be entitled to receive one-fourth of the net proceeds arising from such minerals." In 1825 the Legislative Council decreed that surplus monies of the Nation could be loaned at 6 per cent interest to Cherokee citizens, "provided such person or persons

---

[12] Starr, *History of the Cherokee Indians*, 48f.; *Laws of the Cherokee Nation*, *loc. cit.*

may be fully able to repay the sum or sums loaned and also, shall give bond and two good and sufficient securities, citizens of the nation; and provided, also, that each loan shall not exceed $500 and for a length of time not exceeding six months."[13]

Of utmost importance to the Cherokees in 1825 was the Legislative Council's resolution, passed on November 12, 1825, to establish a permanent capital at New Town to be named New Echota, in memory of the Cherokees' beloved Chota on the Little Tennessee. This permanent capital was to be situated at the confluence of the Coosawattee and the Conasauga rivers—on the south side, where these two streams form the Oostanaula. As estimated by the Cherokees, this capital site was very nearly in the center of the nation and, therefore, accessible to all tribesmen.

At the Legislative Council on November 12, 1825, it was

> *Resolved* . . . That one hundred town lots, of one acre square, be laid off on the Oostenallah River, commencing below the mouth of the creek, nearly opposite to the mouth of the Caunausauga. The public square to embrace two acres of ground, which town shall be known and called Echota; there shall be a main street of sixty feet and the other streets shall be fifty feet wide.
>
> Be it further resolved that the lots when laid off, be sold to the highest bidder. The purchaser's right shall merely be occupancy, and transferrable only to lawful citizens of the Cherokee Nation, and the proceeds arising from the sales of the lots shall be appropriated for the benefit of the public buildings in said town.[14]

Public buildings authorized to be erected at New Echota were a Council House, a Supreme Court building, and a print shop. But at New Echota, also, there would have to be taverns and stores to accommodate legislators and judges when the Legislative Council convened; these necessary buildings were authorized by the Legislative Council, along with permanent homes for the Reverend Samuel

---

[13] *Laws of the Cherokee Nation, loc. cit.*
[14] Starr, *History of the Cherokee Indians,* 49.

Worcester, Elias Boudinot, and Boudinot's printers. Permitted to remain on the site of New Echota were the permanent residences of Elijah Hicks and of other Cherokees built prior to the establishment of the capital.

New Echota's three public buildings, when finished, resembled those of near-by white settlements. But to nineteenth-century Cherokees they must have seemed totally unlike those of the whites; New Echota's public buildings represented to them their nation's progress and its ability to carry out a well-planned educational, cultural, and governmental program.

As described by John Foster Wheeler, an employee of the *Phoenix*, the home of the newspaper was a one-story log structure equipped with "stands, a bank, and cases for the Cherokee type. . . . The latter," according to Wheeler, "was something entirely new as no pattern for a case or cases to accommodate an alphabet containing 86 characters could be found."[15]

The Council House at New Echota—a large, two-storied, rectangular, log structure having brick chimneys, fireplaces, plank floors, glass windows, and a staircase leading to upper rooms where conferences could be held—was to progressive Cherokees a vast improvement over the ancient heptagon and late-eighteenth-century circular council houses. The new Supreme Court building with its elevated platform furnished with a judge's bench, below which were pine-plank benches for jurors, witnesses, officials of the government, and the general public, although agrestic in appearance, was awe-inspiring to most tribesmen in 1829. But to unprogressive Cherokees like Whitepath, all of the New Echota buildings were as ugly and depressing as the white men's customs.

Of these buildings and the capital in general, a New England visitor to New Echota in 1829 rendered this enthusiastic description:

> This neighborhood is truly an interesting and pleasant place; the ground is as level and smooth as a house floor; the center of the nation —a new place, laid out in city form—one hundred lots of one acre

[15] Malone, *Cherokees of the Old South*, 122.

each—a spring called the public spring, about twice as large as our sawmill brook, near the center with other springs on the plat. Six new frame houses in sight besides the Council House, Court House, printing office, and four stores, all in sight of Mr. Boudinot's house; but the stores are continued only during the session of the council, then removed to other parts of the nation—except one steadily continued. The stores in the nation are as large as the best in our town in Litchfield County [Connecticut]; their large wagons of six horses go to Augusta and bring a great load, and you will see a number of them together. There is much travel through this place. I have seen eleven of these large wagons pass by Mr. Boudinot's house in company.[16]

But, though it indirectly referred to the Cherokees' advancement, this laudatory account of their capital did not mention the tribe's top-ranking achievement, the writing and adoption of a new constitution in convention on July 26, 1827. Patterned after the Constitution of the United States, this erudite instrument of governmental organization raised the Cherokee Nation to the high level which it had sought to attain and toward which its progressive leaders had been ceaselessly striving.

Section One of Article Two in the new Cherokee Constitution guaranteed that: "The power of this Cherokee Government shall be divided into three distinct departments; the Legislative, the Executive, and Judicial." Its preamble read:

We, the Representatives of the people of the Cherokee Nation, in Convention assembled, in order to establish justice, ensure tranquility, promote our common welfare, and secure to ourselves and our posterity the blessings of liberty: acknowledging with humility and gratitude the goodness of the sovereign Ruler of the Universe, in offering us an opportunity so favorable to the design, and imploring His aid and direction in its accomplishment, do ordain and establish this Constitution for the Government of the Cherokee Nation.[17]

---

[16] Benjamin Gold to Hezekiah Gold, December 8, 1829, in unpublished research paper "New Echota," by James Puckett.

[17] Starr, *History of the Cherokee Indians*, 55f.

Portions of the constitution were printed in both Cherokee and English in the first issue of *The Cherokee Phoenix* in February, 1828, for the express purpose of informing all the Indians in the Nation of the constitution's provision for their protection and general welfare.

But, unfortunately, the published portions of the Cherokee Constitution were read also by the Cherokees' archenemy in Georgia, Governor Forsyth. Already inflamed by the Indians' achievements, among which was their establishment of a national newspaper, he forwarded this first issue of the *Phoenix* to President Adams at Washington. Along with the paper, he sent a document signed by Georgia legislators protesting the Cherokees' continued occupancy of their ancient homelands and demanding their removal, as provided by the Compact of 1802. After receiving Governor Forsyth's communication, President Adams tried to placate Georgia by sending Colonel Hugh Montgomery to the Cherokee country to effect the peaceable removal of the Indians.

But the Cherokees by then had grown too strong and capable of governing themselves to be moved by Colonel Montgomery's flaccid arguments, which they received in stony silence, their minds focused on more vital matters. Looming on the horizon was the anticipated election in November, 1828, of Andrew Jackson (the well-known Cherokee-hater) to the Presidency of the United States. To prepare themselves for Jackson's expected collaboration with the state of Georgia the Cherokees sought to fill the office of principal chief just vacated by the deaths of both Pathkiller and his successor, Charles Hicks, with a superior executive. The new chief would have to possess almost superhuman ability, and must also be in harmony with the advancement program of the people who firmly believed that the Cherokee Nation must either progress or perish.

That the Cherokees had progressed culturally to a degree unanticipated by anyone in America is proved in a letter written by Harriett Gold Boudinot's father to his brother in Connecticut in 1829. (Mr. and Mrs. Gold had made the long journey to New Echota from Cornwall by horse and buggy.)

We traveled through Orange County into New Jersey; then into Penn. through Easton, Lancaster, Reading, and many other large and beautiful villages . . . then through a part of Maryland and over the Potomac . . . then into Virginia four hundred miles; then crossed Hiwassee River at a place called Calhoun into the Cherokee nation, where an agent of the United States resides to manage the Indian concerns of the Cherokees. We put up at the house of Mr. Lewis Ross. . . . Being a very rainy day we tarried two nights. His house is an elegant white house near the bank of the river, as neatly furnished as almost any in Litchfield County; his family of four pretty children, the eldest a daughter of about twelve years, attending a high school in Tennessee, appeared as well as any girl of her age. Mr. Ross, a brother of the principal chief, has two or three large stores . . . had Negroes enough to wait on us; made us welcome; said he would take nothing from anyone who has connections in the nation. . . . He is part Cherokee, his wife a white woman of the Meigs family, but you would not suspect him or his children to be part Indian. We then traveled about twenty miles and came to Mr. McNair's a white man who married a Cherokee woman, sister of Mr. Joseph Vann, another Cherokee chief. He has a beautiful white house, and about six or seven hundred acres of the best land you ever saw, and Negroes enough to manage it and clear as much as he pleases; raised five thousand bushels of corn; and it would make you feel small to see his situation. Mr. Vann lives in a large elegant brick house, elegantly furnished. We stayed there overnight, and he would take nothing of us.

. . . . We have traveled about one hundred miles in the nation, visited three mission stations, and are much pleased with the missionaries. Mr. Boudinot has much good company and is respected all over the United States, and is known in Europe; he has about 100 newspapers sent him from different parts of the U. S. by way of exchange. . . .

. . . They have two beautiful and interesting children (Elinor and Mary) who would pass in company for full-blooded Yankees. Harriet says . . . she envies the situation of no one in Connecticut. She has a large and convenient frame house, two stories, 30 x 40 on the ground, well done off and well furnished with the comforts of life. They get their supplies of clothes and groceries—they have their year's store of teas, clothes, paper, ink, etc. from Boston, and their sugars, molasses, etc., from Augusta. They have two or three barrels of flour on hand at once.[18]

Mr. Gold could have filled another page with descriptions of residences of other affluent Cherokees, most of whom were mixed bloods. He also could have mentioned full-blood Cherokees who lived in one-room log houses and who still observed the customs of their forebears. But the latter were devoted followers of the Cherokees' mixed-blood principal chief, John Ross, elected to the difficult office in 1828, a month before Andrew Jackson won the Presidential election in the United States.

[18] Benjamin Gold to Hezekiah Gold, in "New Echota," *loc. cit.*

CHAPTER VIII

Cherokee-Georgia Controversy

ONLY AN EIGHTH-BLOOD, Chief John Ross was thirty-eight years old, stood but five feet, six inches in height, and weighed about 150 pounds. He was the grandson of old John McDonald, the Tory agent among the Chickamaugans during the American Revolution, and the son of Daniel Ross, a native of Scotland—as McDonald had been. Married to Molly, McDonald's quarter-blood daughter, Daniel Ross had reared his children like white aristocrats. But, despite their upbringing, they all remained Cherokees to the core. Known also as "Cooweescoowee," Chief John Ross, as an adjutant, had fought with the Cherokee regiment under General Jackson in the Creek war; had served the Nation as president of its National Committee for a decade; and, in 1827, had become president of the convention that adopted the Cherokee constitution—much of which was written by Ross.

Beloved by the common Indians (or "the people," as he called them), Chief Ross had only to tie his horse to a post in the square of any town or village in the Nation to be surrounded by hordes of Indians, most of whom were full bloods living back in the mountains or coves. At the sight of Ross—sometimes attired in white men's clothes with a turban wound around his head in Turkish fashion, and sometimes wearing a black, broad-brimmed planter's hat, boots, and jacket—"the people," many of whom yet wore ancient tribal dress or a variation of it, formed two diagonal lines in the square. There each awaited patiently his turn to "take Chief Ross by the hand," their dark eyes visibly brightening upon encountering Ross's steady blue ones.

Contrary to Ross's defamers, "the people" meant equally as much to Ross as he to them. Throughout his long chieftaincy, Ross alluded continually in addresses and correspondence to the people. "Our country and our people," Ross wrote to John Ridge in September, 1834, "should always be our motto and their will should direct us in the path of duty."[1]

After the election of Andrew Jackson to the Presidency of the United States, the Cherokee council's path of duty became crystal clear to its members as well as to Chief Ross and George Lowrey, Ross's indispensable executive-assistant or second chief. Only one thing would save the Nation from removal, they agreed, and that thing was unity. Consequently, Cherokee leaders preached to the people the doctrine of unity and the dishonor of betrayal, until the mountains and coves reverberated with "United we stand, divided we fall!"—a motto ironically borrowed from George Pope Morris, an American.

Conceivably, Cherokee fear of eviction quickened when Ross had been in office but a year. For on December 8, 1829, President Jackson, in his first annual message to the United States Congress, bluntly bespoke his intention to initiate and propel through Congress, by spring, a bill providing for the removal of Southeastern Indian tribes to lands west of the Mississippi.

Eleven days later, on December 19, the Georgia legislature (inspirited by Jackson's message) passed a series of outrageous laws— or so they seemed to the Cherokees. These laws provided for the confiscation by Georgia of a large section of Cherokee land and its subsequent annexation to Hall, Habersham, Gwinnett, Carroll, and De Kalb counties; the nullification of Cherokee laws within this confiscated area; the prohibition of further meetings of the Cherokee Legislative Council and all other Cherokee assemblies, within

---

[1] Ross Papers, *loc. cit.*

the limits of Georgia; and the arrest and imprisonment of Cherokees who influenced fellow tribesmen to reject emigration west. Georgia's hated laws, which were to go into effect on June 1, 1830, declared contracts between Indians and whites to be null and void unless witnessed by two whites; made it illegal for an Indian to testify against a white man in Georgia courts; and insultingly forbade Cherokees to dig for gold in the Cherokees' newly discovered gold fields near and in present-day Dahlonega and Dalton, Georgia.

When ordered from their own gold fields by the slovenly dressed and brutally inclined Georgia Guard, who cursed and prodded them with pointed sticks or the butts of rifles, Cherokee residents flew into a righteous rage. Reverting to the ancient tribal law of revenge, rioting Cherokees undertook to annihilate the white enemy—not only the Georgia Guard but Georgia intruders equipped with pick-axes, pans, and other gold-digging paraphernalia. To quell the gold-field disturbance, Jackson ordered federal troops into this region but obligingly withdrew them at the request of Georgia's Governor Forsyth, who preferred that the Georgia Guard handle the matter.

The Cherokees seethed with anger and, charged with assault and murder, were arrested, then thrown into filthy Georgia jails. There they helplessly awaited trial by unscrupulous justices of the peace or judges of Georgia's higher courts, who pronounced harsh sentences dictated by Governor Forsyth and his Cherokee-hating supporters.

Georgia's Governor and officials became allied now with President Jackson in his plan to remove approximately sixty thousand Indians living in the Southeast, including the Choctaw, Creek, Chickasaw, Seminole, and Cherokee tribes—a gigantic undertaking even had the tribes been acquiescent.

By May, 1830, Jackson succeeded by a slim margin in pushing through the United States Congress the Indian Removal Bill. Ratified on May 23, the new law irked and disgusted the majority of Americans and a goodly number of Europeans. Especially annoyed by the Jackson-Georgia machine and the removal law were men like William Wirt, the great constitutional lawyer and former attorney general of the United States; Senator Daniel Webster, who had bitterly opposed the bill's passage in the Senate; and Jeremiah Evarts of Boston, one of the founders of the American Board of Commissioners for Foreign Missions and, in 1830, editor of the *Christian Herald.* Wrathful over the injustice done to the Cherokees and their neighbors, Evarts, who had listened angrily to the debates on the Indian Removal Bill in Congress, wrote a series of articles for the *National Intelligencer* (using the pseudonym of William Penn) decrying the attitude of the minority who in both past and present eras had oppressed American aborigines. Also stirred to anger over the Indian situation in 1830 were Chancellor James Kent; Winthrop Sargent; and Honorable Horace Everett, a member of the United States House of Representatives from Vermont. Everett, gaining the floor of the House on May 19, sought to defeat the removal bill by appealing to the conscience of the members of the Georgia delegation:

> . . . Sir, this policy cannot come to good. It cannot, as it professes, elevate the Indians. It must and will depress, dishearten, and crush them. . . . It is all unmingled, unmitigated evil. There is evil on the other side, but none commensurate with that of this compulsory removal. . . . If they (the Indians) are willing after exploring the (new) country, to go, I am willing they should, and will join in making the appropriation. But while the laws exist, beneath which they cannot live, it is in vain to tell me they are willing to go. How do you know it? . . . Unlock the prison doors, and then you can tell . . . I adjure you, Sir, to recede; there is no disgrace in it. Other states, more powerful than Georgia, have receded, on points where their honor and interest were equally involved.
>
> Sir, if Georgia will recede, she will do more for the Union, and more for herself, than if she could add to her domain the lands of all the Indians, though they were all paved with gold.
>
> The evil, Sir, is enormous; the violence is extreme; the breach of public faith deplorable; the inevitable suffering incalculable. Do not stain the fair name of the country: it has justly been said, it is in the keeping of Congress on the subject. . . .[2]

[2] See *Speech of Horace Everett in the House of Representatives of the United States, May 19, 1830, On the Bill for Removing the Indians from the East to the West Side of the Mississippi.*

Editorials in *The Cherokee Phoenix* on Jackson's new law and the Indian question were recopied in publications all over the United States. Preachers of the gospel in the North and East quoted portions of these editorials in their sermons. At a Methodist camp meeting in the South, a minister depicted a scene in Hell in which President Jackson, together with his cohorts, was called to account for the eviction of the Indians from their ancient homelands.

However, despite adverse public opinion, President Jackson continued to seek the eviction of the Southeastern Indians. In the summer of 1830 he urged the Creeks, Choctaws, Chickasaws, and Cherokees—as provided by the Indian Removal Law—to sign individual treaties of removal. But the Cherokees, invited by President Jackson to meet him in August at Nashville to discuss "terms of a treaty," refused. Thereafter, on September 27, 1830, having been betrayed by one of their chiefs and deserted by the other two who had been bribed by United States commissioners, the Choctaws signed the infamous Treaty of Dancing Rabbit Creek. The Chickasaws signed a removal treaty on October 20, 1832; the Creeks, on March 24, 1832; and the Seminoles, on May 9, 1832. But the Cherokees—relying on their white friends and their own educated leaders—held on to their prized independence. Commenting upon this fact to sympathizing Senecas from New York, the Cherokees compared their Nation to a "solitary tree in an open space where all the forest trees around have been prostrated by a furious tornado—save one."[3]

Although Georgia state law forbade it, the Legislative Council of the Cherokees convened at New Echota in July, 1830, and unanimously adopted the following resolutions:

We have no desire to see the President on the business of entering into a treaty for exchange of lands. . . . But we still ask him to protect us agreeable to [federal] treaties . . . provided for our protection. Inclination to remove from this land has no abiding place in our hearts, and when we move we shall move by the course of nature to sleep

[3] Cherokee Delegation to Seneca Delegation, April, 1834, in Ross Papers, *loc. cit.*

under this ground which the Great Spirit gave to our ancestors and which now covers them in their undisturbed repose.[4]

At its meeting in July the council also challenged the right of President Jackson to instruct Colonel Hugh Montgomery, the Cherokee agent, to discontinue the payment of the Cherokees' $6,000 annuity "until arrangements . . . [can] be made by us [the federal government] for the proper distribution to the masses of the nation."[5] To these injustices the Cherokee council replied that the "money due the Cherokee nation every year" was not a gratuity but a payment for the tribe's ceded lands. For this reason, the United States "stands bound to pay the money to the nation."[6]

The council's first concentrated action against the growing removal threat was its vote to expand the power of its principal chief. He was authorized ". . . to employ such counsel or counsels and such other agents as he may think necessary and proper to aid in the conduct of the said proceedings and the arguments of the case or cases, on the part of this nation, or in the offices of citizens of this nation, as he may think proper . . . and he is hereby authorized to draw on the Treasurer of this nation, and issue warrants, for the payment of such counsel fees, and expenses, as he may judge proper and necessary."[7]

That Chief Ross would not find it difficult to procure for his Nation the finest legal counsel in the United States was demonstrated to him upon his return from the New Echota council. Awaiting him at his commodious two-storied dwelling near present-day Rome, Georgia, Ross found a letter from the Cherokees' good friend, Jeremiah Evarts. Evarts' letter contained a valuable digest of the opinions of William Wirt, Chancellor James Kent, Senator Daniel Webster, and Evarts on the Cherokee question:

[4] *Laws of the Cherokee Nation, loc. cit.*
[5] *Ibid.*
[6] *Ibid.* The council estimated that, if distributed per capita, the Cherokees' six-thousand-dollar annuity would be less than fifty cents per person. And some of the Indians would have had to travel 180 miles to collect this amount.
[7] *Ibid.*

We received the *Cherokee Phoenix* of July 3rd, from which we learn that the President wishes to see the Cherokees at Nashville. The following thoughts have occurred to me: would it not be well to appoint a Cherokee delegation to wait on him comprising among others yourself, Major Ridge, and John Ridge, with a view to learn his feelings, and guard against the evil of [his] purchasing of individual Cherokees? Should you think it best to go or send think of the following course.

1. Tell him—Jackson—frankly that you think the U. S. bound to protect the Cherokees against the laws of Georgia; and that you wish to have the matter decided by the Supreme Court.

2. Tell him, that you cannot think of making a treaty until you get a decision on the question. But if you should be mistaken and the court should not sustain your claims you must then do as well as you can.

3. Tell him that you cannot think of making a treaty, till you are advised or requested to do so by a majority of your people—that it is vastly important that you be united as a people—that a permanent division would be attended with great mischief.

4. Give him to understand that you expect whenever you make a treaty it will be made by you *as a nation* and that it will be ratified by the Senate, and that your national character will be hereafter respected.

5. Urge the keeping of intruders away and endeavor to get from him an explicit account of what he means by protecting you in your lands.

If you could get him to commit something to writing, it would be exceedingly desirable. If for instance he would say in writing that he expects to treat with you as a nation, and to have the treaty ratified in the Senate this would be of great benefit to you. . . . After any interviews with him, I would recommend that you write down all he says, and read it over to your number that you may be sure of it being correct. . . . You may be assured that if you get your case fairly before the Supreme Court your rights will be defended. It is so clear a case that the court cannot mistake it. All the great lawyers in the country are on your side.

Again I see that Georgia is arresting Cherokee gold-diggers. Let one of them go to jail, and then bring an action for false imprisonment before a Georgia court, expecting the court to decide against him, and then carry it by writ of error to the Supreme Court of the U. S.

Have you a good safe lawyer in Georgia, whom you can trust? . . .

This is a serious time with you. May the Lord bring you out of all your troubles. Trust your course with Him.[8]

The Cherokees substantially followed the instructions tendered them by Evarts. But, as decreed by the council, a delegation did not visit President Jackson at Nashville. Noting Evarts' question, "Have you a good safe lawyer in Georgia, whom you can trust," Chief Ross, in the summer of 1830, retained the Georgia law firm of Underwood and Harris. At approximately the same time Ross retained William Wirt and Associates of Baltimore to represent the Cherokees, at a set fee to be paid by the Nation. But cut off from the annuity, the Nation was already suffering from pecuniary embarrassment. Consequently, counselors' fees would have to be paid by individual Cherokees with means or possibly by a national loan negotiated with the United States government. But should such a loan be refused it, the Nation could perhaps solicit donations from its many Northern and Eastern sympathizers. Having adopted this attitude, the Cherokee council and Chief awaited further instructions from its distinguished legal counselors, who, directed by William Wirt, went into swift and immediate action.

All set to break Indian-American treaty traditions by settling the controversy according to law, Wirt searched for and found an Indian case that by writ of error could be carried to the Supreme Court of the United States. Assisted by Underwood, Harris, and John Ross, Wirt cleverly appealed the case of George Tassel—a Cherokee convicted of murder and sentenced to be hanged by the Hall County (Georgia) Superior Court. On December 12, 1830, the United States Supreme Court cited the state of Georgia to appear in Washington City and show cause why a writ of error should not be issued in the Tassel case. But Georgia, to show her contempt for federal interference, in state affairs, ignored the summons and expedited Tassel's execution.

Outraged at the Supreme Court's attempt to dictate to Georgia,

[8] Jeremiah Evarts to John Ross, date not distinct on MS but presumably written in middle or latter part of July, 1830, in Ross Papers, *loc. cit.*

Governor Wilson Lumpkin explosively wrote to Jackson on January 3, 1831:

> . . . It appears to me that the rulers of the Cherokees have sufficient intelligence to see the utter imbecility of placing any further reliance upon the Supreme Court to sustain their pretensions. The Supreme Court has as much right to grant a citation to cite the King of Great Britain for any assignable cause as to cite the govt. of Georgia for the manner in which the state chooses to exercise her jurisdiction. Georgia is not accountable to the Supreme Court or any other tribunal on earth unless that is made a crime which is done by virtue of constitutional law.[9]

Possibly William Wirt anticipated Georgia's reaction, because, by March, 1831, Wirt had ready a second Cherokee test to present to the Supreme Court. The Cherokee Nation *v.* Georgia was a request by the Cherokee Nation for an injunction against the state of Georgia for its many violations of Cherokee sovereignty. Wirt's argument was that the Cherokee Nation was an independent sovereign nation and therefore could not be subjected to Georgia laws. Thus, the Supreme Court of the United States should have original jurisdiction of its case and could award an injunction to restrain the state of Georgia from carrying her laws into effect against the Cherokee Nation.

All through the late summer and fall of 1830, William Wirt and Associates had worked to have the case of the Cherokee Nation *v.* Georgia ready at the earliest possible moment. But on November 15, 1830, Wirt confessed to Chief Ross by letter that the case had taken longer to prepare than he had anticipated:

> . . . If the paper I wrote for early in August had arrived in time to have given the necessary notice to the Governor and attorney general I would have tried the Chief Justice singly for the injunction. The unaccountable delay of my letter in reaching you, and the time necessary to collect the documents, has now left so little time between this

[9] In Georgia Governors' Letter Book (1831), Georgia Department of Archives and History, Atlanta.

and the Supreme Court, that the bill [petition] cannot pass before the Supreme Court will be in session, hence it is that, instead of making the motion to the Chief Justice, I now propose to make it to the Supreme Court in full session. I am not sorry for the change. If the whole court concur in granting the injunction, it will have more weight in public estimation than if granted by a single judge. If, on the other hand, they reject it, you will not have been deluded by any false hopes, but will know at once the ground on which you stand. What the fate of the motion will be, it is impossible for any lawyer to predict with certainty; for the case is perfectly new, there being no precedent to guide us. We have now the clear opinion of two of the first lawyers on the continent (Mr. Kent and Mr. Binney) that the court has the power to grant the injunction. In making the motion you have done all that you can do. Your counsel will support it with all the zeal and ability that Heaven has given them and the issue will be with Providence.[10]

But despite Wirt's best efforts, the Cherokees lost their case in the Supreme Court. On March 5, 1831, Chief Justice John Marshall solemnly declared:

> The court has bestowed its best attention on this question, and, after mature deliberation, the majority is of opinion, that an Indian tribe or nation within the United States is not a foreign state in the sense of the constitution, and cannot maintain an action in the Courts of the United States. . . .
>
> If it be true, that the Cherokee nation have rights, this is not the tribunal in which those rights are to be asserted. If it be true, that wrongs have been inflicted, and that still greater are to be apprehended, this is not the tribunal which can redress the past or prevent the future.
>
> The motion for an injunction is denied.[11]

Upon receipt of this news, Chief Ross toured the Nation explaining the Supreme Court's verdict to the people. Returning to the Head of Coosa, Ross found a letter from William Wirt offering "to pursue the contest further if the Nation decided to do so. You know

[10] In Ross Papers, *loc. cit.*

[11] United States Supreme Court Reports, Cherokee Nation *v.* Georgia, 5 Peters 1.

all the considerations pro and con that bear on the question and are perfectly competent to decide it."

Wirt's letter also contained a polite request for payment of $1,000 owed him by the Cherokee Nation. "But," inserted the lawyer, ". . . if you tell me . . . that you are unable to pay fees, I shall solicit you no further on this subject, and you may continue to command my best services."[12]

A dun for the $1,500 owed to Judge William Underwood and Thomas Harris by the Nation was delivered to Chief Ross after Underwood and Harris had ordered the arrest of William Rogers, a mixedblood, who (acting for Ross) had made all the arrangements for the firm's retainment by the Nation.

By great effort Chief Ross managed to pay the Cherokees' legal counselors and to give the Georgia counselors a scathing lecture on Cherokee honesty and stability. "I am certain," Ross wrote to Harris, "that you can have no just grounds to suspect or believe that the authorities of the Nation will turn traitors to their cause and *flee* from *their beloved country to escape these contracts.*"[13]

Reluctant to relinquish their legal counselors, affluent Cherokees agreed to help pay future fees. The Nation's application for a government loan having been rejected in Washington City in February, 1831, these Cherokees knew that the Nation was in straitened circumstances. And, deprived of income from its gold fields, its $6,000 annuity, and a loan from the United States, the Nation would suffer financial embarrassment until afforded relief.

In addition to their legal maneuvers against the forces seeking to effect their removal, the Cherokees made great use of the printed word among their own people and among others in fighting their cause. Special use was made of their newspaper, *The Cherokee Phoenix*. Considered by the Cherokee council to be very nearly as important to the Nation as legal counsel, the *Phoenix* illuminated the "Indian Question" and it made it understandable to "the peo-

[12] Letter of May 28, 1831, in Ross Papers, *loc. cit.*
[13] April 27, 1831, in *ibid.*

ple." And, sent to the four corners of the United States, the *Phoenix* inspirited white newspaper editors in New Orleans, New York, Washington City, Philadelphia, Boston, and Baltimore to recopy its editorials citing Jackson's and Georgia's oppression—a recent example of the latter being the arrest of eleven of the Cherokees' beloved missionaries on July 7, by the Georgia Guard. Required by Georgia law to take an oath of allegiance to the state under penalty of a four-year term of imprisonment in the state penitentiary, the eleven missionaries were put under arrest. Thereupon nine of the eleven capitulated and either took the required oath or agreed to leave the state. But Samuel Austin Worcester and Elizur Butler stood their ground and, after a speedy trial, received sentence on September 15 to four years' imprisonment in the Georgia state prison. The injustice of "the missionary case" was duly heralded to the world by Elias Boudinot, who, since the founding of the *Phoenix*, had been closely associated with Samuel Austin Worcester, Worcester having served as Boudinot's executive adviser.

The council, meeting at Chattooga (in present-day Alabama) in October, 1831, decided to seek funds outside the Nation for the upkeep of the *Phoenix*. Thereupon, the council decreed:

> That the editor of the *Cherokee Phoenix* on his pledge to keep up the circulation of the *Cherokee Phoenix* at his expense during his absence, be authorized and is hereby authorized to take a journey through the U. S. to solicit donations in money from all individuals disposed to . . . aid the Cherokee Nation . . . in its present struggles with . . . all those who are exerting their influence to eject our people from their native land. Be it further resolved that the money so collected shall be appropriated to the support of the *Cherokee Phoenix*.[14]

Another activity of the council and John Ross was to fight possible betrayal of the Nation by its people. But the Cherokee Nation, with few exceptions, throughout 1831–32 remained united. As usual, a

[14] MS—Record of Cherokee council proceedings, or meetings, held on October 31, 1831, in *ibid.*

Cherokee delegation spent the winter and spring in Washington City presenting the Nation's grievances to John Eaton, President Jackson's Secretary of War. The delegation was composed of Ross's hand-picked patriots—John Ridge, John Martin, and William Shorey Coodey—thought by John Ross to be invulnerable to the suggestions of removal which were certain to be made to them by Eaton. Even though John Ross bombarded the members of the delegation with letters designed to stiffen their morale, he actually entertained little fear that Eaton could deter any of them from fighting removal to the death. Nor was Ross apparently apprehensive that the Western delegation in Washington—rumored to be desirous of gaining the Eastern Cherokees' removal so that their own lands would be increased and their own annuity fattened by Congress—would gain its goal. En route to Washington, members of the Western Cherokee delegation had stopped for a while with their Eastern brothers and, upon leaving, had persuaded James Starr and John Walker, Jr., mixed boods, to accompany them to Washington City.

At the time, Starr's and Walker's unofficial visit to Washington City possibly did not seem important to either Ross or the council, who were busy arranging for Worcester's and Butler's case to be presented to the Supreme Court in February by Wirt and his associates. At the Head of Coosa, John Ross awaited news from Boudinot. And when it arrived Ross had every right to feel encouraged and exhilarated.

Acting as Boudinot's secretary, John Ridge, who accompanied his cousin to Philadelphia, wrote the following, under the date of January 12, 1832, to John Ross:

Sir . . . Ere this, you must be already advised of the journey I have undertaken to make to some of the large cities in company with Mr. Boudinot, with a design to draw from the people the expression of public sentiment on the crises of Cherokee affairs . . . and it affords me pleasure to state that the prospects of a great and vigorous expression of indignation from this city, against the cruelties of Georgia and the policy of the United States is now flattering. It will be made either by a public meeting or signatures . . . at their residences, by men appointed for that purpose. Mr. Boudinot's objects are also more understood and measures [are] in . . . [progress] to afford our Nation the relief so much desired.[15]

According to Ridge, Boudinot had received donations of money from Mr. Matthew Cary, a Dr. Ely, and other Philadelphians.

> This day we have dined with Col. McKenney [formerly associated with governmental Indian affairs]. . . . He is apparently as strong a friend as we have. He desires to publish in this city short letters addressed to the President which shall strike him as the lightning strikes the branchless pine. The Cherokees, he said, should be held up. . . .
>
> From this place we design to go to New York, where it is hoped we can get a large meeting to memorialize Congress in our behalf. . . . Onward in the path of duty is my motto. Strongly opposed to surrender our national existence I shall never give it up even unto death. . . . I do hope that our people as usual remain united and continue to depend upon the advice of their chiefs—it is the only way to preserve them and their rights. The U. S. agents who prowl about our country seek to betray them to destruction as well as the Nation. . . .
>
> Mr. Boudinot sends his respects to you.[16]

This was the kind of letter which Chief Ross would have expected from the son of Major Ridge, who had been a formidable enemy of betrayal since his participation in the murder of Doublehead back in 1807. Major Ridge had also been responsible for the Cherokee law—prior to the Nation's advancement—whereby treason became punishable by death.

In the winter and spring of 1831–32, Boudinot, too, appeared to share John Ridge's views against removal. When Chief Justice John Marshall rendered his classic decision that Georgia was in error, that the state laws of Georgia, when applied to Indian matters, were null and void and must give way to federal laws, Boudinot could scarcely contain himself. Boudinot wrote to Stand Watie, his brother, from Boston on March 7, 1832:

[15] *Ibid.*
[16] John Ridge to John Ross, January 12, 1831, in *ibid.*

It is glorious news. The laws of the state are declared by the highest judicial tribunal in the country to be *null* & *void*. It is a great triumph on the part of the Cherokees so far as the question of their rights were concerned. The question is forever settled as to who is right & who is wrong. The controversy is exactly where it ought to be & where we have all along been desirous it should be. It is not now before the great state of Georgia & the poor Cherokees but between the U. S. & the State of Georgia. . . . We can only look & see in this momentous crisis.[17]

But the victory achieved by the Cherokees in Washington did not solve the Nation's problems. Nor did the court's decision bring the immediate release of Worcester and Butler by Georgia. The state perversely refused to release the missionaries for nearly a year after receiving the court's order. And Jackson—so it was rumored—worsened matters by remarking: "John Marshall has rendered his decision; now let him enforce it."

In April friends and relatives of the 626 emigrants who had been enrolled by Ben Currey saw them leave, via the Hiwassee, Tennessee, Ohio, and Mississippi rivers, for the West. And soon the Nation was flooded with letters from these emigrants recounting the failure of the United States government to fulfill its promises concerning rations and supplies made to them through Currey. The long journey west, emigrants complained, had been accompanied by both the illnesses and deaths of loved ones. "Remain where you are" was the message sent to the recipients of emigrant letters.

Up to this time the battle fought by the Cherokees had been waged by all of its leaders. Legal action, newspaper propaganda, and delegations to Washington were all a part of their united campaign to resist removal. On July 23, 1832, however, the specter of disunity haunted the general council held at Red Clay, Tennessee. Indoctrinated with Jacksonian removal propaganda, John Walker, Jr., and James Starr were noticeably friendly to Elisha Chester, a United States commissioner who proferred upon the council a treaty of removal which it immediately spurned. Chester insisted that Cherokee

---

[17] In the Cherokee Papers, Division of MSS, University of Oklahoma.

removal would save the Nation much of the suffering which it would endure by waiting. Noting that Chester's argument caught the attention of Elias Boudinot, John Ridge, Andrew Ross (Chief Ross's brother), William Hicks, William Rogers, and William Shorey Coodey, Starr and Walker surreptitiously added their names to a list of protreaty advocates.

Elias Boudinot's resignation from the editorship of *The Cherokee Phoenix*, a month after the council's July meeting, bespoke his identification with the protreaty faction. Boudinot—seemingly forgetting his anti-removal declarations of the year before—gave as reasons for his resignation the inadequacy of salary, his own failing health, and the Nation's inability to furnish him with the supplies needed to run a national newspaper. In a letter to Ross, Boudinot stated that in his opinion the *Phoenix* had done all that it was supposed to do in defending Cherokee rights and in presenting Indian grievances to the United States people, and that he himself was convinced that the Cherokees should be shown the dangers of their refusal to remove. Boudinot concluded that he could no longer conduct the paper if denied the privilege of discussing those important matters.

> And from what I have seen and heard, were I to assume that privilege, my usefulness would be paralyzed, by being considered, as I have unfortunately already been, an enemy to the interest of my beloved country and people. . . . I should think it my duty to tell them the whole truth, or what I believe to be the truth. I cannot tell them that we will be reinstated in our rights when I have no such hope.[18]

Without equivocation, John Ross and the council accepted Boudinot's resignation, filling his place by the appointment of Elijah Hicks. But, although he possessed depth of character and unquestioned integrity, and he was successful as a businessman, Hicks lacked Boudinot's newspaper experience. And so the *Phoenix* under Hicks's editorship limped painfully along until, on May 31, 1834, it ceased publication.

John Ridge's sudden affiliation with the protreaty faction in the

---

[18] Malone, *Cherokees of the Old South*, 167f.

Nation came to light at the Cherokees' general council in October, 1832. Ridge, as president of the National Committee, introduced a resolution to send a delegation to Washington City in 1832–33 to discuss a treaty of removal with President Jackson. But the council firmly rejected Ridge's proposal and, instead, voted to send a delegation composed of Joseph Vann, John Baldridge, Richard Taylor, and John Ross (as chief and counselor) to Washington City to attend to the Nation's business with the government.

Stoically, John Ross adjured the council and the observers present to stand fast and remain united and all would soon be well. Ross argued that if Henry Clay defeated Andrew Jackson in the November election, the Cherokees' burdens would be lightened. Thereupon Elisha Chester reported erroneously to Jackson in the next mail that the majority of the enlightened half bloods and intermarried whites wanted to make a removal treaty but that the full bloods "were opposed to it, having always followed the advice of Ross and others who did their thinking for them."[19]

Throughout Ross's stay in Washington in 1832–33, his followers back in the Nation kept faith with their beloved chief. Bravely, the people in the mountains donned feathered headdresses, strapped turtle shells filled with pebbles onto their legs and ankles, beat drums, whooped, yelled, and danced all night in the manner of the ancients. The majority got out of hand only when given whisky by whites, who, after getting the Indians arrested for drunkenness by the Georgia Guard, swooped down upon Cherokee property and took possession of it.

Presumably, the Cherokees danced and played ball or chungke to ease their depression. Everywhere there was evidence of Georgia's intolerance and oppression of the Cherokees. Recently, the Georgia legislature had created Cherokee County out of Cherokee land west of the Chattahoochee River and north of the Carroll County line. Included in the new county were the Cherokees' lands that had been previously assigned to five counties. And Georgia now proposed to subdivide this confiscated area into land lots and gold lots, prepara-

[19] Grant Foreman, *Indian Removal*, 245f.

tory to its distribution—by means of a gigantic lottery—to male citizens, widows of veterans, and veterans who could prove that they had lived in the state for four years. In consequence of this Georgia legislation, the people, many of whom were unable to comprehend the meaning of this or that white man's law, were prematurely dispossessed of their homes.

Few complaints, however, passed the lips of Ross's humble followers. But in the Valley Towns in North Carolina, the Reverend Evan Jones and his son began to take the testimonials of oppressed Cherokees who were harassed by Ben Currey, the federal enrolling agent. Upon John Ross's return from Washington, Jones turned these testimonials over to Ross to use as he saw fit.

Whenever he arrived in a town or village—after his sojourn in the United States capital—Ross would tie his horse to a post in the square and calmly advise the people (many of whom had traveled miles afoot and by horse to hear what Ross had to say) to put in their crops, spin cloth, attend mission services, and continue sending their children to the mission schools. He promised that he and the council would keep them informed of affairs attendant to their welfare. Unity, as of yore, remained Ross's slogan.

But in contrast to the faithfulness exhibited by the common Indians toward Ross on these occasions were the sarcastic and envious remarks made by members of the treaty faction. They referred to Ross—behind his back—as "The Delphic Oracle" or "The Diplomatist," and claimed that his one desire was to aggrandize himself at the expense of the misguided and ignorant Indians who hung on his words as though they were "revelations from Heaven." John Ridge's sudden hostility toward Ross remains a mystery even today. But upon Ross's return from Washington in 1833, Ridge was infuriated by the fact that Ross had refused to consider the offer made by the Jackson administration to pay the Cherokees $3,000,000 for their lands in Georgia, Alabama, and Tennessee.

The success of the Treaty party in effecting the final removal of the Cherokee Nation by a fraudulent treaty signed at New Echota on December 29, 1835, by less than one hundred Cherokees stemmed from a secret alliance made by the Treaty party with the Jackson-Georgia removal machine sometime between 1832–35. That this alliance necessitated the betrayal of the Nation by leaders of the Treaty party is a matter of record.

In the large calf-bound volumes containing the outgoing and incoming letters of Georgia governors is the irrefutable evidence that members of the Treaty party secretly joined up with Jackson and Georgia and by so doing were, in the eyes of Ross's party, guilty of treason. But Treaty party members insisted that they were acting for the good of the Nation in that, unless it removed, it would suffer untold misery.

An early example of the Treaty party's alliance with Jackson and Georgia can be found in a letter written by His Excellency Wilson Lumpkin, the governor of Georgia, on February 15, 1833, to Colonel William Williamson, in which Lumpkin informed Williamson that Mr. William Hicks's property should be exempt from confiscation through lottery for the following reasons:

> Mr. Hicks is entitled to quiet and peaceable possession of lots number 209, 181, and 182 of the 15th District of the 3rd Section. . . . My object in calling your attention to this subject, is to remind you . . . that Mr. Hicks has uniformly respected the laws and authority of Georgia and treated her officers and citizens with kindness and respect. . . . And should he be molested in any manner . . . I trust you will be particularly vigilant . . . in affording him every protection.[20]

Ten days later, a letter directed to William Rogers by Governor Lumpkin advised Rogers to report failure to protect the property of members of the Treaty party to Colonel Williamson, "the agent appointed under the late act of the Legislature to superintend the rights and interest of the Natives."[21]

Elias Boudinot's property also was ordered by Governor Lumpkin to be withdrawn from the lottery wheel. In a communication to Ben Currey on December 13, 1834, Lumpkin advised Currey to

[20] In Georgia Governors' Letter Book (1833), *loc. cit.*
[21] *Ibid.*

"assure Boudinot, Ridge, and their friends of state protection under any circumstances. I shall feel it my imperative duty to pay due regard to the situation and afford them every security which our laws will justify or authorize."[22]

In sharp contrast to the treatment accorded the treaty faction, members of the Ross party, together with missionaries Worcester and Butler, were outrageously ousted from their homes by Georgians who had been the fortunate drawers of Cherokee property.

John Ross, upon his return from Washington in April, 1833, found his ailing wife Quatie and their children confined in but two rooms of his large dwelling at the Head of Coosa. Ross's house, outbuildings, corncribs, orchards, livestock, and planted fields had been taken over by lottery winners. Thereupon, Ross was forced to move his family across the line into Tennessee. John Martin's elegant home at Rock Springs, with its marble mantles and hand-carved stairways, eventually went the way of John Ross's property, as did Alexander McCoy's, George Lowrey's, and Elijah Hicks's. Joseph Vann's mansion near Springplace was occupied by the notorious Colonel William Bishop, commander of the Georgia Guard. And, to circumvent ejection, Bishop instructed his guards to shoot down white intruders. Across the road from the Vann house, the Springplace Mission Station, sacred to the Moravians and Christianized Cherokees, became, on December 13, 1833, headquarters for the dissolute Georgia Guard, who converted the chapel into a courthouse and the missionaries' house into a tavern. According to H. G. Clauder, the missionary deposed by order of Colonel Bishop, grogshops were immediately opened on the premises and the once venerated mission station (renamed "Camp Benton") was turned into a "hot bed of vice, and every manner of wickedness."[23]

Georgia lottery drawers obtained Elizur Butler's mission and home at Haweis in January, 1834. And, in February, Samuel Austin Worcester, basking briefly in his hard-won freedom, was ordered by William Springer, Cherokee agent in Georgia, "to evacuate the lot of land no. 125 in the 14th district, of the third section, and to

[22] *Ibid.*

[23] Perrillah and Henry Malone, Unpublished Report of Research Trip to the Newberry Library, Chicago, on Sept. 5–6, 1956. The information on Springplace is from the Payne Papers, V, 1–4, in *ibid.*, courtesy Georgia Department of Archives and History, Atlanta.

SEQUOYAH (George Guess), who devised the Cherokee Syllabary.

CHEROKEE ALPHABET.

CHARACTERS AS ARRANGED BY THE INVENTOR.

R D W Iᵥ G ꟼ ꟼ P Ꮑ Ꮡ У Ꮄ Ꮅ Ꮉ Р Ꮷ M Ꮣ Ꮲ Ꮻ

Ꮃ W B Ꭰ Ꭷ Ꭷ Ꮁ Г A Ꭻ Ꭹ Ꮞ Ꮲ G Ꮖ Ꮜ Ꮜ I Z Ꮽ

Ꮐ Ꭱ Ꮀ Ꮢ Ꭺ Ꮂ Ꮮ Ꭼ Ꮎ Т Ꮆ Ꮝ Ꮸ Ꮷ Ꭻ K Ꮿ Ꮜ Ꮾ Ꮐ

Ꮖ Ꮚ Ꭻ Ꭼ Ꮪ Ꮜ Ꮐ Ꭵ Ꮎ Ꮗ Ꮗ Ꮎ Ꮭ Н Ꮮ Ꮶ Ꮯ Ꮣ

L Ꮏ Ꮝ Ꮬ Ꮳ Ꮛ

CHARACTERS SYSTEMATICALLY ARRANGED WITH THE SOUNDS.

D a	R e	T i	Ꮠ o	Ꭴ u	i v
s ga Ꮝ ka	Ᏼ ge	У gi	Ꭺ go	J gu	E gv
ꝋ ha	Ꭾ he	Ꭿ hi	Ꮄ ho	Г hu	Ꮞ hv
w la	Ꮯ le	Ꮲ li	Ꮈ lo	Ꮋ lu	Ꮑ lv
Ꮽ ma	Ꮷ me	Ꮁ mi	Ꮲ mo	Ᏻ mu	
Ꮎ na Ꮏ hna Ꮐ nah Ꮑ ne	Ꮒ ni	Ꮓ no	Ꮖ nu	Ꮎ nv
Ꮖ qua	Ꮖ que	Ꮘ qui	Ꮖ quo	Ꮗ quu	Ꮛ quv
Ꮝ s Ꮜ sa	Ꮞ se	Ꮟ si	Ꮠ so	Ꮧ su	Ꭱ sv
Ꮣ da Ꮤ ta	Ꮥ de Ꮦ te	Ꮧ di Ꮨ tih	Ꮩ do	s du	Ꮫ dv
Ꮧ dla Ꮬ tla	Ꮮ tle	Ꮐ tli	Ꮯ tlo	Ꮤ tlu	Ꮲ tlv
Ꮳ tsa	Ꮴ tse	Ꮖ tsi	Ꮶ tso	Ꮷ tsu	Ꮷ tsv
Ꮻ wa	Ꮼ we	Ꮅ wi	Ꮎ wo	Ꮎ wu	Ꮚ wv
Ꮽ ya	Ꮞ ye	Ꮏ yi	Ꮅ yo	Ꮿ yu	B yv

SOUNDS REPRESENTED BY VOWELS.

a as *a* in *father*, or short as *a* in *rival*,
e as *a* in *hate*, or short as *e* in *met*,
i as *i* in *pique*, or short as *i* in *pit*,
o as *aw* in *law*, or short as *o* in *not*,
u as *oo* in *fool*, or short as *u* in *pull*,
v as *u* in *but* nasalized.

CONSONANT SOUNDS.

g nearly as in English, but approaching to k. d nearly as in English, but approaching to t. h, k, l, m, n, q, s, t, w, y, as in English.

Syllables beginning with g, except Ꮝ, have sometimes the power of k; Ꭺ, Ꮝ, Ꮿ, are sometimes sounded to, tu, tv; and syllables written with tl, except Ꮮ, sometimes vary to dl.

THE CHEROKEE ALPHABET.

GWY

CHEROKEE

ᎴᎣᎤᎣᎢᎦᎢ.

PHOENIX.

VOL. 1.   NEW ECHOTA, WEDNESDAY JULY 9, 1828.   NO. 20.

EDITED BY ELIAS BOUDINOTT.

PRINTED WEEKLY BY

ISAAC H. HARRIS,

FOR THE CHEROKEE NATION.

At $2.50 if paid in advance, $3 in six months, or $3.50 if paid at the end of the year.

To subscribers who can read only the Cherokee language the price will be $2.00 in advance, or $2.50 to be paid within the year.

Every subscription will be considered as continued unless subscribers give notice to the contrary before the commencement of a new year.

Any person procuring six subscribers, and becoming responsible for the payment, shall receive a seventh gratis.

Advertisements will be inserted at seventy-five cents per square for the first insertion, and thirty-seven and a half cents for each continuance; longer ones in proportion.

☞ All letters addressed to the Editor, post paid, will receive due attention.

[Cherokee syllabary text]

Resolved by the National Committee and Council, That no person shall be allowed to erect or establish a billiard table in the Cherokee Nation, without first obtaining a license from the Treasurer of the Nation, and paying into the Treasury the sum of two hundred dollars as a tax pr. annum, and such license shall not be given for a longer period than one year at a time: and any person or persons, who shall erect or establish a billiard table without first obtaining a license as herein required shall, upon conviction, pay a fine of four hundred dollars, for the benefit of the Cherokee Nation.

New Echota, Nov. 16, 1826.

JNO ROSS, Pres't N. Com.

MAJOR RIDGE, Speaker.

Approved—PATH × KILLER.
his mark,

CHARLES HICKS.

A. McCOY, Clerk of N. Com.

E. BOUDINOTT, Clk. N. Coun.

Resolved by the National Committee and Council, That the resolutions passed Oct. 15th 1825, suspending the poll tax law, and the law imposing a tax on citizen merchants of the Cherokee Nation, be, and the same are [Cherokee syllabary text]

[Cherokee syllabary text]

[Cherokee syllabary text]

SAMUEL AUSTIN WORCESTER, missionary, who devoted a lifetime to translating the Bible and hymns into Cherokee.

The Indian council of 1843 in session at Tahlequah.
From a painting by John Mix Stanley.

CHIEF JOHN ROSS, painted shortly after the signing of the Treaty of
1846. Notice the treaty which Ross is holding.
From a painting by John Neagle.

JOHN RIDGE   MAJOR RIDGE

Illustrations from the Muriel H. Wright Collection

ELIAS BOUDINOT

THE TRAIL OF TEARS, interpreted in a painting by Echohawk.

give the house, now occupied by you up to Colonel William Harden, or whoever he may put forward to take possession of same."[24]

Thus dispossessed, the mission board at Boston advised Worcester to go west with the Cherokees who at frequent intervals were, under pressure from Ben Currey, enrolling for emigration.

The link between Jackson's men and the Cherokee treaty faction was apparent when John Eaton tried to negotiate a treaty with Andrew Ross, John Ross's brother, and his cohorts in Washington in the winter of 1834. By this treaty, the Cherokee Nation was to sell its lands for a consideration so small as to be ridiculous. However, when Andrew Ross attempted to interest the Nation in the treaty, the Nation's defenders rose up in righteous wrath. At a council at Red Clay late in August, the fury of the anti-treaty party vented itself not only upon Andrew Ross but upon John Walker, Jr., who —in the eyes of John Ross's followers—had introduced disunity into the Nation. And Walker, as a result, was murdered.

President Jackson's letter written from the Hermitage on September 3, 1834, directed to Ben Currey and Colonel Hugh Montgomery, further linked the treaty faction with the Jackson-Georgia group. The President wrote:

> I have just been advised that Walker has been shot and Ridge and other Chiefs in favor of emigration and you as agent of the United States government threatened with death.
>
> The Government of the United States has promised them protection. It will perform its obligations to a letter. On the receipt of this, notify John Ross and his council that we will hold them answerable for every murder committed on the emigrating party.[25]

Although it had been in operation for months, the Treaty party was officially organized—according to the dictates of Jackson—on November 27, 1834, at John Ridge's home at Running Waters. The Treaty party's organization was appropriately described by Ben Currey in a letter to Governor Wilson Lumpkin:

[24] Malone, *Cherokees of the Old South*, 180.
[25] In Georgia Governors' Letter Book (1834), *loc. cit.*

SIR—I am now at John Ridge's where a council is to be held on the 27 inst in order to organize a party favourably disposed to Cherokee removal. An election of chiefs in favour of transplanting the tribe will be held . . . and a delegation is to be appointed to go to the city—Washington—to memorialize Congress. . . .

The party about to be organized will require money. Their expenses will not fall short of three thousand dollars in a contemplated visit to Washington City. . . . They desire me to say one season more will give them an entire ascendency over all opposition, provided they receive a hearty support from the states and Gen'l Government and request that you address the President and Sec. of War urging the importance of having a fund to be reached through the draft of the Superintendent to carry on the cause successfully which appears to be gaining formidable support.[26]

The Treaty party's estimation that it would take but "one season more" to give it "an entire ascendency over all opposition," provided it received "a hearty support from the states and Gen'l Government," proved to be amazingly accurate. John Ross, had he been given the opportunity in the fall of 1834 to view the correspondence between the Governor of Georgia and John Ridge, might have saved himself the trouble of accompanying Cherokee patriots to Washington to seek help there for the Nation. For, as the Governor's correspondence with Ridge and others indicates, Ridge's treaty would be the only one accepted by the President—notwithstanding the fact that John Ross's party, in 1835, sought in good faith to treat openly with the government for removal on a basis acceptable to all the Nation, with the exception of the Treaty party.

Aware of the contemplated organization of the Treaty party, John Ross, in September, 1834, attempted to effect a reconciliation between his party and Ridge's. Ross wrote to Ridge:

It is sincerely hoped that every honorable and patriotic man will under the existing state of things unite in exerting an influence among the people with the view of cultivating harmony among one another

[26] November 13, 1834, in *ibid.*

and to suppress as found practicable all causes tending to unnecessary excitement and evil. The general welfare of our much oppressed and suffering people requires it . . . and their peace and happiness demands it of us—and therefore every course calculated to produce strife among the people from partyism should be discarded.[27]

On the eve of their departure for Washington in the winter of 1834, representatives and leaders of the Treaty party and the National (or Ross) party attempted to come to some understanding concerning the respective treaties of removal that each party would support. But the conference was a fiasco, and instead of bridging the differences between the two parties it widened and deepened them. Boudinot asserted that the Ross party's treaty was too vague or general, and the Treaty party's contract was too definite to suit Ross's National party. And so each party went its separate way again.

In Washington City, members of the Treaty party were warmly received by President Jackson, who showed them every courtesy. But government officials had no time for the delegation headed by Ross. However, the latter ascertained while in Washington that the Senate would possibly refuse to ratify a treaty that did not meet the approval of the National party, whose views were shared by a majority in the Senate.

Since the Treaty party had violated the sacred laws of the Nation by putting the Cherokee lands up for sale, the National party had no choice but to try to block sale of the valuable lands for too small a sum. Therefore, when the rival parties were offered but $3,250,000 for their country by the United States government—it was later raised to $4,500,000—Ross demanded that $20,000,000 be paid the Cherokees. But this price the government refused to consider. And, again, the Cherokee question hung in mid-air.

John Ross, on March 22, 1835, wrote to Mr. de Costello y Lanza, chargé d'affaires of Mexico (who at that time happened to be in Philadelphia), informing him that Ross's people would "at once move out of the limits of the United States, provided they could effect an arrangement with your govt. so as to secure them land

[27] September 12, 1834, in Ross Papers, *loc. cit.*

sufficient for their accommodation—and also the enjoyments of equal rights and privileges of citizenship."[28]

Although Ross requested Mr. de Costello to send his reply to Lewis Ross, near Calhoun, Tennessee, the records of the Cherokee Nation do not refer to Costello's answer nor to any further pursuance by Ross of the Nation's voluntary removal to Mexico. However, Costello's reply could have been intercepted by members of the Jackson-Georgia organization. For admittedly Ben Currey, Colonel Nelson, and William Bishop all employed agents to intercept John Ross's mail, as well as the mail that was directed to Lewis Ross and other leaders of the National party.

In March, 1835, the Reverend John F. Schermerhorn, a United States commissioner appointed by President Jackson, accompanied the Treaty party back to the Nation. Schermerhorn's instruction from Jackson headquarters was to get the Ridge party's treaty ratified by the Cherokee people, if possible, before the oncoming Presidential election in November.

By candlelight, on the night of March 29, 1835, a treaty of removal was secretly signed by over a dozen Treaty party leaders in the fastidiously furnished home of Elias Boudinot at New Echota. As prescribed by the Jackson element, the party's next step was to get this document ratified by the people.

The Treaty party did not underestimate the obstacles it would have to surmount to obtain ratification. John Ross's influence over the people would somehow have to be broken. Then, too, Ross's lawyers would have to be persuaded (or bribed) to abandon the National party. Headmen—even Ross—would have to be gotten rid of, possibly by false arrest.

In a lengthy letter to Governor Lumpkin on May 18, 1835, John Ridge coldly outlined the procedure which he would like to see adopted by Lumpkin and Georgia officials "to effect the great objects I have in contemplation . . . I trust that my influence will not be endangered by exposing to the public this communication. *It is*

[28] *Ibid.*

therefore confidential. . . . John Ross is unhorsed in Washington and you must unhorse him here."[29]

The content of this and other Ridge letters now prove beyond any possible doubt his co-operation with the Georgia-Jackson combination. But the National party, at the time unable to gain positive proof of Ridge's collusion, attempted and succeeded in restraining several of its members from killing Ridge. Major Ridge (John's father), Stand Watie, and Elias Boudinot were also candidates for execution by members of the National party. But when reminded that the ancient laws were not to be countenanced in that day of enlightenment, the would-be executioners postponed their plans.

[29] In Cherokee Indian Letters, Talks, and Treaties (1786–1838), WPA Project No. 4341, in Georgia Department of Archives and History, Atlanta.

CHAPTER IX

The Treaty of New Echota

THROUGHOUT THE CHAOTIC AND DEPRESSING MONTHS that preceded the signing of the Treaty of New Echota on December 29, 1835, nine-tenths of the Cherokee people "voted to invest John Ross with full power to adjust the Nation's difficulties in whatever way he might think most beneficial."[1] To this majority Ross remained the Nation's legitimate principal chief and John Ridge was but a self-appointed chief who appeared to be attempting to "sell out" the Nation. Nor did this majority take well to the Jackson-appointed Reverend John F. Schermerhorn, "the loose Dutch Presbyterian minister." To show their contempt for Schermerhorn, Ross's supporters nicknamed him "Skaynooyaynah" (The Devil's Horn).[2]

Chief Ross instructed his people, numbering around 2,600, to attend the Ridge council at Running Waters in July in order to vote against the proposed distribution of the Cherokees' annuity to unauthorized persons. Ross's followers poked fun at Schermerhorn at the council by slyly whispering his new Indian name to members of the Ridge party, who could not resist laughing at it. And Ross's people, refusing to speak to Schermerhorn when he attempted to be

---

[1] Ben F. Currey to Elbert Herring, Esq., commissioner of Indian affairs, May 23, 1835, in Cherokee Indian Letters, Talks, and Treaties, *loc. cit.*

[2] George W. Featherstonhaugh, *A Canoe Voyage up the Minnay Sotor.*

friendly, turned their backs or wandered off to a near-by thicket to receive further instructions on voting from their chief.

Discomfited by this attitude of the very Cherokees whom he sought to influence, Schermerhorn complained to John Ridge that John Ross was the soul of his party. And Schermerhorn was therefore not surprised when the Ross people voted unanimously to reject the annuity-distribution plan.

John Ridge, too, blamed Ross for the distribution plan's rejection. But, anticipating Ross's interference in other vital matters, Ridge, two months before, had written to Governor Lumpkin enlisting his aid in breaking down the power exerted by Ross over the people. Vituperatively, Ridge referred to members of the Ross party as "Halfbreed Nullifiers," "Banded Outlaws," or as "this unholy Aristocracy," who up to then had been permitted to get all the money and avails of Indian treaties:

> . . . The president has assured me that he will stand by this treaty as the Ultimatum of the Government and no other shall be offered to the Cherokee people. But, Sir, the Ross party disbelieve it, & this party composed as it is of Halfbreed Nullifiers wish to change it to suit themselves. They are, by means of falsehoods, in the field, valley, & mountain opposing the ratification of it, as I believe because . . . it is [a] just and honest one. . . . The object is procrastination to outlive Jackson's administration. . . .
>
> . . . There is a remedy in your power, and it is to organize a guard of thirty men placed under the command of Col. Bishop to scour and range in their fortresses & search their caves, and to suppress their secret meetings close to all night dances where the leaders of the Ross Party usually meet with them for consultation. . . . As to the accomplishment of the removal of our people there is no doubt. We are gaining upon the enemy.[3]

Upon receipt of this secret and inflammatory communication from Ridge, Governor Lumpkin issued orders to have pistols, muskets, rifles, and ammunition delivered to William Bishop at Camp Ben-

---

[3] John Ridge to His Excellency Wilson Lumpkin, May 18, 1835, in Cherokee Indian Letters, Talks, and Treaties, *loc. cit.*, 553–56.

ton (formerly Springplace Mission). And the arrests of Whitepath, a venerable and noble chief, Elijah Hicks, James Martin, Thomas Taylor, James Trott, and Walter Adair by the Georgia Guard followed.

Gaining the release of these prisoners proved to be a difficult undertaking for John Ross. At John Ridge's suggestion, Governor Lumpkin had bribed Judge Hooper and William Underwood to abandon the Ross party. Colonel Richard Rockwell and Associates remained the Ross party's sole legal counsel. Therefore, John Ross wrote Colonel Rockwell to secure—if possible—the release of the Ross party's leaders:

> I drop you these hasty lines . . . to say that among those who have been captured and bound over to appear before the court at Cassville by the Georgia military is the White Path a member of the General Council. His offense is unknown and has never been communicated to him by the commanding officer William Bishop. I have given him to understand that you will be in readiness to attend his case should it be presented for trial.
>
> It has been reported that there was a system of operation designed by the oppressors of the people to hatch up lies and falsehoods against the most respectable and influential Cherokee citizens with the view of perplexing their minds and destroying their reputation abroad. And that the notorious George Foot is to be used as one of the base instruments to answer these purposes. But it is hoped that sufficient honesty and justice will be found still to exist in the breast of man. If so, such vile infamous calumniation will but recoil on . . . those who may attempt the abominable project. I trust that you will be a close observer of matters and as far as practicable will endeavor to avert the poisoned dart aimed at your much abused and innocent clients.[4]

John Ross's oft-repeated conviction that there were but two ways to end a controversy—a right way and a wrong way—prompted him to notify Schermerhorn and Ben Currey in September that several weeks before Colonel Bishop and Stand Watie had forcibly "seized and taken away from Elijah Hicks's house the printing press and

---

[4] September 15, 1835, in Ross Papers, *loc. cit.*

types, various books and papers, and other articles belonging to the Cherokee Nation. It has also been stated that this extraordinary proceeding has been performed under your direction in conjunction with that of John Ridge."[5]

Schermerhorn, as could be expected, did not offer to return the kidnapped press or papers. And Boudinot defended the action taken by Stand Watie and Bishop by asserting that since he (Boudinot) had raised the money in the East to buy the press, he felt that it should stay in his possession.

The October council at Red Clay was a dramatic event. Several days before it was scheduled to begin, John Howard Payne, the author of "Home, Sweet Home," arrived at John Ross's humble dwelling near present-day Chattanooga. He bore a letter of introduction addressed to Ross from Colonel Rockwell, who had written:

> Mr. Payne's object in visiting you is to obtain an insight into your national history and copies of such documents as you may have in your possession concerning the traditions of your oppressed people in order that if the race is to be extinguished its history and . . . its wrongs may be preserved. You can safely communicate with Mr. Payne. . . . Should you desire my personal attendance at the approaching council please write me at Milledgeville and I will forthwith come up.[6]

Invited by Ross to begin work on his Cherokee history at once, Payne acquiesced. Thus it happened that he wrote the following vivid account of the preparations for the October council and of the council itself:

> Mr. Ross received me with cordiality. He said he regretted that he had only a log cabin of but one room to invite me to. . . .
> This morning offered the first foretaste of what the next week is to present. The woods echoed with the trampling of many feet: a long and orderly procession emerged from among the trees, the gorgeous autumnal tints of whose departing foliage seemed in sad harmony with the noble spirit now beaming in this departing race. Most of the train

[5] September 15, 1835, in *ibid*.
[6] September 24, 1835, in *ibid*.

was on foot. There were a few aged men, and some few women, on horseback. The train halted at the humble gate of the principal chief: he stood ready to receive them.

Everything was noiseless. The party, entering, loosened the blankets which were loosely rolled and flung over their backs and hung them, with their tin cups and other paraphernalia attached, upon the fence. The chief approached them . . . and each, in silence, drew near to give his hand. Their dress was neat and picturesque: all wore turbans, except four or five with hats; many of them, tunics, with sashes; many long robes, and nearly all some drapery; so that they had the oriental air of the old scripture pictures of patriarchal processions.

The salutations over, the old men remained near the chief, and the rest withdrew to various parts of the enclosure; some sitting Turk fashion against the trees, others upon logs, and others upon the fences, but with the eyes of all fixed upon their chief. They had walked sixty miles since yesterday. . . . They sought their way to the council ground. It was explained to them.

At one moment I observed a sensation among them, and all . . . circled around their chief. Presently an old man [possibly Whitepath, Going Snake, or George Lowrey] spoke . . . each went for his pack, and all resumed their way. There was something in the scene which would have subdued a sterner spirit than mine. . . . Parties varying from thirty to fifty have been passing . . . all day. All seem to contemplate the approaching meeting as one of vital import. I myself, though a stranger, partake of the general excitement.[7]

The general council at Red Clay, attended by both Ross and Ridge Cherokees, assembled as scheduled in the large, open-sided council house at Red Clay that substituted now for the Cherokees' fine modern council house at New Echota. With deep concentration the participants listened to Schermerhorn's presentation of a treaty. "Its most important provisions gave $3,250,000 to the Cherokees for their eastern lands; $150,000 depredative claims (including Creek war losses); restated a guarantee to 13,000,000 acres of western territory granted in treaties of 1828 and 1833 to previously emigrated

---

[7] Grant Foreman, *Indian Removal*, 266f.

Cherokees; and gave an additional 800,000 acres in that same region to those going west." When this treaty came to a vote, it was rejected by the Ross party and rejected also by John Ridge, Elias Boudinot, and leaders of the Ridge party. Thereupon, Schermerhorn raised the amount offered the Cherokees to $5,000,000, or $500,000 more than they had been offered by the Senate the winter before.[8] But by vote this price, too, was rejected.

Neither Ross nor his faithful colleagues had any way of knowing, except by conjecture, that Ridge's and Boudinot's public rejection of Schermerhorn's treaty was done purely for the effect it created. Both Ridge and Boudinot, aware of the penalty one must pay for participation in the cession of lands without the full consent of the Nation, feared assassination and were, therefore, not courting death while attending council with Ross's party. But any impression left by John Ridge and Elias Boudinot at this council that they had abandoned their posts and would thereafter be on Ross's side was proven false by the letter that Ridge wrote to Lumpkin from the council grounds. He informed the Governor of the council's rejection of Schermerhorn's treaty but of the bright prospect of a treaty being consummated—as planned all along—by the Treaty party at New Echota in December:

> A conference is now in session composed of five men of each party . . . to try to compromise and close the treaty but if it can't come to an agreement, the plan is to make a treaty in December. . . . Whatever of protection the U. S. shall promise the friends of the treaty & the Indians who will be moving from the State under it, should not be falsified by the acts of the Georgia citizens. . . . The aggressions of the citizens of Georgia on the enrolled emigrants are increasing which retards our operations very much. I must beg the liberty of referring you to Col. Bishop for a more enlarged view of the proposed policy. He is an individual and an officer who has done more than any other in this country to accelerate the treaty. . . .

[8] Malone, *Cherokees of the Old South,* 181; Grant Foreman, *Indian Removal,* 265; Ross Papers, *loc. cit.*

The Rev. Mr. Schermerhorn will . . . forward you such projects of laws as he deems will be useful on this subject. *My name must be reserved from the public eye.*[9]

Elias Boudinot's letter to Lumpkin, on August 19, 1835, bespoke his fear that the Governor would not, as promised, exempt Boudinot's property from confiscation until after he and his family had moved west. The date of Boudinot's departure was to be set after the Treaty of New Echota was signed in December of that year. Edgily, Boudinot reminded Governor Lumpkin of the Georgia legislature's promise:

> I had occasion sometime since to address you a letter in relation to my house and improvements. . . . On my return from the North I find that Mr. McCoy, who was residing upon the same lot had been removed and . . . Mr. Buchanan . . . had already dispossessed me of my improvements and claims the right of ousting me altogether. It certainly could not have been the intention of the legislature to prejudice the rights and interests of Cherokees under circumstances similar to mine. . . . Already has a part of my farm been taken away. It could not have been the intention of the legislature that the law should operate in this way.[10]

Boudinot was assured by Lumpkin upon receipt of this letter that his property would be protected by the legislature, as promised earlier.

An aftermath of the October council at Red Clay was the arrest of Chief John Ross and John Howard Payne on the night of December 5, 1835, at Ross's home by twenty-five members of the Georgia Guard. The prisoners were forced to mount their horses and, in a cold blinding rain, accompany the guard to Camp Benton. There Payne and Ross were unceremoniously thrown into a dank, dark log cabin that served as a jail. Chained near them was the son of Crawling Snake, speaker of the council, and hanging from the rafters above

---

[9] October, 1835, in Cherokee Indian Letters, Talks, and Treaties, *loc. cit.* (This letter bears no date except 1835. But it had to be written in October at the close of the council meeting at Red Clay.)

[10] Photocopy in Georgia Department of Archives and History, Atlanta.

was the odoriferous decomposing corpse of a Cherokee who had been executed some weeks before. The Guard appropriated Payne's Cherokee history manuscript, which ironically described the Guard as resembling banditti rather than state militiamen. Ross's official papers, too, were taken over by the Guard. Thus outraged, the prisoners remained in the jail until they were reluctantly released thirteen days later by Bishop, who never had preferred any charges against them.

Incensed by his and Ross's treatment at the hands of the military, Payne published a series of articles on the subject in the *Knoxville Register*, the *Georgia Constitutionalist*, and other American newspapers. And readers of these publications gladly took up Payne's hue and cry against the oppression of the Cherokees.

That John Ross did not know the full extent of John Ridge's activities in the Jackson-Georgia conspiracy to gain the Cherokees' removal is indicated by a remark which Ross made to Payne after their arrest: "There is no doubt in my mind but that Currey and Schermerhorn were the instigators of our late treatment by the Georgia guard."[11] Then, too, Ross possibly did not realize that the link between John Ridge and the removal machine dictated both Ridge's and Boudinot's rejection of the treaty presented by Schermerhorn to the general council at Red Clay in October. But, had Boudinot and Ridge not rejected Schermerhorn's treaty publicly, Ross would perhaps not have been impelled to save Ridge's life at that council by frustrating a move of members of the Ross party to assassinate Ridge.

After the council at Red Clay came Schermerhorn's announcement of the coming council at New Echota in December, called for the purpose of gaining signatures to a treaty of removal. At this, a wave of excitement and hostility lashed the Ross people, inciting them to wreak vengeance on the enrollees for emigration and on the white men who confiscated corn (needed by the Indians for food) and distilled it into whisky. Sullenly, Chief Ross's people, obeying his instructions, refused to give to white census-takers the names of their

[11] John Ross to John Payne, January 6, 1836, in Ross Papers, *loc. cit.*

children, or to enumerate their farm improvements, estimate the number of acres they cultivated, or tell how many cattle they owned. For failing to do this, both men and women were stripped, then beaten like animals by the Georgia Guard.

The people living around Dahlonega saw their cattle driven off and sold to buyers who paid for them from pouches filled with gold dust taken from the Cherokees' gold fields. Around New Echota, Cherokee enrollees for emigration went into Mr. Lavender's store and came out laden with food supplies and clothing, while Ross's people scrabbled for food in barren pastures and thickets. But, despite all this, Ross's people refused to go to the New Echota council in December. Instead, they encamped near Lewis Ross's store near the agency or in the neighborhood of the missions, anxiously awaiting news and further instructions from their chief, who, shortly after being released from jail, had hastened to Washington City in company with a delegation authorized by the council to "wait upon" the President and his Secretary of War to ascertain from them how best to terminate the Nation's difficulties.

John Ross was not in the Nation when approximately five hundred Cherokees (including infants and children) assembled at New Echota to witness, on December 29, the signing—by barely one hundred persons—of the disgraceful and fraudulent treaty of removal. By the terms of this instrument, signed by John Ridge, Major Ridge, Elias Boudinot, Stand Watie, and other members of the Treaty party, the Cherokee Nation ceded, relinquished, and conveyed to the United States all the lands owned, claimed, or possessed by the Nation east of the Mississippi River. In consideration for the lands, five million dollars were to be expended, paid, and invested in the manner stipulated and agreed upon.

In exchange for their ancient homelands the Cherokee people received guarantees to western lands already partially occupied by the Cherokees West. These lands were purportedly protected by the stipulation that they should never be annexed by another state or territory without the Cherokee Nation's consent.

Thus was brewed the thin legal substance out of which the Trail of Tears flowed westward. But miraculously, James Adair's dire prophecy (made over a century before) that the Cherokee people were destined to annihilation would not be fulfilled at this time. The Cherokees' tribal vitality would again save them, as it had throughout their history.

CHAPTER X

"The Trail Where They Cried"

JOHN ROSS AND THE CHEROKEE DELEGATION in Washington were admittedly chagrined when the United States Senate—by a single vote—ratified the New Echota treaty, and President Jackson, on May 23, 1836, proclaimed its validity. Until the day the vote was taken Senators Bell, Calhoun, Clay, Webster, and White had assured John Ross that the treaty would not pass the Senate. The treaty's passage can be accounted for by the fact that Senator White unexpectedly changed his vote from "nay" to "yea"—or at least that was how William C. Coodey explained it to Ben Currey:

> I certainly did understand that some of the Senators who voted for the treaty had done so contrary to all expectation, and that one of them (Senator White) voted for it after having spoken against it in the Senate. . . . The most sanguine expectation was indulged that the treaty would be rejected and another formed and this was predicated upon the representations of Senators and members of the House. How far Mr. Ross may have been influenced in his course by the advice of members I cannot say, but my long and intimate acquaintance [with him] forbids the belief that he has at any time been actuated by improper motives. . . . I was not a member of the delegation and did not . . . charge my memory with facts which generally reached me second handed.[1]

[1] July 8, 1836, in Ross Papers, *loc. cit.*

The Senate's ratification of the New Echota tr⟍
line for the final removal of over 15,000 Ross-party⟍
May 23, 1838—precisely two years after the treaty⟍
Thereupon, the Secretary of War notified John Ross that⟍
dent had ceased to recognize any existing government a⟍
eastern Cherokee, and that any further effort by him [R⟍
prevent the consummation of the treaty would be suppressed.⟍

Published all over America, the President's proclamation evo⟍
a storm of protest from citizens in every walk of life. John Q⟍
Adams, a member of the House from Massachusetts, termed the
Senate's acceptance of the New Echota treaty "infamous . . . . It
brings with it eternal disgrace upon the country."[3] Major W. M.
Davis, federal enrolling agent and also an appraiser of Cherokee
improvements, explosively stated to the Secretary of War that the
Treaty of New Echota "is no treaty at all, because not sanctioned
by the great body of the Cherokee and made without their participation or assent. . . . The business of making the treaty was transacted
with a committee appointed by the Indians present, so as not to expose their numbers. . . . The delegation taken to Washington by
Mr. Schermerhorn had no more authority to make a treaty than
any other dozen Cherokee accidentally picked up for the purpose."[4]

General John Ellis Wool, commander of the federal troops dispatched to the Nation to enforce the fraudulent treaty, was so revolted by the prospect of disarming and subjugating the Cherokees
that he asked to be relieved of his onerous task "as soon as circumstances will permit."

The whole scene since I have been in this country has been nothing
but a heartrending one, and such a one as I would be glad to get rid
of as soon as circumstances will permit. Because I am firm and decided,
do not believe I would be unjust. If I could . . . I would remove every

[2] Grant Foreman, *Indian Removal*, 269.

[3] See notes on a speech delivered by "Mr. Chapman of Alabama" in the U. S.
House of Representatives, June 29, 1836, on the New Echota treaty, in Ross Papers,
loc. cit. This is a detached piece—one of the many to be found in Ross Papers
eluding exact classification.

[4] Grant Foreman, *Indian Removal*, 270.

ach of the white men, who, like vul-
unce upon their prey and strip them
from the government of the United
hs, if not ninety-nine out of every
Vest.[5]

ial signed by Cherokee council
of the Cherokees, as well as
ed Cherokee council in Sep-
) do with the distaste which
.eported to the War Department
...π he had met with the Cherokees, but "it is,
...o talk to people almost universally opposed to the
...nd who maintain that they never made such a treaty. So determined are they in their opposition that not one . . . however poor
or destitute, would receive either rations or clothing from the United
States lest they might compromise themselves in regard to the treaty.
. . . Many have said they will die before they will leave the country."[6]

Tennessee volunteers under Brigadier General R. G. Dunlap halfheartedly constructed stockades made of split trees, sharpened and
set in the ground picket-fashion, for use of the troops. Near the
agency at Calhoun and other strategic points they built rows of log
pens, each approximately sixteen feet square and crudely roofed, for
future Cherokee captives. But after attending Cherokee parties and
dances and noting the grace and beauty of the Indian girls (most of
whom had been educated at mission schools or at white seminaries),
the volunteers unwillingly obeyed orders to round up the enrollees
by use of force. Eventually General Dunlap himself became averse
to the use of force. Threatening to resign his commission, Dunlap asserted that he would never dishonor the Tennessee arms "by aiding
to carry into execution at the point of the bayonet a treaty made
by a lean minority against the will and authority of the Cherokee
people."[7]

[5] *Ibid.*, 272.
[6] *Ibid.*, 271.
[7] Govan and Livingood, *The Chattanooga Country*, 92.

Meanwhile, on the floor of the United States Congress, Honorable Henry Wise, a member of the House from Virginia, cogently invited a comparison of John Ross and "Mr. Halsey," a member of the House from Georgia who had tried to belittle Ross. "And," concluded Congressman Wise, "the gentleman from Georgia will not gain greatly by the comparison, either in civilization or morals."[8]

However, President Jackson (soon to be succeeded by Van Buren), paying little heed to public opinion, sternly declared "his settled determination that the treaty should be carried out without modification and with all consistent despatch, and directed that . . . no further communication by mouth or writing should be held with . . . Ross concerning the treaty."[9]

Between 1836–38 approximately 2,000 Cherokees joined the "Old Settlers" or "Cherokees West" in what is today eastern Oklahoma but what was then erroneously referred to by the Cherokees as "Arkansas," a place where it was said the Western sky bent down to touch the land. But remaining in the East were yet 15,000 Ross people who refused to emigrate.

Around January 1, 1837, 600 aristocratic members of the Treaty party availed themselves of the provisions of the New Echota treaty authorizing Cherokees to emigrate themselves. Accompanied by Negro slaves, saddle horses, and droves of fat oxen, these Cherokees traveled overland through Kentucky, Illinois, Missouri, and Arkansas to their new homes, reaching their destination in time to put in spring crops. Possibly the large sum of money, placed (as Lumpkin later boasted) "where it would be most effective," helped ease the self-emigrating Cherokees' journey. White residents of the country through which these emigrants journeyed commented on the fact that they traveled in the manner of white aristocrats—being well mounted, well dressed, and obviously well fed.

The first Treaty-party Cherokees to be emigrated by the government under the New Echota treaty did not fare as well as had the self-emigrants. From Ross's landing a party of 466 persons, on

---

[8] Royce, *The Cherokee Nation of Indians, loc. cit.*, 290.
[9] *American State Papers*, Class V, Military Affairs, VI, VII.

March 3, 1837, embarked for the West in a fleet of eleven flatboats moving in three sections. Following the prescribed water route, they went (via the Tennessee and Ohio rivers) to Memphis and, after crossing the Mississippi at that place, encamped at Montgomery's Point until a pilot could be found to navigate their boats up the Arkansas, a snakelike, treacherous river streaked with disturbing sand bars and cluttered by snags and sawyers. The ascent of the Arkansas achieved, Major Ridge and his party debarked two miles above Fort Smith in order to reach the lands which they intended to settle on Honey Creek near the Missouri line. The remaining emigrants landed at Fort Coffee and from that point entered Cherokee territory adjacent to Fort Gibson.

According to Dr. C. Lillybridge, the emigrants' physician, this party was preyed upon by "colds, influenza, sore throat, coughs, pluerisy, measles, diarrhea, bowel complaint, fevers, toothache, wounds from accidents and fighting, and gonorrhea among the young men."[10] There was also a noted increase in the consumption of whisky, illegitimately sold to the travelers whenever they passed through white settlements.

The second party of Cherokees to emigrate under government supervision, numbering approximately 365, took the overland route through Kentucky, Illinois, and Missouri. Leaving the Cherokee agency near Calhoun on October 14, 1837, this group stopped at Nashville to permit its leaders, Starr and Reese, to pay a respectful call on Jackson at the Hermitage. They reached their Western destination around December 30 of that year, saddened by sickness and the deaths of fifteen of their number—eleven of whom were children.

Back in the old Nation a council, attended by several thousand Cherokees, convened at Red Clay in August, 1837, to receive the latest news from John Ross and the delegation that had been in Washington. Ross had gained permission from Colonel Lindsey (General Wool's successor) for the council to meet, possibly because Lindsey wanted Colonel Mason, a special United States agent, to make "a Talk" to the Cherokees designed to break down their oppo-

---

[10] Grant Foreman, *Indian Removal*, 276.

sition to removal. Present also at the Red Clay council were General Nathaniel Smith from Athens, Tennessee, a successor to Ben Currey, whose death had occurred the preceding winter, and an English visitor who introduced himself as George Featherstonhaugh.

According to Featherstonhaugh, the Red Clay council grounds were alive with Cherokees fending off the rain that fell in torrents:

> I went to the council-house. Great numbers of them were assembled, and Mr. Jones, the missionary, read out verses in the English language from the New Testament, which Bushyhead [the Reverend Jesse Bushyhead], with a singularly stentorial voice and sonorous accent, immediately rendered to the people in the Cherokee tongue, emitting a deep grunting sound at the end of every verse, resembling the hard breathing of a man chopping trees down. . . . This I was told is a universal practice . . . in Cherokee oratory.
>
> When they sang, a line or two of a hymn printed in the Cherokee language was given out, each one having a hymn book . . . and I certainly never saw any congregation engaged more apparently in sincere devotion.
>
> This spectacle . . . led me into reflection upon the opinion which is so generally entertained of its being impossible to civilize the Indian. . . . Here is a remarkable instance which seems to furnish a conclusive answer. . . . A whole Indian nation abandons the pagan practices of their ancestors, adopts the Christian religion, uses books printed in their own language, submits to the government of their elders, builds houses and temples of worship, relies upon agriculture for their support, and produces men of great ability to rule over them. . . . Are not these the great principles of civilization?
>
> They were driven from their religious and social state then, not because they cannot be civilized, but because a pseudo set of civilized beings, who are too strong for them want their possessions![11]

Featherstonhaugh noted the campfires around which Cherokee families huddled, and the public tables loaded down with pots of stewed beef and large bowls of canahomie (or hominy grits) cooked by twenty-four Cherokee families and paid for by the council. Later

[11] *A Canoe Voyage up the Minnay Sotor*, II, 233f.

at the "Talk" delivered by Colonel Mason "in a stand erected near the Council-house," Featherstonhaugh noted that two thousand male Cherokees listened attentively in the rain to Mason's belabored defense of the United States policy as promulgated by Jackson and by Van Buren. But the "Talk" contained dagger-sharp allusions to the government's intentions "to enforce the treaty which the minority had made . . . and even insinuated that the Cherokees' resistance to it was factious. This gave offense, and even Mr. Ross objected to it."[12]

During the remainder of 1837 and the first quarter of 1838, John Ross continued to object vigorously to the federal government's intention to enforce "the treaty which the (Cherokee) minority had made." Authorized by the council, Ross and a delegation, among whom were Situwakee, Whitepath, and Elijah Hicks, again went to Washington in the winter of 1838 to present to the United States Congress a memorial signed by 15,665 persons protesting the treaty. Playing for time, Ross and the delegation proposed to their friends in the House and Senate that they assist the Eastern Cherokees in getting a new treaty introduced in the Congress whereby the Cherokees could retain a portion of their Eastern lands outside the limits of Georgia. Optimistically, Ross wrote to his brother Lewis on February 20—three months before the fateful date set by the President for the Nation's final removal:

> . . . there is much anxiety and restive feeling among the big folks (War Department officials) in regard to the predicament the Cherokee affairs will place them in after the 23rd of May when the Cherokees shall be found still determined not to recognize that dirty paper they have told the Govt. that they never will acknowledge as a "treaty." Our friends in the Senate will move upon this controversy under the dictates of prudence and necessity so as to ensure action and decision upon the point of directing the difficulties to be closed by a new arrangement. It has been deemed best not to urge our memorial upon the House until movements in the Senate shall be developed.[13]

[12] *Ibid.*, 243.
[13] In Ross Papers, *loc. cit.*

As time went on it was rumored that President Van Buren was softening toward John Ross and the Cherokee delegation, whom Van Buren had refused to recognize upon their arrival in Washington in January. But the softening process did not continue, for Van Buren began to receive disconcerting reports from Governor Gilmer (conveyed to him by the Georgia delegation) about the behavior of the common Cherokees. Concentrated in northern Georgia, these Indians were obviously not planning to remove. And the citizens of Georgia were disturbed by their attitude of defiance.

One of Gilmer's "spies" had recently traveled "in a kind of zig-zag direction through the nation." Passing through Forsyth, Cherokee, and Cass counties, he had seen many of the Cherokees repairing their fences and cleaning up their fields, preparatory to planting corn. Some were erecting cabins "as though there was not the least prospect of early removal." They still appeared to entertain the hope of "effecting a new treaty and getting a longer time to remain in this country." The Cherokees around Ellijay were reported to be "saucy, stubborn, and rebellious." They had told Gilmer's spies that they were not going to Arkansas but that the whites had to leave. In De Kalb County between fifty and sixty Cherokees were reported working on the new Western and Atlantic Railroad. Too, the Indians around Ellijay had been seen carrying corn into the mountains, and Clayton's citizens in Rabun County had expressed a fear that the Cherokees in that vicinity—to avoid capture by federal soldiers— "would avail themselves of the opportunity that those large mountains here would afford for secreting themselves." The Indians' contention that the federal troops had been sent to protect them and not the whites irritated the Georgians exceedingly. On February 21, Samuel Tate from Harnageville reported to Gilmer that the Cherokees "dance all night and are not preparing to move. They say they would prefer death to Arkansas." Tate asked for federal troops to be sent to build forts for the whites:

> I assure you . . . the Indians could ruin the whole country if they were to try. There should be one company stationed at Coosawatter [*sic*] that is the strongest Indian settlement in this county and some of them

are very savage. Another betwixt Canton and Ellijay and another betwixt Ellijay and Valley River. It is the mountain Indians that will do mischief. . . . If it is in your power to send troops here I think it would be advisable.[14]

Thus it came about that President Van Buren refused to grant Ross's request for a delayed removal. Instead, as ordered by the President, six-foot-four Major General Winfield Scott was put in command of approximately seven thousand federal and state troops whose job it was to eject the Cherokees from their country on the date set by the treaty.

On March 27, 1838, John Ross received the following notification from the Commissioner of Indian Affairs, C. A. Harris:

> Yesterday the Senate had under consideration the Memorial of the Ross delegation, which by a decision of the majority (36–10) was promptly laid upon the table, every member of the Committee on Indian affairs, except one, voting in the affirmative. These proceedings leave no room to doubt that the legislative branch of the govmt. concurs with the executive and will sanction him in the purpose to carry the Treaty into full effect. You will perceive the importance of giving general circulation of these proceedings in forcible language, the unavoidable conclusion that a ready and cheerful acquiescence on their part can alone save them from serious calamities.[15]

This verdict bestirred nearly two hundred outraged citizens of Marietta, Ohio, to memorialize Congress in behalf of the Cherokees. And in Philadelphia, thousands of Cherokee sympathizers crowded into Pennsylvania Hall, where they vociferously passed and adopted the following preamble and resolution:

> At this time when the liberties of a noble but unfortunate race are about to be closed down by the cupidity of an avaricious people: when a stain is about to be cast upon our National Escutcheon which the tears and regrets of after ages will never be able to remove, it becomes the

[14] In Cherokee Indian Letters, Talks, and Treaties, *loc. cit.*
[15] In Ross Papers, *loc. cit.*

duty of all the friends of humanity to raise their voices against the measures and the men who would thus entail disgrace upon this country and ruin upon its aboriginal inhabitants.

Therefore resolved that we do unequivocally disapprove and indignantly condemn the attempt about to be made by the United States Government for the forcible removal of the Cherokee Nation. Resolved that a copy of the foregoing Preamble and Resolution be forwarded to our representatives in Congress, to the President of the United States, and the Governor of our commonwealth.[16]

But unhappily, when presented to Congress by Judge Southard, these two memorials were laid on the table alongside that signed by 15,665 persons from the Nation. The Cherokee issue, as far as the United States Congress was concerned, was dead. Apprised of this fact, Lewis Ross wrote to his chieftain brother in Washington:

> . . . It is evident that the Gov'mt is determined to move us at all hazzards and it only remains for us to do the best we can. I feel very much afraid that you will fail in making the new Treaty but still hope that you may succeed in placing our affairs in some better footing than they are. I shall anxiously expect to hear from you regularly and hope to hear something of a final adjustment before the 23 May next. I refer you to William S. Coodey for the news of the day with us. Schermerhorn's screw is severely felt by us all.[17]

Plaintively, John Ross's niece and two nephews, writing from schools in Lawrenceville, New Jersey, demanded to know the fate of the Nation. "I was very glad to hear that you were . . . well," eighteen-year-old William Potter Ross (John Golden and Eliza Ross's son, who, in 1838, was preparing for Princeton at Hamill's Classical and Commercial High School at Lawrenceville) wrote his busy uncle in Washington. "But after reading the correspondence between the delegation and Col. Mason . . . I discovered that . . . the actions of . . . men speak in stronger terms than . . . words."[18]

---

[16] This is from an account of a meeting held on May 16, 1838, in *ibid.*
[17] April 12, 1838, in *ibid.*
[18] April 12, 1838, in *ibid.*

From Araminta (Lewis Ross's young daughter who was attending the Lawrenceville Female Seminary), Chief John Ross received a dainty note expressing the girlish hope that "our people will not be moved west."[19] "Dear Uncle," wrote Robert (Araminta's small brother) from his classroom in Lawrenceville, "Do you think there will be anything done for the Cherokees? I hope there will be . . . perhaps you would like a Latin sentence. I will favor you with one. *'Scio Studendum esse nihi'* which is 'I know that I must study.' Now an Indian sentence . . . *'Ka wat lee os, tat gat eh.'* You know the meaning of this. It was sent to me by my Father. 'Peace, peace for the Cherokees. Oh, America, peace for the Cherokees.' "[20] To this letter, little Robert's brother John, a student at Hamill's, added as postscript: "The Congressional session is fast drawing to a close. Have they taken into consideration the Cherokees as a nation? . . . Do you intend to make any further proposition as to making a new Treaty? I ask these questions with a desire of knowing the present position of the delegation at Washington . . . because I am frequently asked these questions."[21]

However plaintive these inquiries from his niece and nephews, who would never again see their old homes but would, upon finishing school at Lawrenceville, go to new, raw homes west of the Mississippi, they perhaps did not clutch the heart of John Ross as did the "wampum letter" which he received from Aitooweyah, the Stud, and Knock Down—all three of whom lived in the Hickory Log district:

> Well now—we are thinking—we who are at home and have sent a message to where you are—this message we consider will add to the strength of your exertions. We the great mass of the people think only of the love we have to our land for . . . we do love the land where we were brought up. We will never let our hold to this land go for we say to you that our father who sits in Heaven gave it to us. [Therefore] . . . the land must be contended for—for if [we] were to let it go it

[19] April 12, 1838, in *ibid.*
[20] March 16, 1838, in *ibid.*
[21] *Ibid.*

will be like throwing away . . . [our] mother that gave . . . [us] birth for [this] is the place where . . . [we] can breathe out the life of . . . [our] existence.[22]

Bitter, but unbeaten, John Ross remained in Washington to collect, if possible, the Cherokees' back annuities and also to arrange for some two hundred old and infirm Cherokees (too feeble to emigrate) to remain in their respective communities as United States citizens. At this critical time Ross also provided for the release of Cherokees in Georgia penal institutions, in order that these prisoners might emigrate west with their people. Perhaps the unpublicized call which Ross paid on Major General Winfield Scott in Washington, too, deserves mention; for it established a relationship between the two that later benefited the Cherokee Nation.

On the occasion of this visit, the Cherokees' diminutive chief not only commanded the statuesque Scott's unwilling respect but won his admiration. Thereafter, when Ross asked General Scott for favors for his people, they were usually granted. Thus, emigrating Cherokees in 1838 were afforded luxuries not afforded many Southeastern Indians who emigrated west between 1832–42.

Having learned a great deal from Ross in Washington about the achievements of the Cherokees, General Scott felt a sympathy for the people whom he had orders to move. And the General's official statements in 1838 reflect his feelings. At the Cherokee Agency at Calhoun, General Scott, on May 10, 1838, addressed a proclamation to the Cherokees that, though firm in tone, exuded kindness and a proper respect for Indian feelings and sensibilities:

Cherokees! The President of the United States has sent me with a powerful army, to cause you, in obedience to the Treaty of 1835, to join that part of your people who are already established in prosperity, on the other side of the Mississippi. . . .

. . . Do not, I invite you, even wait for the close approach of the troops; but make such preparations for emigration as you can, and hasten to this place [Calhoun], to Ross's Landing, or to Gunter's Land-

[22] In *ibid.*

ing, where you will be received in kindness by officers selected for the purpose. You will find food for all, and clothing for the destitute, at either of those places, and thence at your ease, and in comfort, be transported to your new homes according to the terms of the Treaty.[23]

General Scott's orders to his troops—issued a week later, May 17, 1838—advised them:

> The Cherokees, by the advances they have made in Christianity and civilization, are by far the most interesting tribe of Indians in the territorial limits of the United States. Of the 15,000 of those people who are now to be removed—(and the time within which a voluntary emigration was stipulated, will expire on the 23rd instant—) it is understood that about four fifths are opposed, or have become averse to distant emigration; and . . . the troops will probably be obliged to cover the whole country they inhabit, in order to make prisoners and to march or to transport prisoners, by families, either to this place, to Ross's Landing or Gunter's Landing, where they are to be delivered over to the Superintendent of Cherokee Emigration.
>
> Considering the number and temper of the mass to be removed . . . it will readily occur, that simple indiscretions—acts of harshness and cruelty, on the part of our troops, may lead . . . in the end, to a general war and carnage—a result, in the case of those particular Indians, utterly abhorrent to the generous sympathies of the whole American people. Every possible kindness . . . must, therefore, be shown by the troops, and, if, in the ranks, a despicable individual should be found, capable of inflicting a wanton injury or insult on any Cherokee man, woman or child, it is hereby made the special duty of the nearest good officer or man, instantly to interpose, and to seize and consign the guilty wretch to the severest penalty of the laws.[24]

General Scott's detailed orders, although they called for the disarmament of male Cherokees when captured, also demanded that the Cherokees be assured by the troops that at, or beyond, the Mississippi, their cherished firearms would be restored to them. Too,

[23] In *ibid.*
[24] Order No. 25, in *ibid.*

Scott's orders humanely provided for the care of the sick, feeble, lunatic, infants, and "women in a helpless condition."

To expedite Cherokee removal, General Scott efficiently divided the Nation into an eastern district, which embraced North Carolina, the part of Tennessee lying north of Gilmer, Lumpkin, and Union counties in Georgia; a western district, which included Alabama, the residue of Tennessee, and Dade County in Georgia; and a third or middle district, which took in "all that part of the Cherokee country lying within the state of Georgia, and which is not comprised in the two other districts." Ironically, the headquarters for this third district was at the abandoned Cherokee capital of New Echota.

It would be gratifying to report that General Scott's kind and humane proclamation—ordered by the General to be "carefully read at the head of every company in the Army"—was conscientiously carried out by his three thousand regulars and four thousand volunteers. But, sadly, such was not the case. Instead, the roundup and capture of approximately fifteen thousand helpless and unarmed civilized Cherokees and their subsequent imprisonment in rude stockades by Scott's troops were accompanied by rape, robbery, murder, and acts of bestiality on the part of some of the soldiers. A case in point was the unfortunate arrest and tragic execution of Tsali.[25]

The mass ejection from the old Nation of Ross Cherokees, most of whom were captured and imprisoned by Scott's soldiers in June, 1838, was completed by early December of that same year. John Drew's detachment of 153 (increased en route to 245) left for the West on March 17, 1839.[26]

The first Cherokee contingent to be emigrated forcibly by General Scott, numbering around 800, left Ross's Landing for the West on June 6, 1838. Transported in two-decker keelboats measuring

---

[25] See Chapter I, p. 12, of this volume.

[26] A Cherokee MS re migration in 1838–39, containing the number of detachments, the number of emigrants in each detachment, the names of the conductors, and dates of departure from the East and arrival of each detchment in the West is in the Ross Papers, *loc. cit.* This is not a muster roll.

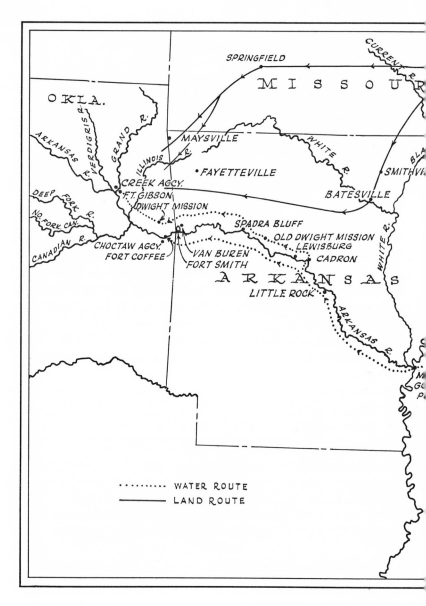

The routes taken by the Chero

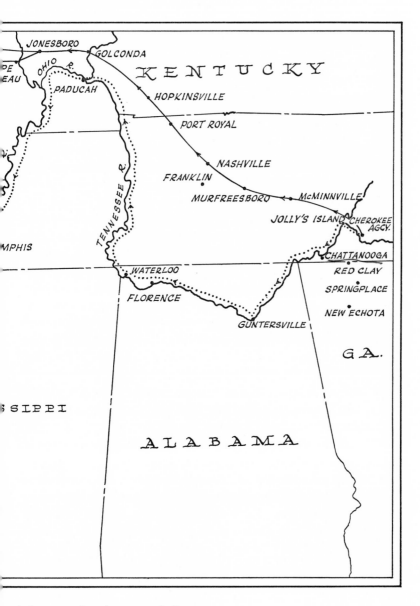

g their removal to the west, 1838–39.

130 feet in length and 20 feet in width and a one-hundred-ton steamboat, this party of unhappy, scantily clad Cherokees traveled to their new homes via the Tennessee, Ohio, Mississippi, and Arkansas rivers. Around June 15, another party, whose exact number could never be ascertained because of their wild behavior, were started from Ross's Landing via water. A third and larger group of 1,071 persons left Ross's Landing in wagons and afoot for Waterloo, where they were put aboard boats provided by the government.

Harassed and angered by the treatment which these June captives (most of whom were from Georgia) received at the hands of white conductors, George Lowrey, the Cherokees' second chief, Lewis Ross, Thomas Foreman, Hair Conrad, and Going Snake petitioned General Scott to delay further emigration until fall when the sickly season should be ended and the summer drought, which held the entire south in bondage, should be broken. Even though these headmen acted (without authority) as spokesmen for John Ross who was still in Washington, General Scott agreeably postponed the emigration of the 13,000 Cherokees remaining in the old Nation until the first of September. But he firmly refused the headmen's request to have the emigrants who had left Ross's Landing on June 17 returned, so as to leave with the others in September. "They have already covered ninety miles of the journey," General Nathaniel Smith, superintendent of Cherokee removal, sharply reminded the petitioners.

When, in the early part of July, 1838, Chief Ross returned to the Nation from Washington, he found Cherokee headmen and common Indians alike penned up in camps like cattle. The majority of captives were sick, discouraged, and grief stricken. But the picture was not all black. The gloom and despair that in June had hung funereally over Camp Butler was now partially lifted by the Reverends John Wickliffe (Kaneeda) and O-ga-na-ya. These native Baptist ministers had somehow gained the commanding officer's permission to erect a rude church adjacent to the camp and fort. In this arbor-like sanctuary Wickliffe and O-ga-na-ya preached night and morning to Cherokee captives. When received into the church, captives were baptized under guard in the near-by river, then, at the point of bayonets, marched back to their disease-infested prisons to seek solace in prayer.

At Camp Hetzel (in present-day Cleveland, Tennessee) the Reverends Jesse Bushyhead and Stephen Foreman, the speaker of the National Council and also native missionary of the American Board, and their families were prisoners. Yet captivity did not deter Foreman and Bushyhead from attempting to keep alive the religious advancement of their people by the deliverance of sermons calculated to restore a captive's faith and hope in God and another world. Backsliders who sought oblivion by imbibing great quantities of whisky smuggled into the camps by white peddlers were prevented by these native ministers from becoming degenerates.

To John Ross, the present condition of his people was not to be countenanced nor permitted to continue. Authoritatively, Ross appointed David Moses, George Still, and David Sanders a committee to report the needs of the people in their respective camps to the officers. Dramshops adjacent to the camps were requested closed by Ross. With the same cool air of dignity which he had displayed when discussing Cherokee affairs in Washington with General Scott months before, John Ross now asked the General to permit the Cherokees to manage and control their own removal in the fall. And to this request Scott unexpectedly gave an affirmative reply. Whereupon John Ross thankfully notified a physician whom he sought to employ for the emigration that arrangements had been made between General Scott and the constituted authorities of the Nation for their removal—"by which the entire control and management will be conducted under the superintendence of the nation."[27]

Having gained a concession granted to no other tribes subject to removal, John Ross made the most of it. After dividing the thirteen thousand Cherokee captives into detachments of one thousand each and on this basis estimating the exact amount of funds required to emigrate each detachment, John Ross presented the figures to General Scott. He at first thought them too high but in the end gave in. Ross reminded Scott in August:

[27] John Ross to unnamed correspondent in 1838 (exact date missing), in Ross Papers, *loc. cit.*

In relation to the daily rations at 16 cts [per person], the estimate is fixed at the rate which the Govt. had already made some arrangements to have them supplied. The addition, however, of sugar and coffee has been made under the estimate which we trust will be reasonable enough.

In our estimate we omitted an item which we deem indispensable but purpose now the addition of soap. The quantity of cost and delivery at the rate of 3 lbs. to every 100 rations at 15 cts. per lb.

Whatever may be necessary in the emigration of our people to their comfort on the way and as conducive to their health we desire to be afforded them.[28]

General Scott's reply to this new request for soap bespoke his willingness to go along with the Cherokee high command, even though by so doing, Scott knew that he would incur the administration's disapproval:

GENTLEMEN:

By your note of this date [August 2, 1838] . . . I perceive that you adhere to the calculation of $158,811, with a slight addition of soap, for the comfortable emigration by land of every thousand Cherokees from this to their new country west of the Mississippi.

As the Cherokee people are exclusively interested in costs as well as the comforts in the removal, I do not feel myself at liberty to withhold my sanction. The estimate therefore of emigration costs submitted to me . . . with the small addition of soap is hereby approved.[29]

At a makeshift council held at the Cherokees' prison camp at Aquohee on the first day of August, 1838, Cherokee headmen who were prisoners there and John Ross incorporated into council records the announcement that Ross, the principal chief of the Cherokee Nation, was empowered to assume the additional title of "Superin-

[28] John Ross, R. Taylor, E. Hicks, E. Gunter, Jas. Brown, Whitepath, and Situwakee to Major General Scott, Aug. 2, 1838, in *ibid.*

[29] Major General Scott to John Ross and members of the Cherokee Committee for Emigration, August 2, 1838, in *ibid.*

tendent of Cherokee Removal and Subsistence." And, in this capacity, Ross was authorized by a council committee (made up of Edward Gunter, Richard Taylor, Elijah Hicks, Situwakee, and Whitepath) acting in behalf of "the people" to make such requisitions for money as from time to time "he may deem necessary for the Cherokee emigration."[30]

When notified by General Nathaniel Smith, former superintendent of Cherokee removal, that General Scott had given Chief Ross permission to take over Smith's duties, former president Andrew Jackson flew into a rage. Angrily, he wrote to Felix Grundy, the attorney general of the United States, from the Hermitage on August 23, 1838:

> The contract with Ross must be arrested, or you may rely upon it, the expense and other evils will shake the popularity of the Administration to its center. What madness and folly to have anything to do with Ross when the agent was proceeding well with the removal on the principles of economy that would have saved at least 100 per cent from what the contract with Ross will cost. . . .
>
> I have only time to add as the mail waits that the contract with Ross *must be arrested*, and General Smith left to superintend the removal. The time and circumstances under which Gen'l Scott made this contract shows that he was no economist, or is, sub rosa, in league with Clay and Co. to bring disgrace on the administration. . . .
>
> P. S. I am so feeble I can scarcely wield my pen, but friendship dictates it and the subject excites me. Why is it that the scamp Ross is not banished from the notice of the administration?[31]

But John Ross, it seems, was neither affected by this outburst of Jackson's nor curbed by General Scott. The total cost of Cherokee emigration, as estimated by Ross and his colleagues, soared to over half a million dollars, but General Scott did not attempt to pare this amount down by the elimination of soap, sugar, or coffee—all of which were considered useless luxuries by the War Department.[32]

---

[30] MS record of a council meeting at Camp Aquohee, August 1, 1838, in *ibid.*
[31] Brown, *Old Frontiers,* 511f.
[32] The cost of Cherokee emigration in 1838–39 was more than $500,000, for it

Uninhibited by Scott, Ross instructed clerks of the Nation to prepare and register the claims of individual Cherokees for adjudication and settlement with the agents of the United States before the emigrants' fall departure. These claims were for houses, firearms, livestock, farm equipment, gristmills, furniture, fruit trees, planted fields, spinning wheels, carpenter and blacksmith tools, and miscellaneous objects owned by the Cherokees—all of which they had been forced to abandon when captured. Toonieyie put in a claim for sheep, pigs, hoes, bedsteads, and cooking utensils; Richard Wilkenson, for sixty-five fruit trees; Sally, a Cherokee woman from the Chickamauga district, claimed the former ownership of six ducks, a plaid cloak, a feather bed, a turkey gobbler, a set of china, two blowguns, a fiddle, garden tools, an umbrella, a coffee pot, and a plow. The claims of the well-to-do Cherokees included not only handsome homes that after the removal became Southern show places owned by whites but blooded race horses, rich household furnishings, immense libraries, and fine silver.

In September, having carefully selected the conductors of the thirteen detachments and their accompanying wagon masters and physicians, and the contractors who were to furnish the emigrants with food and other supplies at various points along the route, John Ross notified Scott that the Cherokees were about ready to embark on their long journey. But because of the extended drought, the day of their departure was again postponed until October.

This delay made it imperative for Ross to ask Scott for additional funds for the subsistence of his people. Food was needed, as well as medical supplies for the sick, coffins for the dead, and clothing for the destitute. John Ross reminded Scott that provision for the poorer class of Cherokees was specified "in the third section of a late action of Congress touching on the removal of the Cherokees."

Happily for Ross, at the height of his straining to meet the burdensome responsibilities attendant to Cherokee removal, he re-

---

kept increasing after this amount was sent to John Ross by the Bank of the United States. Figures assembled by the Office of Indian Affairs in 1839 give the cost of Cherokee emigration in 1838 as $630,000 (see the Ross Papers, *loc. cit.*). But the Office of Indian Affairs warns that these figures are possibly inaccurate.

ceived assurance from Thomas McKenney of Philadelphia that the half-million dollars promised Ross for emigration was on its way:

> DEAR SIR:
>
> I have this moment had a most gratifying interview with Mr. Biddle, President U-States Bank, and have learned from this gentleman what the arrangements are by which you are to be paid the half million dollars that are soon to be placed in your hands. I have been gratified, moreover, by the spirit of kindness toward you and your people by which Mr. Biddle is actuated. It is arranged that this money be conveyed to you by special messenger. Joseph L. Roberts Esq., cashier, a most intelligent and estimable gentleman, will leave this city, in charge of it, tomorrow for Calhoun. It is usual for the issues of this bank to be signed by proxy—but in this case Mr. Biddle has signed them with his own hand and doubtless from respect to you and your people to be filled up in your name. I see in all this strong evidence of personal good will blended with a desire to make the operation as satisfactory to you, as I am sure it will be useful.
>
> It rejoiced me much that you are to receive payment in such sound currency; and to witness a respect toward you and the Cherokees so marked. . . .
>
> I shake hands with you as I have always and wish you health and prosperity; and to your people a rest for your future that shall not in a lifetime be interrupted.[33]

John Ross, having made every effort to prepare his people for the long journey westward, lastly applied to Captain John Page for provisions for himself:

> SIR
>
> Myself and family being a part of the Cherokees to be removed west under the late operations of the military would be entitled to receive provisions from the U. States and not having hitherto applied now request to be supplied. My family consists of thirty-one persons and eighteen horses and oxen . . . you will please to advise me to whom I shall apply for rations.[34]

[33] September 12, 1838, in *ibid.*
[34] August, 1838, in *ibid.*

Carefully, John Ross superintended the boxing and packing of the Cherokee Nation's sacred records, which dated back to 1808, the date of their first written laws. Among these documents was the correspondence between the Cherokee Nation and all the Presidents of the United States from Washington to Van Buren. Preserved also by Ross was his Masonic demission from the Olive Branch Lodge in Jasper, Tennessee. Dated April 11, 1827, the demission stated that Ross, a Master Mason, remained in good standing with the order of Free and Accepted Masons. Of greater importance to Ross doubtlessly was a record of the Cherokee council held on August 1, 1838, in the Aquohee prison camp. Signed by Ross and a Cherokee council committee, this record is unique, for no other tribe of American Indians has been known to hold a recorded council when captives of a white government.

> WHEREAS the title of the Cherokee people to their lands is the most ancient, pure, and absolute known to man its date is beyond the reach of human record: its validity confirmed and illustrated by possession and enjoyment antecedent to all pretense of claims by any other portion of the human race . . .
>
> And WHEREAS the natural, political and moral relations existing among the citizens of the Cherokee nation toward each other and toward the body politic; cannot in reason and justice be dissolved by the expulsion of the nation from its own territory by the power of the United States Government.
>
> *Resolved* therefore by the National Committee and Council and people of the Cherokee nation, in General Council assembled, that the inherent sovereignty of the Cherokee nation, together with the Constitution, laws and usages of the same, are, and by the authority aforesaid, hereby declared to be in full force . . . and shall continue so to be in perpetuity subject to such modification as the general welfare may render expedient.[35]

So it was that part of the Cherokee Nation in the fall and early winter of 1838 took final leave of its ancient and beloved homeland. The first detachment of 1,103 Cherokees to emigrate under their

[35] In *ibid.*

own officers, prior to leaving for the West on October 1, 1838, held a final council at Rattlesnake Springs (near present-day Charleston, Tennessee) and, by unanimous vote, declared their intention to continue their old constitution and laws upon arrival in the West. The officers of this first detachment were John Benge, a descendant of red-haired Chief Bench, who had fought for Cherokee freedom in the eighteenth century. Benge's able and distinguished assistant was George Lowrey, referred to by admiring whites as "the Cherokees' George Washington."

John Burnett, a private in Captain McClellan's company, was an eyewitness to the Cherokees' migration west in 1838. And, in later years, Burnett recalled its horrors:

> ... One can never forget the sadness and solmenity of that morning. . . .
>
> I saw the helpless Cherokees arrested and dragged from their homes, and driven by bayonet into the stockades. And in the chill of a drizzling rain on an October morning I saw them loaded like cattle or sheep into six hundred and forty-five wagons and started toward the west.
>
> ... Chief Ross led in prayer and when the bugle sounded and the wagons started rolling many of the children . . . waved their little hands good-bye to their mountain homes.[36]

Benge's detachment and the twelve that followed it had hard going. Despite the measures adopted by Chief Ross to prevent unnecessary hardships, the thirteen groups under native conductors encountered accidents, disease, death, and discomfort from winter weather. Laboriously, horses, oxen, and footsore emigrants struggled over the Cumberland Range of Mountains, crossed their ancestors' hunting grounds, and, upon reaching the icy Ohio, ferried across it into Illinois.

By the time the emigrants had set up temporary camps at Golconda or at Jonesboro, Illinois, preparatory to crossing the Mississippi, an early and particularly severe winter had rendered their existence

---

[36] "Original Birthday Story of Private John G. Burnett," MS in Cherokee Museum, Cherokee, North Carolina.

almost unbearable. They needed warm clothing, blankets, and additional tents. To alleviate their distress, Lewis Ross, in charge of subsistence, left the detachments at this site and, in company with Lenoir, an agent, hurried to St. Louis to purchase thirty dozen pairs of men's brogans, thirty pairs of white mackinaws, five dozen pairs of boys' brogans, and twenty-three army blankets. The money for these supplies was borrowed by Lewis Ross in St. Louis by pledging his own securities. After the detachments crossed the Mississippi and, from Cape Girardeau, Missouri, threaded their way through Jackson, Farmington, Potosi, Rolla, and Lebanon to Springfield, a small town in the southwestern part of Missouri, they were again in need of supplies. And so from Danford and Brothers at Springfield, Lenoir purchased "96½ yds. striped cotton" and "30 pr. yarn socks" for emigrants who shortly would be traveling in a southwesterly direction to their destination via Aurora, Monett, and present-day Southwest City, Missouri. Some of the people would enter Cherokee country via Rogers, Springdale, Fayetteville, and Prairie Grove, Arkansas.

En route, detachment conductors sent Chief Ross written reports of their progress, setbacks, and disappointments. From Sequatchie Valley, the Reverend Jesse Bushyhead, on October 21, reported that "We have a large number of sick and very many extremely aged and infirm persons in our detachment that must of necessity be conveyed in wagons—our detachment now consists of about 968 or 70 Cherokees." On October 24, Elijah Hicks wrote to Ross from Port Royal near the Kentucky line: "I am almost without officers but shall call on my detachment to fill vacancies that have occurred. My first wagon master died at Woodberry . . . in consequence of, Mr. Hood will perform the duties of Mr. Perry. Whitepath has been in the last stages of sickness . . . and cannot last but a few days. Necowee has given himself up to the bane of death and I have altogether lost his services. Our police has to drive him along the road sometimes fettered." Writing Ross from Mouse Creek on November 4, George Hicks announced that "We are about to take our final leave and kind farewell to . . . the country that the Great Spirit gave our Fathers. . . . we know it is a laborious undertaking but with firm resolutions we think we will be able to accomplish it, if the white citizens will permit us, but since we have been on our march many of us have been stopped and our horses taken from our teams for the payment of unjust . . . debts."

Sometimes John Ross received news of the various detachments from white contractors. Thomas Clark, Jr., hired by Ross to issue supplies to emigrants at Nashville, reported on November 15 that conductors Moses Daniels and James Brown, deterred by the rain, were encamped at Mill Creek "four miles east of here but will leave in the morning." And on December 28, Clark, writing to Ross from the "mouth of the Ohio, Illinois," expressed the hope that Ross would catch up with the detachments when they crossed the Mississippi so as to "dispell the gloom and settle the doubts attendant upon emigration. . . . You are the master workman and it is your peculiar province to come see and determine which I hope you will do."[37] Clark was greatly concerned about the destitute condition of the emigrants in detachments conducted by Peter Hildebrand, Richard Taylor, Moses Daniels, James Brown, and Elijah Hicks, which were stranded between the icy Ohio and Mississippi rivers. It was for these detachments that a purchase of warm clothing was made at St. Louis through the efforts of Lewis Ross.

The frail condition of Quatie, John Ross's wife, prompted Ross to abandon the overland route, taken by the other detachments, at Paducah, Kentucky, and to continue westward by boat. But boat-travel up the Arkansas in early March proved to be more hazardous than land-travel. Sleet, snow, and cold winds from the north forced the detachment which Ross and his ailing wife were in to land and go into camp near Little Rock.

Encamped on a bluff overlooking the Arkansas, Quatie gave her blanket to a sick child who, like Quatie and many other members of the detachment, had contracted a cold. The child to whom Quatie gave her blanket recovered, but Quatie's illness developed into pneumonia and caused her death.

---

[37] Sources which detail Cherokee emigration in 1838–39 are Grant Foreman's *Indian Removal* and the massive collection of Cherokee MSS in Ross Papers, *loc. cit.*

"I was on guard duty the night Mrs. Ross died," Private John Burnett recalled in later years. "When relieved at midnight I did not retire, but remained around the wagon [occupied by Quatie] out of sympathy for Chief Ross and at daylight was detailed . . . to assist in the burial. . . . Her uncoffined body was buried in a shallow grave far from her native mountain home, and the sorrowing cavalcade moved on."[38]

The exact number of lives lost in the 1838–39 Cherokee emigration is not known. Conductors tried to keep strict records of their parties, but this was a difficult procedure in those trying times. The sick were frequently left behind to recover and be picked up by succeeding detachments. However, some of the emigrants, when recovered from illnesses, did not continue their journey—preferring to remain where they were. According to John Ross, 424 emigrants out of his thirteen detachments died en route West in 1838–39. But, as estimated by Cherokee authority Grant Foreman, out of the total of 18,000 Cherokees who went west after the Treaty of 1835, about 4,000 perished—either in stockades prior to removal or on the journey west.[39]

Alluded to as "the Trail of Tears" by Indians of all the Five Civilized Tribes, the journey west was a tragic event that could not easily be erased from the memories of the emigrants or their descendants.

[38] "Original Birthday story of Private John G. Burnett," *loc. cit.*

[39] Starr, *History of Cherokee Indians,* 103; Grant Foreman, *Indian Removal,* 312n.

CHAPTER XI

Discord in the West

UPON ARRIVING IN THE Cherokee Nation West in 1839, approximately thirteen thousand emigrants were issued subsistence rations by the firm of Glasgow and Harrison, government contractors. The provisions were unfit for human consumption—the flour and meal being infested with weevils and the meat, according to Chief Ross, "poor and unhealthy."[1] But when his complaints to Governor Montfort Stokes, the Cherokee agent, and to General Matthew Arbuckle, the doughty old commandant at Fort Gibson, brought no results, Ross purchased supplies for his people from a private agent out of the fast-dwindling sum allotted him by Scott for emigration. On June 10, Ross received the agent's assurance that the provisions were on their way west:

> I have for you corn meal, plank, sash, 10 bbl. rice and one bbl. flour in all about 75,000 lbs. It will require about 12 or 13 teams to haul this . . . away. . . .
>
> According to your desire I made a calculation of the net cost of your last cargo and find that 56 per cent added to the invoice prices will barely reimburse your outlay. On the furniture, ploughs and castings 60 per cent should be added.[2]

[1] Letter of April, 1839, in Ross Papers, *loc. cit.*
[2] W. P. Rowles to John Ross, June 10, 1839, in *ibid*. The "plank" and "sash" referred to here were evidently building materials for houses.

Another unpleasant facet of emigrant life in the West was the hostility displayed by Ridge's Treaty party toward Ross and his people. Shortly after the emigrants' arrival, members of the Treaty party, in high favor with both General Arbuckle and William Armstrong, superintendent of Western Indians, deluged these men with false reports about "the Ross faction." Calculated to create prejudice and dislike among military and agency personnel, the reports did just that.

But these fabrications were discounted from the beginning by Stokes, who did not believe reports that Ross was dishonest while his people were drunkards, capable of crimes ranging from arson to murder. With the exception of Stokes, practically all the military and government personnel believed a tale launched by the Treaty party in late April, 1839, that Situwakee and his mountaineers, settled near Camp Illinois, were planning to attack the camp and massacre its inmates. Excitedly, General Arbuckle dispatched a company of dragoons to the endangered area. But the dragoons saw no evidence of the reported massacre, as the following communication from Captain George A. McCall to General Arbuckle indicates:

SIR—

In obedience to your orders of the 29th to proceed to Camp Illinois and obtain as far as possible all information in relation to the reports of Indian hostilities in that quarter I rode to the residence of John Ross, Esq. and delivered your letter requesting him to accompany me on that duty. At Mr. Ross's house I found many of the principal men of the party recently arrived in this country; and Mr. Ross informed me that they . . . were desirous that the matter should be thoroughly investigated for the satisfaction of all concerned. He at the same time told me the object of the meeting was the settlement of the accounts of the conductors of detachments of the late emigrants, the payment of claims, etc.; and that in the event of his leaving home . . . the meeting must be adjourned; which would lead to considerable inconvenience to a great number of Cherokees. He regretted that the state of things would prevent his accompanying me in person agreeable to your request; but he immediately selected Judge Adair and Mr. Stephen Foreman for that service—and here I would beg leave to remark that

I found them to be men of intelligence and extensive information who evinced . . . every disposition to . . . ascertain the facts in relation to the affair in question.

. . . On my return from [Camp Illinois] I again called on Mr. Ross who desired me to say that he would write to you as soon as practicable on the subject. It may not be amiss to remark that on my journey I observed the Cherokees were very generally employed in building houses, clearing and fencing land and planting.

I also learned that two associations have been entered into by individual Cherokees for the suppression of the sale of whiskey. One was held at Bushyhead's about the first of last week. . . . The other was held at Judge Adair's. . . .

The spirit of the resolutions adopted at both places was to this effect. That all whiskey brought into the Nation by Cherokees should be destroyed and the offenders punished. That if whiskey should be brought in by a white man, it should be taken from him and the fact reported to the commanding officer of the nearest military post. A company of Light Horse was organized consisting of a Captain, Lieutenant and twenty men whose duty it was to carry these resolutions into effect.[3]

Captain McCall's message should have, but did not, arouse Arbuckle's suspicions concerning the falsehoods told him by the Treaty party. Subsequent communications to Arbuckle from Ross proved conclusively that Situwakee, instead of instigating a massacre of white people at Camp Illinois, was among the conductors of the thirteen detachments who, when McCall visited Ross at his home, were peaceably engaged in attending to business pertaining to the late emigration. Refusing to believe Ross, but willing to believe the worst about Ross's people from members of the Treaty party, General Arbuckle again, in late May, dispatched a company of dragoons to the Cherokee settlements adjacent to Arkansas—Arbuckle having heard that a second Cherokee uprising was in the making. But this massacre, like the first, failed to materialize. And it is safe to assume that, because it did not, General Arbuckle was a trifle disappointed, for his dislike of John Ross appeared to be deepening.

The late emigrants outnumbered the Western Cherokees and the

[3] April 25, 1839, in *ibid.*

Treaty party two to one, thereby constituting four-fifths of the total population of the Cherokee Nation West. Paramount among their problems was the perpetuation of their advanced form of government. But unfortunately they discovered that the Western Cherokees expected them to live under their government—a system that, to Eastern Cherokees, seemed entirely outmoded.

Administered by three chiefs and a council, Western Cherokees, lacking a written constitution and having but few written laws, met in council about twice a year at Tahlonteskee, their capital. There in a rustic council house, not far from the mouth of the Illinois River, the Cherokees elected chiefs, councilmen, judges of circuit and district courts, and eight light-horsemen to keep the peace. Divided into but four districts, the Cherokee Nation West embraced seven million acres adjacent to Missouri on the northeast and to Arkansas on the east, with a neutral strip fifty miles wide and twenty-five deep dividing Missouri from the Osage Nation to the west. This sparsely settled region, prior to 1838–39, was about as loosely governed as the old Eastern Nation had been two decades before.

Although Western Cherokees in appearance closely resembled Eastern brothers, environment had affected and changed their habits. They were principally agrarians, who had little time for perfecting a constitution or for revising this or that law. Being neither statesmen nor politicians (perhaps because the conditions under which they lived did not warrant it), Western Cherokees, in addition to farming, owned and operated gristmills and saltworks; and, when life grew dull, they journeyed to the forks of the Brazos River in Texas to trade gunpowder and flint to the wild Comanches for mules and fine horses. Western Cherokees, too, were inordinately fond of gaming and dancing.

Admittedly, they paid small heed to education, although they sent their children to Sequoyah (who operated a saltworks on Lee's Creek) to learn how to read and write the Cherokee language or to Dwight or Fairfield mission schools, established and maintained by church organizations. Nor did religion play an important role in the lives of Western Cherokees in 1839. To them, progress was epitomized by a fenced farm, good crops, pens full of fat hogs, a horse that could beat a neighbor's on a race track, and a comfortable double-log cabin with the walls of its dog-trot hung with fancy bridles, spurs, saddles, guns, and the fishing and hunting equipment of a white frontiersman. In 1838–39 life in the Western Cherokee Nation was decidedly casual, informal, and rustic, as compared with the life led by Eastern Cherokees before removal.

Hopeful of painlessly merging the two governments, Chief Ross accepted the invitation tendered his people by Western chiefs to assemble at Takattokah, or Double Springs, in early June, 1839, to receive the Westerners' hand of friendship. For three days, harmony between the two tribes prevailed on the Takattokah council grounds. Outwardly, all the Cherokees appeared to be brothers—sharing the same campfires, the same blankets. But this harmonious state did not endure, for on the fourth or fifth day of the council Chief John Ross was requested by Western chiefs John Brown, John Looney, and John Rogers to render his views in writing concerning the future government of the now vastly expanded Cherokee Nation. Thereupon Chief Ross, on June 13, submitted the following written resolutions to his Western colleagues:

WHEREAS, the people of the Cherokee Nation East, having been captured and ejected from the land of their fathers by the strong arm of the military power of the United States Government, and forced to remove west of the river Mississippi:

And, WHEREAS, previous to the commencement of the emigration, measures were adopted in general council of the whole nation on the 31st of July and August 1st, 1838, wherein the sentiments, rights, and interests of the Cherokee people were fully expressed and asserted; and, WHEREAS, under those proceedings the removal took place, and the late emigrants arrived in this country and settled among those of their brethren (who had previously emigrated) . . . and, WHEREAS, the reunion of the people, and the adoption of a code of laws . . . are essential to the peace and welfare of the whole Nation . . . therefore,

Be it *resolved,* by the Committee and Council of the eastern and western Cherokees, in General Council assembled, that the three chiefs of the eastern and western Cherokees each, to-wit: John Ross, George Lowry [*sic*], and Edward Gunter, on the part of the Eastern Cherokees and John Brown, John Looney, and John Rogers, on the part of the Western Cherokees, are hereby authorized and required to associate with themselves three other persons, to be selected by them from their respective council or committee, and who shall form a select joint committee, for the purpose of revising and drafting a code of laws for the government of the Cherokee Nation, and they be and are hereby required to lay the same before the general council of the nation to be held at Takattokah on the ———— day of ————, 1839; and which, when approved, shall be immediately submitted to the people for their acceptance.

Be it further *Resolved,* that the respective laws and authorities of the Eastern and Western Cherokees shall continue to be exercised and enforced among themselves until repealed, and the new government which may be adopted, shall be organized and take effect.[4]

Upon receipt of Ross's resolutions, the Western chiefs huffily moved their people to another site on the council grounds and excluded Ross from their council. Sequoyah (George Guess) could possibly have influenced them to accept the resolutions, had it not been for leaders of the Treaty party who recommended their rejection. Thus, Ross's resolutions were not submitted to the people. Instead, John Brown, the first chief of the Western Cherokees, declared that, since the Eastern Cherokees had accepted the hospitality of the Western, union between the two had already been achieved, and that, from then on, the eighteen thousand Cherokees in the West were expected to live under Western Cherokee government.

Since Chief Brown had rendered his decision with finality and had, on June 20, dissolved the council, it seemed futile to John Ross to press the resolutions further. But Sequoyah, with the help of Reverend Jesse Bushyhead, managed to reassemble both factions before they dispersed, and gain their assent to attend a second council for the purpose of founding a new government. With this accomplished, the people—and not their chiefs—voted to adjourn.

On June 22—the day following the council's adjournment—the

---

[4] Resolutions of Eastern Cherokees, implementing a joint council for Eastern and Western Cherokees, dated June 13, 1839, in *ibid.;* see also Starr, *History of the Cherokee Indians,* 108f.

Cherokee Nation reverberated with the shocking assassinations of John Ridge, Old Major Ridge, and Elias Boudinot. Around daylight on June 22, John Ridge was pulled from his bed, dragged into the yard of his home on Honey Creek in the northeastern corner of the Nation, and ruthlessly stabbed to death by unidentified assassins in full view of his distraught wife and children. Major Ridge, at about ten o'clock of that same morning, was shot and killed also by unidentified persons, who fired at Ridge from a precipice overhanging the Arkansas road which he had chosen to take to Vineyard. Boudinot, on that morning, met his death at the hands of a trio of late Cherokee emigrants who urgently requested that he accompany them to the home of Dr. Worcester at Park Hill to obtain medical supplies for their families. Halfway between Boudinot's home and Worcester's the trio, after pinning Boudinot's arms behind him, vengefully slashed him to death with knives and tomahawks.

In a sense, these assassinations were reminiscent of Doublehead's execution by Major Ridge and two accomplices in 1808. Like the Ridges and Boudinot, Doublehead had participated in land cessions to the United States without the sanction of the entire nation, in violation of Cherokee law. Too, the Ridge-Boudinot murders paralleled in some respects the Creek murders of William McIntosh, Tustennugee, and Sam Hawkins, all three of whom had been executed by their people for making land cessions without the consent of the tribe. But the Creek and Cherokee murders differed in this one respect: the Creek murders were authorized by the tribal council, whereas the Cherokee murders, in 1839, were clandestinely planned and executed.

Chief Ross and the National Committee, having returned from the council at Takattokah, were, on June 22, involved with reports, muster rolls, correspondence with the war department, and Lewis Ross's bills for subsistence of emigrants en route west. Gathered at Chief Ross's home near Park Hill, council and committee members, conductors of the various detachments, and clerks of the Nation were overwhelmed with business attendant to the recent removal. But, when apprised of Elias Boudinot's murder, John Ross

225

pushed aside all other matters and dispatched a message to General Arbuckle at Fort Gibson:

> It has become my painful duty to report to you that I have just heard that Elias Boudinot is killed. Upon receiving intelligence of this unhappy occurrence I immediately requested my brother-in-law John G. Ross who accompanied by Mr. Lenoir and others repaired to the place for the purpose of ascertaining the facts with the view of reporting the same to you. They have returned with a message from Mrs. . . . Boudinot confirming the report with the advice . . . for me to leave home for safety, saying that Stand Watie had determined on raising a company of men for the purpose of coming forthwith to take my life. Why I am to be murdered without guilt of any crime I cannot conceive. Therefore with all due respect . . . I trust that you will deem it expedient forthwith to interpose and prevent the effusion of innocent blood by exercising your authority in order that an unbiased investigation might be had in the matter.[5]

Arbuckle's reply hinted that Ross, if not directly implicated in the crimes, was thought to be sheltering the murderers in his home near Park Hill:

> If this is the case, I must believe that you are not apprised of the fact; and if, on inquiry the report made to me on the subject is correct, the troops sent out will take charge of them if turned over and convey them in safety to this post.
> I hope you will avail yourself of the opportunity of the command to visit this Post, as I expect the Chiefs [Western] . . . will be here this evening, or early tomorrow morning.[6]

It is a matter of record that John Ross did not make the mistake of permitting himself to be callously bombarded by questions by the military at Fort Gibson, in the presence of the Western chiefs, concerning crimes committed in a nation whose business it was to apprehend and punish its own criminals. Stoically, Ross maintained

---

[5] June 22, 1839, in *ibid.*
[6] June 24, 1839, in *ibid.*

his dignity and remained in the Nation, attending to his duties. Ross politely answered questions put to him by officers from Fort Gibson who came to see him at Park Hill. But when questioned about the identity of the murderers, he always shook his head.

As can well be imagined, the impact of the Ridge-Boudinot murders was felt by both Indians and whites residing in settlements west of the Mississippi. General Arbuckle sent several companies of dragoons to patrol the Cherokees' boundaries. Oblivious to the fact that crimes committed by Cherokees in the Nation did not come under the jurisdiction of the United States—the murder of Major Ridge was an exception because of its being committed in Arkansas—United States investigators checked and rechecked this clue and that concerning the identity of the murderers. But clues led nowhere. Seemingly familiar with the Cherokee law initiated by Major Ridge and adopted by the Cherokee council a decade before, exacting the death penalty for unauthorized land cessions by members of the tribe, United States investigators still were unable to track down the criminals. And Arbuckle, again aroused by reports of an intended Cherokee massacre on the Arkansas line, urged the governors of Missouri and Arkansas to raise and equip a volunteer brigade to protect their frontiers. Through the military storekeeper at Fayetteville, Arkansas, Arbuckle himself issued a requisition of "132 muskets for Fort Gibson and for Fort Wayne [near the Missouri line] 100 muskets with bayonets, 100 cartridge boxes and belts, 100 bayonet scabbards and belts, 10,000 musket cartridges, and 10,000 flints to be supplied to the citizens of Arkansas."[7]

The furor created by the Ridge-Boudinot murders continued to sweep through the Indian Territory like a frenzied, wind-fanned prairie fire. But on July 1, as planned, around two thousand Cherokees assembled at the Illinois Camp Ground, a mile and a half north of Park Hill, to hasten the organization of a government that would weld Western and Eastern Cherokees into one body and thus provide for the establishment of courts, schools, and churches.

Noting the absence of the three Western chiefs, Sequoyah, one

---

[7] Grant Foreman, *The Five Civilized Tribes*, 302.

of the presidents of the conference, collaborated with John Ross in the composition of a special invitation to Brown, Looney, and Rogers asking them to assist in the closure of the unfortunate breech between the Western and Eastern Cherokees which, if not closed, could result in civil war. To the Western chiefs, Sequoyah touchingly directed these lines:

> We, the old settlers, are here in council with the late emigrants, and we want you to come up without delay, that we may talk matters over like friends and brothers. These people are here in great multitudes, and they are perfectly friendly towards us. They have said, over and over again, that they will be glad to see you, and we have full confidence that they will receive you with all friendship. There is no drinking here to disturb the peace, though there are upward of two thousand people on the ground. We send you these few lines as friends, and we want you to come on without delay, and bring as many of the old settlers as are with you; and we have no doubt but we can have all things amicably and satisfactorily settled.[8]

Sequoyah's efforts brought Chief John Looney into the Ross fold, but Chiefs Brown and Rogers stubbornly stayed away from the Illinois council. Joining the members of the Treaty party, Brown and Rogers arranged a council at Tahlonteskee to begin on July 22. When John Ross, after the adjournment of the conference at the Illinois Camp Ground, appeared at the Tahlonteskee council to explain to the Western chiefs that his convention, on July 12, 1839, had adopted an Act of Union "by which the two parties were declared 'one body politic', under the style and title of the Cherokee Nation," Ross and his colleagues were driven away by the Starrs and Bells, who were heavily armed.[9] Again the grim visage of disunity prevented Western and Eastern Cherokee leaders from becoming brothers. Having banished John Ross, the council at Tahlonteskee then furthered plans for meeting again in October for the purpose of electing new chiefs, passing and adopting resolutions

[8] *Ibid.*, 299.
[9] *Ibid.*

to expel from the Nation all white men sympathetic to John Ross, and increasing the number of light-horsemen to enforce laws of the Western government.

Of utmost significance to Ross's recently united West-East Cherokees was their assembly held at Tahlequah, their new capital, on September 6, 1839. Set like a jewel among gently rolling hills, Tahlequah, like the capital of New Echota, was as nearly in the center of the Nation as seemed feasible to Ross and other Cherokee leaders. Five miles to the north of Park Hill, Tahlequah was convenient both to Dr. Worcester's mission and print shop and to the home of Chief Ross. Ross, at this council, was unanimously elected principal chief of the Cherokee Nation, and David Vann, a Western Cherokee, was elected assistant or second chief.

A new constitution, based on the old, was formally adopted by the council, comprised now of both Eastern and Western Cherokees. Likewise, the benches of the supreme, circuit, and district courts were filled by both Western and Eastern Cherokee judges, though the Western were in the majority. So numerous were the items on its agenda that the Tahlequah council continued in session for almost a month. Before adjourning, council members voted to send a delegation headed by John Ross to Washington to protest the New Echota treaty; to request that it be superseded by a new and better one; to demand payments withheld by the government amounting to $800,000 for spoliation claims; and to explain, as best they could, the circumstances surrounding the unfortunate deaths of the three leaders of the Treaty party.

Following adjournment of the council on October 10, John Ross and William Shorey Coodey, Ross's slim, handsome, young nephew who had written the Act of Union adopted the preceding July, left for Washington. But delegates Joseph Lynch, Elijah Hicks, Edward Gunter, Archibald Campbell, and Looney Price remained in the Nation for another month. They were needed there because Arbuckle's dragoons, bent on apprehending the murderers of Boudinot and the Ridges, were thundering through the countryside questioning all Cherokee officials. Adding to the chaos in the Nation were Tom, Ellis, and Bean Starr. Termed by their enemies "house burners," "horse stealers," and "murderers," this band of Western Cherokee outlaws were further endangering the reputation of the proud Nation, whose prestige, because of the recent murders, was in eclipse, in adjacent Indian Territory. To reinstate the Cherokees with the Creeks, John Ross and others in his party sent lengthy explanations of their troubles to Creek chiefs.

Upon their arrival in Washington in 1840, John Ross and William Shorey Coodey made the unpleasant discovery that Eastern Cherokee prestige was practically nonexistent there. Both President Van Buren and his Secretary of War, Joel R. Poinsett, refused to recognize Ross and Coodey as representatives of the Cherokee Nation, having been apprised by Arbuckle before their arrival that "If he [Ross] had not been prepared to start to Washington on business of much interest as it was understood, to the late emigrants, I would have caused him to be arrested and placed in confinement until the pleasure of the Government was known."[10]

Arbuckle's statement to the Secretary of War that the Western government—headed, as of October 10, 1839, by John Rogers, first chief, John Smith, second, and Dutch, third—was the only lawful government in the Cherokee Nation further discredited Ross and Coodey, even though Governor Montfort Stokes, the Cherokee agent, had previously intervened in their behalf. In a letter to Poinsett, prior to Ross and Coodey's arrival, Stokes had attested to the upright character of Ross and advocated that he be recognized as the principal chief of a majority which represented over four-fifths of the total population of the Nation. Stokes also absolved Ross from having any part in the Ridge-Boudinot murders, asserting that he had known Ross for twenty-five years and knew him to be incapable of either planning or participating in the crimes attributed to him by his enemies.

But Stokes's word against Arbuckle's did not impress the President or the Secretary of War and only resulted in Stokes's suspension from office. Ross and Coodey continued to be ignored by government officials, who sharply censured the decree adopted by the Ross

---

[10] *Ibid.*, 306.

council at the Illinois Camp Ground in July, 1839—the decree which required all signers of the New Echota treaty to appear before the council and answer for their traitorous conduct, under penalty of outlawry. This decree was declared by Van Buren and Poinsett to be not only violent and extreme but to be the main cause of division between the Eastern and Western tribes.

In contrast to the treatment accorded Ross and Coodey in Washington was the warm reception tendered Western delegates Stand Watie, John Bell, and William Rogers by the President and officials of the War Department.

Decked out in gaudy green and mulberry frocked coats, "Cassimere" pantaloons, velvet vests, and handsome beaver cloaks, the three Indians stayed at the Globe Hotel in Washington, where they ran up a sizeable bill which they, personally, did not pay. But Watie paid for some of his and Bell's sartorial equipment with a draft on Glasgow and Harrison. And, according to Grant Foreman, the eminent historian: "Half a dozen bills for the clothing purchased by them were filed with the commissioner by Stand Watie with the view to being reimbursed."

Throughout the first and second sessions of the Twenty-sixth Congress, the status of Ross and the delegation representing the majority did not change, even though Stokes reported to the War Department that on January 15, 1840, around 1,700 Cherokees representing the majority had (in Ross's absence) met at Tahlequah and voted to rescind the decree of outlawry that had been enacted against signers of the New Echota treaty at the Ross council.

Instead, the War Department approved the action of the Old Settlers and the New Echota treaty faction of the Nation who, at a council held at Fort Gibson in February, 1840, adopted "a resolution reported by a special committee, declaring that they were a sovereign and independent people; that John Ross and his partisans would not be permitted to participate in their government except by conquest or by their consent; and that they had no intention of yielding to Ross." The conduct of Ross and his followers was declared by the council at Fort Gibson to be an "unprecedented act of usurpation—we will never acknowledge his government . . . [for]

the only legitimate government of this nation is the one handed down to us by the original settlers of the Cherokee Nation West, and we will to the utmost of our power and ability uphold and defend the same."[11]

The following letter received by Ross in Washington in 1840 from his son James gave Ross the bleak news from home:

> My Dear Father
> Sir
>
> ... The troops has [*sic*] been riding through the country from the time you left the nation untill [*sic*] about a week or two back. They wanted to arrest those murderers as they call them. They have gained nothing by their hunting.
>
> ... There has been more murdering in the nation since you left. The great man Archillah Smith [a signer of the New Echota Treaty] has killed John McIntosh. He stabbed him with a knife. He died instantly after it was done. This was done at Peter Miller's several weeks back. The officers of the Nation has [*sic*] not done anything with him as yet but it will not be long before they will have him arrested and be brought to trial. David Miller has also killed one John Phillips some place near the mouth of the Illinois. He was taken by Ellis Phillips and some few men. I have understood that they killed him without having any trial whatever.[12]

In 1840 a House Committee on Indian Affairs sided with the Ross party. And the resultant majority report, stemming as it did from the committee's thorough examination of both Cherokee and United States official records, was so unflattering to the Chief Executive and the War Department that the House would not permit it to be filed. However, it was released to the press by John Bell, a committee member who had long been a friend of John Ross and the eastern Cherokees.

Charging Van Buren and the War Department with unjustifiable interference in the affairs of the Cherokees, and thereby contributing to the state of unrest, dissension, and anarchy in the Nation, the

---

11 *Ibid.*, 304n., 307f.
12 In Ross Papers, *loc. cit.*

committee held that "interference by the Executive in the affairs of the Cherokee Indians by prescribing any particular form of government or interdicting any system of laws already adopted by the majority, was unconstitutional . . . which, if persisted in, would probably lead to disorder and war."

The President was also severely criticized by the committee for withholding from the majority (or Ross party) the sum of $800,000 due them "on their arrival in the West to pay for spoliation and abandoned improvements . . . until such time as they should agree to abandon the government recently set up by them and acknowledge the rule of the Old Settlers as the only valid government in the Cherokee Nation." Crediting General Arbuckle and the small body of recalcitrant Treaty and Old Settler factions with advocating this plan to Van Buren, the House committee declared that they were "reluctantly compelled to believe, that upon no better or higher suggestions than the hope of operating upon the necessities and avarice of the Indians has the Executive of the United States been influenced in withholding the large sums of money long since due by treaty."[13]

But even after Bell's suppressed report was published, both the President and the War Dapartment continued to snub the government of the majority and to recognize only that of the minority. And it was when he was told of the increase of crimes in the Cherokee Nation that the Chief Executive authorized the War Department to suspend Stokes, the Cherokee agent, then turn the discipline of the Nation over to Arbuckle and the military.

John Howard Payne, who accompanied Ross to the Nation after the latter's lengthy and futile sojourn in Washington in 1840, reported with his usual astuteness the proceedings of the Cherokee National Council, which, in October, 1840, held its first session under the new constitution at Tahlequah:

> In the last week of October the people had all assembled, and the message of their Chief, after being presented to the Committee . . .

[13] Grant Foreman, *The Five Civilized Tribes*, 312.

and the Council . . . was ordered to be produced before them. John Ross accordingly appeared at a sort of rustic forum set up in the open square, with the written message in his hand. . . .

The message was long, but perfectly temperate throughout. It commended the people for having shown so much moderation under their trials, and for having displayed their unanimity in a manner so unquestionable, as must entirely destroy the misconception under which the United States continue to withhold their dues. The Chief explained that the Delegation to Washington had failed . . . because the Government there had been taught to consider the Cherokee nation as disunited; but he exhorted them not to lose patience, for the truth concerning them must speedily be known. . . . He urged their attention to the subject of education, for which the Nation had ample funds in the hands of the President that had never been brought into use, although complaints arose on every side of the want of schools. He referred to the numerous subjects which still call loudly for adjustment with the United States; and among them, the unsettled claim for the balance of the Emigration expense, that so many of the people are interested in so deeply. He exhorted them . . . to continue more scrupulously observant than ever of all their treaty obligations, as the surest means of securing a punctilious regard for their own rights in return. He reminded the people, incidentally, that he himself was . . . interested in the Emigration claim in common with them—having enrolled himself, like the rest; and that he and his family had made the journey under a conductor of his own appointment, and without being in any way a sharer in the emoluments. . . .

The multitude appeared highly pleased with the Principal Chief's address. It was followed by speeches among them, and the whole wound up with a series of resolutions which were adopted unanimously and and enthusiastically.[14]

After William Henry Harrison's brief incumbency, John Tyler became President of the United States on April 4, 1841. John Payne was then employed by the War Department to report further on his stay amongst the Cherokees West. Needless to say, the memorandum prepared by Payne favored the majority. And Tyler, too, as-

[14] *Ibid.,* 314ff.

sured the majority of his support. Approached by Ross and delegates in 1841, Tyler gave them the following guarantee:

> . . . you may assure your people that, so far as I have any power or influence . . . not justice merely shall be done them, but . . . a liberal and generous . . . policy shall be adopted toward them. Upon the ratification of the treaty contemplated, which shall give to the Cherokee Nation full indemnity for all wrongs . . . they may have suffered, establish . . . upon a permanent basis the political relations between them and the United States, guaranty their lands in absolute fee simple, and prescribe specific rules in reference to subjects of the most interesting character, a new sun will have dawned upon them.[15]

But the "new sun" calculated by President Tyler to dawn upon the Cherokee Nation hid behind dark clouds of crime and controversy until 1846—five years from the date Tyler wrote the above communiqué. Between 1841–46, certain members of the tribe reverted to the barbarism of the ancients. When a member of a family or clan met death at the hands of an enemy, the latter was finished off by relatives of the deceased before he could be brought to trial. Thirty-three such murders were reported over a period of nine months in the Cherokee Nation, and drunkenness increased accordingly. Despite the efforts made by law-abiding Cherokees to curb this disorder, crime appeared to flourish on controversy and disunion, a disunion which perilously verged on civil war.

On September 1, 1845, eleven of the Old Settlers and forty-three members of the Treaty party decided to look for homes in Texas, where many of their friends and relatives then lived. Other members of the minority appealed to the United States Congress to divide the Nation and to treat each division as it would a tribe that had no connection whatsoever with the other. So forceful was the argument of this minority that it impelled President James Knox Polk (following the recommendation of the Commissioner of Indian Affairs) to ask Congress on April 13, 1846, to enact legislation

---

[15] Oliver Knight, "History of the Cherokees," *The Chronicles of Oklahoma*, Vol. XXXIV, 180.

providing for the division of the Cherokee Nation and permitting Cherokees who so desired to settle in Texas or elsewhere. And this recommendation by President Polk resulted in the House Committee on Indian Affairs' introducing a bill in the House authorizing division of the Cherokee Nation—one area of the Nation to be occupied by the minority, composed of Western Cherokees (or Old Settlers) and members of the Treaty party; and the other by the majority, who could not be induced by the War Department to abandon either their government or John Ross, their principal chief.

As could be expected, John Ross opposed these propositions. Employing all the political strategy at his command, Ross brought about the defeat of legislation implementing division of the Nation. There followed then in the wake of this defeat a full-dress investigation of the Cherokee controversy by a government commission composed of Colonel Roger Jones, adjutant general of the United States Army, Lieutenant Colonel R. B. Mason of the United States dragoons, and Governor Pierce M. Butler, Stokes's successor.

George Lowrey, acting principal chief of the majority during Ross's absence in Washington, is given credit for rendering assistance to the commission when it met at Fort Gibson to untangle the complex and accumulative controversy. Perhaps without Lowrey the commission's report would not have resulted so soon in the treaty which united the Cherokees. For George Lowrey had the enviable ability of commanding the respect of even his enemies. Noted for his truthfulness, Lowrey's testimony was of tremendous value to the commissioners, who had heard many conflicting versions of the Cherokee controversy prior to their arrival at Fort Gibson.

The resultant treaty, signed on August 6, 1846, in Washington, decreed that the lands in the Cherokee Nation were for the use and occupancy of all the Cherokees; provided for the adjudication of all Cherokee claims as well as the adjustment of other unsettled matters; extended amnesty to fugitives accused of minor and major crimes, provided they returned to the Nation by December 1, 1846; provided for the protection by law of all the inhabitants in the Nation; guaranteed every Cherokee a trial by jury; and promised to reimburse the Nation for sums unfairly deducted by the United

States government from the $5,000,000 owed to the Cherokees in payment for Eastern lands. And, to smooth the ruffled feathers of members of the Treaty party, the Treaty of 1846 stipulated that members of the latter party were to receive $115,000 for all their losses, including the $5,000 to be paid to each of the heirs of the Ridges and Boudinot.

All three factions—the Treaty party, the Westerners, or Old Settlers, and the Eastern people—were represented in Washington at the signing of this tremendously important treaty. And rumor has it that, after the treaty was signed, Stand Watie and John Ross shook hands.

CHAPTER XII

Progress

AFTER THE TREATY OF 1846 the Cherokee Nation enjoyed a golden era of prosperity and progress unsurpassed by its territorial neighbors. In the era that followed the treaty, education, building projects (both private and public), churches and missions, improvement societies, agriculture, domestic arts, and animal husbandry thrived in the Nation. And Tahlequah, the Cherokee capital, together with Park Hill became to the Indian Territory what Boston became to New England at this same date—a center of culture and industry, and a symbol of progress. "The Cherokee have got sense just like the whites, but the Creeks have no sense" was Opothleyohola's comment when the Cherokees' phenomenal advancement, presenting a striking contrast to the lethargy of the broken-spirited Creek emigrants, came to the notice of this chief of the upper Creeks who lived on the Arkansas.[1]

However, Cherokee progress began even before the Treaty of 1846 was signed—the intertribal meeting, or Grand Council, at Tahlequah in 1843 furnishing a notable example. Invited by Chief John Ross, delegates from twenty-one tribes living in or adjacent to the Indian Territory convened in the large council shed in the

---

[1] Ethan Allen Hitchcock, *A Traveler in Indian Territory*, 150.

public square at Tahlequah, in June, 1843, to settle intertribal differences. Termed by Indian leaders "the most important Indian council ever held on the American continent," the Grand Council voted to end the devastating border wars between Indian Territory tribes and to settle intertribal differences by law instead of by bloodshed. As summarized by William P. Ross, the Grand Council's main objective was "to perpetuate peace between tribes; and to encourage agriculture, education; and all useful arts that would in the future promote the comforts of women and children."[2]

Hannah Worcester, Samuel Worcester's third daughter, was only a child when the Grand Council met in 1843. But, when grown, she vividly recalled the dress and behavior of Indian delegates who thronged the large council shed at Tahlequah and for a month smoked, meditated, and eloquently orated. Hannah recalled that the Iowa Indians had strung their garments with little bells that tinkled merrily when they walked.

All manner of Indian dress and behavior were exhibited by the delegates, many of whom were the wild Plains Indians who had been greatly feared by the Five Civilized Tribes who had emigrated west. At the Grand Council, the Plains Indians wore buckskin leggings, robes, and moccasins and carried ornately decorated trade hatchets. The Osages' heads, shaved except for a crested patch on the crown, were as usual ornamented with feathers, and they wore only breechcloths and blankets as had their forebears.

In contrast, the dress of the Cherokees and other emigrants from east of the Mississippi was a mixture of Indian and white attire. Some wore top hats and black morning coats. Others had turbans wound round their heads and wore bright calico Indian hunting shirts which contrasted oddly with their white man's breeches or pantaloons that, in many instances, were quite shabby and threadbare.

Acting as master of ceremonies at the Grand Council, Cherokee leader George Lowrey explained the Indian language of wampum, pipe, and tobacco to the delegates. Presumably Lowrey, as was his

<hr />

[2] Ross, ed., *The Life and Times of Honorable William P. Ross.*

wont at public gatherings, twisted his silk handkerchief around first one hand, then the other, when he was not using it to mop his brow. In translating an alien tongue into Cherokee, Lowrey had the habit of pausing when he could not make out a passage. Twisting his handkerchief, Lowrey would cogitate on the spoken sentence, then curtly exclaim: "Can't go it!" Thereupon, the speaker would be compelled to repeat the sentence until its meaning became perfectly clear to Lowrey, who never passed on to an audience a translation that he did not completely understand.

Hannah Worcester remembered that Chief John Ross spoke to the Grand Council in English and that Ross's speech was translated first into Cherokee, then into Creek, and on and on until it had been translated into eleven languages for the benefit of all the tribal representatives.

In 1843 the problems confronting the Grand Council were numerous and complex; but, because of their superior statesmanship and diplomacy, the delegates settled their differences within a thirty-day period. Thereafter, major intertribal conflicts became practically nonexistent in the Indian Territory. Minor disagreements were settled by laws enacted by the Grand Council. Thus assured of peace, the majority of Cherokees could focus their undivided attention for the next sixteen years on the advancement of the Nation—public education being accorded first place on the agenda.[3]

Prior to 1841, all of the schools in the Nation were either private-subscription schools or mission schools sponsored by religious organizations. Prominent mission schools (after removal) in the Nation were Baptist Mission, north of present-day Westville, Oklahoma; New Springplace, a Moravian mission built on, or near, the site of today's Oaks, Oklahoma; Dwight Mission, near the present Marble City, Oklahoma; and Dr. Worcester's Mission at Park Hill. In connection with the Park Hill Mission, Dr. Worcester operated a printing shop that, between July 18, 1845, and August 18, 1846, printed "276,000 pages of Cherokee school books and tracts; 386,-

---

[3] The account of the Grand Council was drawn from the following sources: Carolyn Thomas Foreman, *Park Hill*, 93; Grant Foreman, *The Five Civilized Tribes*, 367; and Ross, ed., *The Life and Times of Honorable William P. Ross.*

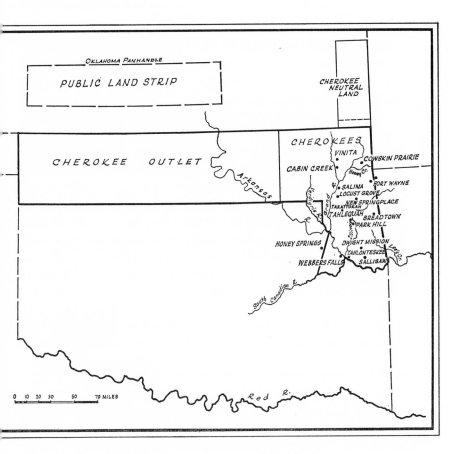

The new home of the Cherokees, west of the Mississippi.

000 in Choctaw and 18,000 in Creek; the largest was a Choctaw spelling book of 108 pages."[4]

By act of council on November 16, 1841, a superintendent of education and eleven public schools were provided for, marking another milestone in Cherokee progress. Two years later, in 1843, seven additional public schools were ordered built by act of council, bringing the total of public schools to eighteen. Appropriately, in 1841, the Reverend Stephen Foreman became the first superintendent of education in the Nation. He was well fitted for the office, having graduated with honors from an Eastern college.

Since many Cherokee children had been orphaned by the removal, the Cherokee council, in 1848, voted an appropriation of $600 for the education of orphans. The next year, appropriations for all elementary public schools were considerably increased by act of council, a sum of thirty dollars being provided for the maintenance of each orphan enrolled in a public school. That same year a Board of Education was created by act of council. The new Board was empowered to hire and dismiss public-school teachers; to supervise the erection of new hewn-log school buildings that were to have floors, windows, and the latest equipment; and to visit schools regularly.

Proud of their public-school system, which they knew to be superior to that of the whites in near-by Arkansas and Missouri, the Cherokees dreamed of having seminaries or high schools; and, by 1851, the dream became a reality. In 1846 the National Council voted appropriations for two seminaries, one for males and the other for females desirous of a higher education. As decreed by act of council, half of the cost of building the two seminaries was to be paid by the Nation, and the other half was to come from the school fund (provided for by treaty in 1835) dispensed by the United States government. Both seminaries were to be supported after completion, as were all the elementary public schools, by the interest on money invested by the Nation in United States registered stocks derived from the sale of Cherokee lands by the federal government. Only the interest from Cherokee investments was used by the Na-

[4] Grant Foreman, *The Five Civilized Tribes*, 367.

tion for education. The Nation took great pride in the fact that the United States government, outside of paying interest on the money it borrowed from the Nation, rendered no support to Cherokee public schools.

When built, the Cherokee Male and Female Seminaries were conceded to be the handsomest and the most pretentious buildings in the Indian Territory or even in the adjacent state of Arkansas. Costing $60,000 each, the seminaries were located in wooded sections within a mile or so of each other. The Male Seminary was three miles northwest of Park Hill, and the Female, about a mile north.

These magnificent public buildings of brick and stone had massive brick columns on three sides and, according to Cherokee historian Emmet Starr, they were each "one hundred eighty-five feet long, one hundred nine feet wide, part two stories and part three stories in height." The bricks used in both seminaries were burned in a kiln on the edge of Park Hill.[5]

Governed by a board of five directors, of which Chief Ross was the ex-officio president, the two seminaries opened their doors to students in 1851. The Cherokee Male Seminary opened on May 6, and the Female, on May 7. The curriculum of the Female Seminary, at Chief Ross's request, was outlined by Miss Mary Chapin, the principal of Mount Holyoke Female Seminary (now College), at South Hadley, Massachusetts. Its second- and third-year students were required to study such subjects as Latin, algebra, botany, vocal music, geography, grammar, and arithmetic. Miss Chapin also selected the faculty of the school. Miss Ellen Whitmore became the first principal of the Female Seminary, and Miss Sarah Worcester (the tall, comely daughter of Dr. Samuel Worcester), Miss Whitmore's assistant. Both of these women were former students at Mount Holyoke.

Upon arriving at her post, Miss Whitmore was scared half out of her wits by the prank of two students, who knocked on her door

---

[5] Information on Cherokee education between 1841–59 is from: Starr, *History of the Cherokee Indians*, 225–46; Ross, ed., *The Life and Times of Honorable William P. Ross*, 74, 76; and Grant Foreman, *The Five Civilized Tribes*, 360, 367, 393, 395, 401, 414.

late one night painted and befeathered like the Plains Indians. However, toward the end of the first year Miss Whitmore, a native of Marlboro, Massachusetts, wrote to Miss Chapin that she liked her work and surroundings:

> The situation is, I think a desirable one in every respect. The salary is large, being eight hundred dollars a year—the school is pleasant—the country delightful—the society of the neighborhood of a superior order, and the religious privileges *good*. . . . Mr. Ross is my constant friend and support—I can go to him at any time and feel sure of his sympathy and aid.

Desirous of obtaining a successor because of her own approaching marriage, Miss Whitmore further reported to Miss Chapin that Chief Ross "is very anxious with regard to my successor. He desires that this seminary should become as much like Holyoke as possible, and hopes that you will send just the right one."[6]

From the pen of Hannah Worcester came this charming description of ceremonies held at the Female Seminary on May 7, to commemorate its opening:

> . . . the large hall and parlor were beautifully decorated, and fragrant with perfume from great bunches of lovely pink azalea or bush honeysuckle. The military band from Fort Gibson was on hand that day, through the courtesy of General Belknap, Post commander at that time. The exercises of the day included . . . the crowning of a May Queen. . . . It was a beautiful ceremony; distant music was heard . . . a troop of young ladies appeared, all in lovely light dresses, escorting their Queen, singing as they marched and gathered around the throne (a bower of vines and flowers) and the Maid of Honor placed the crown (of lovely roses) on her head. In the afternoon when the exercises in the house were over, the band stationed themselves out in the blackjack woods back of the building, and the company, gentlemen and ladies in pairs, promenaded round and round to the music of the band.[7]

---

[6] *The Journal of Ellen Whitmore* (ed. by Lola Garrett Bowers and Kathleen Garrett), 23; Carolyn Thomas Foreman, *Park Hill*, 83.
[7] Carolyn Thomas Foreman, *Park Hill*, 82.

The two seminaries contributed vastly to the reputation which Park Hill enjoyed of being "the Athens of the Cherokee Nation" between 1851–57. After the schools were opened in 1851, two elegant brick churches, a Presbyterian and a Methodist, were built at Park Hill. Resembling a New England meetinghouse, the Presbyterian Church was "crowned with a spire fourteen feet high in which hung a bell with the inscription, 'Park Hill, Cherokee Nation, Reverend S. A. Worcester, Missionary. Holiness unto the Lord.' "[8] The bell had been contributed by George Murrell, Chief Ross's nephew-in-law, whose wealth enabled him to maintain, in addition to his mansion in the Nation called "Hunter's Home," a large plantation in Louisiana to which he and his family repaired for a part of each year.

Another contributor to the Presbyterian Church (and later to the new Methodist one) at Park Hill was Chief John Ross. Other well-to-do Cherokee parishioners of these fashionable churches, too, were generous with contributions.

Tahlequah, as well as Park Hill, profited by the peace and prosperity in the Nation between 1843–59. Incorporated as a town in 1844, Tahlequah soon afterward was transformed from a sleepy hamlet, awake only when the council met, into a bustling year-round capital. Streets were laid out, lots sold, and houses built by Cherokees who realized the commercial and residential possibilities of the town. Catching the spirit of growth, the National Council, in 1844, voted an appropriation of $2,775 to pay James Price, a white man, to erect new quarters south of the Square for the Supreme Court. The brick, two-storied Supreme Court building, when completed, inspirited other innovations. By act of council in 1848, for example, the old headquarters of the committee, the council, and Chief Ross in the Square were torn down and replaced by substantial hewn-log structures. Too, in 1848, Mrs. Susan Taylor hired Mormon artisans, who tarried at Tahlequah on their way west, to build a two-storied brick hotel for the accommodation of her paying guests.

In 1849, Tahlequah merchants, wheelwrights, and blacksmiths

---

[8] *Ibid.,* 99.

were kept busy serving those who passed through the town en route to California gold fields. The forty-niners needed boots, saddles, picks, axes, clothing, shoes for their horses, wheels for their wagons —everything. Succumbing to the gold fever, a number of Cherokees joined the forty-niners when they left. But less adventurous Cherokees opened stores at Tahlequah that catered thereafter to the gold-rush trade.

By 1851, Tahlequah had eight stores, two dentists, and a new attorney at law. The year following, the Council donated land to the Masons on which to erect a two-storied frame building. After its completion, the Masons used the building's second floor, and other religious and civic organizations, its lower. Meetings of the Sons of Temperance were held in the Masonic Building until the outbreak of the Civil War. Also, by act of council in 1852, provision was made for the erection of a national jail.[9]

Implementing Cherokee progress was the establishment of *The Cherokee Advocate* at Tahlequah in 1844. The *Advocate* was the second newspaper to be owned by the Nation and the first to be launched after removal. On September 26, 1844, the first issue of the *Advocate* heralded the important news of the day in both Cherokee and English—as had the old *Phoenix*. But oddly enough, young William P. Ross, its editor, did not publish a news story that would have greatly interested his readers. This neglected item of news was no less than the marriage of Chief John Ross to Mary Bryan Stapler, a Quaker from Wilmington, Delaware. The editor of the *Advocate* was well aware of his chieftain uncle's wedding plans but obviously preferred to let *The New York Tribune* print the story of the nuptials:

> . . . John Ross, the celebrated Cherokee Chief, was married in the President's parlor of this Hotel [Hartwell's Washington House in Philadelphia] last night [September 2, 1844] to Miss Mary B. Stapler of Wilmington, Delaware. He is about 55, and she is only 18 years of

[9] The account of building projects at Tahlequah (1843–52) is based on the following: Grant Foreman, *The Five Civilized Tribes*, 370, 400, 406; and T. L. Ballenger, *Around Tahlequah Council Fires*, 103f.

age; she is a very beautiful girl and highly accomplished. . . . Her father was formerly a highly respected Quaker merchant of this city.

She was given away by her brother and attended by her sister and niece of John Ross as bridesmaids. He had collected several of his daughters and nephews from boarding schools, etc. in New Jersey to be present at the wedding; and after the ceremony a family party of 20 of the Ross's (all half-breed Indians) sat down to a most sumptuous banquet. . . . Ross is considered to be worth half a million dollars. He proposes to sojourn with his beautiful bride at this excellent hotel for a short time; after which he goes straight to his wild home in the South Western prairies.[10]

Ironically, the "wild home in the South Western prairies" to which Chief Ross brought his young bride was "Rose Cottage," a new two-storied white house commanding a fine view of the countryside in the Park Hill area. Roses bordered its mile-and-a-half-long driveway and clambered happily over its fences. Destined to become a show place rivaling Hunter's Home a mile or so distant, Rose Cottage in time had numerous outbuildings, an orchard planted with one thousand apple trees, and stables enough for Ross's horses and those of his guests. Slaves worked the fields and kept Rose Cottage in shipshape, for Ross and his bride were always entertaining guests—Indian agents; the post commander at Fort Gibson; numerous relatives; missionaries; and "the people," who were given a hearty welcome by Ross at his home, and who slept on the floor of the drawing room or wherever they could spread blankets.

The cost of maintaining Rose Cottage frequently prompted Chief Ross's enemies to surmise that he had misappropriated Cherokee funds in order to live in the fine style of a Southern planter. But according to Major Ethan Allen Hitchcock, a government investigator, John Ross did not deserve this criticism. "After much attentive observation," Major Hitchcock reported on December 21, 1841, to Secretary of War J. C. Spencer, "I am of the opinion that John Ross is an honest man and a patriot laboring for the good of his people."[11]

[10] Carolyn Thomas Foreman, *Park Hill*, 29.
[11] Hitchcock, *A Traveler in Indian Territory*, 234.

Possibly Ross's enemies—and they were legion—did not take into account the fact that he derived a portion of his income from the store which he had purchased from R. J. Meigs at Park Hill in 1849, or that the rosewood and mahogany and silver at Rose Cottage had been contributed by his second wife. Too, he supplemented his salary from the Nation with an income from farming and merchandising ventures.

Admittedly, Chief Ross lived on a lavish scale at Rose Cottage, especially after his marriage in 1844. Even so, the elaborate entertainments at Rose Cottage did not surpass the collations given at Hunter's Home by the Murrells. The Murrell's guests sat in handsome red plush chairs and drank from heavy silver goblets that were appropriately engraved with the initial *M*. Waited on by Murrell slaves at table, dinner guests sampled chicken in paste, beef alamode, pickled walnuts, and Maryland biscuits. For dessert, they could have had their choice of floating islands, macaroons, or dumplings (made Indian style) that floated in a sea of delicious blueberry or blackberry juice.

A gracious hostess, Mrs. Murrell, the daughter of Lewis Ross, had herself written a cookbook that was published in Maryland in 1846. In it were reflected both white and Indian cultures, for, wedged in between recipes for fashionable American and French dishes, were recipes for making Indian bread from beans or pumpkins, or for treating illnesses with herbs and roots in the manner of the ancients.[12]

The Rosses and the Murrells contributed equally to the lavish social life at Park Hill. But the seminaries, too, were contributors. Prior to the closing of the seminaries in 1856, there were many elegant weddings, concerts, and collations at the Female Seminary. These social events were duly recorded in *Cherokee Rosebuds*, a school publication whose two youthful editors referred to themselves as "co-editresses." In one of the first issues of *Cherokee Rosebuds*, the "co-editresses" wrote the following editorial on Park Hill:

---

[12] The account of the Murrells' mode of entertaining is based on *Mrs. Murrell's Cook Book*, and on recent interviews with Mrs. Marguerite Clay Ross, curator of the Murrell Mansion, Tahlequah. Mrs. Ross has assembled many interesting new facts about the Murrells and their possessions.

... Instead of rudely constructed wigwams of our forefathers which stood there not more than half a century ago, elegant white buildings are seen. Everything around denotes taste, refinement, and progress of civilization among our people; well may they vie with the long enlightened inhabitants of the east.[13]

An event that never failed to impress the young ladies was the arrival of Chief Ross and his beautifully gowned young wife at the seminary for chapel services. Chief Ross's victoria, with a liveried driver and a black boy in uniform perched on the box, was a splendid and romantic sight for a number of the young ladies who were accustomed to riding in ox-drawn wagons.

But all was not elegance, frivolity, and pomp at Park Hill. At his print shop Dr. Worcester laboriously supervised the printing (in addition to hymn books, almanacs, and translations of the Bible) of hundreds of temperance banners. Children who belonged to "The Cold Water Army" would carry them in the parade around the Square at Tahlequah when the National Cherokee Temperance Society held its meeting.

Hannah Worcester later recalled the fight of the Cherokee leaders and the missionaries against the intemperance that threatened to ruin the Nation:

My father, Dr. Worcester, wrote the songs for the Cherokee Cold Water Army and taught the boys and girls how to sing and march to them; he spent hours and days making for them banners of different devices. Many happy days were spent preparing for and attending the meetings. We sang "Come and Join Our Temperance Army", "Water, Sweet Cold Water", etc. The annual meeting of the Cold Water Army was held at Tahlequah. Some of us had to ride the five miles to Park Hill in the slow clumsy ox-wagon, with the boxes and baskets of provisions for the dinner; while the more fortunate ones went in a four-mule wagon sent through the kindness of . . . Mr. George Murrell, with a Negro driver, to carry thirty or forty children gathered in from the neighborhood.[14]

[13] Carolyn Thomas Foreman, *Park Hill*, 98.
[14] Grant Foreman, *The Five Civilized Tribes*, 387.

Temperance meetings were held all over the Cherokee Nation in the era preceding the Civil War. Hymns, sermons, prayers, and a bountiful repast were features of the large temperance gatherings in the Going Snake, Flint, and Sequoyah districts; since these districts were accessible to Arkansas and Missouri whisky peddlers, they needed the meetings more than some of the other areas.

Mass meetings of Cherokees were held at Tahlequah to protest the continuance of Fort Gibson, for the region around the post was found to be a hotbed of vice and a rendezvous for whisky peddlers. Chief Ross and the Cherokee council petitioned the United States government to do away with the post and to allow the land it was on to be cleaned up and occupied by the Cherokees. In 1857, Fort Gibson was closed—much to the relief of Chief Ross and the National Cherokee Temperance Society.

Agricultural organizations flourished during the reign of progress following the Treaty of 1846. Designed to improve farming methods and to impart knowledge, the Cherokee Agricultural Society encouraged farmers to plant corn instead of cotton. The Society also advocated the planting of orchards, since apples, plums, pears, and peaches did well in Western Cherokee soil. Strawberries, blackberries, grapes, and garden truck were recommended to farmers.

The Cherokee Agricultural Society, working with the Cherokee agent, also encouraged domestic activities among the women. Prizes were awarded for the best pieces of homespun cloth, coverlets, belts, and socks. George Butler, the Cherokee agent, rendered this report to the Commissioner of Indian Affairs in 1853:

> Many of the Cherokee women are neat and industrious housewives, and have acquired many of the finer accomplishments of the whites. Some of them are accomplished needle women; their taste and skill in embroidery may be seen at the Crystal Palace in New York, where has been sent for exhibition a full Indian suit of dressed buckskin beautifully embroidered with silk. This beautiful piece of work was designed and executed by the ladies in the family of Mr. J. M. Payne. The art of manufacturing cloth, both wool and cotton, is carried on to a considerable extent in some families. Some specimens I have seen from

the looms of Mrs. W. A. Adair would hold strong competition for prizes at any of the agricultural fairs of the States.[15]

In 1856, Cherokee financiers were worried about the mounting national debt. The new superintendent of education fumed about the number of schools in the Nation. There were twenty-one elementary schools in operation, and no more were needed, he sternly asserted. He believed that Cherokee youths should be encouraged to till the soil and raise livestock instead of going east to study at medical and law schools, as many of them were doing. The superintendent was possibly concerned—as were Cherokee financiers—over the enforced closing of the seminaries in the fall of 1856 because of the Nation's inability to support them.

Chief Ross, however, remained placid and optimistic. At the meeting of the National Council at Tahlequah in October, 1857, Ross optimistically summed up the progress made by his people in a little over a decade:

> I visited in person during the past summer, the different districts to inform myself of the general condition of the country. The evidence of progress by the Cherokee people furnished by the tour was of the most cheering kind, and contrasts favorably with their condition fifty years ago.
>
> Well cultivated farms, which have yielded abundant crops of grain, and thus affording a full supply for the wants of the people; well filled public schools, large and orderly assemblies, and quiet neighborhoods, which were seen in all the districts, showed marked improvement, and furnish a sure indication of the susceptibility of all classes among the Cherokee people for thorough civilization. To accomplish this work, upon which depends such great interests, it becomes the duty of the National Council to sustain and strengthen our institutions within our own limits, and to guard against every untoward encroachment.
>
> The surest safeguard of the Nation must be found in the respect and confidence of the people; and these can be secured only by its affording that protection to life and property for which it is instituted. . . . Years of trial and anxiety, of danger and struggle, have alone maintained the

15 *Ibid.*, 422.

existence of the Cherokee people as a distinct community; and such must continue to be the case, if we would live as men ourselves, and discharge the debt we owe to posterity.[16]

Two years later—in 1859—George Butler, the Cherokee agent, shared Ross's optimism. Butler reported to the Commissioner of Indian Affairs that the population of the Cherokee Nation was 21,-000 persons, 4,000 of whom were eligible to vote. Living among the Cherokees were 1,000 whites and 4,000 Negroes (including slaves). The Cherokees had 102,500 acres in cultivation. They owned 240,000 head of cattle, 20,000 horses and mules, 16,000 hogs, and 5,000 sheep. Farmers averaged 35 bushels of corn to the acre, 30 of oats, and 12 of wheat. There were, in 1857, 30 (public) schools in the Nation, attended by 1,500 pupils; and the teachers were, with the exception of 2, all Cherokee.[17]

Thus, the Cherokee Nation basked in the warm summer of achievement. Winter and want were forgotten. The war clouds that hung low over the North and South of the United States were, in the parlance of the Cherokees' slaves, "too heavy to tote themselves over the Arkansas." Chief Ross and the Cherokee council in 1859 did not feel that if Civil War, as portended, broke out in the United States, it would touch even the rim of the Cherokee Nation. But in this they were mistaken.

[16] *Ibid.*, 415f.

[17] *Ibid.*, 418f. Emmet Starr *(History of the Cherokee Indians,* 227f.) claimed that there were thirty-two public schools in the Nation in 1858–59 and listed them.

CHAPTER XIII

The White Man's Civil War

In 1860, Chief Ross, at seventy years of age, undertook to keep the Cherokee tribe—and all the territorial tribes, for that matter—neutral. But he found this difficult. For Southern strategists, perceiving that the Indian Territory, lying due west of Arkansas, south of Kansas, and north of Texas, could furnish the South with sustenance for troops, bases for Federal raids, and a highway into Texas, zealously sought to win over the territorial chiefs.

But Chief Ross was not to be easily won. Sternly, he told his people at the October council in 1860: "Our duty is to stand by our rights, allow no interference in our internal affairs from any source, comply with all our engagements, and rely upon [the] Union for justice and protection."[1]

Determined to remain neutral, Ross communicated his views to other territorial chiefs. As noted by William Robertson, a Creek missionary, in a letter to a fellow missionary in March, 1861: "He [Ross] is writing to all the tribes to keep quiet and let the whites settle their own affairs and it is . . . possible that he will succeed in keeping them in a neutral state."[2]

[1] Message of John Ross to the National Council on October 4, 1860, in Ross Papers, *loc. cit.*

[2] William Robertson to Nancy Thompson, March 1, 1861, in Alice Robertson Collection, University of Tulsa.

But in this instance, it seems, Robertson overestimated Ross's influence and underestimated the power of Indian agents and other federal officials in the Territory who had gone secesh. Influenced by pro-Southern Indian Agent Douglas H. Cooper, Indian Superintendent Elias Rector, a number of pro-Southern Texas commissioners, and many of their New England missionaries, the Choctaws and Chickasaws were the first of the Five Civilized Tribes to shift allegience from the Federal government to the Confederate. The Choctaws' and Chickasaws' shift is aptly explained by S. Orlando Smith, a missionary teacher at Spencer Academy in the Choctaw Nation:

> After South Carolina passed her secession ordinance in December 1860 there was a public attempt to excite the Choctaws and Chickasaws as a beginning hoping to bring in the other tribes afterwards. Many of the larger slave holders (who are nearly all half breeds) had been gained before. . . . The country was full of lies about the intentions of the new administration. The border papers in Arkansas & Texas republished from the New York & St. Louis papers a part . . . [of] Hon. W. H. Seward's speech at Chicago during the election campaign of 1860 to this effect "And Indian Territory south of Kansas must be vacated by the Indian." (These words do occur in the report of Mr. Seward's Chicago speech. . . .) This produced intense excitement. . . . "This," they were told, "is the policy of the new administration. The abolitionists want your lands—we [the South] will protect you. Your only safety is to join the South. . . ." The former Indian agent Cooper was a Col. in the rebel service. The oldest missionary [Dr. Kingsbury] who has undoubtedly more influence with the Choctaws than any other white man is an ardent secessionist. . . . I do not like to write such things of my brother missionaries . . . but all the ordained missionaries belonging to the Choctaw & Chickasaw Mission of the Presbyterian Board [with a few exceptions] who remain there . . . [are] secessionists.[3]

Thus influenced, the Choctaws, on February 7, 1861—two days

[3] Annie Heloise Abel, *The American Indian as Slaveholder and Secessionist*, 75-79.

exactly before Jefferson Davis was elected to the office of President of the Confederate States—publicized their intention of supporting the South. The Chickasaw chiefs called an intertribal meeting (or Grand Council) at the Creek council ground near North Fork Town (the site of present Eufaula, Oklahoma) for February 17, to discuss the Civil War and its effect on the tribes. From this, it was generally understood in the Territory that the Chickasaws were on the verge of going secesh along with the Choctaws.

John Ross continued to advocate territorial neutrality, even though he, too, was being urged by propagandists to join the South. The Governor of Arkansas, Henry M. Rector, wrote to Ross on January 29, 1861, that he expected thirteen Southern states to be separated from the Union by March 4:

> Your people, in their institutions, productions, latitude, and natural sympathies, are natural allies in war and friends in peace. . . . Besides this the contiguity of our territory with yours induces relations of so intimate a character as to preclude the idea of discordant or separate action. It is well established that the Indian country west of Arkansas is looked to by the incoming administration of Mr. Lincoln as fruitful fields, ripe for the harvest of abolitionists, free-soilers, and Northern Mountebanks. We hope to find in your people friends willing to cooperate with the South.[4]

Two weeks later, Ross received a similar communication from Indian Superintendent Elias Rector, the Governor's cousin, endorsing Governor Rector's views. "I fully approve of the object the Governor has in view and would ask you to give the matter your favorable consideration."[5]

Before answering either Governor Rector or Superintendent Rector, John Ross sternly instructed delegates William P. Ross, Thomas Pegg, John Spears, and Lewis Downing concerning the course they were to pursue at the Grand Council at North Fork Town:

[4] In Ross Papers, *loc. cit.;* see also United States War Department, *The War of The Rebellion,* Ser. I, Vol. I, 683f.

[5] February 14, 1861, in Ross Papers, *loc. cit.*

In your deliberations it will be proper for you to advise discretion and to guard against any premature movement, on our part, which might produce excitement or be liable to misrepresentation. Our duty is very plain. We have only to adhere firmly to our respective Treaties. By them, we have placed ourselves under the protection of the United States, and of no other sovereign whatsoever. We are bound to hold no Treaty with any foreign power or with any individual State or combination of States, nor with citizens of any State. Nor even with one another, without the interposition and participation of the United States as is evidenced in the case of the Choctaws and Chickasaws. . . . We ought to entertain no apprehension of any change that will endanger our interests. The parties holding the responsibilities of the Federal Government will always be bound to us. And no measures we have it in our power to adopt can add anything to the security we now possess.[6]

With the delegates off to the Grand Council, Chief Ross wrote to Governor Rector on February 22 that the Cherokee people esteemed the friendship of the people of Arkansas but were determined to keep faith with the United States:

I am surprised to be informed by your Excellency that "it is well established that the Indian country west of Arkansas is looked to by the incoming administration of Mr. Lincoln as fruitful fields ripe for the harvest of Abolitionists, Freesoilers, and Northern Mountebanks", as I am sure that the Laborers will be greatly disappointed if they shall expect to find in the Cherokee country fruitful fields ripe for the harvest of Abolitionists etc. And you may rest assured that the Cherokee people will never tolerate the propagation of any such obnoxious fruit upon their soil.[7]

Presumably Chief Ross was highly gratified by the outcome of the Grand Council. Cherokee delegates, upon returning from North Fork Town, reported on March 15 that the Choctaws and Chickasaws had not attended the council, but, in their absence, Cherokee, Creek, and Seminole delegates had harmoniously decided "to do

[6] February 12, 1861, in *ibid.*
[7] In *ibid.*

nothing, to keep quiet, and to comply with our Treaties . . . and whatever may be the exigencies of the future if any should arise we will be found acting in concert and sharing a common destiny."[8]

Informed that the Creek council, convening after the Grand Council, had approved the neutral position taken by intertribal delegates, Ross possibly assumed that the Creeks would continue to repel Southern propagandists and to stand firmly with the Cherokees. But this did not happen. Before the next Grand Council at North Fork Town in April, three Texas commissioners succeeded in winning over mixed-blood Creeks: Chilly McIntosh, Benjamin Marshall, and Daniel McIntosh of the Lower Towns. In fact, Chief Canard of the Lower Towns, prompted by the Texas commissioners, called the Grand Council in April. But the dissenting faction in the Upper Towns, headed by Opothleyohola, continued to stand firmly with Ross and his people.

John Ross, too, was approached by the commissioners before the April council but firmly refused to consider their proposal. "Mr. Ross had some pretty plain talk with the Texas commissioners," Dr. Dwight Hitchcock wrote the William Robertsons from the Cherokee Nation on April 2, 1861. "They said that his was the coldest reception they had met with."[9]

At the April council the Texas commissioners addressed an assemblage of Cherokee, Creek, Sac and Fox, and Quapaw delegates. The Choctaws and Chickasaws again were conspicuously absent, having sent word to the council that high water prevented their attendance. Elected chairman of the council, Creek Chief Motey Canard co-operated with the commissioners, who later reported that they had found the Creeks "Southern and sound to a man."[10] However, the latter statement was not strictly true, for Opothleyohola and his Upper Creeks were as determined as ever to adhere to Creek treaties with the United States government. On this note the Grand Council adjourned uneasily, to meet again in early June.

By May it had become increasingly difficult for John Ross or any

[8] In *ibid.*
[9] In Alice Robertson Collection, *loc. cit.*
[10] Angie Debo, *The Road to Disappearance*, 143.

territorial chief to remain neutral. Apprehensively, Ross noted that Texas troops, ousting the Federal, held all the territorial military posts save Fort Gibson. The latter, having been abandoned by Federal troops four years before, was in Cherokee hands. Elias Rector, it is true, had been replaced by William Coffin, a strong Union man. But Coffin, detained in Kansas, had been unable to take over his active duties as Indian superintendent. Cut off from the United States almost entirely, the Territory had become an island in a Confederate sea. And Southern emissaries seized every opportunity to emphasize this fact.

Thus the spring, summer, and early fall months of 1861 were chaotic, uncertain, and unpredictable in the Territory. In March the secession convention in Arkansas elected Elias C. Boudinot its secretary. A son of the Elias Boudinot who had been murdered in 1839 and a brother of Stand Watie, Elias C. Boudinot had become a resident of Arkansas but had kept in touch with the Cherokee Nation through Watie. Identified with the South as he was, it was natural for Boudinot to encourage Watie to defy Chief Ross, who had forbidden the Cherokees to participate in border warfare or to organize a band of guerrillas for the protection of Arkansas. Watie's men, whose headquarters were in the vicinity of old Fort Wayne, referred to themselves as "Knights of the Golden Circle," but were shortly to change this name to "The Southern Rights party." Violently opposed to Ross and the executive council, the "Knights" contemptuously referred to the Ross party as "that old Dominant party that for years has had its foot on our necks."[11]

Equally active, another organization made up of full bloods, calling themselves "Keetoowahs," was operating in the Nation in 1861 on the side of the Union. Reorganized in 1859 by Evan Jones and his son John, this secret society was ostensibly designed to perpetuate tribal traditions. But it was common knowledge in the Na-

---

[11] Abel, *The American Indian as Slaveholder and Secessionist,* 119; William Penn Adair to Stand Watie, August 29, 1861, in Cherokee Papers, *loc. cit.,* Vol. X, Ser. 3.

The Knights of the Golden Circle existed throughout the South and border states, and only a chapter of it was organized among the Cherokees.

tion that the Keetoowahs had been revitalized by the Joneses to fight slavery. Meeting clandestinely at night in wooded areas, the Keetoowahs wore an insignia of crossed pins, for identification, on their hunting shirts and coats and thus were referred to as "Pins" or "The Pins Indians." Later the Pins were members of the Loyal League.

When Evan Jones and his son, in 1861, were requested by the Baptist Board to leave the Nation for the duration of the conflict between the states, the then unsupervised Keetoowahs reverted to the ways of their fighting forebears. Although pledging allegiance to John Ross and the United States, the Pins at every opportunity savagely attacked the Knights. The resultant clashes portended a division within the Nation, a division that deeply concerned Chief Ross and the executive council, to whom national unity was all important at this critical time.

Noting the dissension developed in the Nation by its warring Pins and Knights, the Confederate government made the most of it. In 1861, Stand Watie was guaranteed by the Confederacy not only arms for guerrilla warfare against the North but also protection against the Pins.

A master stroke of the Confederate government's State Department in its plan to bring all territorial tribes, including the recalcitrant Cherokees, into the fold as quickly as possible was the commission of Albert Pike on March 5, 1861. A New Englander by birth and a veteran of the Mexican War, Pike was practicing law at Little Rock when he received notice of his appointment as an emissary of the Confederate government. An ardent Southern supporter, Pike had represented the Choctaws at Washington and had recently gained a settlement for those Indians of an old claim from the government for $2,981,247.

A second aggressive action of the Confederate Provisional Congress was to create a Bureau of Indian Affairs in March, 1861. This move, in turn, led to the appointment of David L. Hubbard to the office of Indian commissioner of the Confederate states. As his title implied, Hubbard was expected to aid Pike and other Southern agents in aligning the chiefs of territorial tribes with the South, Chief John Ross being Hubbard's immediate target.

Then, to facilitate action in the Territory, the Confederate War Department assigned Brigadier General Ben McCulloch, a former Texas Ranger, to the "command of the district embracing Indian Territory."

Official records of the Confederate states offer proof that all of these appointees—Pike, Hubbard, and McCulloch—were properly informed by Southern experts concerning ways and means of accomplishing their mission. For example, all three knew of the dissenting factions in the Nation and the importance of the arming of Watie's men by the Confederate government.

Pike, Hubbard, and McCulloch were also well aware that, for the last decade, the Cherokee Nation's treasury had been depleted by the vast spending program initiated by the Nation. To raise money for schools, public buildings, and other improvements, the Nation had at various times attempted to dispose of its "Neutral Land" to the United States government for $500,000 with interest from 1835, the date of the Cherokees' acquisition of the land. Embracing 800,000 acres, in a strip twenty-five miles wide extending fifty miles north from the Cherokee boundary, the Neutral Land was of little value to the Cherokees but was apparently of immense value to white squatters from Kansas. Even so, the United States government had refused to pay the interest on the land, and its refusal had balked the sale. Thereafter, the land had become a bone of contention between Cherokees and squatters, a contention that had in times past led to bloodshed.

Cognizant in 1861 of the Cherokees' difficulties over the Neutral Land and also of their depleted treasury occasioned by the nonpayment of Federal annuities, Pike was empowered by the Confederate government to offer the tribe $500,000 *and interest* for their Neutral Land. Hubbard, too, was authorized to use the Neutral Land issue as a weapon to overcome John Ross and the executive council's neutrality.

As for McCulloch, he too was expected to play an important role in winning over the Cherokees. He was to point out the military advantages to be gained by a Cherokee-Confederate alliance and to emphasize the exposed position of the Nation.

Albert Pike met Brigadier General McCulloch at Fort Smith in late May. Conferring with them on this occasion were five or six of Watie's men, whose names do not appear in the official records of the Confederacy. Presumably, Elias C. Boudinot was one of the number, as was Stand Watie. But whatever their names, Watie's men were warmly welcomed by McCulloch and Pike and promised protection from the Pins and ammunition for future guerrilla warfare against the Northern white enemy. Pike also exacted a promise from Watie's men to meet him at a special intertribal council at North Fork Town around June 9.

At this date Pike pretty well knew that the Choctaws and Chickasaws would be at the intertribal council, ready to make a formal treaty with the South. The Lower Towns Creeks, too, were expected to treat with Pike, as were several other territorial tribes to whom invitations had been sent. Pike's invitation was expected to result in a treaty of alliance with the Watie faction, if not with the Ross party.

Pike was to meet McCulloch at Park Hill on June 5, and together they would talk to Chief Ross. In preparation for this interview Pike carefully composed six or seven pages of arguments calculated to break down Ross's resistance. And McCulloch was prepared to inform Ross about what protection he could expect from the Southern military. Both Pike and McCulloch intended also to ask Ross for an audience with the executive council, before which tribunal they were eager to present their case.

While these preparations were in progress at Fort Smith, John Ross was busily answering letters from Arkansas demanding to know where he stood on the war question, now that Arkansas had seceded from the Union. To inquiries made by Mark Bean and a committee of citizens of Boonsboro (Boonsborough) on this subject, Ross replied on May 18, 1861:

> You are fully aware of the peculiar Circumstances of our Condition and will not expect us to destroy our national and individual rights and bring around our hearth stones the horrors and desolations of a civil war, prematurely and unnecessarily. I am—the Cherokees are—your

friends and the friends of your people but we do not wish to be brought into the feuds between yourselves and your Northern Brethren. Our wish is for peace. Peace at home and Peace among you. . . .[12]

To Lieutenant Colonel Kanady at Fort Smith, who had demanded to know his views, Ross wrote on May 17: ". . . under existing circumstances my wish, advice, and hope are that we shall be allowed to remain strictly neutral—our interests all center in peace."[13]

At Park Hill, Chief Ross was required to listen to the arguments presented by Pike and McCulloch. Pike's communiqué knowingly struck at vulnerable spots in Ross's armor of neutrality. For, as authorized by the Confederate government, the communiqué (which was actually a treaty) guaranteed to the Cherokees the fee-simple title and perpetual possession, with the right of disposition, of their whole country; promised to pay to the Cherokees, in case of the loss from any cause of their Neutral Land between Kansas and Missouri, "the purchase money with interest of the 800,000 acres of land lying between Kansas and Missouri"; promised the establishment of Confederate courts in the Territory; and permitted representation in the Congress of the Confederate government—representation that the Cherokees had hoped for. Protection of investments, payment of monies due under existent treaties, and other peripheral benefits were promised the Cherokees if they would make an alliance with the South.[14]

But, after studying Pike's communiqué, Ross stoically replied that he and the executive council had agreed to remain neutral and thus not violate the Nation's treaties with the United States. Ross also refused Pike an audience with the council. Whereupon Pike huffily took off for North Fork Town, presumably expecting better results there. Upon arriving at the Creek council ground, Pike discovered that Watie's men—fearing Ross's vengeance—had decided not to meet him there, but that the Choctaws, Chickasaws, and Creeks were ready to treat.

[12] In Ross Papers, *loc. cit.*
[13] In *ibid.*
[14] See Albert Pike to John Ross, August 1, 1861, in *ibid.*

Meanwhile, Ross informed Brigadier General McCulloch that he would not consider the entrance into the Cherokee country by United States troops an act authorizing armed resistance on the Cherokees' part, since the troops would be those of a government with whom the Cherokees had treaties. This statement so annoyed McCulloch that he left for Sculleyville, where he planned to muster a mounted regiment, even though he knew that the raising of territorial troops would displease Ross.

David L. Hubbard, the new commissioner of Indian Affairs for the Confederacy, was prevented by illness from visiting Ross, but, on June 12, Hubbard wrote to Ross repeating much of what Pike had already said in his June 5 communiqué. Hubbard's language, however, was more forceful than Pike's:

> If the North succeeds you will most certainly lose all. First your slaves they will take from you—that is one object of the war to enable them to abolish Slavery. . . . Another and perhaps the Chief cause, is to get upon your rich lands. . . . It is true they may allow your people small Reserves. They give chiefs pretty large ones, but they will settle among you, overshadow you, and totally destroy the power of your chiefs and your nationality. . . . Go North among the once powerful tribes . . . and see if you can find Indians living, and enjoying power and property & Liberty, as do your people and the neighboring Tribes from the South. If you can, then say I am a liar and the Northern States have been better to the Indians than the Southern States.[15]

Hubbard's letter demanded an immediate answer. To him, Ross replied that the Cherokee Nation expected to keep its treaties with the Union. And to McCulloch, Ross directed this note, under the date of June 17:

> Your demand that those people of the Nation who are in favor of joining the Confederacy be allowed to organize into military companies as Home Guards, for the purpose of defending themselves in case of invasion from the North, is most respectfully declined. I cannot give

[15] In *ibid.*

my consent to any such organization: First, it would be a palpable violation of my position as a neutral; second, it would place in our midst organized companies not authorized by our laws but in violation of treaty, and who would soon become efficient instruments of stirring up domestic strife. . . . As in this connection you have misapprehended a remark made in conversation at our interview some eight or ten days ago, I hope you will allow me to repeat what I did say. I informed you that I had taken a neutral position, and would maintain it honestly, but that in case of a foreign invasion, old as I am, I would assist in repelling it.[16]

In view of Ross's unquestionably sincere determination to keep his people from becoming embroiled in the white man's Civil War, the alliance which the Cherokee Nation made with the Confederate States on October 7, 1861, is very nearly incomprehensible to those students of Cherokee history not in possession of all the facts pertaining to the tribe's capitulation. Actually, the accumulation of events and circumstances left the Cherokee people and Ross no alternative but to go with the South.

On August 1, 1861, Pike curtly notified Ross by letter that he had made formal alliances with the Choctaws, Chickasaws, Lower Towns Creeks, and a number of the Plains Indians:

I do not propose, now, on the part of the Confederate States of America, to enter upon any further argument in regard to the subject [of an alliance] . . . nor to seek to open any further negotiations with the Cherokee Authorities, or again to offer through you, to your people propositions for an alliance offensive and defensive, or of protection on the one hand and wardship on the other. . . .

. . . I wish only, as you have declined ot enter into any arrangement whatever with the Confederate States, even for the purpose of a real neutrality, now and for all future time to exclude the conclusion that the Confederate States will . . . hereafter feel themselves bound to pay the Cherokee People the purchase-money with interest of the 800,000 acres of land lying between Kansas and Missouri. That was offered by me as one of the terms of an alliance, offensive and defensive; which

[16] Abel, *The American Indian as Slaveholder and Secessionist*, 150f.

being rejected, the proposition is now withdrawn forever. . . . In electing to remain neutral and really in alliance with the Northern States,
you will have elected also to look to them for the price of the land, of
which they have already plundered you.[17]

This letter was possibly the determining factor in the decision
reached by Ross and the executive council to make an alliance with
the South. The treaty offered by the Confederacy unquestionably
surpassed any treaty yet made by the Cherokees with the United
States. And, had the South won the war, the Cherokee-Confederate
alliance would have elevated the tribe to an enviable position in
America. But other factors leading up to complete capitulation by
the Cherokees are worthy of notice. By August 10 the battles of Bull
Run and of Wilson's Creek in near-by Missouri had been fought and
lost by the Federals, who appeared to be losing the war. Too, the
battle of Wilson's Creek in Missouri had emphasized the role which
Stand Watie and his men were likely to play in the Civil War—a
role that, if the South were triumphant, would presumably put
Watie in power and the uncommitted Ross in prison. For after the
battle of Wilson's Creek, the Confederate presses had praised Watie
to the skies. According to press reports, Watie's guerrillas had broken
up General Franz Sigel's command by capturing all of his artillery,
save one piece. For this act Watie was made a hero overnight by the
Confederate military. However, Watie's victory incited the Pins to
overt acts of savagery against members of Watie's party.

Conflicts between Watie's men and the Pins had been noted
throughout the summer of 1861. A little over a month before
Watie's victory at Wilson's Creek, a party of his men had attempted
to raise the Confederate Stars and Bars in the public square at Tahlequah but had been stopped by Doublehead and about 150 Pins.

Upon learning of this incident, John Ross and Joseph Vann, the
assistant chief, sent this message to the Pins through Captain Drew:

We greatly regret to hear of difficulties among our people at any
time and particularly so at the present time, when surrounded by the

---

[17] In Ross Papers, *loc. cit.*

commotions that exist among the people of the States. . . . By . . . [unity] alone can we avoid every cause for hostility from either section of the country and upon this policy we ought all to be able to attend to our ordinary affairs and avoid all cause of strife among ourselves.[18]

The Cherokee executive council remained in troubled session much of the summer of 1861. Then, having reviewed every facet of the Nation's situation, the council and John Ross reluctantly concluded that the preservation of its rights and the very existence of the Cherokee Nation demanded an alliance with the Confederacy.

At Tahlequah on Wednesday, August 21, 1861, Chief Ross addressed a convention of about four thousand male Cherokees, declaring that "in view of all the circumstances of our situation, I say to you frankly, that in my opinion, the time has now arrived when you should signify your consent for the authorities of the Nation to adopt preliminary steps for the alliance with the Confederate States upon terms honorable and advantageous to the Cherokee Nation." Ross was emphatic about the importance then, as never before, of unity within the Nation. "Union is strength, dissension is weakness, misery and ruin! In time of war, if war must come, fight together. As Brothers live; as Brothers die!"[19] At the conclusion of this address, resolutions for implementing an alliance with the Confederacy were offered to the convention and were adopted by acclamation.

Immediately after adjournment, Albert Pike was notified by Chief Ross of the Nation's decision, and arrangements were made to negotiate a treaty at the National Council at Park Hill in early October.

Presumably, it was difficult for Ross to inform territorial chiefs who had previously stood with him against a Confederate alliance of the Cherokees' decision. It was especially hard to write to old Chief Opothleyohola and invite him, as suggested by Pike, to the October council for the purpose of treating with Pike. Upon reading Ross's letter, Chiefs Opothleyohola and Oktarharsas believed it to

[18] July 2, 1861, in *ibid.*
[19] *Proceedings* [printed pamphlet], in *ibid.*

be a hoax. To test its validity, the Creek chiefs appended this note to Ross's original letter, then returned it:

> DEAR SIR:
>   We have received a letter from you. . . . In your letter we understand that you and all the Cherokee . . . are in favor with Captain Pike. We don't know whether this is truth or not. . . . we send the same letter.[20]

Even after having been assured by Chief Ross that the letter in question was from him, Opothleyohola firmly refused to attend the council at Park Hill. Preferring to adhere to treaties made with the United States, Opothleyohola and his followers moved to the Little River, intending shortly to head out for Kansas where they hoped to be protected by Federal troops. Broken tribes living in the vicinity of the Little River and other fragmentary tribes in the Territory joined Opothleyohola's band. Leaders of these tribes afterwards carried a message from Opothleyohola to Federal officials in Kansas requesting sanctuary there.[21]

However, Ross's invitations to chiefs of the Shawnees, Senecas, and Quapaws were accepted. In these invitations, Ross referred to the Grand Council meeting at Tahlequah in 1843 when the tribes had resolved to become brothers in order to preserve peace in the Territory. Using imagery freely, in true Indian fashion, Ross affixed his Indian name of "Kooweeskoowee" to the letters.[22]

As the October meeting date drew nearer, the Park Hill area became feverishly active. John Stapler reported to John Ross from Tahlequah on September 25:

> Our Town is filling up with Strangers. Bell's Company arrived late last night . . . C. Boudinot with them; and Stand Watie with his Companies expected tonight. . . . It was remarked in my hearing by

[20] September 14, 1861, in *ibid.*
[21] See Debo, *The Road to Disappearance*, 147–49.
[22] The spelling of John Ross's Indian name varies. But "Kooweeskoowee" is the signature used in the original letters written by Ross to the territorial chiefs in 1861. See the Ross Papers, *loc. cit.*

one of the party that at this time there was no Treaty with any power in existence. . . . Anderson Downing was killed last night. . . . I furnish these items to give you an index to the current at work here.[23]

"The current at work here" referred, of course, to the Watie faction or Southern Rights party, who hoped to overthrow the Ross Party and, by making a treaty with Pike, take over the Cherokee government. "Ross's convention" on August 21, as William Penn Adair called it, was a threat to the plans of the Watie or Southern Rights party. After the Convention, Adair wrote to Stand Watie:

> DEAR FRIEND,
>
> You have doubtless heard all about Ross's convention, which in reality tied up our hands and shut our mouths and put the destiny of everything connected with the Nation and our lives in the hands of the Executive. . . . Pike is disposed to favor us and to disregard the course our executive has taken. The Pins already have more power in their hands than we can bear and if in addition to this they acquire more power by being the Treaty-making power, you know our destiny will be inalterably sealed. It seems we should guard against this. Now is the time for us to strike or we will be completely frustrated. . . . Under these circumstances our Party [the Southern Rights party] want you and Dr. J. L. Thompson to go in person and have an interview with Mr. Pike to the end that we may have justice done us, have this Pin party broken up, and have our rights *provided* for and place us if possible at least on an honorable equity with this old Dominant party that for years has had its foot upon our necks.

In agreement with Adair, James Bell appended this note to his letter:

> DEAR SIR
>
> There is one thing to which Wm. P. Adair has not adverted and that is that Ross has ordered the raising of twelve hundred men, John Drew Col., Tom Pegg Lieut. Col., Wm. P. Ross, Major. Now I have been under the impression that these were commissioned by the

[23] In *ibid.*

Confederate States. It will require a rapid and prompt movement on our part or else we are done up. All of our work will have been in vain, our prospects destroyed[,] our rights disregarded[,] and we will be *Slaves* to Ross tyranny. Write back immediately what we must do, it don't do for you to hold back, declare yourself ready to serve your country in whatever capacity we may want you.[24]

Elias Cornelius Boudinot then lost no time in suggesting to Stand Watie that he make Boudinot a lieutenant colonel in his military organization. "John Ross and you are rivals," Boudinot reminded his uncle from Honey Creek on October 5, 1861. "He has appointed his nephew Lieut. Col. intent on keeping a foothold on the military organization. . . . You have it in your power now to put me in a position where I can do honor to myself and to you. Will you not do it?"[25]

As official records of both sides show, Watie's party did not actively participate in the treaty consummated at Park Hill on October 7, 1861, between the Cherokee Nation and the Confederate government. After the signing of the treaty, Pike presented Chief Ross with the Stars and Bars, to be raised at Ross's discretion in the public square at Tahlequah. And, to erase all ill feeling, Chief Ross shook the hand of Stand Watie. The small delegation of Osages, Quapaws, Shawnees, and Senecas who had signed similar treaties with the Confederacy were reported by Ross to have been in fine spirits afterwards. All of these tribes—save the Osages—had been excused from military service by the terms of their respective treaties.

As explained by John Ross in a letter to Chief Motey Canard after the treaty-making ceremonies at Tahlequah, "they are not expected to furnish any warriors for the service—except the Osages who have agreed to furnish 500 warriors. The others having friends and relatives in Kansas, it was thought best to leave the *door open* for their reception, so soon as they can see their way clear to travel along the *Whitepath* that leads into Our Houses."[26]

[24] August 29, 1861, in Cherokee Papers, *loc. cit.*, Vol. X, Ser. 3.
[25] In *ibid.*, Vol. I, Ser. 2.
[26] October 8, 1861, in Ross Papers, *loc. cit.*

Chief Ross's great desire now was to align all the territorial tribes on the side of the Confederacy. To this end, Ross again urged Opothleyohola and his loyal Creeks on October 11, "to join the other tribes who are now with the Confederacy." But Opothleyohola told Ross's emissary, Joseph Vann, that he simply wanted to live in peace and that he had no design to make war upon anybody.

A week later Ross received the shocking news from Chief Motey Canard written from Camp Losley that Opothleyohola "is more hostile than ever and the Creek slaves are running to him for refuge."[27] According to Chief Canard, Opothleyohola's hostile behavior called for an attack on the loyal Creeks.

Stunned and outraged by the suggestion of an attack on his old friend, Chief Ross wrote to Chief Canard under date of October 20:

> Brothers, we are shocked with amazement at the fearful import of your words. Are we to understand that you have determined to make a military demonstration by force of arms upon Opothleyohola and his followers at the cost of civil war among your own People and therefore involve your red Brethren who are in alliance with the Confederate States? Such a conflict will bring on a warfare inaugurated by you that will not fail to sever the bonds of peace and friendship between us and the other Tribes of Indians who are not in alliance with Opothleyohola. . . . We cannot and dare not therefore give our co-operation to any precipitate action which is calculated to lead to conflict and bloodshed among your people and which would not only injure the prosperity and welfare of the red people but also the common cause of the Confederate States which we have espoused. We beg leave to dissent from you as to the propriety of carrying into effect the intentions in the way of arming you have suggested.[28]

Chief Ross continued to protect Opothleyohola and in early November gained his consent to a meeting either at Lewis Ross's place at the Grand Saline or at Coodey's on the Verdigris. But before Opothleyohola could be conducted by Captains James McDaniel and Porum to either meeting place in the Cherokee Nation, the

[27] In *ibid.*
[28] In *ibid.*

threatened clash between Opothleyohola and Chief Motey Canard had become a grim reality.

The Confederate War Department had placed Pike in command of its newly created Military Department of the Indian Territory. But Pike, after treating with the Cherokees and other tribes at Park Hill in October, had left for Richmond to render a report of territorial alliances to President Davis and the War Department. In Pike's absence, Douglas H. Cooper took over his command: the First Regiment Choctaw and Chickasaw Mounted Rifles; the First Creek Regiment under Colonel Daniel McIntosh; the First Regiment Cherokee Mounted Rifles under John Drew (formerly in command of the Indian Home Guards, organized by order of John Ross to protect the Nation before the treaty with the South had been consummated); the Second Regiment Cherokee Mounted Rifles under Colonel Stand Watie; and Choctaw and Seminole battalions, commanded respectively by Chilly McIntosh and John Jumper.

Made up as it was of many full bloods and Ross-party mixed bloods, Drew's Cherokee regiment was in no mood to obey Cooper's orders to attack Opothleyohola's camp at Red Fork on November 19, after Cooper's men had chased Opothleyohola and his followers out of their camp at Little River. Being former allies of Opothleyohola, Drew's men left the distasteful attack to McIntosh and Jumper's Creek and Seminole battalions, to six companies of Choctaw and Chickasaw Mounted Rifles, and to the Ninth Regiment Texas Cavalry. With Opothleyohola were some 1,575 loyal Creeks (including women and children) and a number of Seminoles, Delawares, Kickapoos, Shawnees, and Wichitas, all of whom were en route to Kansas to obtain Federal military protection.

To justify the attack on Opothleyohola and his followers, Chiefs Canard and Echo Harjo wrote to Ross on November 25:

> On the evening of the 19th inst. a battle was fought at Red Fork. The engagement lasted 6 hours. . . . On the evening before the battle Echo Harjo went to their camps and conversed with them. They proclaimed war, and affirmed they were looking for Cherokees to aid them that they had promised to come to their assistance. They have a

quantity of our property which they are taking northward. Should they be passing through your country please stop them.[29]

Chief Ross's reply was obviously not calculated to please either Canard or Harjo:

> I have received with deep regret the intelligence of your failure to adjust your difficulties with Opothleyohola and his adherents. . . . Brothers—Let us act as men who love our People and their Country . . . and not to be hasty in believing false reports. . . . And if we are united as Brothers and will be true to our own interests we shall not fail to maintain our alliance with the Confederate States with firmness —But will preserve our integrity and Honor as Patriots—invulnerable to all the demons of Hell or their Satellites of Kansas or elsewhere.[30]

The battle at Red Fork on November 19 presaged further defection—if such it can be called—in Drew's regiment. Cooper's Texas and Indian troops pursued Opothleyohola, afterward, to Bird Creek crossing in Cherokee country. There, on December 9, a second indecisive battle was fought, and a number of Drew's mixed-blood officers and full-blood privates either deserted or fought on the side of the enemy. "Captains Vann and Pike went over to Opothleyohola, also several Lieutenants," Lieutenant Colonel William P. Ross informed Chief Ross immediately after the battle. "This news is most painful."[31]

Eluding Cooper for a second time, Opothleyohola's forces, after leaving Bird Creek, pushed determinedly on to Chustenahla in the Osage Hills about twelve miles north of Tulsey, a Creek town that later became Tulsa. The weather had turned very cold, since it was then the latter part of December. Snow covered the ground and harsh winds hallooed through rocky canyons. In some manner Opothleyohola's forces were able to hold onto their possessions—800–900 head of cattle, 250 Indian ponies, and about 190 sheep. But the enemy soon located their hideaway and planned an attack. With

[29] In *ibid.*
[30] November 28, 1861, in *ibid.*
[31] In *ibid.*

The Cherokee Female Seminary near Tahlequah in 1851 (above) and the Cherokee Capitol at Tahlequah (below).

MARY STAPLER ROSS, wife of Chief John Ross.
From a painting by Samuel B. Waugh.

*Thomas Gilcrease Institute of
American History and Art*

Photograph of JOHN ROSS, probably made
while he was in exile in Washington during
the Civil War.

Elias Cornelius Boudinot, Cherokee politician.

STAND WATIE
Civil War Confederate general.

JOHN ROLLIN RIDGE
Cherokee poet.

SALADIN WATIE

*Illustrations from the Division of Manuscripts,
University of Oklahoma Libraries*

The Run into the Cherokee Outlet, September 16, 1893.

FOUR CHEROKEE CHIEFS

CHARLES THOMPSON

LEWIS DOWNING

DENNIS W. BUSHYHEAD

WILLIAM P. ROSS

Illustrations from the Division of Manuscripts,
University of Oklahoma Libraries

Noel Kaho

LYNN RIGGS, author of
Green Grow the Lilacs,
on which *Oklahoma!* was based.

Division of Manuscripts,
University of Oklahoma Libraries

JOHN OSKISON, novelist and
short-story writer.

Hicks Family

ED HICKS, who brought the
first telephone west of St. Louis.

Division of Manuscripts,
University of Oklahoma Libraries

WILL ROGERS, the best-known
Cherokee of them all.

Opothleyohola were Cherokee Captains Vann, Pike, and Scraper and Lieutenants White, Catcher, Eli Smith, Foster, Bear Meat, and Fish, together with a number of Cherokee privates. By then, Cherokee deserters Major Pegg, Adjutant J. S. Vann, Captains Davis and J. D. Hicks, and a number of lieutenants and privates had reached Fort Gibson, where, on December 21, they were dutifully reminded by Chief Ross in a public address of their responsibilities to the Confederacy.[32]

Meanwhile, Opothleyohola, attacked by the enemy on December 26 at Chustenahla, was forced to abandon livestock, wagons, and provisions, and—to avoid capture—flee northward into Kansas in a beating snowstorm. In company with Opothleyohola, Cherokee deserters never forgot the sad scenes enacted on the frozen Kansas campsites of several thousand Indian refugees. Hundreds of frozen limbs and arms were amputated by a Federal army surgeon; mass graves were dug in frozen ground; ponies and mules, unfed for weeks, died and for months remained unburied. Disease (influenza, sore eyes, and fever) caused babies, old people, and even Opothleyohola, to sicken and—under circumstances beyond the control of Indian agents, citizens of near-by Le Roy, Kansas, or the military— to linger miserably until death relieved their suffering.

A heartening sight to Cherokees was the arrival of Reverend Evan Jones, the missionary, who, having been ordered out of the Nation by the Baptist Mission Board some months before, was living for the time being at Lawrence, Kansas. At the request of United States Indian Commissioner W. P. Dole, Jones made a survey of Opothleyohola's camp and thus encountered Cherokee refugees who gave him the news of Chief Ross's capitulation to the Confederacy. On January 21, 1862, Jones wrote to Commissioner Dole:

At the date of my last, I was somewhat discouraged by the confirmation of the report that John Ross had yielded to the pressure which had been brought to bear on him and his people from the seceded States and other quarters. . . . I was unwilling to accept a report which im-

---

[32] "Report of Col. John Drew," in United States War Department, *War of the Rebellion*, Ser. I, Vol. VIII, 16f.

plied anything dishonorable or even unstable in John Ross; because I was so well acquainted with his long settled principles and policy, and with the integrity and firmness of his character, that I could not believe that anything, short of imminent and perilous necessity, could enduce him to abandon the position he had taken at the commencement of the contest. And since I have had free conversations with the Cherokee messengers from Opothleyohola's camp, about the events which have transpired with the last few months, I am satisfied that I was not mistaken in Mr. Ross's character, and—that whatever unfavorable shade may rest on his movements, is the result of causes beyond his control.

I feel the more anxious to have you fully and correctly informed of the state of things in the Cherokee Nation . . . because it must make a great difference in the treatment they ought to receive at the hands of the government.[33]

Jones proceeded then to lay the groundwork for Ross's rescue from the Confederate foe. To Dole, Jones graphically described the animosity and division in the Cherokee Nation stemming from the Treaty of 1835:

And, since the seccession question has been agitated, it has broken out with renewed virulence, though it would not have proceeded to overt acts, but for the incitement of the emissaries of rebellion from Arkansas & Texas and finally from the so-called Confederate States. Under the secession stimulus, this inimical party, last spring raised a military force of five or six hundred, in the interest and for the service of the Confederate States, in defiance of the laws of the Nation.[34]

The defection of portions of each of the neighboring tribes; the pressure of the commissioners and other emissaries of the Confederacy; the occupation of all the territorial forts (except Fort Gibson) by the rebel army; and the declaration made to Ross by McCulloch that, unless the Cherokees would join the Confederacy, he would march his troops into the Territory whenever he deemed it proper to do so, were cited by Jones.

[33] In Ross Papers, *loc. cit.*
[34] *Ibid.*

Certainly no man ever had more zealous representation in court than did Ross when Jones argued his case in the winter of 1862 before United States Indian Commissioner Dole, who had forwarded Jones's communications relating to Ross on to the War Department in Washington. Impressed with Jones's argument, the War Department perfected plans to test Ross's allegiance to the Union, an allegiance thought by Jones to be as strong and firm as before the recent treaty. In order to test Ross and effect his return to the Union, Jones was authorized by Commissioner Dole and Superintendent William Coffin to compose a confidential message from the War Department to be delivered to Ross at the proper time under a flag of truce. Since an early-summer invasion of the Territory was contemplated by the United States War Department, summer seemed the proper time to approach Ross.

As planned by the War Department, Opothleyohola's refugees, clamoring to return to their former homes, were to accompany Federal troops when they invaded the Territory. Organized into an Indian Expedition, the refugees were expected to facilitate the prospective invasion by scouting the northeastern part of the Cherokee Nation, known to be in the hands of Watie's guerrillas and Drew's men. But the latter, according to Jones, would be no problem, for they would join the Expedition, if invited.

To prepare for the summer attack, the Indians were drilled daily by white officers, issued uniforms and caps, and taught how to operate the cannons, which they referred to as "shooting wagons." To the amusement of white officers, the refugees insisted upon drinking great quantities of bullet-proof medicine or the "black drink," chanting weird incantations to the spirits for protection, and frequently punctuating drill practice with war whoops. The small caps worn by privates looked comical when perched atop the Indians' long black hair. And the refugees did not fill out the uniforms issued them, since they were emaciated from a lack of food. But all of the new recruits were eager to learn the white man's military ways.

Meanwhile, on March 6, 7, and 8, in another sector of the Civil War theater, white officers were discovering how sadly neglected had been the Indians' military training. At the Battle of Pea Ridge, or Elkhorn, in northwest Arkansas, when General Samuel Curtis' four huge Union divisions came to grips for three days with General Earl Van Dorn's fourteen thousand Confederates, Pike's Indians, with the exception of Stand Watie's regiment, conducted themselves like seventeenth-century savages. "The amount of effort and of profanity expended by their white officers trying to keep them in line at the front," Horace Greeley later reported, "probably overbalanced the total value of their services; so that, if they chose to depart for their homes soon after the close of the battle, it is not probable that any strenuous efforts were made to detain them."[35]

Pike's Indians were charged by both Union and Confederate War Departments with emitting yells in the heat of the battles that could be heard above the roar of the cannon, with using bows and arrows in lieu of the guns issued them, and with divesting the injured and dead on the battlefields of their scalps (using tomahawks). According to Greeley, Drew's men were "displeased with the falling on their heads of great branches and tops of the trees behind which they had sought shelter; and in fact the whole conduct of the battle . . . to their apprehension, was disgusting."[36]

Since this was the first major engagement by Pike's Indians, their conduct might have been excused had it not been so nortoriously barbaric. Admittedly, Drew's command of full bloods did not want to fight their Northern brothers, and, having been issued worn-out shotguns and rifles and treated with contempt by many of their white allies, they did not deny the charges of barbarism made against them. Both Pike and Ross—although they publicly denounced the Indians' behavior—were somewhat in sympathy with the Indian miscreants who had not been paid for former services by the Confederacy. The uniforms promised them had even been diverted elsewhere. More galling than anything to Ross and Pike was the knowledge that Cherokee troops—in violation of the treaty made with the Confederacy, which distinctly specified that Cherokee troops would not be required to fight on "foreign" soil without

[35] *The American Conflict*, II, 33f.
[36] *Ibid.*

the consent of the Cherokee Nation and its principal chief—had been ordered to Arkansas, leaving the Nation wide open to invasion.

In contrast to the behavior of Drew's men, that of Watie's regiment again drew extravagant praise from the Confederate military. On March 7, at Lee Town, Watie's forces, aided by a few Texans, managed to capture a Federal battery and to withstand the Federals' repeated attempts to recapture it. "I don't know how we did it," declared one of Watie's men afterward, "but Watie gave the order, which he always led, and his men could follow him into the very jaws of death. The Indian Rebel Yell was given and we fought them like tigers three to one. It must have been that mysterious power of Stand Watie that led us on to make the capture against such odds."[37]

Ordered by Van Dorn to occupy Pea Ridge and note any attempt on the part of the enemy to turn the Confederate left flank, Watie and his men complied to the letter. Once during the fray Sigel's cannon shelled both Watie and McIntosh, whereupon Watie's men took temporary shelter in near-by fields and woods. But they shortly returned to the Ridge and held it to the very last of the engagement.

With the deaths of Generals McCulloch and McIntosh, the Confederate army was forced into full retreat in three sections. Watie and his men covered the movement in good order, as did General Joseph O. Shelby. Following the deceptive Shelby, Sigel became confused. Estimating that the Confederate strength was stronger than he had at first thought, Sigel excitedly warned Curtis that Van Dorn might yet rally and surround the Federals.

Upon his return to Camp Stephens, Watie learned that the Indian troops under Pike had been cut off from his command and were wandering around in the hills. Growing tired of the white man's style of fighting, some of Drew's full bloods had returned to Camp Stephens and looted the provision wagon, thus depriving Watie and his men of food. So miscreant had many of Drew's regiment behaved during the Battle of Pea Ridge that Van Dorn, discouraged, had ordered Indian troops back to the Territory. Thereafter, the Indians

---

[37] Frank Cunningham, *General Stand Watie's Confederate Indians*, 60.

were utilized by the Confederate military in guerrilla warfare with instructions to burn bridges, cut off supplies, and otherwise annoy the enemy.

On June 28, the Indian Expedition, having been duly organized in Kansas, left Humboldt. Taking the Military Road out of Baxter Springs, the troops crossed the Quapaw Strip and, unmolested, entered the Indian Territory. The Expedition was commanded by Colonel William Weer, whose forces consisted of the Tenth Kansas Regiment, four companies of the North Kansas Allen's Battery of Six Tenths Parrot Guns, and the First and Second Indian Regiments under Major William Phillips and Colonel John Ritchie respectively. On the lookout for Watie's men, who, mounted on ponies, were known to be thudding down dirt roads in the vicinity of Cowskin Prairie, the First and Second Indian Regiments were ordered to scout the country between the Arkansas border and the Military Road.

A hot July sun added to the discomfort of the Expedition, as did the contaminated water that the men at times were forced to drink. Flies and mosquitoes made both men and horses miserable. But despite these hardships, on July 3, Weer's men surprised an encampment of Drew and Watie's Confederate Indians and Colonel J. J. Clarkson's whites near Locust Grove. After a fierce skirmish, they captured sixty-four mule teams, a Confederate supply train, and one hundred prisoners, among whom were a goodly number of Drew's regiment who invited capture.

As the Expedition struck out across the feverish countryside for Tahlequah, disagreements arose between Colonel Weer and his officers and heightened the tension that already existed in the group. Colonel Weer's sparring partner was usually Colonel F. Salomon, who resented the fact that Weer was taking the Expedition deeper and deeper into the Cherokee country (known to be infested by Watie's guerrillas), apparently oblivious to the distance he was putting between his men and their Kansas supply depots. Weer's lack of perception, so Salomon thought, stemmed from his frequent and generous pulls on the whisky flask. Weer's intemperance concerned his fellow officer.

Fretting at the scarcity of supplies, the lack of water, and the sickness in the camps, Salomon bided his time. Meanwhile, Carruth and Martin, special Indian agents assigned to the Expedition, were taking stock of the Cherokee Nation's resources, the devastation, if any, occasioned by the war, and the crops or lack of them, preparatory to rendering a report to the War Department.

On July 7, Colonel Weer decided it was the opportune time to approach John Ross on the subject of returning to the Union. From his camp on Wolf Creek, Weer dispatched a communiqué to Ross at Park Hill asking for an interview. Delivered to Ross by Dr. Gillpatrick, a surgeon attached to the Expedition, under a flag of truce, the communiqué was promptly answered—but not to Weer's satisfaction. Refusing to grant Weer an interview, Ross reminded him that "under the sanction and authority of the whole Cherokee people" the Cherokee Nation had negotiated a treaty with the Confederate government which it felt honor bound to keep. Accompanying Ross's reply were various documents bearing on the alliance made with the Confederacy, which Ross had included, no doubt, to justify his own and the National Council's previous actions.

Ross's attitude confused Weer, who had received assurance from Evan Jones that Ross and nine-tenths of the Cherokee people, despite outward appearances, remained loyal to the Union. Three hundred of Drew's men and the Cherokee refugees from Opothleyohola's camp who were being returned to their former homes had also assured the Colonel of Ross's loyalty. Thus, Weer referred the matter to General James G. Blunt.

Blunt's reply to Weer (received by the latter on July 12) obviously inspirited him, on July 14, to order Captain H. S. Greeno and his detachment to Park Hill or as near to Park Hill as Greeno deemed advisable. On this same day Weer sent a force, led by Major W. T. Campbell, to examine "the alleged position of the enemy south of the Arkansas." Upon reaching Park Hill, Greeno decided to camp in the vicinity of John Ross's home, which was guarded by some two hundred Ross men. Campbell, after noting the Confederates' activity at Fort Davis, crossed the Arkansas and halted at Fort Gibson and was there joined by Weer to await developments.

Greeno's detachment, made up of one company of whites and fifty Cherokees, encamped two and one-half miles south of Tahlequah, were hard pressed to know what to do next. But as soon as he learned that Colonel Cooper, in command of all the country south of the Arkansas, was concentrating his forces at Fort Davis at the confluence of the Verdigris and Arkansas, Greeno went into action. Commanding his men to make all the commissioned officers who with their men were on guard at Rose Cottage prisoners of war, Greeno boldly ordered the capture and arrest of John Ross.

Having been captured on July 15, Ross and his family, together with all the precious Cherokee records, the Nation's funds, and other valuables, were conducted to Kansas and from there to Washington and Philadelphia under Union escort. Once paroled, Ross established a residence in the two-storied Colonial house at 708 South Washington Square in Philadelphia that belonged to his second wife. There Ross lived for the duration of the war, spending much of his time in Washington on important business for the Nation. Considered by government authorities to be still the principal chief of the once illustrious Cherokee Nation, Ross was treated with the utmost courtesy and respect by President Lincoln and his cabinet. Soon a personal friendship sprang up between Ross and Lincoln, which enabled the exiled Ross to exert an influence on the affairs of his nation. Lincoln even assured Ross with the utmost solemnity in the winter of 1863 that the Cherokees' treaty with the South would never be held against the Nation by the United States government.[38]

Following Ross's arrest and departure from the Nation, the Indian Expedition, in a sense, fell apart. Charging Weer with being "abusive and violent in his intercourse with his fellow-officers, entirely disregarding military usages and discipline, always rash in speech and acts", Colonel F. Salomon, on July 18, arrested his superior officer and arranged to have Weer conducted under guard to Leavenworth to stand trial. Thereafter leaders of the three In-

---

[38] "Memorial of Our National Council, on Behalf of the Hon. John Ross Now and for Over Forty (40) Years, Principal Chief of the Cherokee Nation," Jan. 31, 1866, in Ross Papers, *loc. cit.*

dian regiments (a third had been formed after the Locust Grove victory) decided to consolidate into brigades, with Colonel Robert Furnas in command. Under this arrangement Furnas retained his command of the First Brigade, Lieutenant David Corwin of the Second, and Colonel William A. Phillips of the Third. Colonel Salomon, after Weer's arrest, had withdrawn to Camp Quapaw in the northeast corner of the Nation in order to be near a food depot, good grazing lands, and a pure water supply. He had chosen this location because it enabled his Union forces to patrol the valleys of Spring River, Shoal Creek, and the Neosho or Grand river. The Indian brigades, after their reorganization, moved their headquarters to an area between Horse Creek and Wolf Creek north of the Arkansas River. John Drew and his men were left at Park Hill to protect Ross's holdings, now jeopardized by Confederate forces who held the country south of the Arkansas.

With Fort Gibson, Tahlequah, Park Hill, and practically all the Cherokee country north to the Moravian Mission in Confederate hands, Stand Watie and his men had a field day. Noting that the general store belonging to Daniel Ross and Dan Gunter at Fort Gibson had been unmolested by Federal troops, Watie's men wrecked it, wastefully dumping one hundred hogsheads of sugar on the ground. They then took Daniel Ross and Gunter prisoners. At Tahlequah on August 21, Watie called a council and was elected principal chief of the Cherokee Nation.

Threatened by Watie, Union Cherokees who yet remained in the Tahlequah–Park Hill–Fort Gibson area either swore allegiance to the Confederacy or hid in the woods. Mrs. William P. Ross's mother and sister, occupying Hunter's Hill in its owners' absence, reported to their kin in the East that the day after they left Park Hill for the East, Watie's troops killed two men in the Murrell orchard and a few days later killed several more. Writing from Washington to his son in school at Nazareth, Pennsylvania, William P. Ross gave him this news: "Your grandmother's house at the mill was broken into and all she had was stolen."[39]

[39] November 19, 1862, in *ibid.*

It was a relief to Union Cherokees when General Thomas Hindman (Van Dorn's successor after the former's transfer to another war sector) arrived at Tahlequah and suppressed, for the time being, Watie's guerrillas. Many of the perpetrators of recent atrocities were, by Hindman's orders, deservedly punished before Hindman hurried northward to join General James Rains, Joseph O. Shelby, and Douglas H. Cooper in their scheme to recover the lead mines at Granby, Missouri. Soon afterward Watie, too, left the Tahlequah–Fort Gibson area to participate in skirmishes with Union Indian brigades in the northeast corner of the Nation and over the line into Missouri, Arkansas, and Kansas, where the rebels (both white and Indian) were frequently defeated in the fall and winter of 1862–63. Thus, abandoned for a time—but awaiting the next invader—the Tahlequah–Fort Gibson area, enveloped in gloom and apprehension, became a ghost community—fear haunted.

Meanwhile, in Washington, President Lincoln and John Ross had several conferences. "During the interview which I had the honor to have with your Excellency, the 12th instant," Ross wrote to Lincoln on September 16, 1862, "you requested that the objects of my visit should be communicated in writing. I therefore beg leave, very respectfully to represent. . . ."

The objects of Ross's visit to Lincoln, as summed up in this letter, were to give the President an exact account of why Ross and his people had negotiated a treaty with the Confederacy; to explain why, as soon as the Indian Expedition marched into the country, the great mass of Cherokee people had rallied spontaneously around the authorities of the United States; and to show why the loyal majority were now engaged in fighting under the Union flag. Ross also apprised the President that "The withdrawal of . . . the [Indian Expedition] and [the abandonment of his] people and country to the forces of the Confederate States . . . [had left] them in a position fraught with distress, danger, and ruin."

In conclusion, Ross asked the President for help for his people:

What the Cherokee people now desire is ample military protection for life and property: a recognition by the Government of the obligations of existing Treaties and a willingness and determination to carry out the policy indicated by your Excellency of enforcing the laws and extending to those who are loyal all the protection in your power.[40]

President Lincoln's sympathies and sense of justice seem to have been deeply aroused by Ross—as the following letter, written by Lincoln to General Samuel Curtis on October 10, 1862, indicates:

> I believe some Cherokee Indian regiments, with some white forces operating with them, now at or near Fort Scott, are within your department and under your command. John Ross, Principal Chief of the Cherokees, is now here an exile, and he wished to know, and so do I, whether the force above mentioned could not occupy the Cherokee country consistently with the public service. Please consider and answer.[41]

General Curtis' reply to Lincoln was not exactly reassuring. "I doubt," Curtis immediately wrote, "the expediency of occupying ground so remote from supplies, but I expect to make rebels very scarce in that quarter pretty soon."[42]

However, Union forces did step up action in the Indian Territory in October. Late in that month, General James G. Blunt's Kansas Division attacked the Confederate forces of General Cooper near Fort Wayne. Although Stand Watie stood up to Blunt's superior numbers with his usual fire and fury, the Union troops won. And Watie covered Cooper's retreat to Fort Davis.

After this, Colonel William Phillips occupied Fort Gibson, and, according to the former Hannah Worcester, Phillips would now hold the country from the South. When Phillips was not tearing down the two blockhouses at the fort and using them to build other fortifications, he was fighting off the attacks of Watie's guerrillas,

---

[40] In *ibid.*
[41] Morris L. Wardell, *A Political History of the Cherokee Nation,* 157.
[42] *Ibid.*

who roamed the Nation and burned, pillaged, and carried off the property of loyal Cherokees. A refugee in Kansas, Mrs. William P. Ross, wrote to her schoolboy son in 1863: "You know your papa's and grandpa's store was burnt and they lost between 40 and $50,000 worth of goods."[43] In a later letter to her son, Mrs. Ross bemoaned the fact that they were now homeless:

> Where we will find another home I cannot say, but I still intend to go back to the Nation, but whether there will be peace, safety and pleasure living there for a long time to come is doubtful. At best things will be changed. Many of our friends have been scattered abroad upon the world. Others dead, yet others are estranged one from the other.[44]

In February, 1863, the National Council (composed of Ross men) held a meeting at Cowskin Prairie and protested Watie's claim to the title of principal chief bestowed upon him at Tahlequah the preceding August. Acting for Ross, Thomas Pegg presided as chief at this council, which officially abrogated the treaty made with the Confederacy; voted to depose all Cherokee officials who were disloyal to the Union; and, in accordance with Lincoln's policy, abolished slavery. Deciding that it was of utmost importance to keep in touch with the Union government, the council also voted to send a delegation to Washington (Chief Ross, already there, could counsel with delegates Evan Jones and Captain James McDaniel). Meeting again in May, the council passed an act empowering Riley Keys and William Potter Ross to receive and dispense funds received from the Union government to 1,200 starving refugees. But, obviously, the starving refugees in the Tahlequah area had received some help before this, for Mrs. William P. Ross had commented in a letter to her son on February 23, 1863:

> Your papa is at Mayesville or was a few days ago . . . but expected

---

[43] May 13, 1863, in Ross Papers, *loc. cit.*
[44] August 31, 1863, in *ibid.*

to go down to Park Hill with some wagons and 100 men taking flour to the poor people there. Watie's men have acted very badly indeed since we left. They took all of Uncle Robert's things and gave them away and Aunt Min's too and robbed Mrs. Gunter's House when she was dying.[45]

Hannah Worcester was one of the white people at Park Hill who looked forward to the flour and food supplies' being brought to that area by William Potter Ross and his company of one hundred loyal Cherokees. She wrote to her sister, Mrs. A. E. W. Robertson, on May 12, 1863:

> I am dependent on what is given me for bread, but we have not suffered yet. They are now expecting a large Train loaded with flour to supply the people. Hundreds of women and children, now without bread and salt, eagerly waiting for the Train. . . . I fear that many will actually starve this year.[46]

The victories of the Union army at Gettysburg and Vicksburg in the summer of 1863 had their parallel that same summer in the Indian Territory. The Battle of Honey Springs, fought in the Creek country on July 17, 1863, and lost by the Confederacy, marked the turning point in territorial warfare. Confederate Colonel Cooper's original plan was to capture Fort Gibson. Consequently, he concentrated his Creek, Choctaw, Chickasaw, and Cherokee forces, together with a squadron of Texas cavalry, at Honey Springs to wait there for reinforcements promised him from Fort Smith—planning when they arrived to take the Texas Road to the fort and capture it without difficulty. But Cooper's plans went astray.

Anticipating Cooper's attack, Union forces from Fort Gibson, reinforced by those of General Blunt, attacked Cooper at Honey Springs (near present-day Muskogee, Oklahoma) before Cooper's reinforcements arrived and so put the Confederates to rout. Pain-

---

[45] In *ibid.*

[46] In Alice Robertson Collection, *loc. cit.*

fully and slowly the defeated forces withdrew to camps in the Choctaw and Chickasaw nations, leaving the greater part of the Indian
Territory in the hands of the Federals, who, encouraged by their
decisive victory, immediately occupied Fort Smith.

Alarmed at the turn of the Confederate tide, Stand Watie appealed for aid to S. S. Scott, commissioner of Indian affairs, at Richmond:

> The history of military operations in this country and in the State of
> Arkansas, directly affecting the interests of our people, gives just cause
> for complaint. The Indian troops who have been true to the South
> from the very first have been treated in many instances as though it
> were immaterial whether or not they were paid promptly or equipped
> as thoroughly as other soldiers. Money specially obtained for them has
> more than once been appropriated to the use of other commands. Cloth-
> ing, procured at great trouble and expense, to cover the nakedness of
> Indian troops has . . . been distributed among less necessitous soldiers.
> . . . In April last a small force of hostile Indians, Negroes, and one
> battalion of Kansas troops, in all about 2,000 men, took possession of
> Fort Gibson. . . . They have held this place, and consequently the
> Cherokee Nation, ever since, almost unmolested.[47]

Watie expressed regret in this communication that families of the
Confederate Indians had been forced to flee the Nation and seek
refuge in camps in the Chickasaw and Choctaw nations and in the
state of Texas. Among the refugees were Watie's wife Sarah and
their four younger children—Saladin (Watie's eldest son, who, at
fifteen, had been made a captain) remained until the end of the war
with his father.

Mrs. Watie, torn by anxiety for both her son and husband, often
expressed the wish during her exile in Texas that she would die.
In the fall of 1863, hearing about Watie's acts of vengeance in and
around Tahlequah, she grew more depressed. Fearing that her husband would kill William Potter Ross, whom his men had pur-

---

[47] Cunningham, *General Stand Watie's Confederate Indians*, 103f.

portedly captured, Mrs. Watie urged that Ross's life be spared—not on account of her sympathy for him but because his death would hurt Ross's poor old mother.

Watie's reply to Sarah, written from his camp near North Fork Town on November 12, 1863, should have relieved her concern over Ross. However, Watie's recitation of his other acts of vengeance could not have been reassuring to Sarah, to whom Watie had once said, "I am not a killer":

> I went to Tahlequah and Park Hill. Took Daniel Hicks and Ross. Would not allow them killed because you said William Ross must not be killed on old Mrs. Jack Ross's account. Killed few Pins in Tahlequah. They had been holding Council. I had the old Council house set on fire and burned down. Also John Ross's house. Poor Andy Nave [related to Chief Ross] was killed he refused to surrender and was shot by Dick Fields. I felt sorry as he used to be quite friendly toward me before the war. . . . Another scout has since been made to Tahlequah under Butler [the notorious James Butler]. He returned today. They found some negro soldiers at Park Hill killed two and two white men. They brought in some of Ross's negroes. . . . Since Steele's & Cooper's retreat from Fort Smith I have been placed in command of [all] the Indian troops but Choctaws.[48]

Appalled at Watie's activities, Dr. Dwight Hitchcock wrote to the William S. Robertsons on November 25, 1863:

> The history of the last four weeks is a sad one. . . . On the night of the 28th of October Watie with 80 to 100 men visited Tahlequah and Park Hill. . . . Andrew Nave was shot and stabbed. . . . One Cherokee soldier was killed at Tahlequah—another a few miles above. Daniel Hicks, John A. Ross, Jack Cooston, and Marion Holderman, 6th Kansas . . . were made prisoners. Many houses were utterly emptied. I lost almost all I had. . . . Mother lost the mementoes of her dead children. . . . The Chief's house was burned to ashes. . . . on the 31st of October Shelby passed Dwight [Mission] with the remains of his

---

[48] In Cherokee Papers, *loc. cit.*

deserted army from Missouri and on the next day made a junction with Cooper at the mouth of the Sallisaw. Moving down the Arkansas, they menaced Fort Smith, but were met by our forces and compelled to . . . retreat toward Red River.[49]

According to Dr. Hitchcock, Jim Butler's men had in their recent raid pulled the shoes off the feet of little orphaned children who were being cared for at Park Hill by Mrs. Palmer.

A Ross man, Hitchcock did not tell the Robertsons that the Pins were keeping up with the atrocities committed by Watie, Butler, and other Confederate guerrillas. They too were on "a mission of the devil"—as Hitchcock termed the mission of Jim Butler and Watie—throughout the fall months of 1863. "Hannah was down last week," Hitchcock wrote to the Robertsons from Fort Blunt, "[and] I can well believe it when she says 'it seems all the time like one great funeral.' "[50]

Stand Watie's admirers—and they were legion in 1864 as they are today—were tremendously impressed by his war achievements. On May 10, 1864, Watie rose to the rank of brigadier general in the Confederate army, a military honor accorded no other Indian at that date. On June 15, 1864, Watie captured a steamboat ascending the Arkansas loaded heavily with Federal supplies for Fort Gibson. This act of Watie's prompted General Maxey to exclaim: "Watie and his men have been from the beginning as true as the needle to the North star."[51]

Toward the end of the war, Brigadier General Stand Watie's uniform was threadbare, and Mrs. Watie was planning to make him a new one that would compliment his rank. But before she could get started, General Watie, assisted by General Richard Gano and his Texas Brigade, had the great good fortune to capture, on September 18, 1864, a Federal wagon train packed with enough food and

[49] In Alice Robertson Collection, *loc. cit.*

[50] *Ibid.*

[51] See Ohland Morton, "Confederate Government Relations with the Five Civilized Tribes," *Chronicles of Oklahoma*, Vol. XXXI, Nos. 2 and 3 (Autumn, 1933), 317.

clothing for two thousand men. Valued at $1,500,000, the wagon train—consisting of 250 big heavy wagons and 740 mules—was captured at Cabin Creek (in present-day Mayes County, Oklahoma). Apprised of his deed, Mrs. Watie wrote to her husband. "I thought I would send you some clothes," she laconically commented, "but I hear that you have done better than to wait on me."[52] But from General Douglas this last important encounter between the Federals and the Confederates in the Indian Territory drew more extravagant praise:

> The brilliancy and completeness of this expedition has not been excelled in the history of the war. Firm, brave and confident, the officers had but to order and the men cheerfully executed. The whole having been conducted with perfect harmony between the war-torn veteran Stand Watie, the chivalrous Gano, and their respective commands.[53]

The houses of the Confederate Congress passed a joint resolution of thanks to General Watie and General Gano. It was signed on January 23, 1865, by President Davis. But Stand Watie's star was to attain even greater brilliance when, after Lee's surrender at Appomattox on April 9, 1865, Watie held off from surrender until June 23, 1865. By so doing, he went down in history as the last Confederate general to give up the fight.

The Civil War now having come to an end, the Cherokee Nation faced another era of rebuilding. But in its new government John Ross was destined to have little part. Grief-stricken by the death of his beloved wife in Philadelphia on July 20, 1865; by the death of his eldest son in a Confederate prison camp; and by the devastation which his Nation had suffered from a war that he had not wanted, Ross's health suffered. But his unconquerable spirit miraculously enabled him to stay alive a little longer. Having been the Cherokees' principal chief for nearly forty years, he could not abandon his Nation until a fair and equitable treaty had been negotiated between it and the United States. After that, he could lay his many burdens down forever.

[52] *Ibid.*, 318.
[53] *Ibid.*, 317f.

CHAPTER XIV

The Oft-inked Treaty Pen

In 1865, the treaty pen having now supplanted the sword, five United States commissioners—appointed by President Johnson to negotiate treaties of "friendship and amity" with territorial Indian nations and tribes—headed for Fort Smith to prepare for the peace council scheduled to open there on the morning of September 8.

En route to the Fort Smith council from Philadelphia around the same time was delegate Chief John Ross, who, when his boat was but a day's distance from Fort Gibson, wearily penned the following lines to his sister-in-law:

Steamer Iron City
Five miles below Van Buren
August 31, 1865

Dear Sister Sarah:

I trust you have read . . . my hasty notes . . . mailed on the way for the loved ones of 708 [South Washington Square, Philadelphia]. . . . In these letters you were all advised of our safe voyage. We were detained at Little Rock about eight hours unloading freight etc. In the meantime some of us [the Cherokee delegation that had been in Washington on the Nation's business] paid our respects to Genl. Reynolds and Col. Nelson. . . . We were informed by the Genl that Genl Harney [one of the United States commissioners] had left that morning for

Fort Smith and that the other commissioners from Washington [Dennis Cooley, the New Indian commissioner; Elijah Sells, Southern superintendent; Thomas Wistar, a Pennsylvania Quaker; and Ely Parker, a Seneca Indian, who had been a member of Grant's staff in the late war] . . . were not expected to reach Fort Smith until the 5th of September.

The river [Arkansas] is in a good boating condition. If no unforeseen accident prevents, the Captain says we will reach Fort Gibson tomorrow afternoon. The boat shakes—and my mind is not sufficiently composed to write as satisfactorily as I could wish under other circumstances.

I know that I am fast approaching my country and my people [after an absence of three years] and that I shall soon meet with my dear children [by first marriage], relatives, and friends who will greet me with joyful hearts. But where is that delightful home and the matron of that once happy family who so kindly and hospitably entertained our guests—alas, I shall see them no more on earth. The loved wife and mother is at rest in the Heavenly mansions prepared for the redeemed, and the family Homestead ruthlessly reduced to ashes by the hand of rebel incendiaries, and . . . I am here journeying . . . alone to find myself a stranger and homeless in my own country. . . . The picture is painful to my feelings.[1]

The aged Principal Chief of the Cherokees was forced by fatigue bordering on collapse to abandon his plan to attend the opening sessions of the council on September 8, and to remain with relatives at the Murrell house near Park Hill until the middle of the month. Ross sent Second Chief Lewis Downing to the Fort Smith council in his stead. Accompanying Downing were delegates Christie, Reese, Pegg, Flute, Conrad, Fish, Chee-Chee, William P. Ross, Baldridge, White Catcher, and a half-dozen other loyal or Union Cherokees.

At Fort Smith these men learned that Stand Watie's Southern Cherokee delegates would not be present for the opening sessions of the council, as they were holding a council with Southern Choctaws, Creeks, Seminoles, Chickasaws, and other fragmentary tribes in or

[1] In Ross Papers, *loc. cit.*

adjacent to the Territory at Armstrong Academy in the Choctaw Nation to the south. But despite their absence, the commissioners decided to open the Fort Smith Council on schedule.

Commissioner Cooley, chairman of the commissioners and also "presiding president" of the council, in his opening address charged his Union audience with "crimes of secession," accusing them of being traitors to the Union cause. Stung by his accusations and pronouncement that, because of their defection, territorial tribes and nations would be required by the federal government to forfeit both tribal lands and tribal annuities, Cooley's audience revolted. Silas Armstrong, chief of the Union Wyandots, angrily declared that the council had already fallen far short of his expectations. And why had Cooley not reserved his "talk" for the real enemies of the federal government, the absent Southern Indians, due to arrive at the council in a few days? Other delegates bitterly maintained that they were not empowered by their people to negotiate treaties with the federal government, but had come to the council expecting to renew peaceful alliances with the federal government and not to be accused by it of defection. Their people had sacrificed their all for the Union, and they were not traitors.

Permitted to air these grievances at the afternoon session of the council, the Indians made the most of the opportunity. Eloquently, the Cherokees argued their case, reminding the commissioners that, although their Nation had made a necessitous treaty with the Confederacy on October 7, 1861, it had abrogated that treaty in February, 1863, and from then on two troops had fought on the Union side. But obviously the Cherokees' argument had little effect on Cooley. When they had finished, he viciously attacked their absent chief, accusing Ross of being an enemy of the United States, and thus unworthy of consideration or pardon by the President, even though individual deserving Cherokees would be pardoned.

Harshly, Cooley read aloud to the council the names of the nations and tribes who, because of their former alliances with the Confederacy, had now "forfeited and lost all their rights to annuities and lands."[2] Understandably, the Cherokees were at the end of Cooley's

[2] Annie Heloise Abel, *The American Indian under Reconstruction*, 187f.

black list, since they had held out longer against the Confederacy than any of the Southern Indians and had been the last tribe in the nation to sign a Confederate treaty. Having thus disposed of Chief Ross and the Cherokees for the time being, Cooley next gave his audience a digest of the instructions handed him by James Harlan, secretary of the interior, prior to his (Cooley's) departure from Washington. Harlan's orders were calculated to break down any resistance to the drastic provisions contained in the treaties to be proffered the delegates. Cooley, as directed by Harlan, prefaced the submission of these treaties with the following unctuous and high-sounding statements:

. . . Under the terms of the treaties with the United States Congress of July 5, 1862, all these nations and tribes have now forfeited and lost all their rights to annuities and lands. The President, however, does not desire to take advantage of or enforce the penalties for the unwise actions of these Nations.

The President is anxious to renew the relations which existed at the breaking out of the rebellion.

We as representatives of the President, are empowered to enter into new treaties with the proper delegates of the tribes located within the so-called Indian territory, and others . . . living west and north of the Indian territory.

Such treaties must contain, substantially, the following stipulations:

1. Each tribe must enter into a treaty for permanent peace and amity with themselves, each nation and tribe, and with the United States.

2. Those settled in the Indian territory must bind themselves, when called upon by the government, to aid in compelling the Indians of the plains to maintain peaceful relations with each other, with the Indians in the territory and with the United States.

3. The institution of slavery . . . must be forthwith abolished, and measures taken for the emancipation of all persons held in bondage, and for their incorporation in the tribes on an equal footing with the original members, or otherwise provided for.

4. . . . a stipulation in the treaties that slavery, or involuntary servitude, shall never exist in the tribe or nation, except in punishment of crime.

5. A portion of the lands hitherto owned and occupied by you must be set apart for the friendly tribes now in Kansas and elsewhere, on such terms as may be agreed upon by the parties, and approved by the government.

6. It is the policy of the government . . . that all the nations and tribes in the Indian territory be formed into one consolidated government, after the plan proposed by the Senate of the United States, in a bill [Harlan's bill railroaded through the Senate in March, 1865, a few days before he received the appointment to the cabinet post of secretary of the interior] for organizing the Indian territory.

7. No white person, except officers, agents, and employees of the government, or of any internal improvement authorized by the government, will be permitted to reside in the territory, unless formally incorporated with some tribe, according to the usages of the land.[3]

A majority of the delegates asked the commissioners to permit them a leisurely examination of the treaty's contents. But the Cherokee delegates, having a deeper understanding than the others of the true meaning of the document, refused point-blank to sign it, unless the commissioners agreed to insert the following statement in the record:

> We, the loyal Cherokee delegation, acknowledge the execution of the treaty of October 7, 1861; but we solemnly declare that the execution of the treaty was procured by the co-ercion of the rebel army.[4]

Upon receipt of this statement, Cooley and the other commissioners rightfully assumed that Chief John Ross had crossed the Arkansas River and was somewhere in the vicinity of the council house dispensing advice to the Cherokee delegates. Whereupon the commissioners apprised Secretary Harlan by wire of Ross's arrival and their intention to refuse to recognize him as the Cherokees' principal chief.

"I am satisfied in view of the facts and circumstances . . . ," Harlan replied, "that it would be for the benefit of the great Cherokee Na-

[3] *Ibid.,* 187ff.
[4] *Ibid.,* 199.

tion that their present Chief John Ross be deposed from his said office of principal Chief of the Cherokee Nation."[5]

Tension tightened in council circles when Southern Cherokee delegates, together with Southern Choctaw, Chickasaw, Creek, and Seminole delegates, arrived. Prominent at all the sessions thereafter was thirty-one-year-old Elias Cornelius Boudinot. As spokesman for Stand Watie and the other delegates, Boudinot courted the favor of the commissioners by his flow of eloquence and his amiable attitude toward the controversial points of the treaty—the elevation of Negroes to the status of citizens in the Nation excepted.

The intention of the federal government, as clearly stated in the treaty, was to form all the nations and tribes in the Indian Territory into one consolidated government, after the plan proposed by the Senate in Harlan's bill. Obviously, Boudinot did not react unfavorably to this suggestion, as did Ross. Ross, a master-analyst of Indian bills introduced in the Congress, had heard Harlan's bill debated in the Senate in February and early March. Aware of its design, Ross had opposed the bill before its passage, thereby incurring Harlan's animosity. But Boudinot, either unmindful or unaware that the bill, as incorporated into the present treaty, would divest territorial nations and tribes of the cherished right to manage their own affairs and thus eventually terminate individual governments, approved heartily of Harlan's bill. He termed it "one of the grandest and noblest schemes ever devised for the red man and entitles the author to (as I believe he will soon receive) the lasting gratitude of every Indian."[6]

Neither did Boudinot seem to resent the presence at the Fort Smith Council of railroad lobbyists. Employed by railroad companies to acquire right of ways through the Territory by fair means or foul, these persons were an abomination to Chief Ross, who had studied their operations in Washington for the past three years (and even before the late war).

Agitated by the lobbyists and by the proposed treaty, Chief John

---

[5] *Ibid.*, 201n.
[6] Wardell, *A Political History of the Cherokee Nation*, 193.

Ross hastened to the council at Fort Smith, arriving there on September 15. His grim presence in the council room created a stir among both the commissioners and the Southern Cherokees. At sight of Ross, Boudinot redoubled his efforts to please the commissioners. And the latter, having received approval from Harlan of their plan to denounce Ross, instructed Chairman Cooley to read aloud the following statement at the afternoon session of the council:

> WHEREAS, John Ross, an educated Cherokee, formerly chief of the nation, became the emissary of the States in rebellion and, by means of his superior education and ability as such emissary, induced many of his people to abjure their allegiance to the United States and to join the States in rebellion. . . .[7]

The indictment of John Ross by the commissioners that followed was designated to ruin Ross and, thereafter, to rid the admininstration in Washington of his unwelcome interference in territorial affairs. Seated in the council room among his faithful supporters, John Ross heard himself referred to by Cooley as an enemy of the United States, as a charlatan who pretended to be the principal chief of the Cherokee Nation but was not, and as a poisoner of the minds of both Cherokee and Creek delegates.

Like a hammer on flint, Cooley's voice penetrated the ears of his audience as he prefaced his accusations repeatedly with the word "Whereas":

> . . . WHEREAS, we believe him still at heart an enemy of the United States and disposed to breed discord among his people, represent the will and wishes of the loyal Cherokees, and is not the choice of any considerable portion of the Cherokee nation for the office which he claims, but which by their law we believe he does not in fact hold; and
>
> WHEREAS, the Agent and Superintendent have recommended that the said Ross be deposed and not recognized by the Government as the principal chief of the Cherokee nation, and the Commissioner of Indian Affairs having approved the same. . . .

Now therefore, we the undersigned Commissioners sent by the Presi-

[7] Abel, *The American Indian under Reconstruction*, 199n.

dent of the United States to negotiate treaties with the Indians of the Indian territory and southwest . . . do approve the above recommendation and decision and refuse as commissioners . . . to recognize said Ross as chief of the Cherokee Nation.[8]

Having accomplished his mission, Commissioner Cooley invited the Southern delegates to express their views. But before they could do so, Chief Ross addressed the chair. "May I make a few remarks?" Ross inquired. Given permission, Ross grimly faced his accuser:

Sir, I deny the charges asserted against me. I deny having used any influence either with the Cherokees, Creeks, or any other persons to resist the interests of the Indians, or of the Government of the United States. . . . I claim to be as loyal a man as any citizen of the United States. . . . I have been forty odd years Chief of the Cherokees, elected time after time. They re-elected me in my absence and I came on to the council at my advanced age, after burying my wife and burying my son. I had three sons in your army, also three grandsons and three nephews. If I had been disloyal I would not have shrunk from going in the direction where the enemies of the United States were. I came on with the hope that I might be useful to my people, to those of my people who had separated from the Nation, [and] to the Government of the United States. I came here not for the purpose of resisting the policy of the United States. If we have rights, we ought to be permitted to express them. I never recommended any other course than that which could be sustained consistent with the laws of the United States. I have been three years residing in Washington. I have been in communication with the Department [of the Interior], Sir [and] with the President. With Mr. Lincoln, I was constantly in communication, and up to the last moment [of Ross's stay in Washington] I communicated with the present President [of] the United States.[9]

Chief Ross's defense of his character on this occasion was long remembered by both white and red men who heard it. And, since his speech was published in the *New York Herald*, it was widely

[8] *Ibid.*, 200n.

[9] *Ibid.*, 203n.

circulated, as was Elias Cornelius Boudinot's diatribe against Ross that followed. For no sooner had Ross resumed his seat at the council than Boudinot gained the floor. Seizing this priceless opportunity to discredit Ross, Boudinot vindictively accused Ross of fomenting dissension in the Cherokee Nation. "I will show you," Boudinot said, "the deep duplicity and falsity that have followed him [Ross] from his childhood to the present day, when the winters of 65 or 70 years have silvered his head with sin; what can you expect of him now?"[10]

Perceiving that Boudinot's attack on Ross was obviously the resumption of a factional feud of long standing, Cooley adjourned the council until the day following. But Boudinot had sufficiently impressed Cooley to command his favor. For the remainder of the council Boudinot and Cooley were frequently seen talking together. Ross and his delegation were often snubbed by Cooley and his colleagues, possibly because Ross's delegation stubbornly refused to sign the treaty unless the commissioners would agree to incorporate into their records the delegates' statement regarding the Cherokees' treaty with the Confederacy.

Reluctantly, on September 18, the commissioners yielded on this point. But they adamantly refused to withdraw the charges made by Commissioner Cooley against Ross, as demanded by the delegates.

Signed by the Cherokees and other territorial tribes, the Fort Smith treaties were considered by the President to lack permanency until officially signed in Washington. Informed of this fact, the Union Cherokees called a council at Tahlequah in October to elect delegates to the Washington council and to address a memorial to the President in behalf of Chief John Ross, who had been so shamefully humiliated at Fort Smith. Cut to the quick by the indignities that had been heaped upon him and the aspersions cast upon his character by Cooley, Chief Ross collapsed after the council.

Chief Ross's niece, Mrs. William P. Ross (the former Molly Ross), fumed:

> I feel so angry at those commissioners. He [Uncle] talked so much about the way they had treated him. It is *shameful* and a disgrace to

10 *Ibid.*, 205n.

President Johnson to approve the course they took at the Council. The Cherokees say that white people have no right to take away the chief they have voted into office for so many years. I fear we will have much trouble for the way Uncle has been treated.[11]

Confined to his bed at the Murrell house, Ross's condition alarmed his relatives, who summoned Dr. Brown from Park Hill. The latter attentively prescribed remedies for the ailing seventy-five-year-old chief and then sat beside his bed night and day for almost a week, unwilling to leave Ross until he showed signs of improvement. But Ross's malady was partially heartbreak and sorrow, and Dr. Brown knew no remedy for that.

Able in late November to accompany the Cherokee treaty delegation to Washington, Ross wrote to his sister-in-law in Philadelphia that "so soon as I shall get out of the woods to be heard, I will make my defense against the foul aspersions that have been published by designing men to injure my reputation by placing me in a false position to subserve Policy and their own sinister motives."[12]

Chief Ross and the Cherokee delegation succeeded in obtaining an interview with President Johnson shortly after arriving in Washington in January. Upon being admitted to the President's office in the White House, Chief Ross, observing the amenities, introduced members of the delegation to the President. At this meeting also were Secretary Harlan and Commissioner Cooley. As planned by the delegation, Thomas Pegg delivered to President Johnson the lengthy handwritten memorial that had been carefully prepared by the Cherokee National Council "in behalf of the Honorable John Ross now and for over forty years principal chief of the Cherokee Nation."[13] Courteously Pegg requested that the President read the memorial vindicating Ross and its accompanying documents bearing on the Cherokees' relationships with the Confederacy. When Pegg had finished, Delegate McDaniel addressed the President and re-

[11] To her son "Will," October 2, 1865, in Ross Papers, *loc. cit.*

[12] November 12, 1865, in *ibid.*

[13] January 31, 1866, in *ibid.* The memorial contains the promise made Ross by President Lincoln not to hold the Cherokee treaty with the South against the Nation.

viewed all the disquieting circumstances that had compelled Chief Ross to align the Cherokee Nation with the Confederacy. Asked by his people if a treaty made by the Cherokees with the Confederacy would be binding or permanent, Ross had told them on the eve of the convention at Tahlequah, August 21, 1861:

> We are in the situation of a man standing alone upon a low naked spot of ground, with the water rising rapidly all around him. He sees the danger, but does not know what to do. If he remains where he is, his only alternative is to be swept away and perish. The tide carries by him, in its mad course, a drifting log. It perchance comes within reach of him. By refusing it he is a doomed man. By seizing hold of it he has a chance for his life. He can but perish in the effort, and may be able to keep his head above water until rescued or drift to where he can help himself.[14]

McDaniel explained to the President:

> We comprehended the import and force of the figure. The people saw and adopted the only means within their reach for self-preservation and an alliance was formed under duress with the rebellious states and the schemes of the rebel Cherokees [Southern Rights Cherokees] were thereby thwarted and so we drifted along in hardships, dangers, and death, in support of the Union cause until we reached the shore to stand upon the ground of our original rights.[15]

After McDaniel had spoken, President Johnson remarked that the government would act justly toward the Cherokees and that he would read the "papers" submitted for his consideration.[16]

Both Secretary Harlan and Commissioner Cooley then had the floor. Denying that he had used the word "depose" in regard to Ross, Cooley contended that he had simply said at the Fort Smith

[14] *Ibid.*; see also John Ross to Sarah, 1866, in *ibid.*

[15] John Ross to Sarah, 1866, in *ibid.* (This letter gives an exact account of the parts played by the commissioners, Ross, and the Cherokee delegation at the White House on January 15, 1866—a most revealing MS.)

[16] *Ibid.*

Council that the commissioners would not recognize Ross as the Cherokees' chief on that particular occasion.

When it came Chief Ross's turn to speak, he sharply refuted Cooley's statement, insisting that "depose," not "recognize," had been the word used by the commissioners in relation to himself. Reciting verbatim the talk between himself and the commissioners, Chief Ross explained to the President that parts of this particular conversation were not contained in the documents presented to him by the commissioners.

In a letter written by Chief Ross to his Philadelphia sister-in-law shortly after this audience with Johnson, he told her:

> At an interview with Secretary Harlan yesterday I protested *against* the propriety and self-respect of negotiating thru Commissioner Cooley on the ground of his committal to the rebel Cherokees [and] of his prejudice unjustly cherished against myself. And I have urged the Secretary to conduct the negotiations himself with us: And he has finally agreed to do it and to commence as soon as his other duties will permit him to devote a part of his time to us—and he will notify us of the time when he will be ready to meet us on the business. The city is full of Indians of various tribes—among them Stand Watie and son Saladin. Dick Fields and Joab Scales have arrived to associate, I suppose, with Boudinot and Wm. P. Adair. I feel myself as standing upon firm ground. . . . Time will soon indicate whose official authority is resting upon a sandy foundation.[17]

In the months that followed, the rival Cherokee delegations in Washington waged a battle royal over the treaty that awaited their signatures. Boudinot's Southern delegation demanded that the treaty provide for the division of the Cherokee Nation into two separate units, each having its own government. So divided, Southern Cherokees would occupy the Canadian District and an area lying between the Grand and Arkansas rivers, over which "the old dominant party" or Union Cherokees would have no jurisdiction whatsoever. Chief Ross's delegation, on the other hand, argued that division of the Nation would weaken and possibly shorten its life.

[17] *Ibid.*

As noted by Washington officials, the two Cherokee delegations were as far apart as the poles and, judged by their actions, would never resolve their differences. But these officials did not know John Ross! Possessing an unbelievable amount of political acumen and experience, Ross figuratively moved mountains to prevent the division of the Nation, just as he had prior to the Treaty of 1846. "He is as artful as ever," wrote J. W. Washbourne, secretary of the Southern delegation, to Joab A. Scales in June, 1866, "and tho' he [Ross] is personally powerless, he can work through agents, as you and I know to our cost."[18]

By saying that Ross was "personally powerless," Washbourne was alluding to the illness that, since March, had confined Ross to his hotel bed. But this illness had not prevented Ross from directing the activities of the Union delegation, nor from conferring with the Secretary of Interior, nor from striving with might and main to eliminate or soften the treaty submitted to the Cherokees.

On one occasion Secretary Harlan, Commissioner Cooley, and Elijah Sells had called on Ross at his humble hotel, located on the corner of Pennsylvania and Eighth streets, to wish him a speedy recovery.

"I learn, Mr. Ross, that you are seventy-five years of age and have served your nation over fifty," Commissioner Cooley observed.[19]

Ross replied from his sickbed:

> Yes, Sir. I am an old man and have served my people and the government of the United States a long time, over fifty years. My people have kept me in the harness, not of my own seeking, but of their own choice. I have never deceived them; and now I look back, not one act of my public life rises up to upbraid me. I have done the best I could, and today upon this bed of sickness, my heart approves all I have done. And still I am John Ross, the same John Ross of former years. Unchanged! No cause to change![20]

[18] Wardell, *A Political History of the Cherokee Nation*, 195.
[19] Daniel Ross to Brother [William P. Ross], April 3, 1866, in Ross Papers, *loc. cit.*
[20] *Ibid.*

Continuing to be confined to his bed in Washington, Ross frequently thought of John, his son by his second marriage. "It affords me exceedingly great pleasure," Ross commented in a dictated letter to his sister-in-law on April 4, 1866, "to be assured by John of his determination to put his shoulder to the wheel. This is well said. And yet I would have him remember and keep constantly before him that it is the long pull and the steady pull after all that achieves in life the most—in other words that it is uniform effort, day in and day out, that makes the man."[21]

Ross's advice to his son could well have been heeded by the delegates and United States commissioners who, day after day, attempted to come to some agreement concerning the Cherokee treaty. As usual, the independent Cherokees lagged behind the other four civilized tribes, who, by the middle of June, 1866, had all signed treaties, even though these treaties required them to make unpleasant concessions, such as granting right of way to railroad companies through territorial lands, admitting emancipated slaves and free Negroes to citizenship in their respective tribes, and opening tribal lands to Indians on neighboring reservations.

But, eventually, Cherokee delegates and United States officials came to an agreement. On July 19, 1866, the Cherokees signed the treaty that has been termed by present-day political analysts "a three-cornered treaty between the Department of the Interior and the southern and northern Cherokees."

Summarized, the Cherokee Treaty of 1866 abrogated the Confederate treaty of alliance of October 7, 1861; abolished slavery forever; proclaimed a general amnesty; and repealed confiscation laws imposed on southern Cherokees during the war and restored to these Cherokees their confiscated property. The 1866 treaty permitted Cherokees who so desired to occupy the Canadian District, "and, in case this did not furnish sufficient land, the area north of the Arkansas River lying between the Grand River and the Creek boundary—even farther north if necessary."[22] Freed slaves and free

---

[21] In *ibid.*

[22] Wardell, *A Political History of the Cherokee Nation*, 203.

Negroes were accorded the privileges of citizenship and the occupancy of land in the Canadian District and the area between the Grand and Verdigris rivers.

The Northern delegates lost their fight against organization of the territory—as did all the territorial tribes. But Harlan's bill was modified somewhat; and, although the territorial tribes were required by treaties to send delegates to a general council, at least the rigid rule of a white territorial governor was not imposed on them.

The establishment of United States courts within the territory struck at the very heart-core of John Ross and the other Cherokee delegates, who had hitherto lamented the fact that Cherokee cases were referred to white judges in the United States District Court in Arkansas instead of to native judges in a district court in the Nation.

Ceding their Neutral Land and the Cherokee Strip to the United States in trust (to be sold in due time) did not make Cherokee delegates cringe, but the erection of military posts within the Nation by the United States did. For this provision in the treaty bespoke the federal government's intention to police the Nation, as it had unsuccessfully done before.

The treaty's greatest foe, Chief John Ross, did not, however, live to see the chaos resulting from an agreement that at best could only be termed a compromise. For less than a fortnight after the Treaty of 1866 was signed, Chief John Ross's spirit departed this world. Ross died on August 1, 1866, in Washington City, and, until other more suitable arrangements could be made by the Cherokee National Council, his body rested in Brandywine Cemetery at Wilmington beside Mary, his second wife.[23] Thus the difficult reconstruction problems, outgrowths of the Treaty of 1866, became the heavy burdens of John Ross's successors who, like him, would strive mightily to keep alive the once great Cherokee republic for at least another forty years.

[23] Ross, ed., *The Life and Times of Honorable William P. Ross*, 261.

CHAPTER XV

Reconstruction and Statehood

FOLLOWING THE DEATH of Chief John Ross, the Cherokee National Council at its November meeting at Tahlequah elected William Potter Ross to the vacant office of principal chief—a difficult and trying office in normal times but one rendered more difficult in 1866 by postwar problems attendant to reconstruction. After acknowledging the honor bestowed upon him by the council, the new Chief enumerated a few of the difficulties confronting the Nation: the Treaty of 1866; the bitter enmity between Northern and Southern Cherokees; and—not to be minimized, certainly—the pinching poverty of the Cherokee people. He continued:

> The treaty concluded at Washington by the delegation of the Cherokee Nation, on the 19th of July, 1866, having met the approval, and being signed by the President of the United States, is now the supreme law. Whatever may be our opinion as to the justice and wisdom of some of the stipulations it imposes, we have full assurance that the delegation obtained the most favorable terms they could, and it is our duty to comply in good faith with all its provisions. By this course the Cherokee people will not only perform a simple duty but may be able to render harmless those articles of the treaty which, regardless of our constitution, changes its provisions and clearly contains the germs of future strife and division.[1]

[1] Ross, ed., *The Life and Times of Honorable William P. Ross*, 2f.

As emphasized by Chief Will Ross, the troublesome articles of the Treaty of 1866 were Article Eleven, granting a right of way "to any company or corporation which shall be duly authorized by Congress to construct a railroad from any point north to any point south, and from any point east to any point west of and which, may pass through the Cherokee Nation"; Article Twelve, providing for a general or intertribal council, "consisting of delegates elected by each nation or tribe lawfully residing within the Indian Territory," to be convened annually by the United States and to be organized as prescribed by the United States; and Article Thirteen, authorizing the establishment of a court or courts by the United States in the Indian Territory, "with such jurisdiction and organized in such manner as may be prescribed by law."

The railroads, argued Chief Will Ross, would menace the Nation by their acquisition of land needed by the Cherokees and, also, by encouraging white settlement. Article Twelve portended the dangerous organization of the Indian Territory into one patterned after federal territories, as previously suggested by the Harlan Bill. And Article Thirteen, providing for the establishment of a United States court or courts, presaged the curtailment of the judicial powers of the Five Tribes.

Amendments to the Cherokee constitution—rendered necessary at this time by the Treaty of 1866—related to the modification of such boundary lines of the Nation "as may be made necessary by the 17th article of the treaty concluded at Washington on the 19th day of July, 1866." The treaty also provided for the acceptance by the Cherokees as citizens of the Nation "all freedmen who have been liberated by voluntary act of their former owners or by law, as well as all free colored persons who were in the country at the commencement of the rebellion, and are now residents therein, or who may return within six months, and their descendants."[2]

Following Chief Will Ross's address to the council, a resolution was offered providing that the amendments to the constitution be submitted to the Cherokee people at a general convention on No-

[2] Starr, *History of the Cherokee Indians,* 170–77.

vember 26, at Tahlequah. Several days later, on that date, Chief Will Ross addressed the convention:

> Friends and Fellow Citizens:
>
> You have been called together . . . for the purpose of making known to you the provisions of the treaty, concluded at Washington on the 19th day of July last, and of obtaining your ratification of certain amendments to the constitution of the Nation which seem to be required, in part, by that treaty. The objects of the meeting are, therefore, important, while the circumstances under which it is held possess more than ordinary interest. For the first time for more than five years the people are assembled in general convention. For the first time since the war have you all met as friends and brothers. I most devoutly thank the Great Ruler of the Universe that it is my privilege to address you as one people. I thank Him that amidst the carnage, the horror and the desolation of those long, dark years of conflict, we have not been swept entirely off the face of the earth.[3]

Perceiving that the Southern Cherokees were not well represented, Chief Ross stressed the importance of unity, the kind of unity that would give strength to the Cherokees' reduced numbers and to the Nation:

> Cherokees! If you firmly resolve to become one people, you will become one people. . . . We are all possessors of a common inheritance so let us enjoy it. . . . Let us look forward to the pleasing landscape of the future . . . and not back upon the dark valley of the past, with its lost friends, blighted hopes and sad and fearful associations. . . . Never did we have more to live for, to labor for, and to gain.

The remainder of Ross's speech was reminiscent of the addresses made to the people in the past by Chief John Ross:

> Let the young men of this nation remember that idleness leads to poverty, to dissipation, to strife, to violence, to murder, to the gallows . . . [and] that industry is honorable and leads to contentment, to com-

[3] Ross, ed., *The Life and Times of Honorable William P. Ross*, 55–57.

petence, to success, and distinction. Although there are many sad and silent hearthstones, not all the first born in the land have been smitten. There are still many children left. These must be educated. . . . The means of a common school education in the English language . . . are within the reach of nearly, if not quite, all the children of the country. . . . We cannot stand still! We must go forward or backward.[4]

Two days later, on November 28, the required amendments to the constitution were ratified by the convention.

But Chief Will Ross's conciliatory attitude toward the Treaty of 1866, displayed in his address to both the council and the convention, was not echoed by Elias Cornelius Boudinot, who, in behalf of the Southern Cherokee delegation, had on July 25, 1866, written Stand Watie from Washington:

> We have been beaten; that is to say we have not been successful in securing an absolute separation. I am in doubt as to the proper course to pursue. Adair and the others wish to defeat the treaty the Rosses have signed, but I incline to the opinion that the better policy would be to accept what he put in their treaty as it does not commit us to anything, and gives us a good chance to renew the demand for a division at a more favorable opportunity.
>
> The treaty grants a general amnesty, declares confiscation laws void, and gives the Ross party no jurisdiction over us in civil and criminal cases before the courts. They shoulder all the responsibility of the negro matter. We get none of the money. I haven't time nor patience to explain.[5]

Boudinot's bitter sentiments were shared by hundreds of Southern Cherokee families who had refugeed in Texas or in the Choctaw and Chickasaw nations during the war. Reluctant to return to the Nation now that another Ross was at its head, a number of Southern Cherokees did not return until the termination of Will Ross's first administration in August, 1867. Upon learning then that the Ross party (or National party, as it was later called) had split into two

---

[4] *Ibid.*, 57f.
[5] Edward Everett Dale and Gaston Litton, *Cherokee Cavaliers*, 247.

warring factions, known as the Downing party and the Ross party, Southern refugees began drifting back to the Nation. Pending the election of a new principal chief on the first Monday in August, 1867, these refugees, realizing that they stood no chance of electing a chief from their own ranks, supported Lewis Downing. They hoped that the Downing party's candidate for chief would win over "Bill Ross," as Southern Cherokees contemptuously called the late chief's nephew and present chief.[6]

According to Chuweska Fodder, an eyewitness, the 1867 election was anything but peaceful. Fights, participated in by both men and women, were the order of the day at the polls. Even after it was announced that Downing had won over Ross, sporadic fighting broke out in the nine districts of the Cherokee Nation between "Downing men" and "Ross men."

With Chief Downing in office, practically all the Southern Cherokees moved back to the Nation. Downing, although supported by the Pins, was infinitely less obnoxious to the Southern Cherokees than Ross, whose education at Princeton was known to have been arranged by his late chieftain uncle (at one of the most critical periods in the history of the Nation) with a view to preparing him for the office of principal chief.

Understandably, Southern Cherokees settled in the Canadian District, even though their property was elsewhere. "I don't like the idea of throwing myself in the arms of the Pins across the river and have therefore rented twenty acres here," was William Boudinot's explanation of why he had settled near Webbers Falls, where his law practice was slow and unremunerative. Upon their return to the Nation from Texas and Watie's former camp on Red River, the Stand Waties settled near the Boudinots and other Southern Cherokees in the vicinity of Webbers Falls. Poor as the proverbial field mouse, Stand Watie's sole ambition now seemed to be to eke out sufficient income from farming and other small business enterprises to educate his children, who, while in Texas, had not attended school regularly. Watica, a youth of about seventeen, was sent by

---

[6] *Ibid., passim.*

Watie to Cane Hill College at Cane Hill, Arkansas. Minnehaha, or "Ninnie," two years or so younger than her brother, attended a boarding school at Fort Smith for a time. And Jacqueline, about eleven, obtained her belated education at Webbers Falls.

Among the Southern Cherokees who repossessed property near Fort Gibson were the Scrimshers, the Adairs, the Clem Rogerses (parents of Will Rogers, the humorist), the Woodalls, and the Agnews. According to John Martin Adair, who was ten at the time, his mother, after returning to the Nation, dug up the china dishes that she had buried before her flight to Texas. But Adair, in after years, could not recall what ever became of the Widow Lipe, who, when her husband had been killed in the first battle of Bayou Menard, and the Pins afterward had cut off his fingers to obtain his rings, had sewn up all the gold she owned in her dress and "hit out" for New York, presumably to live with her kin.[7]

Mrs. Mary Cobb Agnew, her memory as bright as a new silver dollar in 1937, remembered vividly how the country around Fort Gibson looked when she returned to it after the war:

> The houses and cabins had been burned. Fields had grown up into thickets of underbrush. The hogs and cattle which the soldiers had not killed had gone wild in the woods and canebrakes. People had to start life anew—build log cabins, clear ground, plant crops, build fences.[8]

Anderson Bean, an emancipated slave residing at Fort Gibson in postwar days, recalled years later that the Negroes who were made Cherokee citizens were so intimidated by intermarried whites and Cherokees that they were afraid to venture out on the streets after dark. Bean also remembered the cholera epidemic that viciously attacked the Cherokee Nation in 1867:

> It wasn't anything for someone to say, "So and so is dead." And you would say, "No, he ain't dead. I was just talking to him an hour ago,"

[7] Interview: John Martin Adair, in the Indians-Pioneer Papers, Vol. I, Frank Phillips Collection, University of Oklahoma.

[8] Interview 5978, in *ibid.*, Vol. VI.

and the answer was, "Makes no difference; he's dead now." Some claimed that the muskrats that came up on the river boats were what started the cholera. The government moved us Negroes out on Four Mile Creek until the cholera was over.[9]

Northern Cherokees who returned to the Nation after its occupation by Union forces were certainly not affluent but generally speaking were better off than their Southern neighbors, whose return to the Nation lagged behind their own by several years. Chief Ross's aristocratic wife, for example, wrote to her son Will at school in the East on March 3, 1866, from Fort Gibson that she had recently "managed to find enough to get up a fine supper" for some of the officers at the fort. To her son, Mrs. Ross described the new fences that had been built around their house and other changes that had taken place: "Papa and I got into the wood wagon (we have no carriage now) and went out about 5 miles and got a good many cedar trees and set them out in the yard."

Since it was difficult for her to procure strawberry plants, Mrs. Ross instructed her son to send strawberry seed, which he was to procure by pressing strawberries between a cloth. "The seed will stick to the cloth and you can send some in a letter."[10]

In the early days of reconstruction, when, as a Cherokee wit commented in the *Advocate*, "money was as scarce as angels' wings or hen's teeth," the poverty of the Nation was somewhat alleviated by the Cherokees' land cessions to the United States government. As provided by the Treaty of 1866, the Cherokees, coincident with the signing of the treaty, ceded their "Neutral Land" in Kansas and the narrow strip of land lying along the thirty-seventh parallel, also within the state of Kansas. After cession, these lands were held in trust by the United States until sold to white settlers for the benefit of the Cherokee Nation. This negotiation (one of the few beneficial transactions made by the Cherokees with the United States government) permitted the Cherokees to have in operation thirty-two public or national schools in 1867, forty-two in 1869, and sixty-four in

---

[9] Interview 5030, in *ibid.*, Vol. VI.
[10] In Ross Papers, *loc. cit.*

1870, with appropriations of "8,200, $16,400, $25,000 respectively for their support."[11]

By the twenty-third article of the Treaty of 1866, it was stipulated that 15 per cent of all funds due the Cherokee Nation by the United States, "or that hereafter may accrue from the sale of their lands by the United States, was to be invested and the interest applied to the orphan fund." Thus, an institution for Cherokee orphans was put into operation in 1872, with its temporary headquarters at the Male Seminary near Park Hill. In this pillared old sanctuary, once the pride of the Cherokee Nation, approximately ninety orphans were temporarily housed, fed, clothed, and taught the three *R*'s by as competent teachers as could be found in the Nation. Maps, blackboards, and all the latest school equipment were utilized in educating children of school age, orphaned by the recent war, at an annual expense of $65 per pupil. The necessity for making education available to these children can be realized by a perusal of the census taken in the Cherokee Nation after the war. The census report showed that the population of the entire Nation was approximately 13,566, as compared to 18,000 before the war, and that the war left one-third of the Cherokee women widows and one-fourth of the children in the Nation orphans.[12]

But education was not the only postwar project sponsored by the Cherokees. Religion, thought by Cherokee leaders to be essential to human welfare, took its rightful place in the reconstruction of the Nation. Authorized by the council, Chief Will Ross, in 1866, invited Congregationalists, Presbyterians, both Southern and Northern branches of the Methodist church, Baptists, and Moravians to return to the Nation.

Among the native ministers who resumed their work with the Cherokees following the war was the Reverend Stephen Foreman. Returning from Texas in 1866, Foreman repaired the old Boudinot house near Foreman's Park Hill home and converted it into a church, to which he gave the name "Church in the Woods."

[11] Ross, ed., *The Life and Times of Honorable William P. Ross*, 75.
[12] *Ibid.*, 78f.

Springplace having been burned by the enemy, Moravian ministers E. J. Mock and Wesley Spaugh conducted temporary services in the dining hall of the Female Seminary (its large classroom had been damaged by the storage of provisions for troops). And it was in the reception room of the Female Seminary that the Reverend Mock, on June 1, 1867, conducted services for Chief John Ross, whose remains had, by order of the Cherokee National Council, been returned to the Nation for burial in the Ross family cemetery adjacent to the former site of Rose Cottage.

Southern Methodists created a new circuit in the Nation in 1868, whereupon the Reverend John Harrell wrote to Major B. Davis, Cherokee agent: "The present year has been one of great prosperity. Park Hill . . . and several other places have been favored with revivals of religion and some 311 have been added to our communion."[13]

Camp meetings in other areas of the Nation were well attended after the war. John Alcorn (in 1937) remembered attending camp meetings in the vicinity of Lee's Creek that sometimes lasted for two months. Another favorite site was on Evansville Creek near the Chalk Bluff bridge. According to old-timers, these meetings were held after the crops were harvested, when the people had a little leisure in which to partake of the spiritual nourishment for which they hungered during the uncomfortable reconstruction period.

On the Cherokees' agenda, in addition to the furtherance of education and religion, were the rehabilitation and construction of public buildings. Tangible monuments to Cherokee reconstruction that are standing today are the old brick capitol building in the Square at Tahlequah, which, at present, serves Cherokee County as a courthouse, and the Administration Building of Northeastern State College, also at Tahlequah. The latter edifice, built before statehood, was once the new Female Seminary—a replacement of the old, which burned in 1887.

Other postwar monuments to Cherokee rehabilitation—many of

13 Carolyn Thomas Foreman, *Park Hill*, 146.

these are gone now—were a national jail or prison; an asylum for the insane, deaf and dumb, blind, and indigent persons of the Nation; a home for orphans at Salina; a telephone company with headquarters at Tahlequah, the first to be organized in the Mississippi Valley west of St. Louis; and an up-to-date opera house.

These and other landmarks were tangible evidence that the Cherokees were overcoming postwar handicaps and going forward in their characteristically headlong but motivated style. In 1876, as noted by Indian Agent Marston, the Nation's schools "stood as a monument to . . . [Cherokee] progress in civilization; they reflected credit on the natives and particularly on the religious societies through whose teachings the Cherokees were first led to appreciate the benefits of education. Extensive additions were made to the seminaries in 1876."[14] Both Male and Female Seminaries after the war graduated men and women who later became oustanding citizens of Oklahoma.

The wonder of the successes obtained by the Cherokees in rebuilding their nation after the Civil War is multiplied a hundred times over when one considers the handicaps under which they labored between 1866–1900. The poverty that forced once prosperous Cherokees to walk instead of ride, to weep instead of smile, to mend instead of sew, to whitewash instead of paint was a small burden to them, in comparison with the fear that eventually they might be deprived of self-government by the dissolution of their constitutional nation.

Of little moment, for example, when compared to the catastrophe of governmental dissolution, was the invasion of the Cherokee lands by cattlemen from Texas, who periodically grazed their herds en route from Texas to Northern markets on the Cherokee Outlet lands. The Cherokees solved this problem by charging cattlemen so much a head for grazing privileges. And, in 1883, having disposed of all but approximately 8,000,000 acres of Outlet lands to the Osages, Kaws, Pawnees, Oto-Missouris, and Tonkawas for a large sum, the Cherokees leased their remaining Outlet lands for a term of five

---

[14] *Ibid.,* 152.

years at $100,000 per year to the Cherokee Strip Livestock Association. The first payment of $50,000 in silver, delivered to Cherokee lessors at Tahlequah on October 1, 1883, by an agent of the Livestock Association, was long remembered by the poorer Cherokees, who since the war had been drinking a parched-corn brew in place of coffee, and pounding corn into meal with a mortar and pestle in the manner of the ancients.

The general council—provided for in Article Twelve of the Treaty of 1866, and at first feared by Will Ross and Cherokee leaders— did not lead to the reorganization of the Indian Territory but rather, by 1875, was a dead issue, for the simple reason that the United States Congress discontinued appropriations for its support. The explanation given by federal officials for the termination of funds for the council was that the Osages and the Five Tribes "used it [the general council] as a medium for memorials and protests, in faultless English, against railroad schemes and land grabs; and the bewildered nomads of the plains, fighting for their existence against odds they could not understand, came [to the general council] for sympathy and advice."[15]

Delegates to the council could not deny these charges. Meeting at Okmulgee, the Creek capital, in June, 1870, for the purpose of devising ways and means to resist the "adventurous spirit of the white man," delegates from the Creek, Seminole, Chickasaw, Osage, and Cherokee nations adopted a resolution against the territorial bills then pending in the United States Congress, and "strengthened the Compact of 1843 by the provision that the principal chief of any member tribe might call an intertribal council."[16] Elected president of the general council, Will Ross, from that date on, fought for territorial freedom. His weapon was the pen, which, in his hands, was more powerful than the fiery sword.

A general council called by the United States the following fall at Okmulgee was attended by delegates from all the Five Tribes, the Osages, and several small territorial tribes. The council was

---

[15] Debo, *The Road to Disappearance*, 209.
[16] *Ibid.*, 205.

properly conducted, with Superintendent Hoag serving as president and delegates receiving pay for attendance, as provided by the United States Congress. Tractably, the council offered to mediate a peace with the Plains Indians, then hostile to the United States, and adopted a committee report containing statistical information on the natural resources and agricultural progress in the Territory, but protested strongly against the reorganization of the Territory by the United States. Pulling away from the control which Superintendent Hoag attempted to impose on them, council members adopted a constitution for a united government of their own choice. It would be headed by a governor elected by qualified voters; have a general assembly of a senate and house of representatives elected from the various tribes, whose duties it would be to legislate on intertribal matters; and have a territorial judiciary system. But this proposed government did not appeal either to President Grant or to the Congress unless its constitution could "be amended so that the Congress would have a veto over all legislation, and the executive and judicial offices . . . would be appointed by the President."[17]

Thus shorn of its glory and power, the general council's plan for a territorial government was eventually abandoned by all the delegates, save the Creeks. After a few more meetings, the general council was discontinued in 1875.

William P. Ross, author of many of the memorials and protests against railroad schemes and land grabs presented to the council, was a distinguished and able rhetorician. Ross was also angry at the railroads. For in 1871, the Missouri, Kansas, and Texas Railroad Company, without the consent of the Cherokee council, had extended its line from Chetopa, Kansas, to Choteau Station. From that point it had built into the Creek Nation, establishing the terminal town of Muskogee before building to Eufaula and eventually, in 1873, to Colbert's Ferry on Red River. Then in September, 1871, the Atlantic and Pacific Railroad had entered the Nation from Seneca, Missouri, and formed a junction with the "Katy's" north-south line at Vinita, where its progress was halted, by order of the Cherokee

[17] *Ibid.*, 206.

council, until 1880. Incensed by the disorder and vice brought by the railroads to the Nation, by their disregard of Cherokee property rights, and by their demand for right of ways through the heart of the Nation, in 1872, Will Ross, in a protest signed by members of the general council and addressed to the Congress, referred to the railroad companies as "soulless corporations [who] hover like greedy cormorants over this territory and incite Congress to remove all restraint and allow them to swoop down and swallow over 23,-000,000 acres of the land of this territory, destroying alike the last hope of the Indians and the honor of the government."[18]

Designed by the general council to defeat the rash of territorial bills before the Congress, the protest was aimed directly at *House of Representatives Document Number 2635* (a bill to organize the Indian Territory without the consent of the territorial tribes), *House of Representatives Document Number 3086*, and *Senate Document Number 1244*. Accompanying the "Protest of the Indian Delegates" (compiled by Will Ross) was a comparative chart of the territories, both federal and Indian, under the protection of the United States. This chart bore out Ross's assertion that

> Indian Territory, in population, number of acres cultivated, products, wealth, valuation, and school statistics, is equal to any organized territory of the United States, and far ahead of most of them. It has a smaller area than any other and a larger population than any except Utah and New Mexico. It has more acres of land under cultivation than Washington Territory, over one-third more than Utah, and more than twice as many as Colorado or Montana; and the number of bushels of wheat, corn, and other farm products raised in the Indian Territory is more than six times greater than either Utah, New Mexico, or Colorado.

Unquestionably, the "Protest of the Indian Delegates" helped defeat *House of Representatives Document Number 2635*, for the protest also argued that

[18] Ross, ed., *The Life and Times of Honorable William P. Ross*, 120.

Cherokees with a population of 15,000 have two boarding schools and sixty day schools—three of which are for the children of freedmen —with an average attendance of 1,948 pupils, sustained at a cost of $25,000 last year [1871].

The Creeks, numbering 15,000, have three missions and 2,050 church members. . . . They have one boarding school and thirty-one day schools, attended by 860 pupils, at a cost of $14,258 for the past year.

The Choctaws and Chickasaws, numbering 20,000 have three missions and 2,500 church members. They have two boarding schools and forty-eight neighborhood day schools. Thirty-six of these are sustained by the Choctaws at a cost of $36,500; fourteen by the Chickasaws at a cost of 33,000 last year.[19]

However, this protest and its successors did not deter the Congress from discontinuing the general council. Pointing up as it did the resources and development of the Territory, the protest possibly inspirited Congress to cease its appropriations to the council; to dismiss Indian agents assigned to each of the tribes; and, in 1874, to put the Five Civilized Tribes under the jurisdiction of a commissioner in charge of Union Agency at Muskogee.

After this had been done, the Cherokees presumably realized that the United States was preparing to extinguish Indian titles and absorb territorial tribes into a new state of the Union. Elected to fill out the unexpired term of Lewis Downing after the latter's death in 1872, Chief Will Ross, in an address delivered to the National Council and the people on November 5, 1873, predicted the ultimate dissolution of territorial tribal governments by the United States:

The results anticipated from the change in . . . [Indian–United States] relations, are the gradual blending of the Indians under the same form of government . . . the allotment of their lands in severalty, the gradual extinction of all civil distinction between them and citizens of the United States, and their [the Indians'] ultimate absorption as a portion of their [the United States] population.[20]

[19] *Ibid.*, 142–43.
[20] *Ibid.*, 60.

By 1889 the prediction made by Ross over a decade before was nearing its fulfillment. The railroad companies were getting a firmer grip on the Territory, and their influence in Washington was growing. In league with the railroads was none other than Elias Cornelius Boudinot, who, after the Treaty of 1866, spent much of his time in Washington. By consorting with railroad officials, by promoting dubious deals in the Nation, and by doing everything in his power to open the Territory to white settlement, Boudinot became a symbol of betrayal to both Southern and Northern Cherokees, who united in fighting the opening of the Territory to whites.

On March 2, 1889, a bill was pushed through Congress and subsequently rushed to President Grover Cleveland authorizing the President to admit white settlers to an area in the Territory, 1,887,-796 acres in extent, referred to as "the Unassigned Lands." Located in very nearly the center of the Territory, the Unassigned Lands had, in January, 1889, been sold to the United States by the Creeks and Seminoles and included a part of the Creek land settled by the Cheyennes and Arapahoes. Ratified by President Cleveland at the end of his administration, the opening of the Territory to white settlement was proclaimed on March 23, 1889, by President Harrison during his third week in office. On April 22 white settlers made the first run into an area that today embraces the major portions of six Oklahoma counties—Payne, Logan, Kingfisher, Canadian, Oklahoma, and Cleveland. A year later, on May 2, 1890, Congress passed an Organic Act for the Territory of Oklahoma, as these six counties and a seventh in the Panhandle (Beaver County) were now to be known. Thus did the Indian Territory exist for over a decade side by side with the Territory of Oklahoma settled by whites.

Understandably the same pressure exerted by white settlers on Congress to procure the Unassigned Lands and a portion of the Panhandle led to the admittance of white settlers to other areas in the Indian Territory. The Cherokee Nation therefore did not benefit from the new lease which it made with the Cherokee Strip Cattle Association in 1888. For the act ratified by President Cleveland which had provided for the opening of the Unassigned Lands was amended. The Springer Amendment authorized the President to appoint a commission to make deals with all the Indians in the Territory who could be persuaded to dispose of their lands. The original act had specified that the Cherokees be offered $1.25 per acre for the Cherokee Outlet. Now, to prevent the Cherokees from leasing the Outlet to the Cherokee Strip Cattle Association, the President gave notice to both Cherokees and association that, pending the United States commissioners' negotiations with the Indians, cattle would not be permitted to graze the Outlet.

The commissioners' negotiations resulted in the Cherokees' relinquishment of the Outlet to the United States. By an act approved by the Congress on March 3, 1893, and ratified by the Cherokee Nation on May 17, the Cherokee Outlet—embracing approximately 6,574,487 acres—was sold to the United States for the sum of $8,595,736.12. Opened to white settlement on September 16, 1893, the Cherokee Outlet run was conceded by eyewitnesses to have been the most spectacular of all the runs made in the Indian Territory. One hundred thousand people, by train, on horseback, afoot, and in vehicles of every description, reached the immense Outlet lands on the appointed day. Stampeding across its rich grasslands, they feverishly staked out claims in an area now included in twelve counties and parts of counties extending across the northern part of present Oklahoma from Osage County to the one-hundredth meridian.

The Congressional act of March 3, 1893, also empowered the Dawes Commission to treat separately with the Five Civilized Tribes and to procure from these tribes agreements for allotment of lands in severalty and the subsequent dissolution of tribal governments preparatory to Oklahoma statehood.

The Cherokees (especially the Keetoowah full bloods) refused to co-operate with the Dawes Commission, the United States Geological Survey, or any of the agents who sought to persuade them to accept the federal government's revolutionary proposition. Mary Cobb Agnew's thoughts on the matter—delivered in 1937—furnishes an example of the opinion held by a majority of the Nation in 1894:

We Indians got our homes rebuilt [after the Civil War] and were doing well when the government took another shot at us and set up the Dawes Commission in 1894. We owned all the land as a whole and could farm all we wanted to as long as we didn't infringe on a neighbor's land. We had a good government of our own just like we had back in Georgia, but the white man wanted our land just as they wanted it in Georgia.

Again there was much discussion. The white people called us barbarians, half-wits, said we couldn't run our business, etc. So they sent men out to enroll all the citizens of the Cherokee Tribe. I and all my kin enrolled without any trouble, for I saw and so did Mr. Agnew, that if we were to get anything it would be necessary to enroll. . . . I am an old woman who has lived a long time and if there ever was a race of people that was downtrodden it was the Cherokees. . . . I knew every principal chief of the Cherokees from John Ross to Tom Buffington. Something always arose to cause the chiefs more worry than the President of the United States has today [1937]. The white man all the time wanted to get all the Indians had and the worries of the chiefs were to help the people. The chiefs of the Cherokees were men and smart men.[21]

The principal chiefs of the Cherokee Nation of Mary Cobb Agnew's day (Chief John Ross excepted) were Lewis Downing, William P. Ross, Charles Thompson or Ochalata, Dennis W. Bushyhead, Joel Mayes, Colonel Johnson Harris, Samuel Houston Mayes, Thomas Buffington, and William C. Rogers. Out of this number only Will Ross and Dennis Bushyhead were elected by the National party. The others were elected by the Downing party, which was eclipsed for a time in the early 1880's by the Union party. Reorganized in 1887, the Downing party thereafter elected every principal chief of the Cherokee Nation until statehood.

In the chaotic and uneven era preceding statehood, party lines surprisingly gave way to the common concern felt by the Nation over its future. Regardless of party, Cherokees united to combat the dissolution of the cherished Cherokee government. Eloquently, Elias Cornelius Boudinot, the nephew and namesake of the man who had (prior to his death in 1890) argued for the opening of Indian Ter-

---

[21] Interview 5978, Indian-Pioneer Papers, *loc. cit.*

ritory to white settlement, addressed Congressional committees in Washington in behalf of his people, who protested the dissolution of their government. At the same time, the people whom Boudinot represented refused year after year to attend the meetings arranged by the Dawes Commission at Muskogee or elsewhere. But after the passage of the Curtis Act, the Cherokees were forced to change their tactics. Reluctantly, on January 7, 1899, Cherokee delegates, meeting with the Dawes Commission, agreed to submit to the vote of the people "an agreement which provided for: 1) the allotment of lands in severalty, 2) the continuation of the executive and legislative branches of the Cherokee government until allotment had been completed."[22]

On January 31, 1899, a majority of the Cherokees voted for this agreement. But when it reached Washington, its ratification by the Congress failed. A similar compact—the outcome of negotiations in Washington in 1900—was ratified by the Congress on March 1, 1901, but when it was submitted to the Cherokee people on April 29, it was defeated. Eventually the Secretary of the Interior, admittedly impatient over the delay and action of the Cherokees, decreed that the work of enrolling some 41,000 recalcitrant Cherokees would proceed under the general provisions of the Curtis Act. Thereupon agents, appointed by the Dawes Commission in the spring of 1902, attempted the forcible enrollment of the Cherokees. But the full bloods in the eastern hills, nearly all of whom were members of the Keetoowah Society, would not submit to the process. Hiding from the agents in inaccessible and out-of-the-way places known only to Keetoowahs, they eluded capture as long as possible. And many of these full bloods when captured purportedly preferred imprisonment to enrollment. But the majority of Cherokees, in a special election called by Chief Thomas Buffington on August 7, 1902, approved by vote the third agreement proffered by the United States and were duly enrolled. These Indians each selected an allotment of 110 acres of "average land" from the tribal domain. By the end of the summer of 1902 the Dawes Commission reported the receipt

[22] Gaston Litton, *History of Oklahoma*, I, 484.

of "nearly fifty thousand applications of Cherokees, Shawnees, Delawares, by blood and intermarriage, and freedmen for entry on the Cherokee rolls."[23]

As in the case of all the Five Tribes, Cherokee enrolling centers were jammed with white applicants, who glibly asserted that they were of Cherokee descent. Sometimes they merely said, "quarter," "eighth," or "sixteenth" when interrogated. The weeding out of whites soon became a puzzling and onerous burden to enrolling agents, for the Five Tribes were bleaching out and the appearance of mixed bloods frequently belied their Indian heritage. It was estimated that 300,000 persons, instead of the 100,000 Indians known to be entitled to enrollment, showed up at the centers before the rolls of the Five Tribes were closed.

Even though the Cherokee government was to have been dissolved by March, 1906, "it was continued in modified and restricted form under an act of Congres until June 30, 1914, when all business in the division of tribal properties was finished. Principal Chief William C. Rogers, chosen in the last election (1903), continued in his office until 1917 to sign the deeds in the transfer of Cherokee lands."[24]

The dissolution of territorial tribal governments and the allotments of Indian lands in severalty to each citizen of the Five Tribes marked two of the most momentous milestones in the history of Oklahoma, a state whose admission to the Union was officially proclaimed by President Theodore Roosevelt on November 16, 1907.

On that date President Roosevelt, after signing the proclamation in the presence of Oklahoma dignitaries and other witnesses with a quill plucked from the wing of an Oklahoma eagle, announced with typical gusto, "Oklahoma is a state."[25] Telegraphed to Guthrie, former capital of the Oklahoma Territory and then temporary capital of the new-born state of Oklahoma, President Roosevelt's message was read by Charles H. Filson to a vast assembly of Oklahoma citizens congregated on the grounds of the Carnegie Library.

[23] *Ibid.*, I, 485.
[24] Wright, *A Guide to the Indian Tribes of Oklahoma*, 73.
[25] Litton, *History of Oklahoma*, I, 506.

Following this, a mock marriage service between Miss Indian Territory and Mr. Oklahoma Territory was performed by the pastor of a Guthrie church. Impersonating the bride, Mrs. Leo Bennett (of Cherokee descent) wore a floor-length satin gown, an exquisite picture hat, and carried in her gloved hands a mauve-colored chrysanthemum. Mr. C. G. Jones, as her groom, was properly attired in a morning coat and striped trousers. At the conclusion of this unique ceremony, the Whittaker Orphans' Home Band appropriately played the national anthem, after which the assembly witnessed the inauguration of Oklahoma's first governor, Charles N. Haskell. After solemnly taking the oath of office, Haskell opened his inaugural address with this eloquent but vigorous statement: "When the brilliant rays of this morning's sun spread over the land it lighted forty-five sovereign states between the two oceans. The sun will set tonight and its last rays will light a grander federation composed of forty-six states."[26]

As citizens of the newest state in the Union, the Cherokees, in 1907, stood at the threshold of a new era, a new beginning. And, contrary to popular expectation, the majority of Cherokees dominated a large section of the state of Oklahoma. Aware that they were by education, experience, and training qualified to do so, Cherokee leaders assumed the responsibilities of citizens of the United States and Oklahoma immediately after statehood. Cherokees participating in the Constitutional Convention were Clem Rogers, James Swarts, the Reverend Henry Cloud, Charles Frye, A. S. Wyley, O. H. Brewer, W. Littlejohn, J. Copeland, and J. T. Edmondson.[27] And in the United States Congressional race of 1907—the first in Oklahoma—James S. Davenport, tribal attorney and former speaker of the Cherokee House of Representatives, won over Frank G. Hubbard, a white resident of Muskogee. In 1907, too, Charles D. Carter, of Choctaw-Cherokee descent, easily defeated Loren G. Disney by 29,856 to 15,925 votes.

Elected to the United States Senate from Oklahoma in 1907 was

[26] *Ibid.,* 507.

[27] Starr, *History of the Cherokee Indians,* 183.

Robert Latham Owen, one-eighth Cherokee. Born at Lynchburg, Virginia, Senator Owen was the son of a railroad president and of Narcissa Chisholm Owen, a Cherokee. Educated in private schools at Lynchburg and Baltimore, Owen later graduated with honors from Washington and Lee University at Lexington, Virginia, and shortly afterward moved to the Cherokee Nation. Fearless and independent, Owen became a beloved national figure, and one of the giants of the United States Senate, prior to his retirement from that body on March 3, 1925.

After statehood, Cherokee physicians and surgeons Francis B. Fite and W. Thompson, together with their Cherokee colleagues who in territorial days had organized the Indian Territory Medical Association, merged the Indian Territory and Oklahoma Territory Medical Associations, thus bringing into existence the Oklahoma State Medical Association.

Cherokee educators, newspaper editors, and ministers of the gospel contributed to the upliftment and betterment of both whites and Indians residing in the new state of Oklahoma. Thus did the Cherokees—a race of people whose origin is enshrouded in mystery, whose four-century-old (recorded) history is one of repeated defeats and repeated victories—triumph over the dissolution of their tribal government.

But the coin has two sides. After statehood, full-blood Keetoowahs retreated to the flinty hillsides and valleys in eastern Oklahoma, where they sought to keep alive ancient tribal traditions and by this method shut out reality. Eastern Oklahoma Cherokees have yet a long road to travel, if they are to overtake the more progressive members of their proud race. But they may yet throw aside their present lethargic habits, abandon their listless contemplation of the future, and, like Sequoyah, explore the unknown. For, given the proper incentive, no mountain, it seems, is too high to climb, no current too swift to swim, if one is a Cherokee.

Bibliography

I. MANUSCRIPT MATERIALS

British Museum, Library, Department of Manuscripts

Letter from Major Charles Gale to English correspondent, November 2, 1711, in "F. Fairfax Discourse of Witchcraft" (Unpublished MS No. 32,496). [This is an account of Indian atrocities at Charlestown and of the enslavement by the English of thirty-nine Indian women and children in 1711.]

Cherokee Museum, Cherokee, North Carolina, Manuscripts Collection

"Original Birthday Story of Private John G. Burnett, Captain Abraham McClellan's Company, 2nd Brigade, Mounted Infantry, of Cherokee Removal, 1838–39."

Georgia Department of Archives and History, Atlanta

Cherokee Indian Letters, Talks, and Treaties (1786–1838). Vols. I, II, III, WPA Project No. 4341.

File 2, Loose Papers—Ross, John.

Georgia Governors' Letter Books (Incoming and Outgoing Letters, 1831, 1834–38).

Malone, Perillah and Henry. Report of Research Trip to the Newberry Library, Chicago, on September 5–6, 1956.

Unclassified letters relating to missionaries and Cherokees.

Murrell Mansion, Tahlequah, Oklahoma

Entries in Ross Family Bible (1865, 1866).

National Archives, Washington, D. C.

Microcopy No. 234, Roll, 75. [This includes the Henderson Roll and claims of Cherokee emigrants, 1835–38. The General Services Administration, National Archives and Records Service, can now furnish microfilm copies of the Letters Received by the Office of Indian Affairs, 1824–81 (on Microcopy No. 234). Microcopy No. 247 includes rolls with copy of Papers of the Continental Congress; Indian Treaties, 1748–86; Ordinances of the Congress, 1781–88; Reports of Committees on Indian Affairs and Lands in the Western Territory, 1776–88; and other valuable material relating to the Cherokees.]

Philadelphia, Pennsylvania, City Hall

Will of Andrew Duché, 1778. No. 112 (photocopy).

Privately Owned MS

Journal of Elijah Hicks, 1844. Courtesy Hammond G. Riggs, Jr., Tulsa, Oklahoma.

Smithsonian Institution, Bureau of American Ethnology, Manuscripts Collection

Cherokee Relations with the United States Government, MSS No. 1882, 1882–a, 1882–b, 2936, 4198.

Mooney, James. Bibliography of sources relating to the culture and history of the Cherokees [possibly contains references not published in Mooney's Cherokee papers], MS No. 3723.

Payne, John Howard. Extracts from MS on Cherokees, MS No. 3723. [This MSS Collection also contains maps, photographs, linguistic data, kinship charts, information on wampum belts, census reports, unpublished notes, and letters relating to the Cherokee Indians by contributors to B. A. E. publications.]

Thomas Gilcrease Institute of American History and Art, Manuscripts Collection

[Chicken, Col. George]. Journal of the Commissioner of Indian Affairs, 1725. Transcript from Public Record Office, London.

Fyffe, William, to Brother John, February 1, 1761 (letter).

Ross Papers.

University of Oklahoma. Division of Manuscripts and Frank Phillips Collection

Cherokee Papers. Division of Manuscripts.

Indian-Pioneer Papers (116 vols. and Table of Contents). Frank Phillips Collection.

University of Tulsa

Alice Robertson Collection.

Stevenson, James F. "Stand Watie in the Civil War." (Unpublished thesis, Tulsa, 1948.)

Tyner, Howard. "The Keetoowah Society in Cherokee History." (Unpublished thesis, Tulsa, 1949.)

II. UNITED STATES GOVERNMENT DOCUMENTS AND RECORDS

American State Papers. Indian Affairs, Vol. IV; Military Affairs, Vols. VI, VII.

Bureau of American Ethnology. Frederick Webb Hodge, ed. *Handbook of American Indians North of Mexico. Bulletin No. 30.* 2 Pts. Washington, 1907, 1910.

————. John Swanton. *The Indians of the Southeastern United States. Bulletin No. 137.* Washington, 1946.

————. *Bulletin No. 145.* Washington, 1900.

————. Royce, Charles. *The Cherokee Nation of Indians. Fifth Annual Report.* Pt. 2. Washington, 1887.

————. *Seventh Annual Report.* Washington, 1885, 1886.

————. *Eighteenth Annual Report.* Washington, 1900.

————. *Nineteenth Annual Report.* Pt. 1. Washington, 1897–98.

Commissioner of Indian Affairs. Annual Reports (1895, 1896).

Congress, House of Representatives. 76 Cong., 1 sess., *House Exec. Doc. No. 71*, January 3, 1939.

————, ————. 82 Cong., 2 sess., *House Report No. 2503*, Serial 11583.

————, Senate. 23 Cong., 1 sess., *Sen. Exec. Doc. No. 512.* 5 vols.

————, ————. 25 Cong., 1 sess., *Sen. Exec. Doc. No. 27.*

Kappler, Charles J. *Indian Affairs: Laws and Treaties.* 3 vols. Washington, 1904.

Smithsonian Institution. *Annual Report to the Board of Regents.* Washington, 1956.

Supreme Court Reports. Cherokee Nation *v.* Georgia. 5 Peters 1.

————. Mitchel *et al. v.* United States. 9 Peters 748.

————. Worcester *v.* Georgia. 6 Peters 512.

War Department. *The War of the Rebellion: A Compilation of the*

Official Records of the Union and Confederate Armies. Ser. I, Vols. I, VIII.

III. NEWSPAPERS AND MAGAZINES

The Cherokee Advocate (Tahlequah, Cherokee Nation), 1873–74.

The Chronicle of the Early American Industries Association, November, 1934, January, 1935.

Columbian Centinel, Massachusetts Federalist (Boston), November 2, 1799.

The Courier (New Orleans), April 27, 1838.

The Indian Chieftain (Vinita, Cherokee Nation), April 27, 1883.

The Muskogee Phoenix, October 15, 1948.

New York Observer, August 14, 1830.

Niles' Weekly Register (Baltimore), Vol. XXXVIII, Ser. 4, March, 1830–September, 1830; (Baltimore), Vol. LI, Ser. 5, September, 1836–March, 1837; (Washington), Vol. LIV, Ser. 5, March, 1838–September, 1838.

The Panoplist, 1807–1809.

Richmond Dispatch, August 29, 1883.

The Sequoyah County Times (Sallisaw, Oklahoma), 1957.

The Tulsa World, 1959–61.

Twin Territories (Muskogee, Indian Territory), 1902–1903.

IV. BOOKS

Abel, Annie Heloise. *The American Indian as Participant in the Civil War.* Cleveland, 1915.

————. *The American Indian as Slaveholder and Secessionist.* Cleveland, 1915.

————. *The American Indian under Reconstruction.* Cleveland, 1925.

Adair, James. *History of the American Indians.* London, 1775.

Adams, James Truslow, ed. *Dictionary of American History.* 6 vols. New York, 1940.

Alvord, Clarence Walworth, and Lee Bidgood. *The First Explorations of the Trans-Allegheny Region by the Virginians, 1650–1674.* Cleveland, 1912.

American Heritage Book of Indians. New York, 1961.

Ballenger, T. L. *Around Tahlequah Council Fires.* Oklahoma City, 1945.

Bartram, William. *Travels through North and South Carolina, Georgia, East and West Florida, the Cherokee Country, the Extensive Territories of the Muscogulges or Creek Confederacy, and the Country of the Choctaws.* London, 1792.

———. *The Travels of William Bartram.* Ed. by Francis Harper. New Haven, 1958.

Bass, Althea. *A Cherokee Daughter of Mount Holyoke.* Iowa, 1937.

———. *Cherokee Messenger.* Norman, 1936.

Battey, George M., Jr., *A History of Rome and Floyd County.* Atlanta, 1922.

Bohn, Cassimir. *Bohn's Hand-Book of Washington.* Washington, 1854.

Bourne, Edward Gaylord, ed. *Narratives of the Career of Hernando de Soto.* 2 vols. New York, 1904.

Bowers, Lola Garrett, and Kathleen Garrett. *A. Florence Wilson, Friend and Teacher.* Tahlequah, 1951.

Briggs, Herbert W., ed. *The Law of Nations; Cases, Documents, and Notes.* New York, 1942.

Brinton, Daniel G. *The Lenape and Their Legends with the Complete Text and Symbols of the Walum-Olum.* Philadelphia, 1885.

Brown, Catherine. *Memoir of Catherine Brown, A Christian Indian of the Cherokee Nation.* Ed. by Rufus Anderson. Boston, 1828.

Brown, John P. *Old Frontiers.* Kingsport, Tennessee, 1938.

Bruner, Joseph. *Who's Who among Oklahoma Indians.* Oklahoma City, 1928.

Butterfield, Roger. *The American Past.* New York, 1947.

Caldwell, Mary French. *Andrew Jackson's Hermitage.* Nashville, 1933.

Calendar of Virginia State Papers, 1652–1869. 11 vols. Richmond, 1875–93.

Catlin, George. *The North American Indians.* 2 vols. London, 1876.

Candler, Allen D., ed. *Colonial Records of Georgia, 1738–1744,* 26 vols. Atlanta, 1904–16.

Cherokee Hymns Compiled from Several Authors. Park Hill, 1844.

Constitution and Laws of the Cherokee Nation. Tahlequah 1852, 1880.

Corden, Seth K., and W. B. Richards. *Oklahoma Red Book.* 2 vols. Oklahoma City, 1912.

Cotterill, R. S. *The Southern Indians.* Norman, 1954.

Couch, Nevada. *Pages from Cherokee Indian History.* St. Louis, 1884.

Cunningham, Frank. *General Stand Watie's Confederate Indians.* San Antonio, 1959.

Cushman, H. B. *A History of the Choctaw, Chickasaw, and Natchez Indians.* Greenville, Texas, 1899.

Dale, Edward Everett, and Gaston Litton. *Cherokee Cavaliers.* Norman, 1941.

Debo, Angie. *And Still the Waters Run.* Princeton, 1940.

⸻. *The Road to Disappearance.* Norman, 1941.

Dinwiddie, Robert. *Dinwiddie Papers.* Ed. by R. A. Brock. 2 vols. Richmond, 1883–84.

Donaldson, Thomas. *United States Census Office, 11th Census, 1890 . . . Eastern Band of Cherokees of North Carolina.* Washington, 1892.

Drake, Francis, ed. *The Indian Tribes of the United States.* Philadelphia, 1884.

Drake, Samuel B. *The Aboriginal Races of North America.* Boston, 1848.

Eaton, Rachel Carolina. *John Ross and the Cherokee Indians.* Chicago, 1921.

Everett, Horace. *Speech of Horace Everett in the House of Representatives of the United States, May 19, 1830, On the Bill for Removing the Indians from the East to the West Side of the Mississippi.* Washington, 1830.

⸻. *Speech of Horace Everett in the House of Representatives of the United States on the Cherokee Treaty, May 31, 1838.* Washington, 1838.

Featherstonhaugh, George W. *A Canoe Voyage up the Minnay Sotor.* 2 vols. London, 1847.

Fernow, Berthold. *The Ohio Valley in Colonial Days.* Albany, 1890.

Fitzgerald, Mary Newman. *The Cherokee and His Smokey Mountain Legends.* Asheville, North Carolina, 1946.

Fitzpatrick, H. L., ed. *The Oklahoma Almanac, 1957.* Norman, 1957.

Foreman, Carolyn Thomas. *Indians Abroad.* Norman, 1936.

⸻. *Indian Women Chiefs.* Muskogee, 1954.

⸻. *Oklahoma Imprints.* Norman, 1936.

⸻. *Park Hill.* Muskogee, 1948.

Foreman, Grant. *Advancing the Frontier.* Norman, 1933.

⸻. *The Five Civilized Tribes.* Norman. 1934.

⸻. *Fort Gibson.* Norman, 1936.

⸻. *Indian Removal.* Norman, 1932.

⸻. *Indians and Pioneers.* New Haven, 1930.

⸻. *Sequoyah.* Norman, 1938.

Foster, George Everett. *Reminiscences of Travel in Cherokee Lands.* Ithaca, New York, 1898.

———. *Se-quo-yah, the American Cadmus and Modern Moses.* Philadelphia, 1885.

———. *A Story of the Cherokee Bible.* Ithaca, New York, 1899.

Fries, Adelaide L., ed. *Records of the Moravians in North Carolina, 1752–1820.* Raleigh, North Carolina, 1922.

Gabriel, Ralph Henry. *Elias Boudinot, Cherokee, and His America.* Norman, 1941.

Gittinger, Roy. *The Formation of the State of Oklahoma, 1803–1906.* Norman, 1939.

Goode, William H. *Outposts of Zion.* Cincinnati, 1863.

Govan, Gilbert E., and James W. Livingood. *The Chattanooga Country (1540–1951).* New York, 1951.

Greeley, Horace. *The American Conflict: A History of the Great Rebellion in the United States of America, 1860–'65.* 2 vols. Hartford, 1877.

Greenleaf, Ben. *Cherokee Almanac.* Park Hill, 1860.

Hansen, Harry, ed. *The World Almanac, 1960.* New York, 1960.

Hargrett, Lester. *Oklahoma Imprints.* New York, 1951.

Harrington, Mark R. *Cherokee and Earlier Remains on Upper Tennessee River.* New York, 1922.

Hart, Carroll, and Mrs. Lilla M. Hawes. *Georgia Date Book, 1959.* Boston, 1959.

Hawkins, Benjamin. *Letters of Benjamin Hawkins, 1796–1806.* Collections of the Georgia Historcial Society, Vol. IX. Savannah, 1916.

Haywood, John. *The Natural and Aboriginal History of Tennessee up to the First Settlement Therein by the White People in the Year 1768.* Nashville, 1823.

Hewatt, Alexander. *An Historical Account of the Rise and Progress of the Colonies of South Carolina and Georgia.* 2 vols. London, 1779.

Heye, George Gustave. *The Nacoochee Mounds in Georgia.* New York, 1874.

History of Tennessee. Nashville, 1887.

Hitchcock, Ethan Allen. *A Traveler in Indian Territory.* Ed. by Grant Foreman. Cedar Rapids, Iowa, 1930.

Honey, W. B. *The Old English Porcelain.* New York, 1946.

Houston, Sam. *The Autobiography of Sam Houston.* Ed. by Donald Day and Harry Herbert Ullom. Norman, 1954.

James, Marquis. *The Life of Andrew Jackson: Border Captain—Portrait of a President.* Garden City, New York, 1938.

Jefferson, Thomas. *Writings of Thomas Jefferson.* 10 vols. New York, 1892–99.

Jenyns, Soame. *Later Chinese Porcelain.* New York, 1951.

Langer, William L., ed. *An Encyclopedia of World History.* Boston, 1940.

Lanman, Charles. *Letters from the Alleghany Mountains.* New York, 1848.

Leitner, Leander, ed. *The Walum Olum.* Brooklyn, 1952.

Litton, Gaston. *History of Oklahoma.* 4 vols. New York, 1957.

Logan, John Henry. *A History of the Upper Country of South Carolina, from the Earliest Periods to the Close of the War of Independence.* Vol. I. Columbia, S. C., 1859.

Loomis, Augustus W. *Scenes in the Indian Country.* Philadelphia, 1859.

Looney, Rella Watts, ed. *The Chronicles of Oklahoma: Cumulative Index . . . 1921–1959.* Oklahoma City, 1961.

Lumpkin, Wilson. *The Removal of the Cherokee Indians from Georgia.* New York, 1907.

McCoy, Isaac. *History of Baptist Missions.* Washington and New York, 1840.

McKenney, Thomas L., and James Hall. *History of the Indian Tribes of North America.* 2 vols. Philadelphia, 1855.

McReynolds, Edwin C. *Oklahoma: A History of the Sooner State.* Norman, 1954.

Madison, James. *The Writings of James Madison.* 9 vols. New York, 1900–10.

Malone, Henry Thompson. *Cherokees of the Old South.* Athens, Georgia, 1956.

Missouri Pacific Railway Company. *Statistics and Information Concerning the Indian Territory, Oklahoma Territory, and the Cherokee Strip.* St. Louis, 1889.

Morris, Richard B. *Encyclopedia of American History.* New York, 1953.

Morse, Jedidiah. *Report to the Secretary of War on Indian Affairs.* New Haven, 1822.

Murrell, Mrs. George. *Mrs. Murrell's Cook Book.* Walnut Hill, Montgomery, Maryland, 1846.

North Carolina Colonial Records. 26 vols. Raleigh, North Carolina, 1886–90, 1909–14.

Nuttall, Thomas. *Nuttall's Journal of Travels into the Arkansas Territory, October 2, 1818–February 18, 1820.* Vol. XVIII of Reuben Gold Thwaites, ed., *Early Western Travels.* Cleveland, 1904–1907.

O'Beirne, H. F., and E. S. O'Beirne. *The Indian Territory: Its Chiefs, Legislators, and Leading Men.* St. Louis, 1892.

Owen, Narcissa. *Memoirs of Narcissa Owen (1831–1907).* Washington, 1907.

Parker, Thomas Valentine. *The Cherokee Indians.* New York, 1907.

Parris, John. *My Mountains, My People.* Asheville, North Carolina, 1957.

———. *Roaming the Mountains with John Parris.* Raleigh, North Carolina, 1955.

Parton, James. *People's Book of Biography.* Hartford, 1868.

Payne, Betty, and Oscar Payne. *Dwight Presbyterian Mission.* Tulsa, 1954.

Peake, Ora Brooks. *A History of the United States Indian Factory System: 1795–1822.* Denver, 1954.

Preston, Thomas W. *Historical Sketches of the Holston Valleys.* Kingsport, Tennessee, 1926.

Rackham, Bernard, and Herbert Reed. *English Pottery.* New York, 1924.

Ramsey, J. G. M. *The Annals of Tennessee to the End of the Eighteenth Century.* Kingsport, Tennessee, 1926.

Ranke, Vinetta Wells. *The Blackburn Genealogy.* Washington, 1939.

Richardson, James D., ed. *Messages and Papers of the Presidents, 1789–1897.* 10 vols. Washington, 1896–99.

Robertson, James Alexander, ed. *True Relation of the Hidalgo of Elvas, 1557.* 2 vols. De Land, Florida, 1933.

Roosevelt, Theodore. *Winning of the West.* 4 vols. New York and London, 1889–96.

Ross, Mrs. William P., ed. *The Life and Times of Honorable William P. Ross of the Cherokee Nation.* Fort Smith, 1893.

Sass, Herbert Ravenal. *Hear Me, My Chiefs!* New York, 1940.

Schoolcraft, Henry R. *Indian Tribes of North America.* Philadelphia, 1860.

Schroeder, John Frederick, and B. J. Lossing. *Life and Times of Washington.* 4 vols. Albany, 1903.

Scott, Graham Williamson. *The American Craftsmen.* New York, 1940.

Setzler, Frank. *Cherokee County, North Carolina—Antiquities*. Washington, 1941.

Smith, W. R. L. *The Story of the Cherokees*. Cleveland, Tennessee, 1928.

Speck, Frank G. *Decorative Art and Basketry of the Cherokees*. Milwaukee, 1920.

————, and Leonard Broom, in collaboration with Will West Long. *Cherokee Dance and Drama*. Berkeley, 1951.

Stambaugh, Samuel C. *A History of the Cherokee from the Period of Our First Intercourse with Them down to the Present Time—1846*. Washington, 1849.

Starkey, Marion L. *The Cherokee Nation*. New York, 1946.

Starr, Emmet. *Cherokees "West," 1794–1839*. Claremore, Oklahoma, 1910.

————. *History of the Cherokee Indians*. Oklahoma City, 1921.

Thoburn, Joseph B., and Muriel Wright. *Oklahoma: A History of the State and Its People*. 4 vols. New York, 1929.

Thomas, Cyrus. *The Cherokees in Pre-Columbian Times*. New York, 1890.

Timberlake, Henry. *Lieut. Henry Timberlake's Memoirs*. Ed. by Samuel Cole Williams. Johnson City, Tennessee, 1927.

————. *Memoirs of Lieut. Henry Timberlake*. London, 1765.

Ulmer, Mary, and Samuel E. Beck. *To Make My Bread*. Cherokee, North Carolina, 1951.

Underwood, Thomas Bryan, and Moselle Stack Sandlin. *Cherokee Legends and the Trail of Tears*. Knoxville, 1956.

Walker, Robert Sparks. *Torchlights to the Cherokees*. New York, 1931.

Wardell, Morris L. *A Political History of the Cherokee Nation, 1838–1907*. Norman, 1938.

Washburn, Cephas. *Reminiscences of the Indians*. Richmond, 1869.

Whitmore, Ellen. *The Journal of Ellen Whitmore*. Ed. by Lola Garrett Bowers and Kathleen Garrett. Tahlequah, 1953.

Williams, Samuel Cole. *Beginnings of West Tennessee in the Land of the Chickasaws, 1541–1841*. Johnson City, Tennessee, 1930.

————. *Dawn of Tennessee Valley and Tennessee History*. Nashville, 1937.

————, ed. *Early Travels in the Tennessee Country*. Nashville, 1928.

————. *History of the Lost State of Franklin*. Nashville, 1933.

————. *Tennessee during the Revolutionary War.* Nashville, 1944.

Wilson, James Grant, and John Fiske, eds. *Appleton's Cyclopaedia of American Biography.* 6 vols. New York, 1887–89.

Wright, Muriel H. *A Guide to the Indian Tribes of Oklahoma.* Norman, 1951.

————. *Springplace, Moravian Mission, Cherokee Nation.* Guthrie, Oklahoma, 1940.

V. ARTICLES

Baillou, Clemens de. "The Chief Vann House, the Vanns, Tavern and Ferry, *Early Georgia,* Vol. II, No. 2, 3–11.

————. "Excavations at New Echota in 1954," *Early Georgia,* Vol. I, No. 4, 19–29.

Ballenger, T. L. "Colored High School of the Cherokee Nation," *Chronicles of Oklahoma,* Vol. XXX, No. 4, 454–62.

————. "The Cultural Relations between Two Pioneer Communities," *Chronicles of Oklahoma,* Vol. XXXIV, No. 3, 286–95.

————. "Joseph Franklin Thompson," *Chronicles of Oklahoma,* Vol. XXX, No. 3, 285–91.

Beeson, Leona Selman. "Homes of Distinguished Cherokee Indians," *Chronicles of Oklahoma,* Vol. XI, No. 3, 927–41.

Benton, Joseph. "Some Personal Remembrances about Lynn Riggs," *Chronicles of Oklahoma,* Vol. XXXIV, No. 3, 296–301.

Britton, Wiley. "Some Reminiscences of the Oklahoma Cherokee People," *Chronicles of Oklahoma,* Vol. VI, No. 2, 163–77.

Brown, Frances Rosser. "When East Met West," *Chronicles of Oklahoma,* Vol. XXX, No. 4, 417–19.

Brown, John P. "Eastern Oklahoma Chiefs," *Chronicles of Oklahoma,* Vol. XVI, No. 1, 3–35.

Chapman, Berlin B. "How the Cherokees Acquired and Disposed of the Outlet," *Chronicles of Oklahoma,* Vol. XV, No 1, 30–49; Vol. XV, No. 2, 205–25; Vol. XV, No. 3, 291–321; Vol. XVI, No. 1, 36–51; Vol. XVI, No. 2, 135–62.

Condon, Glen. "Yes, We Have Indians," *Tulsa World* (Sunday Magazine), May 5, 1957.

Crockett, Bernice Norman. "Health Conditions in Indian Territory, 1830 to Civil War," *Chronicles of Oklahoma,* Vol. XXXV, No. 1, 80–90; Vol. XXXVI, No. 1, 21–39.

Croy, Homer. "Will Rogers of the Movies," *Oklahoma Today*, Vol. XI, No. 1, 4–33.

Davis, Harry. "Theatre of the People," *Unto These Hills* [drama program], 39.

Ferebee, Percy B. "Western North Carolina Associated Communities," *Unto These Hills*, 18.

Foreman, Carolyn Thomas. "An Early Account of the Cherokees," *Chronicles of Oklahoma*, Vol. XXXIV, No. 2, 141–58.

———. "The Light-Horse in the Indian Territory," *Chronicles of Oklahoma*, Vol. XXXIV, No. 1, 17–43.

———. "The Lost Cherokee Treaty," *Chronicles of Oklahoma*, Vol. XXXIII, No. 2, 238–45.

———. "Miss Sophia Sawyer and Her School," *Chronicles of Oklahoma*, Vol. XXXII, No. 4, 395–413.

Frye, Maggie C. "Indian Eloquence," *Oklahoma Today*, Vol. XI, No. 1, 28–29.

Garrett, Kathleen. "Music on the Indian Territory Frontier," *Chronicles of Oklahoma*, Vol. XXXIII, No. 3, 339–49.

———. "Worcester, the Pride of the West," *Chronicles of Oklahoma*, Vol. XXX, No. 4, 386–96.

Gatchet, A. S. "Indian Tribes Settled in the Cherokee Nation," *Indian Chieftain*, February 9, 1893.

Harmon, G. D. "The North Carolina Cherokees and the New Echota Treaty," *North Carolina Historical Review*, Vol. VI, No. 3, 237–53.

Harrington, Janette. "Forerunners," *Presbyterian Life*, Vol. V, No. 17, 11–13.

———. "Missions Are People," *Presbyterian Life*, Vol. V, No. 17, 23.

———. "A New Land to Be Won," *Presbyterian Life*, Vol. V, No. 17, 14–16.

Johnson, N. B. "The American Indian as Conservationist," *Chronicles of Oklahoma*, Vol. XXX, No. 3, 333–40.

Knepler, Abraham Eleazer. "Education in the Cherokee Nation," *Chronicles of Oklahoma*, Vol. XXI, No. 4, 378–401.

Knight, Oliver. "Cherokee Society under the Stress of Removal," *Chronicles of Oklahoma*, Vol. XXXII, No. 4, 414–28.

———. "History of the Cherokees," *Chronicles of Oklahoma*, Vol. XXXIV, No. 2, 159–82.

Lackey, Vinson. "New Springplace," *Chronicles of Oklahoma*, Vol. XVII, No. 2, 178–83.

La Farge, Oliver. "The Enduring Indian," *Scientific American*, Vol. CCII, No. 2, 37–45.

Lindquist, G. E. E. "Indian Treaty Making," *Chronicles of Oklahoma*, Vol. XXVI, No. 4, 416–48.

Love, Paula, ed. "The Best of Will Rogers," *Oklahoma Today* (Fall Issue, 1959), 26–27.

Loye, Dave. "Cherokee Country," *Oklahoma Today*, Vol. IX, No. 4, 10–36.

Ludlum, Robert. "Gideon Blackburn," *A Train of Thought from Blackburn College*, Vol. VI, No. 6 (February, 1954).

———. "More about Gideon Blackburn," *A Train of Thought from Blackburn College*, Vol. IX, No. 3 (November, 1956).

McGinty, J. Roy. "Symbols of a Civilization That Perished in Its Infancy," *Early Georgia*, Vol. I, No. 4, 14–17.

Malone, Henry T. "New Echota—Capital of the Cherokee Nation," *Early Georgia*, Vol. I, No. 4, 12–15.

———. "The Cherokees Become a Civilized Tribe," *Early Georgia*, Vol. II, No. 2, 12–15.

Meserve, John Bartlett. "Chief Thomas Mitchell Buffington and Chief William C. Rogers," *Chronicles of Oklahoma*, Vol. XVII, No. 2, 135–46.

Mooney, James. "The Cherokee Ball Play," *American Anthropologist*, Vol. III, No. 2, 105–32.

Morton, Ohland. "Confederate Government Relations with the Five Civilized Tribes," *Chronicles of Oklahoma*, Vol. XXXI, No. 2, 189–204; Vol. XXXI, No. 3, 299–322.

Murchison, A. H. "Intermarried Whites in the Cherokee Nation . . . 1865–1887," *Chronicles of Oklahoma*, Vol. VI, No. 3, 299–327.

Parris, John. "The Tsali Story," *Unto These Hills*, 33.

Roberts, Mrs. W. E., Sr. "Civil War Proved a Detriment to Five Civilized Tribes," *The American Indian*, Vol. I, No. 7, 10, 15.

Routh, Eugene Coke. "Early Missionaries to the Cherokees," *Chronicles of Oklahoma*, Vol. XV, No. 4, 449–65.

Self, R. D. "Chronology of New Echota," *Early Georgia*, Vol. I, No. 4, 3–5.

Street, James. "The Great Smokies," *Unto These Hills*, 35f.

Thiessen, Val. "Cherokee Cadmus," *Oklahoma Today*, Vol. XI, No. 1, 8–10.

Thoburn, J. B., ed. "Letters of Cassandra Sawyer Lockwood: Dwight Mission," *Chronicles of Oklahoma*, Vol. XXXIII, No. 2, 202–37.

Travis, V. A. "Life in the Cherokee Nation a Decade after the Civil War," *Chronicles of Oklahoma*, Vol. IV, No. 1, 16–30.

Wecter, Dixon. "History and How to Write It," *American Heritage*, Vol. VIII, No. 5, 24–27, 87.

Wenger, Martin A. "Three Cherokees . . . to See the 'King, Their Father,' " *The American Scene*, Vol. III, No. 4, 6–7.

Williams, Samuel Cole. "An Account of the Presbyterian Mission to the Cherokees," *Tennessee Historical Magazine*, Ser. II, Vol. I, No. 2.

Wright, Muriel H., ed. "The Journal of John Lowery Brown," *Chronicles of Oklahoma*, Vol. XII, No. 2, 177–213.

———. "Report to the General Council of the Indian Territory Meeting at Okmulgee in 1873," *Chronicles of Oklahoma*, Vol. XXXIV, No. 1, 7–16.

———. "Seal of the Cherokee Nation," *Chronicles of Oklahoma*, Vol. XXXIV, No. 2, 134–40.

———. "The Wedding of Oklahoma and Miss Indian Territory," *Chronicles of Oklahoma*, Vol. XXXV, No. 3, 255–64.

Index

of which *The Cherokees* is the sixty-fifth volume, was inaugurated in 1932 by the University of Oklahoma Press, and has as its purpose the reconstruction of American Indian civilization by presenting aboriginal, historical, and contemporary Indian life. The following list is complete as of the date of publication of this volume:

1. Alfred Barnaby Thomas. *Forgotten Frontiers:* A Study of the Spanish Indian Policy of Don Juan Bautista de Anza, Governor of New Mexico, 1777–1787. Out of print.

2. Grant Foreman. *Indian Removal:* The Emigration of the Five Civilized Tribes of Indians.

3. John Joseph Mathews. *Wah'Kon-Tah*: The Osage and the White Man's Road. Out of print.

4. Grant Foreman. *Advancing the Frontier, 1830–1860.* Out of print.

5. John Homer Seger. *Early Days among the Cheyenne and Arapahoe Indians.* Edited by Stanley Vestal.

6. Angie Debo. *The Rise and Fall of the Choctaw Republic.*

7. Stanley Vestal (ed.). *New Sources of Indian History, 1850–1891.* Out of print.

8. Grant Foreman. *The Five Civilized Tribes.* Out of print.

9. Alfred Barnaby Thomas. *After Coronado*: Spanish Exploration Northeast of New Mexico, 1696–1727. Out of print.

10. Frank B. Speck. *Naskapi:* The Savage Hunters of the Labrador Peninsula. Out of print.

11. Elaine Goodale Eastman. *Pratt:* The Red Man's Moses. Out of print.

12. Althea Bass. *Cherokee Messenger:* A Life of Samuel Austin Worcester. Out of print.

13. Thomas Wildcat Alford. *Civilization.* As told to Florence Drake. Out of print.

14. Grant Foreman. *Indians and Pioneers:* The Story of the American Southwest before 1830. Out of print.

15. George E. Hyde. *Red Cloud's Folk:* A History of the Oglala Sioux Indians.

16. Grant Foreman. *Sequoyah.*

17. Morris L. Wardell. *A Political History of the Cherokee Nation, 1838–1907.* Out of print.

18. John Walton Caughey. *McGillivray of the Creeks.*

19. Edward Everett Dale and Gaston Litton. *Cherokee Cavaliers:* Forty Years of Cherokee History as Told in the Correspondence of the Ridge-Watie-Boudinot Family. Out of print.

20. Ralph Henry Gabriel. *Elias Boudinot, Cherokee, and His America.*

21. Karl N. Llewellyn and E. Adamson Hoebel. *The Cheyenne Way:* Conflict and Case Law in Primitive Jurisprudence.

22. Angie Debo. *The Road to Disappearance.* Out of print.

23. Oliver La Farge and others. *The Changing Indian.* Out of print.

24. Carolyn Thomas Foreman. *Indians Abroad.* Out of print.

25. John Adair. *The Navajo and Pueblo Silversmiths.*

26. Alice Marriott. *The Ten Grandmothers.*

27. Alice Marriott. *María:* The Potter of San Ildefonso.

28. Edward Everett Dale. *The Indians of the Southwest:* A Century of Development under the United States. Out of print.

29. Adrián Recinos. *Popol Vuh:* The Sacred Book of the Ancient Quiché Maya. English version by Delia Goetz and Sylvanus G. Morley from the translation of Adrián Recinos.

30. Walter Collins O'Kane. *Sun in the Sky.*

31. Stanley A. Stubbs. *Bird's-Eye View of the Pueblos.*

32. Katharine C. Turner. *Red Men Calling on the Great White Father.*

33. Muriel H. Wright. *A Guide to the Indian Tribes of Oklahoma.*

34. Ernest Wallace and E. Adamson Hoebel. *The Comanches:* Lords of the South Plains.

35. Walter Collins O'Kane. *The Hopis:* Portrait of a Desert People. Out of print.

36. Joseph Epes Brown. *The Sacred Pipe:* Black Elk's Account of the Seven Rites of the Oglala Sioux. Out of print.

37. Adrián Recinos and Delia Goetz. The Annals of the Cakchiquels. Translated from the Cakchiquel Maya, with *Title of the Lords of Totonicapán*, translated from the Quiché text into

Spanish by Dionisio José Chonay, English version by Delia Goetz.

38. R. S. Cotterill. *The Southern Indians:* The Story of the Civilized Tribes before Removal.

39. J. Eric S. Thompson. *The Rise and Fall of Maya Civilization.*

40. Robert Emmitt. *The Last War Trail:* The Utes and the Settlement of Colorado.

41. Frank Gilbert Roe. *The Indian and the Horse.*

42. Francis Haines. *The Nez Percés:* Tribesmen of the Columbia Plateau. Out of print.

43. Ruth M. Underhill. *The Navajos.*

44. George Bird Grinnell. *The Fighting Cheyennes.*

45. George E. Hyde. *A Sioux Chronicle.*

46. Stanley Vestal. *Sitting Bull:* Champion of the Sioux, A Biography.

47. Edwin C. McReynolds. *The Seminoles.*

48. William T. Hagan. *The Sac and Fox Indians.*

49. John C. Ewers. *The Blackfeet:* Raiders on the Northwestern Plains.

50. Alfonso Caso. *The Aztecs:* People of the Sun. Translated by Lowell Dunham.

51. C. L. Sonnichsen. *The Mescalero Apaches.*

52. Keith A. Murray. *The Modocs and Their War.*

53. Victor W. von Hagen (ed.). *The Incas of Pedro de Cieza de León.* Translated by Harriet de Onis.

54. George E. Hyde. *Indians of the High Plains:* From the Prehistoric Period to the Coming of the Europeans.

55. *George Catlin: Episodes from "Life among the Indians" and "Last Rambles."* Edited by Marvin C. Ross.

56. J. Eric S. Thompson. *Maya Hieroglyphic Writing:* An Introduction.

57. George E. Hyde. *Spotted Tail's Folk:* A History of the Brulé Sioux.

58. James Larpenteur Long. *The Assiniboines:* From the Accounts of the Old Ones Told to First Boy (James Larpenteur Long). Edited and with an introduction by Michael Stephen Kennedy.

59. Edwin Thompson Denig. *Five Indian Tribes of the Upper Missouri.* Edited and with an introduction by John C. Ewers.
60. John Joseph Mathews. *The Osages:* Children of the Middle Waters.
61. Mary Elizabeth Young. *Redskins, Ruffleshirts, and Rednecks:* Indian Allotments in Alabama and Mississippi, 1830–1860.
62. J. Eric S. Thompson. *A Catalog of Maya Hieroglyphs.*
63. Mildred P. Mayhall. *The Kiowas.*
64. George E. Hyde. *Indians of the Woodlands:* From Prehistoric Times to 1725.
65. Grace Steele Woodward. *The Cherokees.*

The Cherokees has been set in Linotype Caslon Old Face of 11½ points on a 13-point body. This face was originally designed and cut by William Caslon in England in the eighteenth century, where it enjoyed widespread popularity. Early transplanted to the American colonies, Caslon remained the most commonly used type face throughout the Colonial period, and is for this reason traditionally suited to American historical works and to writings on the American Indian.

UNIVERSITY OF OKLAHOMA PRESS

NORMAN